Discover Historic California

A Travel Guide to Over 1,800 Places You Can See

George and Jan Roberts

Gem Guides Book Co.

315 CLOVERLEAF DRIVE, SUITE F
BALDWIN PARK, CA 91706

First Edition 1986
Second Edition 1988
Revised Edition 1990
Fourth Edition 1994

Maps by George Roberts and John Mayerski

Library of Congress Catalog Card Number: 94-76113

ISBN 0-935182-74-8
(Previous ISBN 0-935182-35-7)

INTRODUCTION

Discovering places where California history was made.

Fifty years after Columbus discovered America, California's first landmark was established . . . the landing place of Juan Rodriguez Cabrillo, the Portuguese navigator who landed at San Diego Bay and claimed his discovery for Spain. Next came Sir Francis Drake, who landed north of San Francisco (at Drake's Bay) in 1579 and made claim to California for the Queen of England.

The Russians also came to California, established settlements, built Fort Ross, and raised their flag over California's soil. But it would be the Spanish who, in 1769, would be the first to colonize California by founding the first mission at San Diego.

The first overland trail into California was opened by Jedediah Strong Smith in 1826. Next came the emigrants, the Mexican War, the Bear Flag Revolt, the raising of "old glory" at Monterey in 1846, and the discovery of gold in 1848.

It was that famous discovery of gold at Sutter's Mill in Coloma that sparked the growth of California. Mining camps sprang up throughout the "Mother Lode" territory and the "Golden State" earned its nickname by yielding gold almost as far south as the Mexican border. Forty-niners came by overland trail, by ship around the Horn, and across the Mojave Desert through Death Valley.

Within the next decade, Butterfield stages were traveling the length of California, the Pony Express reached Sacramento and the building of the first transcontinental railroad began.

These events, and over 1,000 others that are significant in California's history, are commemorated throughout the state and designated as registered state historic landmarks.

Discover Historic California takes you there. With this guide you'll know where the landmark is, the event that took place and other historical sites that are nearby. Also included are many places of historical interest that have not been designated as "official" state landmarks, but have had a part in California's history.

Among these are coastal lighthouses, preserved historic districts in many towns, living museums where the past is brought to life, ghost towns, operating pioneer railroads, historical museums and local landmarks.

Use this guide to plan a day's outing, weekend trip or a vacation. As you travel to these historical places . . . explore the area . . . you'll discover another side of California

Traveling with *Discover Historic California*

Areas of California that include registered state landmarks or historical places of interest have been arranged into 76 travel regions in this guide. Main highways and roads leading to these sites are identified along with nearby cities and towns.

REGION NUMBER

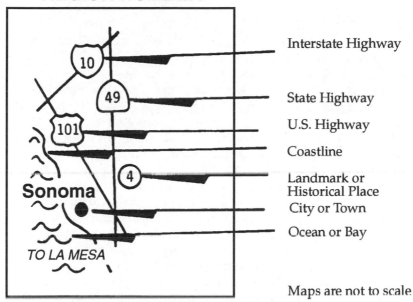

Interstate Highway

State Highway

U.S. Highway

Coastline

Landmark or Historical Place

City or Town

Ocean or Bay

Maps are not to scale

Immediately after each Region Map is a listing of all the state landmarks and places of historical interest in that region. Listings are in numerical order by locations on the map. Number ① on the map is number ① on the listing, etc. When two or more listings have the same number, it means that they are all in the same area on the map.

Sites that have been registered as State Historical Landmarks are identified by the initials "SHL" after the name of the landmark.

A few important points:

STATE LANDMARK SIGNS . . . The absence of a state landmark sign doesn't necessarily mean that you missed the landmark. Some sites are not identified with state plaques. If the actual site of a landmark is inaccessible, its landmark sign could be placed at a more public location, such as a park or alongside a highway.

PRIVATE PROPERTY . . . Some landmarks are on private property and not open to the public. Please respect the property owner's right to privacy.

OPERATING HOURS . . . State Parks, National Parks and privately operated facilities may be closed during certain times of the week, have limited hours and may be inaccessible under adverse weather conditions.

CALLING AHEAD . . . Telephone numbers have been included whenever possible. If you plan to make a special trip to see one particular site, it would be advisable to call ahead.

FEES . . . Entrance fees are charged at some parks and privately operated facilities to cover their operating costs.

ACCURACY OF INFORMATION . . . Extensive research was conducted to insure the accuracy of information included in this guide. Historic buildings are sometimes relocated, damaged by the elements or destroyed. Others are renovated, opened to the public for the first time, designated a state monument, etc. If you let us know when you find a change, or a better address for a site, we'll include an update in the next printing of this guide.

WANT MORE INFORMATION . . . Several publications are listed at the end of this guide that you can refer to for more history about these sites. Many chambers of commerce, visitors bureaus and historical societies are active throughout California and are an excellent source for information.

PLACES INCLUDED ON MAP . . . Maps shown in this book are drawn to focus on historical sites in the region. Roads, towns and cities that do not contribute to that theme may be excluded.

ACKNOWLEDGMENTS

Hundreds of organizations and groups provided material that was used to write this travel guide. You'll find many of their names in the pages of this book . . . for they are the chambers of commerce and historical museums across the state that furnish historical tour information to those who visit their cities.

Libraries were another source for good research material. Staff in the reference departments made a special effort to help us. Our local library, Whittier Main, was especially helpful.

California Department of Parks and Recreation, who administers the registration of historical landmarks, was our primary source for historical landmark information. Their cooperation has made it possible for us to include in this guide the most recently designated state landmarks.

This book is dedicated to our children:
Jeff, Scott, Patrick and Jennifer,
who made traveling to California's historic places
a real family adventure.

These circled numbers represent the general area covered by the 76 Region maps that are part of this guide. The Table of Contents lists each region, by number, and the page number in the guide where it can be located.

CALIFORNIA

TABLE OF CONTENTS

xvi

REGION 1

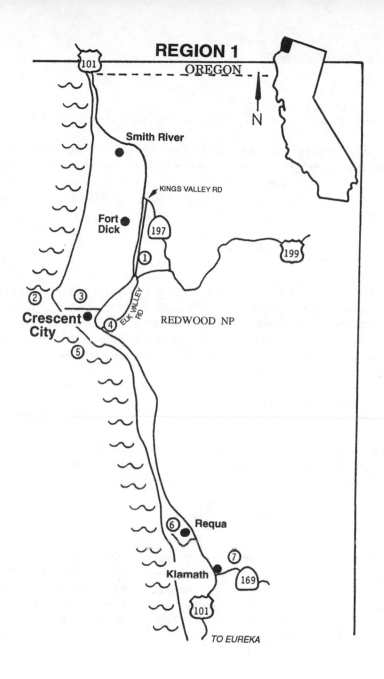

OREGON

Smith River

KINGS VALLEY RD

197

199

Fort
Dick

①

② ③

Crescent ④ ELK VALLEY RD
City REDWOOD NP

⑤

⑥ Requa

⑦

Klamath 169

101

TO EUREKA

N

1 - Camp Lincoln   SHL 545
4241 Kings Valley Road, 6 miles northeast of Crescent City off U.S. 101

This U.S. military post was established in 1862 by the California Volunteers to keep the peace between Indians and the area's white settlers. The post was abandoned in 1870 when the Indians were relocated. The former Commanding Officer's Quarters remain and is now used as a private residence.

2 - St. George Reef Lighthouse
7 miles off the coast, northwest of Crescent City

St. George Reef Lighthouse was among the most expensive ever built, taking years to complete because of the treacherous storms and dangerous reefs that surround the station. Closed in 1975, after less than 85 years of service, it stands as a tribute to the men who served there and endured the isolation and severe weather conditions.

3 - Tolowa Indian Village Site   SHL 649
Pebble Beach Drive, south of Pacific, Crescent City

Tolowa Indians had one of their major villages at this site where they remained until the late 1800s. None of the structures remain to be seen that were originally built at this location.

3 - Brother Jonathan Cemetery   SHL 541
9th Street and Pebble Beach Drive, Crescent City

Before the St. George Reef Lighthouse was constructed to warn passing ships of the dangerous submerged reef that lies six miles off the coast northwest of here, the steamer *Brother Jonathan* struck the reef in a sudden storm and most of those on board drowned. Many of those who perished in this tragedy on July 30, 1865, were buried in this town's cemetery.

3 - Redwood National Park Museum
1111 - 2nd Street, Crescent City (707) 464-6101

The history of this region of Northern California, and the 106,000-acre Redwood National Park, is featured in the displays at this museum.

3 - Del Norte County Historical Society Museum
577 "H" Street, Crescent City (707) 464-3922

Housed in the 1926 sheriff's office and jail, this museum depicts the county's marine, mining and lumber history.

3 - SS *Emidio* SHL 497
On the waterfront at Front and "H" Streets, Crescent City

The 10,745-ton General Petroleum Corporation tanker, the SS *Emidio*, was the first ship to be torpedoed and shelled by a Japanese submarine off the West Coast during World War II. Five men lost their lives in the attack on December 20, 1941, which took place about 200 miles north of San Francisco. The ship broke-up on the rocks off Crescent City. Pieces of the hull reached the city's harbor and are preserved at this memorial.

4 - Crescent City Plank and Turnpike Road SHL 645
U.S. 101 at Elk Valley Road, Crescent City

A wagon road was built in 1858 by the "Crescent City and Yreka Plank and Turnpike Company" connecting Crescent City and Waldo, Oregon. This road was used primarily to supply goods to the gold fields and towns in the interior. Sections of the original plank road are visible along Howland Hill Road.

5 - Battery Point Lighthouse SHL 951
Battery Point at the end of "A" Street, Crescent City (707) 464-3089

The Battery Point Lighthouse (Crescent City Lighthouse) was put into service in 1856 and staffed until it was automated in 1953. In 1964, the lighthouse survived the tidal wave that destroyed a large section of Crescent City and stands today as it did a hundred years before. No longer a functioning lighthouse, it is preserved as a maritime museum and is accessible to the public at low tide. Among the museum's featured exhibits is the ship's bell from the sidewheeler *Brother Jonathan*, which sank near this site July 30, 1865, in America's worst peacetime sea disaster.

6 - Requa
Del Norte County Historical Society (707) 464-3922
Redwood National Park, north bank of Klamath River, 3/4 miles west of Requa

A large settlement of Yurok Indians, one of the many different tribes that inhabited this region, lived here by the mouth of the Klamath River. An original Indian dwelling has been restored and is maintained by the historical society.

6 - Trees of Mystery Park
15500 U.S. 101, South Klamath (707) 482-2251 or (800) 638-3389

The legend of Paul Bunyan is one of the interesting redwood sculptures featured in this storyland park. The surrounding redwood groves contain the "Family Tree," "Fallen Giant" and the largest known "Cathedral Tree." Northwest Indian artifacts, baskets and costumes are exhibited in the park's Indian museum.

7 - Site of Fort Ter-Wer   SHL 544
Site at intersection of Terwer Riffle Road and Klamath Glen Road, east of Klamath off Hwy 169

In October, 1857, Lt. George Crook and his men built Fort Ter-Wer at this site. A few months earlier, they had established Fort Crook in Shasta County. U.S. military presence was needed to maintain peace between Indians and white settlers in these two areas.

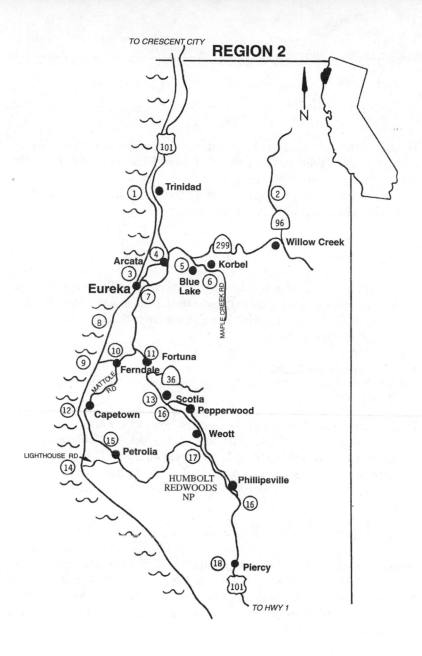

TO CRESCENT CITY

REGION 2

N

101

● Trinidad ①

②

96

299 ● Willow Creek

Arcata ④
③ ⑤ ● Korbel
Eureka ● ⑦ Blue ⑥
Lake

MAPLE CREEK RD

⑧

⑩ ⑪ Fortuna
⑨ Ferndale
MATTOLE RD 36

⑬ ● Scotla
⑫ Capetown ⑯ ● Pepperwood

● Weott

⑮ ● Petrolia ⑰

LIGHTHOUSE RD
⑭ HUMBOLT
REDWOODS
NP ● Phillipsville

⑯

⑱ ● Piercy

101

TO HWY 1

5

1 - Trinidad SHL 216
U.S. 101, north of Arcata, Chamber of Commerce (707) 677-0591

The first town to be settled by Americans along the northern coast of California was Trinidad in 1850. Trinidad became a major supply center for the surrounding gold camps. When mining activity ended, Trinidad's population dwindled. Today it is one of California's smallest incorporated cities.

1 - Trinidad Head SHL 146
Plaque on the beach, U.S. 101, Trinidad

A 1775 Spanish expedition, under the command of Bruno de Heceta, erected a wooden cross at this site and took possession of this land in the name of Carlos III of Spain. The granite cross that now marks this site was erected in 1913.

1 - Trinidad Head Lighthouse
Off U.S. 101, about 20 miles north of Eureka, on a slope overlooking the ocean, Trinidad

Established in 1871, this lighthouse has been in continuous use for more than a century. Its lens was removed in 1948 when the lighthouse was automated and is now available for closer inspection at a replica of this structure built in Trinidad's park. In 1914 the highest tidal wave ever recorded covered this 196-foot high beacon.

1 - Site of Yurok Indian Village SHL 838
Monument at Ocean and Edwards Streets, Trinidad

Spanish explorers who landed here in 1775 first discovered the prehistoric Yurok Indian village of Tsurai. A reservation was established for the Yurok in 1855, but most chose to live at the village that they occupied until 1916. A monument to this ancient Indian tribe was erected overlooking the site of Tsurai.

2 - Hoopa Tribal Museum
Hoopa Valley Indian Reservation, Hoopa Shopping Center on Hwy 96, 12 miles north of Willow Creek (916) 625-4110

This Indian museum features a collection of Hupa, Yurok and Karuk Indian artifacts, local Indian basketry, ceremonial regalia, tools and redwood dugout canoes. Some of the museum's artifacts are used in traditional tribal ceremonies by local Indians.

3 - Samoa Cookhouse
On Samoa Road, west of U.S. 101 over the Samoa Bridge, between Eureka and Arcata (707) 442-1659

Built in 1900, Samoa Cookhouse is the last surviving cookhouse in the West. Meals are still served lumber camp style at long tables covered in oil cloth. Early culinary items are featured in their museum and dining rooms. Historic relics from the lumber and logging industries are also displayed.

3 - Eureka   SHL 477
Chamber of Commerce, 2112 Broadway, Eureka (707) 442-3738

Established in 1850 to serve the mining camps, Eureka's importance as a lumber shipping port made it the economic center of the region and by 1856 it was named the county seat of Humboldt County. The town has more than 100 Victorian style homes and restored buildings of various architectural styles built from 1850 to 1902. A guide to some of these buildings is available from the Chamber of Commerce.

3 - Humboldt Bay Maritime Museum
1410 Second Street, Eureka (707) 444-9440

A modified replica of the George McFarlan home, originally constructed at this site in 1852, now houses the collection of the Humboldt Bay Maritime Museum. This museum chronicles Humboldt Bay's contributions to the Pacific Coast's maritime heritage.

3 - Eureka's Old Town District
1st, 2nd and 3rd Streets, "C" to "G" Streets, on the waterfront of Humboldt Bay, Eureka Tour reservations (707) 445-2117

Restored buildings in an 1800s atmosphere can be found in this historic district of Eureka. Romano Gabriel's Sculpture Garden, a collection of wooden figures and forms representing people who made the headlines during his lifetime, have been restored and are exhibited in Old Town.

3 - Clarke Memorial Museum
240 "E" Street, Eureka (707) 443-1947

Housed in the 1900 Bank of Eureka Building are artifacts from Humboldt County collected by Cecil Clarke, who taught history for 36 years at Eureka High School. Collections include clothing from the 1840s to the 1940s, antique weapons, Victorian furnishings and maritime displays. One of the largest collections of Indian basketry in Northwestern California is housed in one wing of this museum.

3 - Carson Mansion
143 "M" Street, Eureka (707) 445-2117

Called the "most ambitious" Victorian house built north of San Francisco, this 18-room mansion is one of the most photographed houses in America. Built in 1884-1885 of hardwood and redwood, it has many interesting hand-carved features that can be seen on the building's exterior. Operated as a private club, Carson Mansion is not open to the public, but its elaborate appearance can be enjoyed from many outside vantage points.

4 - Camp Curtis SHL 215
Sign on Frontage Road to U.S. 101, 1 and 1/2 miles north of Arcata

After Fort Humboldt was established in 1853, many other posts were built in the outlying region to protect settlers from Indian raids. Camp Curtis was the headquarters of the Mountain Battalion State Militia between 1863 and 1865, which established the last of the Indian reservations and brought an end to fifteen years of Indian warfare and bloodshed on both sides.

4 - Arcata
Chamber of Commerce, 1062 "G" Street, Arcata (707) 822-3619
Historical Sights Society of Arcata (707) 822-3619

The city of Arcata was once the home of California's noted short-story writer, Bret Harte. His home at 927 "J" Street is among 15 featured Arcata historical houses. A guide to these homes is available from the Chamber of Commerce, or the Historical Sites Society of Arcata, at (707) 822-1274.

4 - Jacoby Building   SHL 783
780 - 7th Street, Arcata   (707) 822-1758

Augustus Jacoby built the basement and first story of this structure in 1857, and for the next seven years it served as a refuge during occasional Indian raids. Various businesses that supplied the region's mines occupied the building until it was sold in 1880. This restored structure is considered among the most beautiful buildings on the Northern California coast.

5 - Arcata and Mad River Railroad Company   SHL 842
Blue Lake depot, Blue Lake   (707) 668-5576

The oldest rail line on the Northern California coast was the Arcata and Mad River Railroad Company, which served the area between Humboldt Bay and the Trinity River mines. The beginning of this line in 1854 is commemorated at the Blue Lake railroad depot. Affectionately called the "Annie and Mary," in honor of two of the railroad's employees in 1907, it is the oldest continuously operated line west of the Rocky Mountains. This railroad company is now part of the North Coast Railroad.

6 - Old Arrow Tree   SHL 164
1 mile east of Korbel on Maple Creek Road

Tribes of Indians that once lived along this region peppered the bark of this redwood tree with arrows. The tree is believed to have been a symbol of peace or a boundary between the neighboring camps.

7 - Humboldt Harbor Historical District   SHL 882
Harold Larson Vista Point, Humboldt Hill Road, east of U.S. 101, Eureka

Discovery of Humboldt Bay was made in 1806 by men under the command of Captain Jonathan Winship. This outstanding natural harbor became a major Northern California shipping port in the late 1800s.

7 - Fort Humboldt State Historic Park   SHL 154
3431 Fort Avenue, Eureka (707) 445-6567

Fort Humboldt was established in 1853 to provide protection for settlers of this region. Frequent skirmishes between Indians from the surrounding mountains and the "white men," who settled here during the 1850s, usually resulted in innocent men on both sides being killed. Among the soldiers who served at this fort during this period of unrest was Ulysses S. Grant. He was a captain when stationed here in 1854. An original fort structure has been restored and is now used as a museum. Relics from the period 1850-1860 are exhibited.

8 - Table Bluff Lighthouse
Woodley Island Marina at Lighthouse Ranch, south of Eureka
(707) 444-9440

From 1892 to 1972 this was a functioning lighthouse protecting ships from a dangerous reef offshore. In 1981 the main part of the structure was relocated to the Woodley Island Marina in Eureka, and today is maintained by the Humboldt Bay Maritime Museum.

9 - Centerville Beach Memorial Cross   SHL 173
On Centerville Beach, 7 miles west of Ferndale via Centerville Road

On January 6, 1860, the steamer *Northerner* struck a hidden rock off Cape Mendocino causing the loss of 38 lives. The wrecked steamer drifted to Centerville Beach where its remaining passengers and crew were saved. This cross was erected in honor of those who lost their lives at sea in this tragedy.

10 - Ferndale   SHL 883
West of Fortuna on Mattole Road (707) 786-4477

Settled in 1852, Ferndale became the agricultural center of Northern California. The prosperity of the community is reflected in the quality construction of its Victorian style homes, churches and businesses. Spanning one half mile across the Eel River to the village entrance is the 1911 Fernbridge, the largest concrete structure of its time. A walking guide of Ferndale's Victorian Village is available from any shop along Main Street.

10 - Ferndale Museum
Third and Shaw Streets, Ferndale (707) 786-4466

Ferndale Museum features rooms set in the Victorian Era, logging and farm equipment, an operating seismograph, and a working forge from the town's original blacksmith shop.

11 - The Depot-Fortuna's Museum
1 Park Street, off Main Street, Fortuna (707) 725-2495

This restored 1900 railroad depot contains displays of early historical items from the Fortuna area.

12 - Cape Mendocino Lighthouse
Cape Mendocino, off U.S. 101, near Mattole Road, south of Capetown

The 1860 wreck of the steamer *Northerner* and the loss of 38 lives at sea helped speed the completion of this lighthouse which began operating in 1868. Standing 422 feet above the shoreline it is one of the country's highest lighthouses. An automated signal has been installed and the old lighthouse is no longer in use. The light station is not open to the public.

13 - Pacific Lumber Company Museum
Main Street, Scotia (707) 764-2222

A 1920 bank building constructed entirely of redwood now houses the museum of the Pacific Lumber Company. Old logging equipment, tools, equipment, and an old switchboard are displayed. Passes are available for self-guided tours of the Pacific Lumber Company's mill.

14 - Punta Gorda Lighthouse
South of Lighthouse Road, west of Mattole Road

In 1907, the coastal liner *Columbia* sank sixteen miles south of here with the loss of 87 lives. As usually happened after a shipwreck, public outcry demanded the construction of a lighthouse to prevent future disasters. Less than forty years after it was put into service, Punta Gorda lighthouse was replaced with a lighted whistle buoy and the station abandoned.

15 - California's First Drilled Oil Wells   SHL 543
Monument in Petrolia, south of Ferndale via Mattole Road

The first crude oil produced from drilled oil wells in California came from an oil field located near here on the North Fork of the Mattole River. In June 1865, the first crude oil was shipped to an oil refinery in San Francisco.

16 - Avenue of the Giants
33-mile route between Phillipsville and Pepperwood off U.S. 101 (707) 946-2229

Coast redwood trees along this highway are the tallest trees in the world, some towering to heights of 350 feet. Some of the interesting points along this historic route are: the One Log House, Drive Thru Tree, Chimney Tree, The Hobbitt and the Eternal Tree.

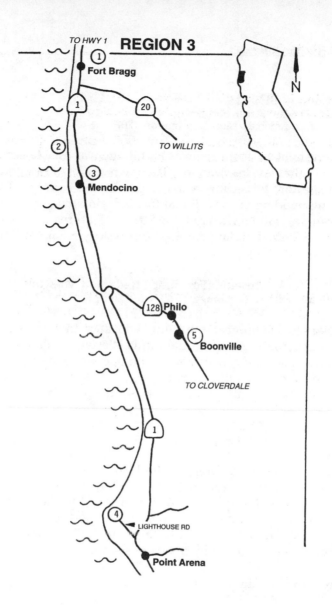

REGION 3

TO HWY 1

① Fort Bragg

1

20

TO WILLITS

②

③ Mendocino

128 Philo

⑤ Boonville

TO CLOVERDALE

1

④ LIGHTHOUSE RD

Point Arena

N

13

1 - Fort Bragg SHL 615
Marker at 321 Main Street, Fort Bragg
Chamber of Commerce Visitor Information (707) 961-6300

In 1857 the military post known as Fort Bragg was established on the Mendocino Indian Reservation. The town of Fort Bragg grew up around the fort to become a major city in the county. The last remaining building of the original fort is maintained by the city of Fort Bragg at 430 North Franklin Street. Pictures and narrative reports inside the building tell the fort's history from 1857 through 1864.

1 - Guest House Museum (Fort Bragg Redwood Museum)
343 North Main Street, Fort Bragg (707) 961-2840

This logging and lumber museum is located in the 1892, C. R. Johnson, guest house, next to California Western Railroad's Skunk Depot. Georgia-Pacific, which owns and operates one of the world's largest redwood sawmills in Fort Bragg, also operates passenger trains on the century-old Skunk line between Fort Bragg and Willits.

1 - Weller House Museum
524 Stewart Street, Fort Bragg (707) 964-3061

The oldest house in Fort Bragg is the 1886 Victorian home built for lumber businessman Horace Weller. Only the finest available redwood was used in the construction of this three-story mansion. Interior paneling came from the heartwood of old growth redwoods—wood that can never be duplicated. Tours of this private residence can be scheduled by calling in advance.

2 - Point Cabrillo Lighthouse
West of Hwy 1, Mendocino

Constructed in the early 1900s, this lighthouse was staffed until 1970 when an automatic beacon was mounted on its roof. The design of this old structure looks to be more like a church than the traditional tower lighthouse. Point Cabrillo Light Station is closed to the public.

3 - Ford House (Mendocino Headlands State Park Visitor Center)
735 Main Street, Mendocino (707) 937-5804 or (707) 937-5397

Mendocino Area Parks Association maintains the 1854 home of J. B. Ford as their local visitors' and interpretive center. Ford discovered this region's redwoods and selected the site where he constructed a sawmill shipped here from the East. History of this region's logging industry is displayed, and information about Mendocino's nineteenth century houses is available from park staff.

3 - Mendocino Presbyterian Church SHL 714
44831 Main Street, Mendocino   (707) 937-5441

Built in the 1860s, this is one of the oldest Protestant churches in continuous use in California and the best known landmark in the area.

3 - Mendocino Historical Research/Kelley House Museum
45007 Albion Street, Mendocino (707) 937-5791

The history of Mendocino's early settlers is exhibited in this restored 1861 pioneer home. Historical photographs and facts about the town's early buildings are maintained in this museum's library.

3 - Temple of Kaun Ti (Chinese Joss House) SHL 927
45160 Albion Street, Mendocino

One of the oldest Chinese houses of worship in continuous use is the Temple of Kaun Ti, built here in the late 1850s. Original furnishings are still in use throughout the temple. This Chinese Joss House is the only remaining Chinese temple on the North Coast.

4 - Point Arena Lighthouse and Museum
Lighthouse Road, west of Hwy 1, Point Arena (707) 882-2777

At 115 feet, Point Arena Lighthouse is among the tallest on the coast. The original structure, built in 1870, was destroyed in the 1906 earthquake. Its replacement, built the following year, is operated as a museum and is open for tours. It was from this station that a Japanese submarine was spotted just after the bombing of Pearl

Harbor in December 1941. That same submarine torpedoed the tanker *Emidio* off Cape Mendocino a few days after this sighting.

5 - Anderson Valley Historical Museum
Highway 128, Schoolhouse exit, 1 mile north of Boonville (707) 895-3207

Housed in the 1891 one-room Con Creek School are the collections of the Anderson Valley Historical Society, including Pomo Indian basketry, stone tools and artifacts found in Anderson Valley. The history and culture of this region's agricultural community and lumbering industry are exhibited in additional structures.

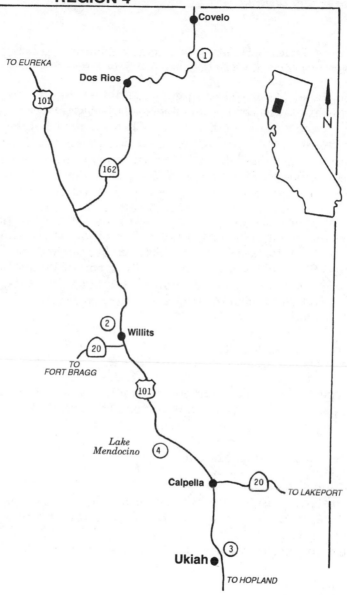

1 - Round Valley SHL 674
Marker at Inspiration Point on Hwy 162 between Dos Rios and Covelo

Round Valley Indian Reservation was established in this valley in 1858 to raise cattle for the Mendocino Indian Reservation at Fort Bragg. Nine different Indian tribes still make their home on this historic site.

2 - Willits Historic Sites
U.S. 101

Victorian-style homes, restored buildings in the downtown area and the Willits Country Mall are part of Willits' historical district where many of these structures from the 1800s can be seen in their original settings. Stage robber Black Bart was also a part of Willits' historic past. He would hide behind the now famous Black Bart Rock, south of town off U.S. 101, and rob the Wells Fargo Stages that traveled the old stage road.

2 - California Western Railroad
299 East Commercial Street, Willits (707) 459-5248

Passenger travel on the century-old California Western Railroad line is regularly scheduled between Willits and Fort Bragg on the Skunk line which boards at this historic depot.

2 - Mendocino County Museum
400 East Commercial Street, Willits (707) 459-2736

This historic museum features Pomo and Yuki Indian baskets, furniture, clothing, tools, machinery and other relics from Mendocino County's early history. Displays show all aspects of life in the county and the changes that have taken place over the years.

3 - Sun House SHL 926
431 South Main Street, Ukiah (707) 462-3370

Constructed in 1911, this Craftsman-style redwood bungalow was the home of ethnologist Dr. John W. Hudson and his wife, the well-known artist, Grace Carpenter Hudson. Docents from the neighboring Grace Hudson Museum conduct regular tours of Sun House which has been completely furnished with items reflecting the lifestyle of this famous couple.

3 - Grace Hudson Museum/The Sun House
431 South Main Street, Ukiah (707) 462-3370

In October 1986, the Grace Hudson Museum opened as an art, history and anthropology museum to house the collections of the Hudson's Sun House. Dr. John Hudson's research on the California Pomo Indians, and paintings of Pomo Indian life by Grace Hudson, are the featured exhibits. Tours of the neighboring Sun House are conducted by docents from the museum.

3 - Held-Poage Memorial Home and Research Library
603 West Perkins Street, Ukiah (707) 462-6969 or (707) 462-2039

Indian artifacts, toys, kitchen antiques and historical records of Mendocino County are featured in this 1903 home now operated as a museum and research library by the Mendocino County Historical Society.

Held-Poage Memorial Home. Courtesy of Mendocino County Historical Society

3 - Moore's Flour Mill
1550 South State Street, Ukiah (707) 462-6550

This water-powered flour mill uses an 18-foot wooden water wheel and two century-old millstones to grind various types of grain into flour. The millstones in this operating mill can be viewed through a window in the visitor area.

3 - Ukiah Vichy Springs Resort   SHL 980
2701 Vichy Springs Road, Ukiah (707) 462-5900

Day's Soda Springs, the first mineral springs resort in this region of California, was established in 1854 by William Day. Colonel William Doolan acquired the resort in 1867, added the Vichy Springs Hotel, and was active in the development and settlement of the region. Although the resort has undergone changes in name and ownership, it remains today as the oldest continuously-operating thermal mineral springs resort in California.

4 - Pomo Visitor Center
Marina Drive, Pomo Day Use Area, north end of Lake Mendocino (707) 485-8685

The round shape of this center is symbolic of the ceremonial dance house used by the Pomo Indians of this region. Exhibits, films and demonstrations depict the 5,000-year history of Mendocino County's first inhabitants.

Mendocino County's Historic Wineries

The introduction of grapes to California's agriculture more than a century ago has produced some of the world's finest wines in the Mendocino-Napa-Sonoma region. Many of these old wineries offer tours of their facilities and usually advertise their locations along the main highways.

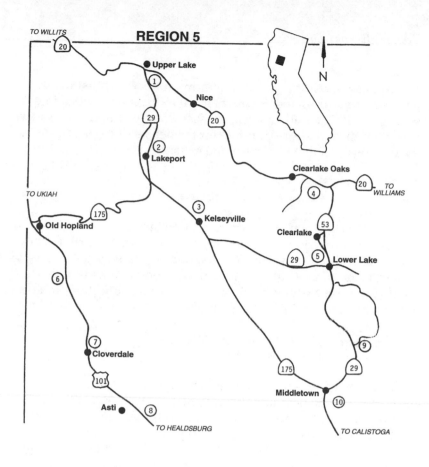

TO WILLITS

20

● Upper Lake

1

Nice

29

20

2

● Lakeport

Clearlake Oaks

20 TO WILLIAMS

TO UKIAH

4

175

● Old Hopland

3

● Kelseyville

53

Clearlake ●

29 5 Lower Lake

6

7

● Cloverdale

9

101

175

29

Asti ● 8

Middletown ●

10

TO HEALDSBURG

TO CALISTOGA

N

---

1 - Upper Lake
Junction of Hwy 20 and Hwy 29, north of Lakeport
Lakeport Visitor Center, 875 Lakeport Boulevard, Lakeport (800) 525-3743

Upper Lake's Main Street has been restored to a style reminiscent of the 1860 frontier days when this town was first settled. An early settler of this area was Benjamin Dewell, one of the men who made the first Bear Flag that flew over California in 1846 during the Bear Flag Revolt.

1 - Bloody Island SHL 427
Reclamation Road and Hwy 20, south of Upper Lake

The murder of two early settlers, Stone and Kelsey, by Indians in

1849 was answered by an attack of army soldiers against the Indian inhabitants of this island. More than 100 Indians were killed in what was later called the "Bloody Island Massacre." It wasn't even known for sure if the Indians responsible for the deaths of Stone and Kelsey were on this island at the time of the massacre.

2 - Old Lake County Courthouse SHL 897
Lake County Museum, 225 North Main, Lakeport (707) 263-4555

In 1870 this courthouse was erected to replace the former building that was destroyed by fire. While this new county courthouse was being built, the county seat was temporarily moved to the city of Lower Lake. Lake County museum is housed within this old courthouse and features a Pomo Indian basket collection, tuleboat and exhibits of early Lake County history.

3 - Stone and Kelsey Monument SHL 426
West end of Main Street, Kelseyville

Charles Stone and Andrew Kelsey used local Indian labor to build their adobe home near this site in the late 1840s. It is believed that Andrew and his brother, Benjamin, forced Indians to work for them in the gold fields, which cost many Indians their lives from starvation, exposure and disease. In the fall of 1849, the Indians rebelled and took the lives of Charles Stone and Andrew Kelsey.

4 - Sulphur Bank Mine SHL 428
Hwy 20 at Sulphur Banks Road, east of Clearlake Oaks
Clearlake Chamber of Commerce (707) 994-3600

Two million pounds of sulphur was mined here between 1865 and 1869. In 1873 the first quicksilver was mined and for over seventy years the mine was an important producer of mercury.

5 - Lower Lake's Stone Jail SHL 429
Main Street, Lower Lake

The town of Lower Lake built this stone jail from locally quarried rock in the 1870s, after the city had been the temporary county seat for two years. It was the smallest jail built in the United States.

5 - Anderson Marsh State Historic Park
Highway 53, north of Hwy 29, between Clearlake and Lower Lake (707) 994-0688 or (707) 279-4293

Scottish immigrant John Still Anderson and his family settled the 1300 acres encompassing this marsh in 1885 and built the ranch buildings which are being used today by the Anderson Marsh Interpretive Association. In 1982, 870 acres of the marsh were purchased by the state. Preserved are several large prehistoric Indian sites and six separate wildlife communities.

6 - Squaw Rock SHL 549
6 miles south of Hopland on U.S. 101

The Indian village of Sanel existed here long before the city, which became Hopland, was settled near this site in 1859. According to Indian Legend, an Indian maiden, Sotuka, leaped from this precipice upon her faithless lover, Chief Cachow, and the woman sleeping by his side, bringing death to all three. In later years this place was called "lovers leap."

7 - Cloverdale Museum
215 North Cloverdale Boulevard, Cloverdale (707) 894-2067

Cloverdale's museum is housed in an 1870s pioneer home which is furnished with Victorian antiques. Various pieces of authentic 1800s furniture have been restored, including an old organ and an antique bed. Old photographs, pioneer paintings and a large collection of household items are on display. Information about this region's early settlers and their homes can be obtained from museum staff.

7 - Icaria-Speranza Commune   SHL 981
27620 Asti Road (on west side of road, 1/4 mile south of U.S. 101), south of Cloverdale

A colony of French immigrants, led by the Dehay and Leroux families, established Icaria-Speranza, an experiment in utopian society, at this 885-acre site in 1881. They followed the teachings of French philosopher, Etienne Cabet, and built a society based on social beliefs, high family values and a strong emphasis on education. It would be the last Icarian community started in the United States. The Icaria schoolhouse was built at this site in 1882.

In 1886, a few months before the colony was disbanded, the schoolhouse and an acre of land was deeded to the Icaria School district.

8 - Italian Swiss Agriculture Colony   SHL 621
River Road off U.S. 101, Asti

One hundred Italian immigrants established an agricultural colony here in 1881. They planted vineyards on a 1,500-acre tract and six years later, built a 7,500-square foot winery. The winery, which can still be toured, became world famous for its award winning wines produced under the name Italian Swiss Colony.

9 - Stone House SHL 450
5 and 1/2 miles north of Middletown on Hwy 29 at Spruce Grove Road

Robert Sterling, whose wife was the first white woman in the valley, built this stone house in 1853-1854. It was torn down forty years later and rebuilt of the same stone.

10 - St. Helena Toll Road   SHL 467
Monument on Hwy 29 at south edge of Middletown

St. Helena Toll Road was built in the 1860s to replace the steeper "Old Bull Trail" that ran between Middletown and Calistoga over Mount St. Helena.

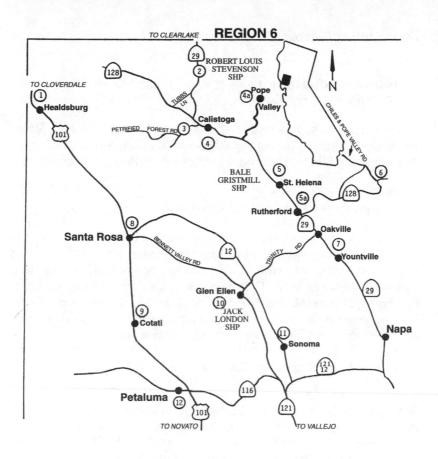

1 - Walters Ranch Hop Kiln   SHL 893
6050 Westside Road, Healdsburg

In the early 1900s, this region was a major Western United States hop-growing area. Among the last remaining relics from that era is this stone hop kiln that was once part of Sol Walters' pioneer ranch.

1 - Healdsburg Museum
221 Matheson Street, Healdsburg   (707) 431-3325

Healdsburg's restored 1910 Carnegie Library building became the permanent home of the Healdsburg Museum in 1989. It houses an impressive range of artifacts and documents related to northern Sonoma County history. Collections include Pomo Indian basketry and crafts, Nineteenth Century weapons, tools, costumes and crafts. Exhibits describe local Pomo Indian culture, the Mexican rancho era, and the infamous Healdsburg squatter's land wars.

2 - Robert Louis Stevenson State Park   SHL 710
5 miles north of Calistoga on Hwy 29   (707) 942-4575

Robert Louis Stevenson spent time here in a miner's cabin with his new bride, Fannie Van de Grift Osborne, in the late spring of 1880. It was memories of that time, around the tunnels of the Silverado mine, that he took with him to France where he wrote "Silverado Squatters." The site of the bunkhouse is marked in this state park.

3 - Old Faithful Geyser of California
1299 Tubbs Lane, Calistoga   (707) 942-6463

This region of California, well-known for its hot spring resorts, is home to the state's only regularly erupting geyser. Fed by a hot, underground river, "Old Faithful" emits 60-foot showers and vapor every 40-45 minutes.

3 - Petrified Forest   SHL 915
4100 Petrified Forest Road, off Hwy 29, west of Calistoga   (707) 942-6667

The volcanic eruption of Mt. St. Helena millions of years ago brought these trees down and covered the area in lava and ash. These preserved trees, turned into stone, were discovered in 1871, and the area opened to visitors. Trees 3 - 12 feet in diameter and 100 feet long were uncovered as the site was excavated over the next 60 years.

4 - Nancy Kelsey's Home Site   SHL 686
4531 Foothill Boulevard (Hwy 128) and Diamond Mountain Road, Calistoga

The first woman to cross the plains, Nancy Kelsey, arrived in California in 1841 and built a home with her husband, Benjamin. All that remains of their home is the hearthstone, which is being preserved on private property.

4 - Site of York and Hudson Cabins   SHL 682 and SHL 683
Foothill Boulevard (Hwy 128) and Lincoln Avenue, Calistoga

Two pioneers, John York and David Hudson each built themselves a cabin on sites that are diagonally across the street from each other. York's redwood log cabin stood on land where he planted this region's first wheat crop. Neither one of these 1845 era cabins remain today.

4 - Napa Valley Railroad Depot   SHL 687
1458 Lincoln Avenue, Calistoga   (707) 942-6332

The second oldest remaining depot in California is the restored, 1868, Southern Pacific Depot in Calistoga. Sam Brannan helped bring the railroad here by getting others interested in financing the line. When the line began operating, 3,000 people came from San Francisco to the grand opening of Sam Brannan's resort. Retail stores now operate within this historic structure.

4 - Sam Brannan Cottage (Brannan Cottage Inn)
109 Wapoo Avenue, Calistoga   (707) 942-4200

Sam Brannan built a hotel and 25 cottages at this site in the 1860s as a summer resort. This meticulously renovated cottage, now a bed and breakfast inn, is the only Sam Brannan cottage remaining at its original location. Nearby at 1712 Lincoln Avenue (Pacheteau's Hot Springs Resort) is Sam Brannan's original hot springs.

4 - Sam Brannan Store SHL 648
Wapoo and Grant Streets, Calistoga

In 1859, Sam Brannan erected this building as a general store to support his thriving resort business. His original building still stands on the same site where it was constructed more than a century ago. It has been operated more recently as a private care home.

4 - Sharpsteen Museum and Sam Brannan Cottage SHL 685
1311 Washington Street, Calistoga (707) 942-5911

Historical scenes of the early days of Calistoga are the featured exhibits at this museum. Temporary exhibits of local historical interest are shown throughout the year. A guide to historical places of interest in Calistoga is published by the museum. On the grounds of the museum is one of the original twenty-five cottages built by the town's founder, Sam Brannan, when he established his famous resort hotel. Robert Louis Stevenson spent time in this cottage in the 1880s as a guest of Sam Brannan's resort.

4 - Schramsberg SHL 561
Schramsberg Road, off Hwy 29, southeast of Calistoga (707) 942-4558

A series of tunnels were built into these hills by Jacob Schram when he began Napa Valley's first hillside winery in 1862. The original house and winery have been well-preserved and can be toured by appointment.

4A - Litto's Hubcap Ranch SHL 939
6654 Pope Valley Road, northwest of Pope Valley

Emanuele Damonte began building Litto in 1942. During a span of 30 years he carefully arranged over 2,000 hubcaps, 200 bird houses, pull-tops, bottles and other recycled materials into arrangements that would become one of California's exceptional twentieth century folk art environments.

Rhine House. Courtesy of Beringer Vineyards, photo by Richard W. Warton.

5 - Beringer Brothers Winery   SHL 814
2000 Main Street, St. Helena (707) 963-7115

Jacob Beringer, who had been employed at the Charles Krug Winery as foreman, selected this site for a winery in the late 1870s. Hundreds of feet of tunnels were cut into these limestone hills for the cellars and winery. Large oak casks are used to store wine in these cellars where the temperature stays at an almost constant 58 degrees Farenheit year around.

5 - Rhine House
2000 Main Street, St. Helena (707) 963-7115
Business Office, 1000 Pratt Avenue, St. Helena

The winery offices and tasting room of the Beringer Vineyards were built in 1885, by Frederick Beringer, who founded the historic Beringer Winery with his brother Jacob in 1876. Many features of the Beringer estate in Germany were duplicated here.

Charles Krug Winery Historic Carriage House which contains the wine library. Courtesy of the Seagrams Classics Wine Co.

5 - Charles Krug Winery SHL 563
2800 Main Street, St. Helena (707) 963-2761
Visitor Center (707) 963-5057

Charles Krug made the first commercial wine in California in 1858 and built a stone wine cellar in what is now the oldest operating winery in the Napa Valley.

5 - Napa Valley Museum
Vintage Hall, 473 Main Street, St. Helena (707) 963-7411

Local art and artifacts representing the history, art and natural history of the Napa Valley are exhibited in a second floor gallery located in the 1912 St. Helena High School building. Other well-maintained 1890s buildings line the city's historic Main Street.

5 - Silverado Museum
1490 Library Lane, St. Helena (707) 963-3757

The life and works of Robert Louis Stevenson are exhibited here in original manuscripts, photographs and artifacts that depict the life of this author.

A leaf from the original manuscript of Jekyll and Hyde. Robert Louis Stevenson's desk. Books from Stevenson's personal library. Courtesy of the Silverado Museum, St. Helena.

5 - Old Bale Mill   SHL 359
Bale Grist Mill State Historic Park, 3369 North St. Helena Hwy
(707) 963-2236

This historic water-powered gristmill, known as the Bale Mill, was constructed in 1846 using locally available materials. Lumber used in the mill's construction came from nearby forests. Millstones were quarried from the hills behind the mill. For the next 25 years, settlers would bring their grain to this mill to be ground into flour. Bale Mill was restored to its original condition and is preserved as part of this historic state park.

5A - Wine Discovery Center
St. Supery Winery, 8440 St. Helena Hwy, Rutherford (707) 963-4507

A gallery of interactive wine exhibits at this modern winery offers visitors a full sensory experience of the wine making process. Grapes can be tasted direct from the vine in the winery's one-acre demonstration vineyard. The Atkinson House, a completely restored 1882 Queen Anne style home, shows the lifestyle of valley residents a century ago. Silver, crystal and the library of the former owner are displayed.

6 - Chiles Mill   SHL 547
3 and 3/4 miles north of Hwy 128 at junction of Lower Chiles Valley Road, and the Chiles and Pope Valley Road

The first American flour mill in Northern California was erected here by Joseph Chiles in the 1840s. The old mill fell into ruins after being abandoned for many years. Only the site of this historic mill remains today.

7 - Yount's Blockhouse, Adobe and Mills   SHL 564
Stone Monument at site on Yount Mill Road, 1 mile north of Yountville

George Yount settled in this region of Napa County in the early 1830s where he constructed a Kentucky-style blockhouse with living quarters upstairs and a fort on the first level. Over the next few years Yount built an adobe, gristmill and sawmill at this site. The contributions of this early pioneer are commemorated at the site where his structures once stood.

7 - Grave of George C. Yount SHL
George C. Yount Pioneer Cemetery, Lincoln and Jackson Streets, Yountville

An emigrant from North Carolina, George Yount came to California in 1831 where his skills as a hunter, trapper and craftsman enabled him to obtain two Mexican land grants in the Napa Valley. Yount was highly respected by the Indians, mission Padres and Mexican officials, and was regarded as a good host by travelers that came this way. The grave of George Yount is marked in this cemetery, where he was laid to rest in 1865.

7 - Veterans Home of California SHL 828
California Drive and Hwy 29, Yountville (707) 944-4918

Veterans of the Mexican War founded this home for elderly and disabled veterans in 1884. The state of California has owned and maintained the home since 1897.

8 - Hood House SHL 692
7501 Sonoma Hwy, Santa Rosa (707) 539-6660

William Hood constructed this building from bricks he fired on this site in 1858. His house was purchased by the state in the early 1940s and is now a part of the California Youth Authority as a detention facility.

8 - Robert Ripley Memorial Museum
490 Sonoma Avenue, Santa Rosa (707) 524-5233

Creator of "Ripley's Believe it—or not!," Robert L. Ripley, was a native of Santa Rosa and is memorialized in this museum. Memorabilia from Ripley's travels around the world are exhibited along with many personal items. Even this building is an example of Ripley's cartoons—for it was built from a single redwood tree . . . believe it, or not!

8 - Sonoma County Museum
425 - 7th Street, Santa Rosa (707) 579-1500

Santa Rosa's former post office building was moved to this location in 1979 and converted into a county museum. A collection of cultural, historic and artistic exhibits from Sonoma County are displayed.

First Floor Lobby, Sonoma County Museum. Courtesy Sonoma County Museum.

8 - Luther Burbank Home and Gardens   SHL 234
200 block of Santa Rosa Avenue, Santa Rosa (707) 524-5445

Pioneer horticulturist Luther Burbank lived here for 50 years conducting plant breeding experiments to improve the quality of plants and to increase the world's food supply. In these gardens, and on his 18-acre experimental farm outside Sebastopol, Burbank introduced more than 800 new varieties of plants, fruits, vegetables, nuts and grains. His home, original furnishings, greenhouse, carriage house and gardens are open to the public. Arbor Day in California is celebrated on March 7, the anniversary of Luther Burbank's birthday.

8 - Jesse Peter Memorial Museum
1501 Mendocino Avenue, Santa Rosa (707) 527-4479

Indian artifacts from California's Native American Indian tribes are the featured exhibits of this museum.

9 - Cotati's Downtown Plaza SHL 879
U.S. 101, Cotati

The center of the town of Cotati was laid out in a hexagon shape with each of the six streets on the outside of the hexagon named for the six sons of the area's first white settler, Dr. Thomas Page. Only one other city, Detroit, Michigan, was designed in the same hexagonal street pattern as this 1897 city.

10 - Jack London State Historic Park SHL 743
2400 London Ranch Road, 1 and 1/2 miles west of Glen Ellen (707) 938-5216

This ranch was the home of the celebrated author, Jack London, from 1905 until his death at age 40 in 1916. Included on these grounds are his grave, the ruins of "Wolf House" and the "House of Happy Walls." "Wolf House" was completed by London in 1913, but was destroyed by fire just before he and his wife were to move in. All that remains are the walls and chimneys, which were constructed of native volcanic stone. The "House of Happy Walls" was built by his wife, Charmain London, three years after his death as a memorial to him. It now houses a museum of London's art works which he collected from the South Pacific and furnishings from his original study.

11 - San Francisco Solano Mission Vineyard (Sebastiani) SHL 739
389 Fourth Street East, Sonoma (707) 938-5532

The first vineyard in Sonoma County was planted here by mission Fathers in 1825. General Vallejo acquired the vineyards after secularization of the mission in 1835 and produced prize-winning wines. In the early 1900s, Samuele Sebastiani, an Italian immigrant, purchased this property on which the family continues to produce fine wines. The winery operates an Indian artifact museum and exhibits a large collection of carved casks at this historic site.

11 - Site of Union Hotel and Union Hall   SHL 627
Napa Street and First Street West, Sonoma

A two-story stone hotel and meeting hall were built here to replace the single story adobe and frame buildings that were damaged by fire in 1866. In 1955, both buildings were razed and a bank constructed on this site.

11 - Salvador Vallejo Adobe   SHL 501
417 First Street West, Sonoma

Salvador Vallejo, brother of General Vallejo, lived in this adobe home until the summer of 1846 when he and the General were temporarily taken prisoners in the Bear Flag Revolt. A second story was added to the building when it became a boarding school for the Presbyterian Cumberland College from 1858-1864.

11 - Sonoma Depot Museum
270 First Street West, Sonoma   (707) 938-9765

Sonoma's original train depot was destroyed by fire in 1976. Funds were raised and this replica was constructed the following year. It now houses the Sonora Valley Historical Museum with furnishings and decor of the 1880s. Historical artifacts are displayed in realistic settings.

11 - Swiss Hotel   SHL 496
18 West Spain Street, Sonoma

This adobe home was built for General Vallejo's brother and his wife who came here in 1840. It became the Swiss Hotel in the late 1880s. Preserved as part of Sonoma State Historic Park, the Swiss Hotel operates as a restaurant in an early 1900s setting.

11 - General Mariano Vallejo's Home   SHL 4
West Spain Street and Third Street West, Sonoma   (707) 938-1578

General Vallejo, founder of the Pueblo de Sonoma and an outstanding man of his day, built his frame house which he named "Lachryma Montis," on this site in 1851-1852. After California became independent of Mexico, General Vallejo was chosen to be a member of the Constitutional Convention of California which was held in Monterey in 1849. He lived here until his death in 1890. A collection of Vallejo's memorabilia is housed in a museum maintained in the nearby Swiss Chalet.

11 - Sonoma Barracks   SHL 316
Corner of Spain and First Street East, Sonoma

Sonoma Barracks was erected in 1836, by General Vallejo, as quarters for the Mexican soldiers that defended the Pueblo de Sonoma. This building was the headquarters of the Bear Flag Party, who ultimately proclaimed California a republic, and raised the "Bear Flag" over Sonoma's plaza in June 1846.

11 - Bear Flag Monument   SHL 7
Spain and First Street East, Sonoma

Concerned that Mexico was planning to drive American settlers out of California, Captain John Fremont and a party of 33 men made a surprise attack against the Pueblo de Sonora and captured General Vallejo in June 1846. Since their action didn't represent the United States, the American Flag could not be raised. Instead, the "Bear Flag of the California Republic" was created and raised over Sonoma. Three weeks later American forces landed in Monterey and declared California a territory of the United States. On July 9, 1846, the Bear Flag was replaced with the "Stars and Stripes" by Lt. Joseph Revere, grandson of Paul Revere.

11 - Nash Adobe   SIIL 667
579 First Street East, Sonoma

John Nash was taken prisoner here in 1847 by Lt. William Tecumseh Sherman when he refused to give up his post as alcalde to Lilburn Boggs. Lewis Adler, a pioneer merchant in Sonoma, lived in this home with his wife Nancy in 1848. Nancy Adler's great-granddaughter restored the adobe in 1931.

11 - Sonoma State Historic Park
20 East Spain Street, Sonoma (707) 938-1578

Six buildings have been preserved as part of the Sonoma State Historic Park with another four in the same area designated as State Historical Landmarks.

11 - Mission San Francisco Solano SHL 3
114 East Spain Street, Sonoma

The last of the 21 California Franciscan missions was established here in 1823 on the advice of California's Mexican Governor Arguello who wanted to check the advance of Russian settlements into the California interior.

11 - Blue Wing Inn SHL 17
133 East Spain Street, Sonoma

General Vallejo had this two-story adobe inn constructed in the early 1840s to accommodate emigrants and travelers that came to the Pueblo de Sonoma. It later became one of the first hotels in Northern California. Kit Carson and Ulysses S. Grant are among the famous guests who stayed at this hotel.

11 - Buena Vista Winery SHL 392
18000 Old Winery Road, Sonoma (707) 938-1266

The first wine grapes grown in California, from European vine cuttings, were in Colonel Agoston Haraszthy's Buena Vista Vineyard in 1857. Colonel (Count) Haraszthy was also the first to use California redwood for wine tanks. The cellars he tunneled into these limestone hills can be seen today at this historic winery.

11 - Sonoma Gaslight and Western Railroad Train Town
On Broadway, 1 mile south of Sonoma's town square (707) 938-3912

Fifteen-inch gauge live-steam locomotives and diesel replicas are used to transport visitors on tours of this 10-acre railroad park. The park depicts a mountain mining district as it might have been in the late 1800s with trees, lakes, bridges, tunnels and buildings. Railroad shops and full-size equipment are also on display.

11 - Temelec Hall   SHL 237
220 Temelec Circle, 3 miles southeast of Sonoma

This 20-room house, with its nine fireplaces, was built using forced Indian labor, by Captain Granville Swift, a member of the Bear Flag Party. Constructed of stone from local quarries, it was said to have cost more than $250,000 when it was built in 1858, making it the most expensive house in the county. It is still in use today as a community center in a privately owned retirement community.

Buena Vista Winery, yesterday and today. Courtesy of Buena Vista Winery Vineyards.

12 - Petaluma Adobe SHL 18
Petaluma Adobe State Historic Park, 3325 Adobe Road, Petaluma
(707) 762-4871

Between 1834 and 1844 General Vallejo built one of the state's finest adobe houses on his 66,000-acre ranchero. This immense building was his headquarters for cattle ranching and farming. Within its walls were facilities for supporting this large operation: tannery, smithy, gristmill, meat curing, basket making and other similar operations. The quality of the building's original construction can be seen in this completely restored adobe structure.

General Mariano Vallejo's Adobe. Courtesy of Petaluma Adobe State Historic Park.

12 - Petaluma Historic Walking Tour
Chamber of Commerce, 215 Howard Street, Petaluma (707) 762-2785

The city of Petaluma was settled in the 1850s. Many of the city's older buildings were constructed by those first settlers. The downtown area has: "Iron Front" buildings from the late 1800s; stone and brick buildings from the early 1900s; and false front stucco structures.

12 - Petaluma Historical Library and Museum
20 Fourth Street, Petaluma (707) 778-4398

Housed in this 1904 Carnegie Library are historical exhibits of Petaluma from the 1850s. A unique feature of this building is its free standing stained glass dome—the only one of its type in the state. A guide to the city's other historic buildings is available from museum staff.

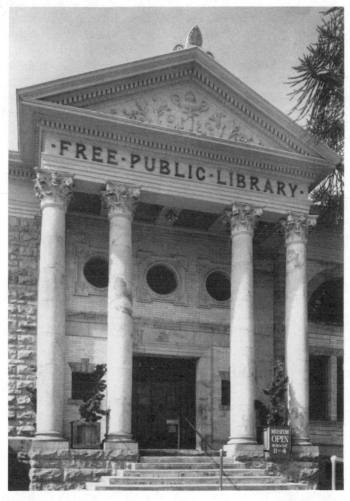

Petaluma Library/Museum. Courtesy of the Petaluma Area Chamber of Commerce.

REGION 7

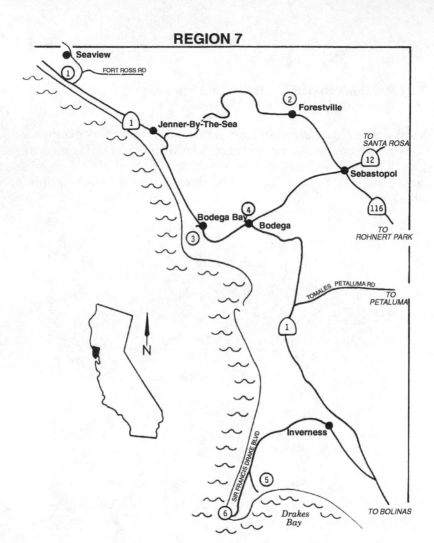

1 - Fort Ross State Historic Park   SHL 5
19005 Coast Highway, 13 miles north of Jenner-By-The-Sea   (707) 847-3286

Fort Ross was built by Russians in 1812 as the center of their settlement in this region of California. Russians came here primarily to trap sea otter for its fur, but also successfully farmed the land. Russia's flag flew over this colony until 1841 when they sold all their holdings to Captain John Sutter. The original 1836 commandant's house has been preserved along with many structures rebuilt with original materials including the Russian Orthodox chapel, Kuskor House and Call House.   Original furnishings used during the Russian occupation of this fort are exhibited in this state park

2 - Cooper's Sawmill   SHL 835
Mirabel Park, 2 miles north of Forestville on Mark West Creek, off River Road

The first known commercial water-powered sawmill was built here in 1834, by Captain John Cooper, brother-in-law of General Vallejo. Nothing remains today of his sawmill or the redwood home he built on his Rancho El Molino. A plaque commemorates this pioneer California enterprise.

3 - Bodega Bay and Harbor   SHL 833
Doran Park, off Hwy 1, south of Bodega Bay   (707) 875-2211

Bodega Bay was named for Spanish explorer, Juan Francisco de la Bodega who explored this region in October 1775. In the early 1800s, Russian trappers who hunted sea otter off the California Coast established their settlement here. With the departure of the Russians in 1841 and the arrival of American settlers, the principal activity of this area changed to lumbering. An 1861 Catholic Church and 1873 schoolhouse are among the early settler's buildings still remaining.

4 - St. Teresa's Catholic Church   SHL 820
Bodega Hwy near Bodega Lane, Bodega

Constructed of redwood, in 1859-1860, St. Teresa's has served this community continuously for more than a century. It is one of the oldest buildings in this region of California.

5 - Drakes Bay
Stone Cross on Drakes Beach, Point Reyes National Seashore
(415) 663-1092

When Sir Francis Drake landed along this shore in 1579, he claimed California for Queen Elizabeth I of England. Although the exact location of his landing cannot be determined, the plate of brass he nailed to a post when he set foot on California soil has been found. It is on display at the Berkeley campus of the University of California. A stone cross commemorating Drake's landing has been erected in this preserved area.

6 - Point Reyes Lighthouse
End of Sir Francis Drake Boulevard, Point Reyes National Seashore, off Hwy 1, Point Reyes (415) 669-1534

The many shipwrecks caused by this area's persistent fog made it imperative that a lighthouse be placed here. In 1870, Point Reyes Lighthouse opened with a thousand-prism lens towering almost 300 feet above the sea. This station was staffed for more than a century until it was replaced with an automated light, and fog signal, in 1975. Today, it is operated as a historical site by the National Parks Service.

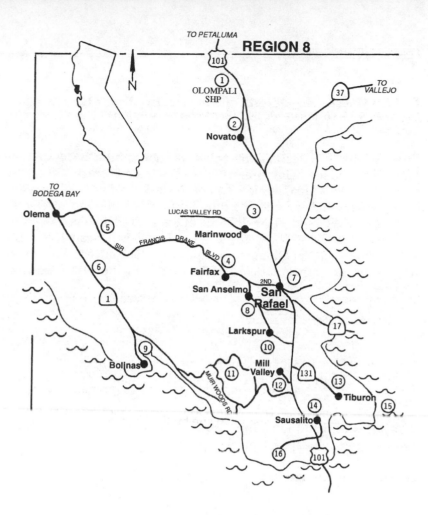

1 - First House Erected North of San Francisco Bay   SHL 210
Olompali State Historic Park, 8901 Redwood Hwy, north of Novato, west of
U.S. 101 (415) 456-1286 weekdays or (415) 892-3383 weekends

Ruins of the 1776 Ynitia adobe, the first house built north of San
Francisco Bay, are being preserved at this State Historic Park. Its
owner, Camilo Ynitia, was the son of the last chief of the Olompali
Coast Miwok Indians and the only California Indian to receive a
Mexican Land Grant. A small battle of the Bear Flag Revolt of 1846
took place at this site, with the loss of one American life. An
archaeological dig at Olompali uncovered a 1567 silver sixpence, a
relic from Sir Francis Drake's 1579 visit with the Coast Miwok
Indians.

2 - Novato History Museum
815 DeLong Avenue, Novato (415) 897-4320

The restored circa 1850 home of Novato's first postmaster, Henry F.
Jones, houses the city's museum of history. Memorabilia from
Hamilton Air Force Base, which operated here from 1928 to 1975, is
displayed in the museum's Hamilton Room. Antique furniture,
dolls, dresses, hand fans, furs, toys, tools, and a collection of old
photographs and maps are displayed.

2 - Marin Museum of the American Indian
2200 Novato Boulevard, Miwok Park, Novato (415) 897-4064

This museum of the American Indian stands on the site once
inhabited by California Coast Miwok Indians. Aboriginal house pits,
the ruins of an adobe constructed in the 1830s and the remains of a
stone reservoir can be seen on these grounds. Featured in the
museum are photographs, Indian artifacts and archaeological
material that pertains to Indians that once lived here.

3 - Miller Creek School Historical Sites
2255 Las Gallinas Avenue, Marinwood

Adjacent to the Miller Creek School are the Old Dixie Schoolhouse
and the Miwok Archaeological Preserve. The Old Dixie Schoolhouse
was built as a one room schoolhouse in 1864 and continued to be
used until 1958. It was moved to this location in 1971 and restored.

Visits to the old school can be arranged by calling (415) 479-8881. Evidence of Coast Miwok Indians has been found in several shell mounds along Miller Creek; prompting local residents to preserve the area. Artifacts found in these mounds are displayed in the Miller Creek School. For tours of the mound call (415) 883-4310.

4 - Site of the "Lord Fairfax" Home   SHL 679
Marin Town and Country Club, south end of Pastori Avenue, Fairfax

Charles Fairfax, California Assemblyman and Speaker of the Assembly, moved here with his wife in the late 1850s when he was Clerk of the State Supreme Court. Known as "Lord Fairfax," because of his royal ancestry, his home was the social center of this region. The last political duel in California was fought here, by two members of the state legislature, at an 1861 party given by Lord Fairfax. Nothing remains today of the Fairfax home.

5 - Pioneer Paper Mill   SHL 552
Samuel P. Taylor State Park, Sir Francis Drake Boulevard, 4 miles southeast of Olema (415) 488-9897

Pacific Coast's first paper mill was erected here by Samuel Taylor in 1856. For almost 40 years the mill shipped paper to San Francisco and other West Coast cities. Taylor was proud of the natural beauty surrounding his mill and encouraged friends to come and camp in the area. Eventually, "Camp Taylor" was established as a public resort. His son later built the Hotel Azalea to room the many visitors to this pioneer resort.

6 - Olema Lime Kilns   SHL 222
East side of Olema Creek, 100 yards west of Hwy 1, 4 and 1/2 miles south of Olema

James Shorb and William Mercer were believed to have used these stone kilns in the 1850s to produce lime from the limestone hills in this area. No record exists to establish who constructed these kilns or when they were built. Several 1850s buildings remain in the nearby town of Olema including the Olema Inn which once operated as the Nelson Hotel when this was a stage stop.

7 - Marin County Civic Center SHL 999
East of U.S. 101, 2501 Civic Center Drive, San Rafael. For tour information (415) 499-7407

The Marin County Civic Center is the last major work of Frank Lloyd Wright, the largest constructed project of his career, and the only one built to house institutions of government. Wright's beliefs in democratic values are expressed in his design of the futuristic-looking complex: a 580-foot long, three-story Administration Building; and an 880-foot long, four-story, Hall of Justice, set off at an angle and joined together by a central, 80-foot diameter, rotunda.

7 - St. Vincent's School for Boys SHL 630
1 St. Vincent Drive, San Rafael (415) 479-8831

Don Timoteo Murphy, appointed administrator of Mission San Rafael by General Vallejo, willed more than 300 acres of his land to the Archbishop of San Francisco in 1853 for the building of a school. St. Vincent's School for Boys was established two years later by the Sisters of Charity of St. Vincent de Paul. It is now operated as a home for disturbed young boys.

7 - Mission San Rafael Archangel SHL 220
1104 - Fifth Avenue, between Court and "B" Streets, San Rafael (415) 454-8141

Mission San Rafael was the twentieth of the 21 missions founded by the Franciscan Padres in Alta California. After secularization in 1834, the neglected mission deteriorated until nothing of the original buildings remained. A replica of the mission was built near the original site in 1949. Three of the mission's original bells hang outside the chapel entrance in one wing of this replicated mission. The other wing contains the mission museum. St. Raphael's Catholic Church is located on the site of the mission's first chapel.

7 - Marin County Historical Society Museum (Ira Cook House)
Boyd Park, 1125 "B" Street, San Rafael (415) 454-8538

Constructed in 1879, as a guest house by Ira Cook, it now serves as the home of Marin County Historical Society's Museum. Local artifacts, memorabilia and photographs are displayed from Marin County's early pioneer settlers

7 - China Camp State Park SHL 924
247 North San Pedro Road, San Rafael (415) 456-0766

China Camp, with 10,000 residents, was among the most populous of the Chinese settlements in the San Francisco Bay area between 1874 and 1910. Chinese fishermen introduced commercial fishing to this region, using Chinese junks and nets to catch tiny bay shrimp, which they exported in large quantity to China. Four of the buildings erected when the settlement was first established are preserved in this state park.

7 - Falkirk Community Cultural Center
1408 Mission Avenue, San Rafael (415) 485-3328

Furnishings from the late 1800s are featured in this 1888 Victorian mansion. On the grounds of this museum are sculpture gardens and an arboretum.

Falkirk Community Cultural Center, San Rafael. Photos by Robin Rothstein (interior) and Gary Sinick (exterior).

8 - San Francisco Theological Seminary
2 Kensington, San Anselmo (415) 258-6500

San Francisco Theological Seminary was originally established in San Francisco's City College in 1854, as a training center for the Presbyterian ministry. It moved three times before permanently locating here in 1891-1892. Tours of this pioneer California seminary can be arranged by calling the Administration Office.

9 - Bolinas Museum
48 Wharf Road, Bolinas (415) 868-0330

History of west Marin county's shipping, lumbering and dairy industry, and collections of regional artifacts are on display.

9 - Bolinas Lighter Wharf 221
2 miles north of Bolinas at junction of Hwy 1 and Olema-Bolinas Road

Lumber from mills in the surrounding area was delivered to this lagoon by wagon to be transported by ship to San Francisco. At this wharf, wood was transferred to lighters (barges) and taken out to ships anchored in the deeper offshore waters. Bolinas wharf was a major link in the transportation of lumber to San Francisco in the 1850s. Some of the century-old buildings are still being used.

9 - Audubon Canyon Ranch
Bolinas Lagoon Preserve, 4900 Hwy 1, 3 miles north of Stinson Beach (415) 868-9244

A thousand acres of a former dairy ranch with forests of Douglas Fir and Coast Redwood have been preserved here as a wildlife sanctuary for the once, "nearly-extinct" Great Egrets and Great Blue Herons. Local Native American history, and an introduction to the Preserve, is presented in the Display Hall inside the converted milking barn.

10 - Green Brae Brick Kiln SHL 917
125 East Sir Francis Drake Boulevard, Larkspur

Remillard Brick Company, once the largest brick manufacturer on the West Coast, operated this kiln until 1915. Remillard bricks, which were last produced in 1968, can be found in many of San Francisco's landmarks, such as Ghirardelli Square.

11 - Muir Woods National Monument
Muirwoods Road off Hwy 1, southwest of Mill Valley (415) 388-2595

More than 500 acres of redwoods, the tallest trees in the world, are preserved in this part of our National Park system. It. was here, in 1945, that 500 people attended a ceremony to commemorate the forming of the United Nations in San Francisco. A monument to that occasion, and to President Franklin D. Roosevelt, was erected in a Cathedral-like setting of towering redwoods a half mile into the park along the main trail.

12 - Old Mill   SHL 207
Old Mill Park, Cascade Drive at Throckmorton Avenue and Old Mill Street, Mill Valley (415) 383-1370

The town of Mill Valley was named after Marin County's first sawmill which was built here in the 1830s by John Reed (Read). Remains of Reed's old saw mill are now preserved in Old Mill Park. Reed also ran the first ferry boat operation in the San Francisco Bay.

12 - Mill Valley Outdoor Art Club   SHL 922
1 West Blithedale Avenue, Mill Valley (415) 388-9886

During the late 1800s a summer resort was operated here at what was then known as Blithedale. Residents, concerned about the increasing number of campers and others who came to this area for its recreational value, formed the Outdoor Art Club in 1902 to preserve the area's natural environment. The club has its headquarters in this redwood building.

13 - Lyford House
376 Greenwood Beach Road, Tiburon (415) 388-2524

Built in 1876, this restored Victorian home is on an 11-acre section of the National Audubon Society's 900-acre sanctuary. Tours of this home, which is furnished in late 1800s period antiques, can be arranged by calling the Society.

Lyford House. Courtesy of Richardson Bay Audubon Center, Tiburon.

Old St. Hilary's Landmark. Tiburon. Courtesy of Old St. Hilary's Landmark Society, photo by Phillip L. Molten.

13 - Old St. Hilary's Historic Preserve
Located above the intersection of Alemany and Esperanza Streets, overlooking Tiburon (415) 435-1853

Artifacts from early California settlers are displayed in this 1888 Carpenter-Gothic style "Old St. Hilary's in the Wildflowers Church." This is one of the few buildings of this style still in its original condition in California.

13 - The China Cabin, 1866 Social Saloon of the SS *China*
52-4 Beach Road, Belvedere (415) 435-1853

The SS *China*, an 1866 wooden, side-wheel, transpacific steamship, which was also rigged for sail, was designed and built by William Webb, the leading 19th century American naval architect. In 1886, after thirty round trips to Yokahama and Hong Kong, the ship was taken out of service. The social saloon and two attached staterooms were removed and barged here where they were used as part of a residence for 90 years. In 1978, an extensive restoration of the Victorian-style Social Saloon was completed. Its walnut woodwork, cut-glass floral window panes, oil-burning brass chandeliers with crystal prisms, and 22k gold trim made this one of the finest passenger ship accommodations in the world. The China Cabin operates today as a maritime museum, and for use again as a social saloon.

The 1866 Social Saloon of the SS China. Courtesy of Old St. Hillary's Landmark Society, photo by Phillip L. Molten.

14 - San Francisco Bay Delta Model
2100 Bridgeway, Sausalito (415) 332-3870 or (415) 332-3871

This two-acre scale model of the entire San Francisco Bay and River Delta region was built by the U.S. Corps of Engineers in 1956. It is hydraulically operated and used to determine and analyze bay characteristics and behavior under various conditions. It is one of the largest working scale models in the world.

15 - Angel Island State Park SHL 529
Can only be reached by ferry from San Francisco or Tiburon, for Ferry service information call (415) 435-1915 or (415) 435-2131

Named by Spanish explorer, Juan Manuel de Ayala in 1775, Angel Island has served as a quarantine station for new immigrants to America and as a wartime detention facility for Japanese and Italian prisoners of war during World War II. Indian dwelling sites and several military buildings from the 19th and 20th centuries can be seen along the park's twelve miles of trails.

16 - Point Bonita Lighthouse
Alexander Avenue exit off U.S. 101, take Conzelman Road and follow signs to Lighthouse, call ahead for tour hours (415) 331-1540

Established in 1855, the original Point Bonita Light Station was replaced by this masonry building in 1877. Shortly after the lighthouse was opened, the West Coast's first fog signal was placed here—an iron cannon which had to be fired every half-hour when there was fog. The cannon was replaced with a more efficient signal two years later. This station was staffed until 1980 when it became the last of California's stations to be automated.

The Historic Point Bonita Lighthouse, Marin Headlands. Courtesy of U.S. Dept. of the Interior, National Park Service, photo by Richard Frear.

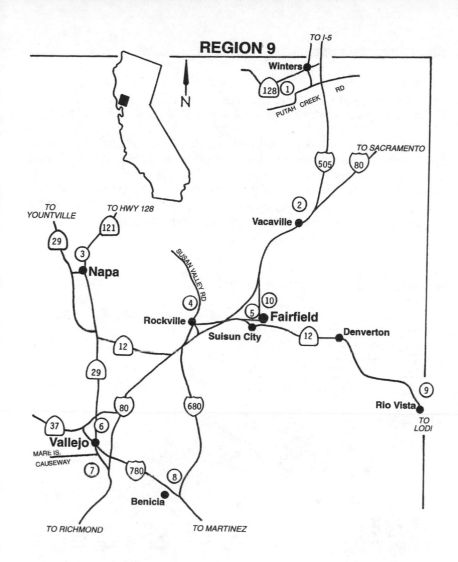

REGION 9

TO I-5

Winters

128   1

PUTAH   CREEK   RD

TO SACRAMENTO

505   80

2

Vacaville

TO
YOUNTVILLE

TO HWY 128

29   121

3   Napa

SUSAN VALLEY RD

4

10

Rockville   5   Fairfield

Suisun City   12   Denverton

12

29

80   680

37   6   Rio Vista

Vallejo   TO
LODI

MARE IS.
CAUSEWAY   7   780   8   9

Benicia

TO RICHMOND   TO MARTINEZ

N

55

1 - University of California Experimental Farm   SHL 804
2 miles southwest of Winters, off Putah Creek Road

Solano County's first American settler, John Wolfskill, arrived here in 1842 with one of his brothers and their 96-head of cattle. A true horticulturist, he planted acres of nuts and seeds and began the county's first orchards. More than 100 acres of the Wolfskill Ranch were willed to the University of California in 1937 to be used as an experimental agricultural farm. University buildings now stand on the site of John Wolfskill's family home.

2 - Vacaville Museum
213 Buck Avenue, Vacaville (707) 447-4513

Vacaville's museum is located in a historic residential area of the city in the midst of old Victorian homes. Artifacts from the beginning of Solano County in the 1850s, photographs, flat irons from across the United States and lingerie are among the museum's featured collections. A guide to the city's historical buildings is available at the museum.

"Solano Women" exhibit, Vacaville Museum. Courtesy Vacaville Museum, photo by James D. Toms

2 - Pena Adobe   SHL 534
Pena Adobe Road, east off I-80 in Pena Adobe Park, Vacaville
(707) 449-5198 or (707) 449-5390

Governor Pio Pico made a substantial land grant to Juan Vaca and Juan Pena who emigrated here from New Mexico in 1842. They both built adobe houses, but only the Pena adobe remains today. It has been restored to its original condition and furnished with mid-1800 pieces. The Pena adobe is considered to be one of the oldest structures in the state. Local historical artifacts are housed in the Mowers-Goheen Museum adjacent to the adobe.

3 - First Presbyterian Church   SHL 878
1333 Third Street, Napa

Pioneer architects R. H. Daley and Theodore Eisen designed this building that was erected as the First Presbyterian Church. This church has been in continuous use since it was constructed in 1874.

3 - Napa County Historical Society Research Library and Museum
1219 First Street, Napa (707) 224-1739

This is the oldest library in the state still being used for its original purpose. The 1901 Goodman Library Building houses the research library and collections of the Napa County Historical Society. Historical documents and photographs, Chinese period clothing, old pistols, stationery of old Napa Valley businesses, authentic Native American baskets, and old grocery baskets are exhibited.

4 - Rockville Stone Chapel   SHL 779
Suisun Valley Road and Rockville Road, Rockville

Benicia's Reverend Sylvester Woodbridge, who came to California as a missionary from New York, laid the cornerstone for this Methodist Episcopal Church building in 1856. In 1929, ten years after the last services were held, the building was donated to the Rockville Public Cemetery. It was restored in 1940, as a pioneer memorial, and remains on these grounds as a cemetery chapel.

Historic Key System streetcar No. 352 now back in service at the Western Railway Museum at Rio Vista Junction. Photo by Harre W. Demoro.

"Boat" car from Blackpool, England. Courtesy of the Western Railway Museum, photo by Harre W. Demoro.

5 - Western Railway Museum
5848 Hwy 12, Suisun City (707) 527-9440

An 1886 New York City "EL" is among the 100 vintage electric and steam railroad exhibits on the grounds of this 23-acre museum. Electric trolleys and rail cars operate year-round on two-mile tours of the displays. Antique gasoline engines, steam threshers and early automobiles are also exhibited.

6 - Vallejo Naval and Historical Museum
734 Marin Street, Vallejo (707) 643-0077

The history of Vallejo and nearby Mare Island Naval Yard is displayed in photographs, documents, relics from the 1850s and memorabilia. The museum is housed in the old Vallejo city hall, the town's only building listed on the National Register of Historic Places. Inside is a working 40-foot Navy periscope from the USS *Baya*. Group tours of Mare Island Naval facility can be arranged through this museum.

6 - Site of Second State Capitol Building SHL 574
219 York Street, Vallejo

General Vallejo granted land to the state and agreed to build a capitol building, schools, churches and other structures if the state would move the capitol from San Jose to this location. The capitol was located here for two years between 1851 and 1853, but the financing Vallejo needed to fulfill his agreement with the state did not materialize, and the capitol moved to Benicia. The frame building that Vallejo constructed no longer stands.

6 - Vallejo Architectural Heritage District
Vallejo Chamber of Commerce, 2 Florida Street, Vallejo (707) 644-5551

Preserved within the Vallejo Architectural Heritage District are almost two dozen, pre-1900 homes built in various architectural styles popular before the turn-of-the-century. A guide to these homes is available from the Chamber of Commerce.

7 - U. S. Naval Shipyard SHL 751
Mare Island Causeway, west of Hwy 29, Vallejo (707) 646-4465
Heritage District (707) 644-7649

The Navy's first shipyard on the Pacific Coast was established in 1854 under the command of Commander David Farragut, who later became a Civil War hero and the Navy's first full admiral. The battleship *California* was one of more than 500 ships built at this yard. Preserved on this military facility is the Navy's oldest chapel; and an 1856 cemetery, containing the graves of sailors of eight nationalities. The daughter of Francis Scott Key is also buried here. Mare Island tours can be arranged by calling the Public Affairs Office, or by contacting the Vallejo Naval and Historical Museum at (707) 643-0077.

8 - Fischer-Hanlon House   SHL 880
135 West "G" Street, next to Benicia Capitol State Park, Benicia
(707) 745-3385

Swiss immigrant, Joseph Fischer, moved the unburned half of a hotel from another site to this lot which he purchased in 1858. He converted the hotel into a home for his family by adding a front porch, additional rooms on the rear of the structure and several outbuildings behind the old hotel. The house, with its original furnishings and family clothing, was given to the state of California in 1968 by Fischer's three nieces, the Hanlon daughters.

8 - Benicia-Capitol State Historic Park   SHL 153
101 West 1st Street, Benicia City Park (707) 745-3385

Benicia's city hall, designed to resemble a Greek temple, was offered to the state for use as a capitol building in the early 1850s. The state capitol, known in those days as the "capitol on wheels" moved here in 1853. It was the third location in as many years. A year later, the capitol moved again to what would become its final destination . . . Sacramento. This building was used as the county seat of government until 1859 and is now preserved as a state historic park. Reconstructed furniture, from the 1850s, and historic exhibits are on display in this restored building.

8 - Site of Benicia Seminary   SHL 795
153 West "I" Street, Benicia

In 1852, one of the first Protestant girl's schools in the state was established on this site. For more than 30 years the Benicia Seminary graduated quality students, many who went on to successful teaching careers in other schools. Reverend Cyrus and his wife, who owned the Seminary for six years, founded the famous Mills College of Oakland. Nothing remains of the old Seminary building that once stood here.

8 - Benicia Historic Tour
Benicia Chamber of Commerce, 601 - 1st Street, Benicia (707) 745-2120

A guide to Benicia's 21 historical points of interest is available from the Chamber of Commerce.

8 - Site of First Protestant Church in California   SHL 175
Benicia City Park, Military West Street and 1st Street, Benicia

California's first Protestant Church was erected on this site in 1849 by Reverend Sylvester Woodbridge, a missionary sent here from New York. He also established the first school in Benicia, which was one of the first in California. The building was abandoned in 1871 and no longer stands.

8 - First Masonic Hall in California   SHL 174
106 West "J" Street, Benicia

In 1850, the first Masonic Hall built in California was erected here. For two years, when Benicia was the county seat, the first floor of the building was used as the county courthouse. Ownership of the building changed several times until it was reacquired in 1950 and was once again used as a Masonic Lodge.

8 - St. Paul's Episcopal Church   SHL 862
120 East "J" Street at 1st Street, Benicia

Captain Julian McAllister, Commander of the Benicia Arsenal, designed this unique church in 1859. Built by workmen from the Pacific Mail and Steamship Company, the church's ceiling is like an inverted ship's hull. It has been in continuous use since 1860.

8 - Benicia Barracks   SHL 177
2024 Camel Road, Benicia (707) 745-5435

This was one of the first military bases established in California, by the U.S. Army, in 1849. The Army's headquarters were established in what was planned to be the central military post in this section of California. These barracks were abandoned in 1908 and became part of the Benicia Arsenal.

8 - Benicia Arsenal   SHL 176
2024 Camel Road, Benicia (707) 745-5435

A small wooden powder magazine was erected here in 1851 to serve as an ordinance supply depot for the U.S. Army. Two years later, construction of an additional fifteen frame and stone buildings, was begun. One building constructed in 1857 was a magazine with 4 and 1/2-foot thick stone walls. Still standing in excellent condition are the post hospital, two warehouses and the clock tower building, which were all constructed of stone.   Seven frame buildings constructed in the 1880s, are also preserved in this complex. Two of the famous officers stationed here were Lieutenants William Tecumseh Sherman and Ulysses S. Grant.

8 - Benicia Camel Barn Museum
Camel Road, Building #9, 2nd floor, Benicia (707)745-5435

During the period 1858-1863, the U.S. Army experimented using camels as pack animals in the desert region of Southern California, but the camels' tender feet couldn't adapt to the area's rocky soil. In 1864, the camels were sent here to be sold. Today, four buildings on the grounds of the Benicia Arsenal comprise the Camel Barn Museum Complex. The complex consists of two Camel Barns, an Engine House and a Powder Magazine. Museum exhibits and artifacts tell the history of the U.S. Army Arsenal and the city of Benicia.

Benicia Camel Barn. Courtesy of Benicia Camel Barn Museum.

8 - Site of Matthew Turner/James Robertson Shipyard   SHL 973
Foot of West 12th Street, Benicia   (707) 746-0213

Matthew Turner, the most prodigious shipbuilder in North America, relocated his shipyard from San Francisco to Benicia in 1882. The yard's ways, on which 169 of his 228 vessels were built and launched, are visible at low tide along with the remains of the whaler, *Stamboul*, which was used as a shipyard work platform. James Robertson purchased the yard from Turner in 1913 and operated it until 1918.

9 - Rio Vista Museum
16 North Front Street, Rio Vista   (707) 374-5169

Artifacts from Rio Vista, farm pieces, costumes and antique furniture are exhibited in the historical collection of this museum.

10 - Travis Air Force Museum
2nd Street and Travis Avenue, Building 80, Travis Air Force Base
(707) 837-2801

The centerpiece of California's newest air museum is a 1912 biplane built by two brothers in San Francisco. Among the museum's featured indoor exhibits are: one of the original engines from Howard Hughes' giant eight-engine *Spruce Goose*; a B-17 bomb sight used during World War II; and an F-105 Gatling gun. A collection of military aircraft are on display including a B-52, C-124 and the C-56 that once transported President Franklin Roosevelt.

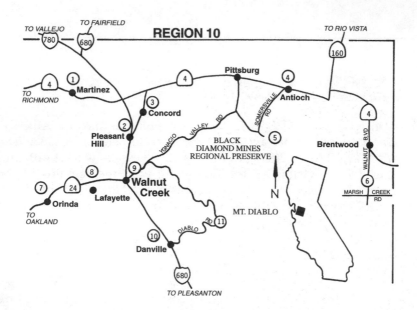

The map shows:

TO VALLEJO — 780
TO FAIRFIELD — 680
TO RIO VISTA — 160
TO RICHMOND — 4
Martinez ① 4
Pittsburg 4
Antioch 4 — SOMERSVILLE RD
Concord ③
Pleasant Hill ② — IGNACIO — VALLEY RD
BLACK DIAMOND MINES REGIONAL PRESERVE ⑤
Brentwood — WALNUT BLVD
⑧
Walnut Creek ⑨
⑦ 24
Lafayette
Orinda
TO OAKLAND
MT. DIABLO ⑪ — DIABLO RD
N
MARSH CREEK RD ⑥
Danville ⑩
680
TO PLEASANTON

---

1 - Site of the Murder of Dr. John Marsh   SHL 722
4500 block of Pacheco Boulevard, Martinez

The first doctor to practice medicine in the San Joaquin Valley was John Marsh, who arrived here in 1837. He treated the Indians when they were sick, and they in turn helped build his first adobe home and farm his land. To other than the Indians, he was known to be unfair in the payment he demanded for his services. He became so disliked because of the way he treated his Mexican neighbors that he was murdered by three former employees on this road, between his home and the town of Martinez, on September 24, 1856.

1 - Vicente Martinez Adobe   SHL 511
4202 Alhambra Avenue, Martinez   (510) 228-8860

Built on the Rancho El Pinole in 1849 by Vicente Martinez, this adobe was later sold and was the home of employees of the John Muir Ranch. It has been restored as part of the John Muir National Historic Site.

64

*John Muir Home and
National Historic Site.
Photo courtesy of
John R. Harris.*

1 - John Muir National Historic Site   SHL 312
4202 Alhambra Avenue, Martinez   (510) 228-8860

John Muir explored the mountains of California in the late 19th century, to discover how nature created them, and to promote their preservation. His writings and his dedication to the conservation movement established preservation as a national land policy. John Muir's foresight is responsible for the protection of wilderness areas and the establishment of many of the National Parks we enjoy today. This 17-room mansion was Muir's home from 1888 until his death in 1914. His home, and original furnishings of the period, are preserved by the National Park Service.

1 - John Swett Ranch
Hill Girt Ranch, end of Millthwait Drive off Alhambra Valley Road, Martinez

Built on the Rancho El Pinole in 1849 by Abilino Altamarano, this preserved adobe was part of the John Swett Ranch. Swett was the superintendent of public instruction from 1863 to 1867 and did more in his career as a teacher and administrator than any other man for California's public education system.

1 - Martinez Historical Museum
1005 Escobar Street, Martinez (510) 228-8160

History of Martinez is displayed in the 1890 "Borland Home," which is both the county museum and home of the Martinez Historical Society.

1 - Alhambra Cemetery
Martinez Regional Shoreline, turn left on Escobar from Alhambra, right onto Talbert, and left on Carquinez

Joseph Walker, a trailmaker and guide, who brought many emigrant parties over Walker Pass in Kern County, is buried here in Contra Costa County's oldest cemetery with other pioneers of this area.

1 - Historic Martinez
Chamber of Commerce, 620 Las Juntas, Martinez (510) 228-2345

Throughout the city are many 1865-1910 homes in every style of Victorian and turn-of-the-century motif. A retail directory to downtown Martinez, published by the city, includes a listing of thirteen of Martinez's historic sites. A guide to these buildings is available from the Chamber of Commerce.

2 - Diablo Valley College Museum
321 Gold Club Road, Pleasant Hill (510) 685-1230, Ext. 257

In addition to Indian anthropological exhibits, this museum has a collection of old scientific instruments (including a working seismograph) and sea life native to the region.

3 - Fernando Pacheco Adobe   SHL 455
3119 Grant Street, Concord

This adobe house was built in 1843 by Fernando Pacheco on 1,500 acres given him by his father, Salvio Pacheco. It was restored in 1941 and is listed on the National Register of Historic Places.

3 - Salvio Pacheco Adobe SHL 515
2050 Adobe Street, Concord

The first two-story adobe home built in this valley was constructed in 1853, by Salvio Pacheco, on this part of his 18,000-acre land grant. After the 1868 earthquake, Salvio offered residents of the nearby town of Pacheco tracts of land surrounding his adobe for one dollar a lot. The town, which grew up around his adobe, was later called Concord. Today, his original adobe houses the Associates National Bank.

4 - Antioch Historical Sites
Chamber of Commerce, 608 West 2nd Street, Antioch (510) 757-1800

Antioch Historical Society has preserved many of the town's original buildings from the late 1800s. A guide to Antioch's history is available through the Society.

5 - Mount Diablo Coal Field SHL 932
Black Diamond Mines Regional Preserve, Somersville Road off Hwy 4, Antioch

This was the leading coal producing region in the state from 1848 until the early 1900s. The mining ghost towns that once flourished here are gone, but the Black Diamond Mines Regional Preserve contains the century-old Rose Hill cemetery, an archeological site, and coal mine openings that were once part of the Somersville, Stewartville and Nortonville mining areas.

6 - Brentwood Home of Dr. John Marsh
Southwest of Brentwood via Walnut Boulevard at Marsh Creek Road

This 14-room house was built for Abbie Marsh, the young wife of Dr. John Marsh who was one of California's first physicians. Abbie never lived here as she died before it was completed in 1856. This three-story, stone and brick home was one of the first permanent buildings in this county and has remained a landmark since its completion.

7 - Joaquin Moraga Adobe SHL 509
24 Adobe Lane, Orinda

Joaquin Moraga, grandson of the founder and first commandante of the Presidio of San Francisco, built this adobe in 1841 on the land grant given to his grandfather Jose Joaquin Moraga. His home was restored to its original condition in 1941 and is now the oldest house in the county.

8 - Lafayette Historical Points of Interest
Chamber of Commerce, 100 Lafayette Circle, Lafayette (510) 284-7404

The Chamber of Commerce has a guide to 15 local historical places of interest including: buildings erected in the 1800s, a pioneer cemetery, Indian burial grounds, an 1853 gristmill wheel and old schoolhouses.

9 - Shadelands Ranch Historical Museum
2660 Ygnacio Valley Road, Walnut Creek (510) 935-7871

Built in 1902, this home of pioneer fruit farmer, Hiram Penniman, is preserved and furnished with many pieces of the family's original furniture. Walnut Creek Historical Society occupies part of the home for its displays and exhibits.

Shadelands Ranch Historical Museum. Photo courtesy of Brad Rovanpera.

9 - Alexander Lindsay Junior Museum
1901 - 1st Avenue, Walnut Creek (510) 935-1978

Interesting exhibits, primarily for children, are featured, including Indian artifacts, geological exhibits and other collections.

10 - Pedro Fages Trail   SHL 853
Marked at 856 Danville Boulevard, Danville

The Pedro Fages expedition through Contra Costa County in 1772 was in search of a land route to Point Reyes—a goal that they would not achieve. Instead, they blazed trails into areas of the state that had never been seen by white men before and opened the way for pioneering settlers. Part of that original trail is commemorated here.

10 - Tao House/Eugene O'Neill National Historic Site
Access to park by reservation only (510) 838-0249

Tao House, the home of playwright Eugene O'Neill, has been restored and refurnished to reflect the atmosphere of the period when he wrote some of his most significant works. This National Historic Site honors his accomplishments, which include: Pulitzer Prizes for *Beyond the Horizon, Ana Christie, Long Day's Journey into Night* and *Strange Interlude*; and the the 1936 Nobel Prize for literature.

11 - Mount Diablo State Park   SHL 905
Diablo Road, 5 miles east of Danville off I-680 (510) 837-2525

Mount Diablo has long been a landmark used by California's explorers. In 1851, the top of Mount Diablo was chosen as the starting point for the United States survey of California's lands. The base and meridian lines that intersect at the top are referred to in the legal descriptions of two-thirds of California's real estate. Many of California's great mountain ranges can be viewed from the top of Mount Diablo.

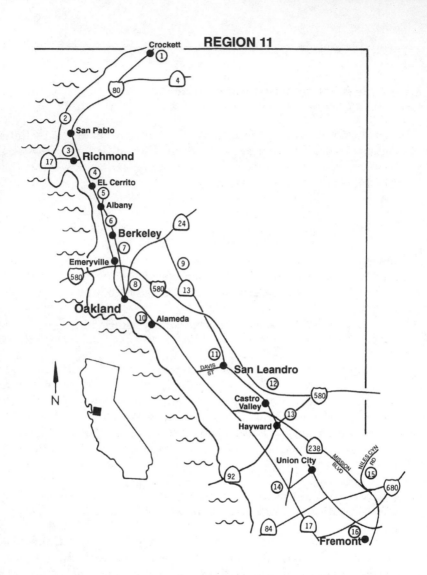

1 - Thomas Edwards Homestead   SHL 731
900 Loring Avenue at Ralph Street, Crockett (510) 787-2178

Thomas Edwards built this home on the site of an old Indian village in 1867 using timbers that came around the Horn. "The Old Homestead," as it was called in those days, was the center of the town of Crockett and the community's first building.

2 - East Brother Lighthouse
117 Park Place, Point Richmond (510) 233-2385

Century-old East Brother Light Station was automated by the U.S. Coast Guard in 1969. In 1980 its ornate buildings were converted into an island inn where overnight guests enjoy turn-of-the-century accommodations. Day tours of the station can be arranged by calling the keeper.

2 - Alvarado Adobe   SHL 512
#1 Alvarado Square, San Pablo (510) 215-3080

The original adobe erected at this site in 1842, was the home of Governor of California, Juan Bautista Alvarado, from 1848 until his death in 1882. He acquired ownership when his wife, Martina, inherited the property in 1851. The original adobe was razed in 1954. A replica of the home was reconstructed and features a Rancho-era bedroom and Victorian parlor. History of the region and Native American artifacts are displayed. A bunkhouse and the Blume House, a 1905 folk-Victorian style furnished farmhouse, are part of this complex.

3 - Richmond Museum
400 Nevin Avenue, Richmond (510) 235-7387

Richmond's past is displayed in historic photographs, artifacts and antiques, including early fire-fighting equipment. Models of ships show the city's historic link with the sea.

1910 Carnegie Library building, home of Richmond Museum. Courtesy of Richmond Museum.

4 - The Castro House at El Cerrito   SHL 356
El Cerrito Plaza, San Pablo Avenue, El Cerrito

Don Francisco Castro brought to this land the first herd of cattle and planted the region's first fruit trees in 1826. His adobe home stood here until it was destroyed by fire 130 years later. His original property, on which this adobe was built, is now within the grounds of the El Cerrito shopping center.

5 - Albany Historical Tour
Albany Chamber of Commerce, 1108 Solano Avenue, Albany
(510) 525-1771

A guide to Albany's historical points of interest is available from the Chamber of Commerce. Included in the tour are local homes and other structures from the early 1900s.

6 - University of California - Berkeley Campus   SHL 946
2200 University Avenue, Berkeley (415) 642-5215

The oldest campus of the University of California was established here in 1868 by the state legislature. Historic Founders' Rock, at the La Loma entrance, is the spot where the trustees of the College of California, who gave the land and founded the university, stood in 1860 and dedicated this land to be used for education.

72

6 - Lawrence Hall of Science
University of California, Centennial Drive near Grizzley Peak Boulevard, Berkeley (510) 642-2858

The work of Ernest O. Lawrence, U.C. Berkeley's first Nobel Laureate, and inventor of the cyclotron, is commemorated here with Lawrence memorabilia and artifacts related to early cyclotron development. The center also features science exhibits and "hands on" planetarium shows in the Holt Planetarium.

Lawrence Hall of Science. Courtesy of University of California, Berkeley.

6 - Piedmont Way   SHL 986
Piedmont Avenue between Gayley Road and Dwight Way, Berkeley

This section of Piedmont Avenue was the first residential street in the nation proposed and adopted to the natural scene by Fredrick Olmstead, the "Father" of landscape architecture in America. Olmstead was the principal designer of such well-known landmarks as New York's Central Park, and the Washington D.C. Zoological Gardens. He planned this scenic stretch of Piedmont Avenue in 1865 as a broad, centrally divided avenue with an overarching canopy of street trees and garden-filled setbacks. His urban landscape ideas were adopted by designers for years to come and his proposal to preserve wilderness values at Yosemite, by making the area a "public reservation," laid the foundation for the nation's system of national parks and wilderness areas.

Judah L. Magnes Museum, in the renovated Burke Mansion, Berkeley. Photo courtesy of Andrew Partos.

6 - Berkeley City Club   SHL 908
2315 Durant Avenue, Berkeley

Julia Morgan, architect of William Randolph Hearst's San Simeon castle, designed this building, constructed in 1929, for the women of the Berkeley City Club. This club was founded in 1927 to contribute to the social, civic and cultural progress of the city.

6 - Judah L. Magnes Memorial Museum/Jewish Museum of the West
2911 Russell Street, Berkeley   (510) 849-2710

This historic mansion is the home of the Western Jewish History Center. Its collections include ritual objects, costumes, Holocaust collection and artifacts from Jews of India and North Africa.

7 - Ancient Shell Mound Site   SHL 335
Shell Mound Street, east of I-580 at Powell Street, Emeryville

Prehistoric Indians used this site as a camping ground. The accumulation of their disposed shells from clams, oysters and other shellfish, formed what was known as the Emeryville Mound. Eventually this disposal area covered hundreds of thousands of square feet. Before the mound was leveled in 1924, for construction of a factory, University of California researchers excavated the mound and removed skeletal remains which were placed in its Museum of Vertebrate Zoology.

8 - Dunsmuir House and Gardens
2960 Peralta Oaks Court, Oakland (510) 562-0328

Alexander Dunsmuir had this 37-room, Classical Revival mansion built in 1899 as a gift for his mistress of 20 years, whom he was then planning to marry. Neither he, or his wife, lived in this home. He died six weeks after their wedding and she died eighteen months later. I. W. Hellman, founder of the Wells Fargo Bank, lived here until 1961, when the estate was acquired by the city of Oakland. This three-story home has many outstanding features including a Tiffany glass dome over the central staircase.

8 - Northern California Center for Afro-American History and Life
5605 San Pablo Avenue, Golden Gate Library, Oakland (510) 658-3158

The history of blacks in Mexico and the Western United States is displayed in photographs and artifacts.

8 - St. James Episcopal Church SHL 694
1540 - 12th Avenue, Oakland (510) 533-2136

This church has held regular services since its founding in 1858. The original structure now annexes the present church.

8 - Site of the College of California SHL 45
13th and Franklin Streets, Oakland

The College of California was established in 1853 as the Contra Costa Academy at Broadway and Fifth Streets. They moved to this four-block site after being incorporated as a college. Trustees of the college offered to donate their land in Berkeley to the state if the legislature would establish a university there. The University of California was formed in 1868. It used the facilities of this college until their first building was completed in Berkeley in 1873.

8 - First Unitarian Church of Oakland SHL 896
Southeast corner of 14th and Castro Streets, Oakland (510) 893-6129

Walter Mathews, distinguished Oakland architect, designed this Victorian-Romanesque styled structure for the First Unitarian

Church. Erected in 1890 this church's outstanding feature is its stained glass windows by Goodhue of Boston.

8 - Paramount Theater SHL 884
2025 Broadway, Oakland (510) 893-2300

Opened in December 1931, the Paramount Theater is said to be one of the finest examples of "Art Deco" movie houses in the United States. Typical of the movie palaces built during the rise of the motion picture industry, it has been completely restored and registered as a National Historic Landmark.

8 - Site of St. Mary's College SHL 676
Broadway and Hawthorne, Oakland (510) 631-4000 or (510) 273-8350

St. Mary's College was formed in San Francisco in 1863. From 1889 until 1928 the college was located in the brick building that stood here. In 1928 the college moved to Moraga.

8 - Jack London Square
Foot of Broadway at the Waterfront, Oakland (510) 893-7884

Named for California's famous writer, Jack London, this site includes the old "First and Last Chance Saloon," a favorite spot that London frequented. It is still operating and has a collection of his memorabilia. A sod-roofed cabin from the Yukon Territory, where London spent one winter, has been relocated here and restored. It contains artifacts from his life and work.

8 - Oakland Hotel
260 - 11th Street, Oakland

Built in 1912, this U-shaped hotel was one of the most elegant of the West Coast hotels. Three presidents stayed here, as well as many Hollywood stars and celebrities of the period. It was used by the Army as a V. A. Hospital during World War II. Today it is a senior citizen's complex.

8 - Oakland Museum
1000 Oak Street, Oakland   (510) 273-3401 or (510) 834-2413

Three museums are housed in this four-block complex: Art, History and Natural Science. Also featured at this museum is an extensive section on Western America historic environments.

8 - Camron-Stanford House
1418 Lakeside Drive, Oakland   (510) 836-1976

Erected in 1876, this two-story Victorian mansion was the home of the Oakland Public Museum from 1907-1969. It has been restored to its original condition and now contains decorative arts and furnishings, period rooms, artifacts, and household items, from the years 1875 to 1885.

Interior Camron-Stanford House, Oakland. Courtesy of Camron-Stanford House Preservation Association, photo by Brad Bussey.

Camron-Stanford House. Courtesy of Camron-Stanford Preservation Association.

8 - Lake Merritt Refuge
Lakeside Park, Belleview Avenue, North shore of Lake Merritt, Oakland

Lake Merritt, covering 160-acres, was formed in 1869 when a dam was constructed at this site. That same year, the state made the lake a wild fowl refuge—the first in the nation. Lake Merritt is a registered National Historic Landmark and the only salt water lake, and wild fowl preserve, located in the middle of a city.

8 - Peralta Hacienda Site   SHL 925
2511 - 34th Avenue, Oakland

The first permanent settlement on the east side of San Francisco Bay, following the missions, was here at Rancho San Antonio. Luis Peralta, who received his Mexican land grant from the last Spanish governor of California, had an adobe built in 1820, where his four sons would stay whenever they visited the rancho. The original adobe was demolished in 1897 and some of its bricks were used in the construction of other buildings.

8 - Mills Hall   SHL 849
Mills College, 5000 MacArthur Boulevard, Oakland (510) 430-2255

Dr. Cyrus Mills and his wife established the Benicia Seminary in 1865 and moved it to this site in 1871. This four-story wooden building was once considered the most beautiful educational building in the state. In 1885, the name of the seminary was changed to Mills College. Today, it continues to be one of the leading women's colleges in the country.

9 - Joaquin Miller Home and Park   SHL 107
Exit east off the Warren Freeway (Hwy 13) at Joaquin Miller Road to 3590 Sanborn Drive, Oakland (510) 238-6888 or (510) 273-2267

The City of Oakland purchased this estate in 1919 in order to preserve the home and grounds of Joaquin Miller, California's "Poet of the Sierras." Miller lived in this area, which he called, "The Hights" from 1886, until his death in 1913. The home, which he built himself, he called "The Abbey." He planted trees and built the stone monuments located on these grounds. The last monument he erected was to General Fremont, who stood here and named the famous "Golden Gate" in 1864. His home has been a registered as a National Historic Landmark.

9 - Site of Blossom Rock Navigation Trees   SHL 962

Thomas J. Roberts Recreation Area, 10570 Skyline Boulevard east of Joaquin Miller Park, Oakland (510) 635-0138, extension 2200

Navigators guiding their ships through San Francisco Bay in the 1800s used two redwood trees that stood at the top of the ridge behind this park as a visible landmark. By sighting these trees and aligning them with Blossom Rock, a natural hazard in the Bay, a hazard line was drawn, giving the ship's captain a route of safe passage around Blossom Rock. In April 1870, the U.S. Corps of Engineers blew the top off Blossom Rock and removed this dangerous obstacle from the sea lanes.

9 - Rainbow Trout Species Identified   SHL 970

Redwood Regional Park, 7867 Redwood Road, Oakland (510) 635-0138, extension 2200

In March 1855, Dr. W. P. Gibbons, founder of the California Academy of Sciences, identified a new species of fish collected from San Leandro Creek, which he called rainbow trout. By the early 1900s this prized game fish was found throughout the world. Direct descendants of the original rainbow trout, described in 1855, still thrive in Redwood Creek, a tributary of San Leandro Creek.

9 - Pardee Home Museum

672 - 11th Street, Oakland (510) 444-2187

Three generations of Pardee family history is preserved in the restored Italianate-style villa that Dr. Enoch H. Pardee, and his wife, Mary, built in 1868. Enoch Pardee, and his only child, George, were both mayors of Oakland. George was elected Governor of California in 1903, and worked actively for resource conservation until his death in 1941. Over 60,000 objects collected by the Pardee family are exhibited including: furniture, California paintings, candlesticks, musical instruments, pottery, religious artifacts and an extensive collection of scrimshaw.

Pardee House c. 1870, carriage house in background. Photo courtesy of the Pardee Home Foundation.

Restored Pardee Home Museum. Photo courtesy of the Pardee Home Foundation.

10 - Site of the China Clipper Flight Departure SHL 968
Main Gate, U.S. Naval Air Station, Alameda

The first commercial transpacific flight departed from the Pan American Airlines, Alameda Terminal, on November 22, 1935. Six days later, after stops at Pearl Harbor, Midway Island, Wake Island and Guam, this inaugural flight was completed in Manila. This China Clipper flight by a Martin M-130 opened the Pacific airways to future commercial flights and ushered in a new era in transportation.

10 - Camino of Rancho San Antonio SHL 299
Santa Clara Avenue through Alameda

Camino of Rancho San Antonio was the old Mexican road that connected the mission at San Jose with Oakland to the north. The approximate route of this old Mexican trail is followed by Santa Clara Avenue.

10 - Alameda Terminal First Transcontinental Railroad SHL 440
Lincoln and Webster, Alameda

On September 6, 1869, the first transcontinental train of the Central Pacific Railroad, to reach San Francisco Bay, arrived at this terminal in Alameda. This building served as the western terminal until Oakland's station was completed two months later. The Alameda terminal no longer exists, but Oakland's terminal, at 464 Seventh Street, has been remodeled and is still in use.

10 - Croll Building SHL 954
1400 Webster Street, Alameda

This well-known Alameda landmark was constructed as a hotel in 1883. It soon became a popular lodging place for boxers who trained at nearby Neptune Beach. This Nationally Registered Historical Landmark was converted into offices and retail stores in 1981.

11 - San Leandro Oyster Beds   SHL 824
Mulford-Wicks Landing, west end of Marina Boulevard, San Leandro

During the 1880s and 1890s a successful oyster industry was located in San Leandro at what is now the San Leandro Marina. Oysters were harvested from these beds in such numbers that it became the state's single most important fishery. Pollution in the San Francisco Bay brought an end to this business around 1912.

11 - Ingnacio Peralta Home   SHL 285
561 Lafayette Avenue, San Leandro (510) 562-7144

Alameda County's first brick house was built in 1860 for Ignacio Peralta, one of the four sons of the original Rancho San Antonio grantee, Don Luis Peralta. This beautifully preserved example of Spanish architecture is now used as the Alta Mira Club House.

11 - Best Tractor Company
800 Davis Street, San Leandro

Daniel Best began producing steam tractors after purchasing the San Leandro Plow Company in 1886. His son, C. L. Best, built a tractor company at this site in 1916. Ten years later it merged with the Holt Brothers to become the Caterpillar Tractor Company.

11 - Little Shul
642 Dolores Avenue, near Bancroft Avenue, San Leandro (510) 357-8505

Originally located at 59 Chumalia Street, this 1889 Jewish synagogue was moved here and now stands behind Temple Beth Sholom. It is the oldest synagogue still standing in Northern California.

11 - Rancho San Antonio   SHL 246
Root Park, East 14th Street, North of Davis, San Leandro

Pablo Vicente de Sola, last Spanish governor of Alta California, gave the 43,000-acre land grant, Rancho San Antonio, to Don Luis Peralta in 1820 as a reward for almost 40 years of outstanding service in the army. Peralta, who came to California with the Anza expedition in 1775-76, helped establish the missions at Santa

Cruz and San Jose. In 1851, a few years before his death, Peralta divided this estate among his four sons who settled the land with their families.

11 - Estudillo Homesite SHL 279
550 West Estudillo Avenue, San Leandro. St. Leander's Church
(510) 895-5631

Jose Estudillo built an adobe house near the San Leandro Creek in 1836-1837 and became the first white settler of the San Leandro area. His second home was built on this site about 10 years later. It was used temporarily as San Leandro's courthouse after the city was named the county seat in 1855. St. Leander's Church, and a priest's residence, now stands on the site of the Estudillo family's last home.

12 - First Public School in Castro Valley SHL 776
Redwood Road between James and Alma, Castro Valley

The first public school in Castro Valley was built here on land donated by Josiah Brickell in 1866. The original one-room schoolhouse is gone, but has been replaced by another school on this same site.

13 - McConaghy Estate
18701 Hesperian Boulevard, Hayward (510) 278-0198 or (510) 276-3010

In addition to the 1886 home, which includes furnishings of the period, this estate has a collection of carriages, wagons and tools displayed in the outbuildings behind the main house.

13 - Hayward Area Historical Society Museum
22701 Main Street, Hayward (510) 581-0223

History of southern Alameda County is exhibited in the former 1927 brick post office building. Part of the restored post office is included in the museum. Household and personal items of the region from the turn-of-the-century, antique fire fighting equipment from 1860 and 1923, and historic photographs are displayed.

14 - Nation's First Successful Sugar Beet Factory   SHL 768
Northeast of Alvarado on Dyer Street, Union City

The first successful sugar beet processing plant in the country was built here in 1870 by E. J. Dyer. The factory is now closed.

14 - Site of First County Courthouse   SHL 503
Union City Boulevard and Smith Street, Alvarado District, Union City

The building that stood at this site was the first county courthouse when Alameda County was formed in 1853, from portions of Contra Costa and Santa Clara Counties. The town of Alvarado, which is now Union City, was designated as the first county seat.

15 - Vallejo Flour Mill   SHL 46
Fremont City Park at the northeast corner of Mission Boulevard and Niles Canyon Road, Niles

Jose Vallejo, older brother of General Mariano Vallejo, received a Mexican land grant of almost 18,000-acres in 1842, on which he erected two flour mills. The stone foundation of the second mill, and the stone aqueduct built to bring water one mile to the mill, can still be seen at this park.

16 - Mission San Jose   SHL 334
43300 Mission Boulevard, Fremont   (510) 657-1797

Mission San Jose, the 14th mission founded by the Franciscan Padres, was established at this site in June 1797. It became one of the largest and most prosperous of the California missions. Over the years a number of earthquakes caused major damage to the mission, resulting in three successive structures being erected on this site. Of the original mission, only the padres' living quarters remain today. St. Joseph's Church was rebuilt after the 1868 earthquake and contains elegant crystal chandeliers, murals, religious paintings and a gold leaf altar. Restoration of the other mission buildings began in 1916.

16- Leland Stanford Winery SHL 642
1250 Stanford Avenue, Fremont (510) 656-2340 or (510) 656-2340

Governor Leland Stanford purchased the Warm Springs estate of Clemente Columbet, in 1869, where he planted orchards and vineyards. The Stanford winery is now operated by the Weibel Vineyards, which use some of the original buildings of the estate.

16- Shinn House Historic Park
1251 Peralta Avenue, Fremont (510) 791-4340

Memorabilia of the Shinn family is displayed in this 1876 redwood ranch house built by James Shinn. Gardens surrounding the house include some of this pioneer nurseryman's specimen trees.

16- Higuera Adobe
47300 Rancho Higuera Road, Fremont (510) 657-6848

This one and a half-story adobe was one of the seven built about 1840 on the Higuera grant. A total restoration of the adobe was completed in 1978. Replicas of original furnishings are displayed.

16- Ardenwood Historic Farm
34600 Ardenwood Boulevard, Fremont (510) 796-0663

Farm life, as it was near the turn-of-the-century, is demonstrated for visitors to Ardenwood, the farm that George Patterson established in the 1870s. Draft horses pull wagons, rail cars and plows. Docents, in period attire, perform farm chores. Antique pieces of farm equipment have been restored. And, the farmhouse, with its beautiful Queen Anne style addition, and several outbuildings, are open for tours.

16- Coyote Hills Regional Park
8000 Patterson Ranch Road, west of Fremont (510) 795-9385

Four Indian shell mounds, spanning a period of 2,200 years of Native American habitation, are preserved within this wildlife sanctuary. Park naturalists conduct group programs at the largest of the four Indian sites.

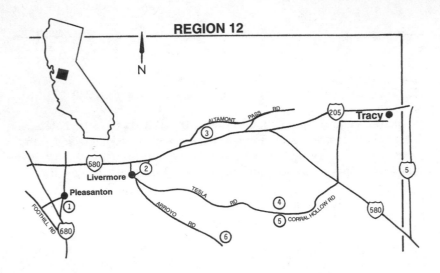

1 - Pleasanton
Pleasanton Chamber of Commerce, 450 Main Street, #202, Pleasanton
(510) 846-5858

Pleasanton's first settler was Augustine Bernal, who in 1850 built an adobe home that still stands. This pioneer adobe and other historic buildings are listed in a guide that is available from the Chamber of Commerce.

1 - Amador-Livermore Valley Historical Society Museum
603 Main Street, Pleasanton (510) 462-2766

Housed in Pleasanton's 1914 Town Hall, this museum features displays of tools, Indian and local artifacts, household items and historic photographs.

1 - Francisco Solano Alviso Adobe SHL 510
Meadowlark Dairy Farm, Foothill Road at Bernal Avenue, Pleasanton

This adobe, constructed around 1844-1845, was the first built in Pleasanton Valley. It is reported to have been used by General John Fremont as his headquarters during the Battle of Sunol Canyon.

2 - Robert Livermore Monument   SHL 241
Robert Livermore Park, 4700 East Avenue, Livermore

Less than a mile north of here is the Robert Livermore home site, where he built the first wooden building in Livermore Valley, in 1849. He constructed the home from timbers that were shipped around the Horn. Livermore was an established rancher and the first man, after the Mission Fathers, to plant vineyards and orchards in this region. This monument was erected to honor the efforts of this early pioneer.

2 - Concannon Vineyards   SHL 641
4590 Tesla Road, Livermore (510) 447-3760

Established in 1883, and still in operation, Concannon Vineyards made sacramental and commercial wines of superior quality, from the vineyards planted here. The success of these pioneer wineries soon brought an additional two dozen wineries to this valley.

2 - Wente Bros. Winery   SHL 957
5565 Tesla Road, Livermore (510) 447-3603

This pioneer winery was founded in 1883, by Carl Wente, in Livermore Valley. Today it holds the distinction of being the oldest, continuously operated, family-owned winery in the state.

3 - Altamont Pass Windfarms
I-580, east of Livermore

Windmills were first used in this area by farmers in the early 1900s, primarily to pump water. Today, more than 4,000 windmills have been installed here in the world's largest collection of windmills. Together, they generate enough electrical energy to meet the needs of 27,000 California homes year around.

4 - Corral Hollow   SHL 755
9 miles southwest of Tracy on Corral Hollow Road

Evidence of an ancient Indian encampment was discovered in this arroyo and the surrounding hills. This location was also part of the old Spanish trail of the 1700s, and the route taken by '49ers heading for the southern mines during the Gold Rush. Later, this region became an important coal mining area with the discovery of coal in 1856.

5 - Carnegie   SHL 740
9 miles southwest of Tracy on Corral Hollow Road

The town of Carnegie was established when the Carnegie Brick and Pottery Company was constructed in the 1800s. White glazed firebrick was produced here until the early 1900s. A series of man-made and natural disasters ruined the owners of the company financially, causing the close of their business in 1911. Only the abandoned dumps of the Tesla Coal Mine remain in this area.

6 - Cresta Blanca Winery   SHL 586
Wente Bros. Winery, 5050 Arroyo Road, Livermore (510) 447-3603

Cresta Blanca wine, produced from the vineyard planted here by Charles Wetmore in 1882, won highest honors at the 1889 Paris Exposition. It was this success that brought California wine makers their first international recognition. This pioneer winery has been renovated and reopened as the Wente Bros. Sparkling Wine Cellars.

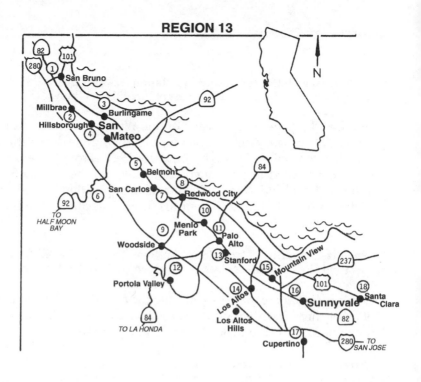

Portola Expedition Route

In 1769, Gaspar de Portola, and a 60-member expedition party, traveled north from San Diego in search of the bay of Monterey. During this expedition they twice reached the harbor of Monterey Bay, but failed to recognize it as such. Their search took them further north where they discovered San Francisco Bay.

This historic expedition is commemorated at several locations along the trail that he blazed through California.

1 - Temporary Detention Camps for Japanese-Americans SHL 934
Tanforan Park, Huntington Avenue, west of U.S. 101, San Bruno

Japanese and Japanese-Americans on the West Coast were ordered to report to temporary detention camps following the declaration of war against the United States, by Japan, in 1941. From these camps, they were relocated to permanent camps across the United States until the end of World War II. The Japanese population here reached a maximum of 7,816 in the six months that this facility served as an assembly center.

2 - Portola Expedition Camp (San Andreas Lake) SHL 27
Hillcrest and Skyline Boulevard, east side of San Andreas Lake, Millbrae

Portola's expedition camped at this site the evening of November 4, 1769, after their first sighting of San Francisco Bay. The site where they camped is now inundated by San Andreas Lake.

3 - Anza Expedition Camp SHL 48
San Mateo Creek near Barroilhet Avenue and Hwy 82, Burlingame

Juan Bautista de Anza explored the San Francisco peninsula to locate sites for a mission and a presidio to quarter the Spanish Garrison. Anza, and his party of men, camped along this route in March 1776. Two of those campsites have been commemorated; one here at Burlingame and one at San Mateo.

3 - Burlingame Railroad Station SHL 846
Burlingame Avenue and California Drive, Burlingame (415) 343-2732

Erected in 1894, this Mission Revival style structure used roof tiles from two missions; the Mission San Antonio de Padua at Jolon, and the Mission Dolores Asistencia at San Mateo. This building, with its early 18th century roof tiles, can be seen at its original location.

4 - Carolands SHL 886
565 Remillard Road, Hillsborough

Willis Polk, who designed the 43-room mansion known as "Filoli" in Woodside, supervised construction of this American Renaissance style chateau for Harriet Pullman Carolan, heiress to the Pullman

Railroad Car company fortune. It was later acquired by Countess Lillian Remillard Dandini of the Remillard Brick Company. This once lavish chateau is now in disrepair.

4 - Anza Expedition Camp   SHL 47
Arroyo Court, north side of 3rd Avenue, San Mateo

Juan Bautista de Anza explored the San Francisco peninsula to locate sites for a mission and a presidio to quarter the Spanish garrison. Anza, and his party of men, camped along this route in March 1776. Two of those campsites have been commemorated; one here at San Mateo and one at Burlingame.

4 - "The Hospice"—Site of the Mission Dolores Outpost at San Mateo   SHL 393
Baywood and El Camino Real (Hwy 82), San Mateo

This outpost was one of several built around 1800 to serve the Mission San Francisco de Asis (Mission Dolores). It was used primarily as a hotel for travelers between Santa Clara and the mission in San Francisco. This outpost was abandoned, and in 1849 was used as a store and public house. It was destroyed in the 1868 earthquake and only its roof tiles were saved. They were later used in the construction of the Burlingame Railroad Station in 1894.

4 - San Mateo County Historical Museum
1700 West Hillsdale Boulevard, San Mateo   (415) 574-6441

History of San Mateo County area is displayed through a variety of exhibits. Artifacts, mammoth teeth, dioramas of the various cultures that once lived here, and historical items from the period after this county was formed in 1856, are on display. This museum also has an impressive horse drawn carriage collection.

5 - George Center Mansion
1219 Ralston Avenue, Belmont   (415) 591-4270

Built in 1906, this house was known as the "Twin Pines Mansion." This once luxurious private residence is now the home of the San Mateo County Arts Council. Contemporary works of art, from local artists, are featured in this historical home.

5 - Ralston Hall   SHL 856
1500 Ralston Avenue, Belmont (415) 508-3501, Ext. 201

William Ralston, Founder of the Bank of California, and eminent San Francisco financier, acquired a modest villa from Count Leonetto Cipriani and expanded it into this 88-room mansion. In addition to the stone carriage house still remaining on these grounds, Ralston added extensive outbuildings, including a Turkish bath and a bowling alley. This restored mansion, with its hall of mirrors, crystal chandeliers and grand staircase, contains many 19th century antiques, and is a registered National Historic Landmark. Tours can be arranged through The College of Notre Dame.

6 - Portola Expedition Camp (Crystal Springs Lake)   SHL 94
Junction of I-280 and Hwy 92, south of Hillsborough

The November 5, 1769, camp of the Portola Expedition, and the trail they followed south along San Francisco Bay, is now covered by the Crystal Springs Reservoir.

7 - San Carlos Depot
Old Country Road at San Carlos Avenue, San Carlos

Southern Pacific Railroad constructed this depot in 1888, the same year that the San Carlos Land Company was formed to finance development of a town around the depot. This depot stands today in almost the same condition as when it was first built.

8 - Union Cemetery   SHL 816
Addison Street at Woodside Road (Hwy 84), south of El Camino Real, Redwood City

Established in 1859, the name of this cemetery reflects the sympathies of the people who lived here before the Civil War conflict.

8 - Lathrop House
627 Hamilton Street, Redwood City (415) 365-5564

San Mateo County's first clerk and assessor built this 11-room, two-story, Gothic Revival house in 1863. In 1905 it was moved to this location and completely restored to its original condition. Now it is the home of the Redwood City Historical Association and is operated as a museum. Victorian furnishings and Civil War period items, reflecting the time Civil War General Patrick Conner lived here, are exhibited.

9 - Portola Expedition Camp (Woodside) SHL 92
Next to the Filoli Mansion, Canada Road and Edgewood, Woodside

Portola's Expedition camped here on their return trip to San Diego, which began November 11, 1769.

9 - Site of Former Town of Searsville SHL 474
Junction of Portola Road and Sand Hill Road, Woodside

Searsville Lake now covers the site of the town of Searsville that grew up here in the mid-1850s. John Sears built his home in 1854, which later became a hotel known in the area as the "Sears House." It became a popular place for lumberjacks and teamsters, and the town of Searsville was settled around the hotel. Building of the dam that formed Searsville Lake brought an end to the "Sears House" in the early 1890s. The site of the town is marked by this monument.

9 - Site of San Mateo County's First Sawmill SHL 478
La Honda Road near Alambique Creek, Wunderlich County Park, west of Woodside

In 1848, on the bank of Alambique Creek, Charles Brown constructed San Mateo County's first sawmill. Nearby stands the adobe he built in 1839. The design of this sawmill was similar to the one built for John Sutter in Coloma, where gold was discovered in 1848.

9 - Filoli SHL 907
North of Edgewood on Canada Road, north of Hwy 84, Woodside
(415) 366-4640 or (415) 364-2880 for tours

In 1916 this 2 and 1/2-story mansion, with a 16-acre garden, was designed by the famous California architect, Willis Polk, for William Bourn. Bourn was the founder of the Greystone Winery, and a member of the family that owned the Empire Gold Mine. He and his wife lived in this 36,000-square foot, Georgian Revival, brick home until their deaths in 1936. William Roth, heir to the Matson Shipping fortune, purchased this estate in 1937. In 1975, Mrs. Roth donated it to the National Trust for Historic Preservation. Tours of the gardens, and some of the 43 rooms in the main house, can be arranged. Filoli was the estate filmed for the television series "Dynasty."

9 - Woodside Store   SHL 93
471 Kings Mountain Road, northwest of Hwy 84, Woodside (415) 851-7615

The first store between San Francisco and Santa Clara was opened in 1854, by Dr. R. O. Tripp and M. A. Parkhurst. Extensive lumber operations took place in this area, with 15 sawmills operating within a few miles radius of this store. The Woodside Store became the center of the region's social and business activity. It has been preserved as a county and state historical site and is now operated as a museum. Many of the store's original equipment and furnishings are on display.

Woodside Store. Courtesy of San Mateo Historical Association.

10 - Capidro   SHL 939
262 Princeton Road, Menlo Park

An elaborate maze of cement walls and arches, and a garden planted with roses, geraniums and fig trees, was designed and constructed by John Guidici over a forty-five year period. He embedded the walls with brightly decorated ceramic tiles, shells from local beaches and recycled material to create one of California's outstanding twentieth century folk art environments.

10 - Menlo Park Railroad Station   SHL 955
1100 Merrill Avenue, Menlo Park (415) 325-2818

The community of Menlo Park was established in the 1850s by Dennis Oliver and D. C. McGlynn, who acquired ownership of a 1,700-acre tract which they named for their former home in Ireland. Completion of the San Francisco-San Jose Railroad, through Menlo Park, in 1863, brought about construction of this station. It has been restored by the Menlo Park Chamber of Commerce which has its offices in this historic building. The town of Menlo Park that grew up around the station became the home of many of the state's prominent citizens, one of whom was Governor and U.S. Senator, Milton Latham.

10 - Church of the Nativity
210 Oak Grove Avenue, Menlo Park (415) 323-7914

The first Catholic church built in Menlo Park is this well-preserved 1872 Victorian Gothic Revival style structure.

10 - Portola Journey's End   SHL 2
Hwy 82 at San Francisquito Creek, Menlo Park

Portola's expedition established a base camp here on November 6, 1769, on the opposite bank from the old redwood known as "El Palo Alto." On November 10, 1769, Portola made the decision to end his search for Monterey Bay and return to San Diego. Five years after the Portola expedition, another Spanish explorer, Don Rivera, would also camp at this site and sketch "El Palo Alto" on the Spanish map of San Francisco.

11 - Hostess House   SHL 895
University Avenue and El Camino Real, Palo Alto

This building was originally erected at Camp Fremont in Menlo Park, where it served as a meeting place for servicemen during World War I. After the war, the building was relocated and became the first municipally sponsored community center in the nation.

11 - John Adams Squire House   SHL 857
900 University Avenue, Palo Alto

Constructed in 1904, this house is an outstanding example of Greco-Roman Classic Revival architecture. It was among the early Palo Alto houses that survived the disastrous 1906 earthquake.

11 - Professorville Historic District
Addison, Cowper, Emerson and Embarcadero Streets, Palo Alto

Living quarters were constructed for the faculty of Stanford University using a continuous skin of shingles for the walls and roofs. Construction of these homes took place between 1890-1920.

11 - Pioneer Electronics Research Laboratory   SHL 836
Channing Avenue and Emerson Street, Palo Alto

The "Father of Radio," Dr. Lee de Forest, devised the first vacuum tube amplifier and oscillator at this laboratory in 1911-1913. It is from this birthplace of electronics that the radio industry began.

11 - Palo Alto Junior Museum
1451 Middlefield Road, Palo Alto (415) 329-2111

The first children's museum in the United States was dedicated here in 1941. Historical items and exhibits of special interest to young people are the main features of this museum.

11 - "El Palo Alto"
Alma Street and Palo Alto Avenue, Palo Alto

In 1769, Gaspar de Portola discovered this area and named this redwood tree "El Palo Alto" (the tall stick). A later exploration party sketched this tree on their official Spanish map of San Francisco. This famous tree has also been reproduced on the seal of Stanford University.

11 - Casa de Tableta   SHL 825
Alpine and Arastradero Roads, Palo Alto

This old wooden saloon was built in the 1850s at the junction of two well-traveled pioneer roads. Early settlers and local Mexicans frequented this place which has continued to operate under various names and ownerships.

11 - Birthplace of "Silicon Valley" SHL 976
367 Addison Avenue, Palo Alto

David Packard's garage at the rear of this property is the birthplace of the Hewlett-Packard Company, and the conerstone of "Silicon Valley," the world's first high-technology region. Dr. Frederick Terman, a radio communications professor at Stanford University, urged his students to work for, or start their own, electronics companies in the surrounding area, instead of heading East to established firms. In 1938, with Terman's encouragement and financial help, William Hewlett and David Packard began developing their first product, an audio oscillator, in this garage. In 1953, under Terman's leadership, Stanford University set aside 660 acres to create Stanford Research Park, a high-technology industrial park. Terman and Packard teamed-up to recruit corporate tenants, and when Hewlett-Packard took a lease in 1954, it became the nucleus for Silicon Valley. Within 30 years the park was fully leased by 90 tenant firms; and another 1,100 companies settled in Silicon Valley.

11 - Co-Invention of the Integrated Circuit SHL 1000
844 East Charleston Road, Palo Alto

Robert Noyce, a pioneer in the evolution of modern electronics, began experimenting with transistors while a student at Grinnell College. After earning his Ph.D. from M.I.T., Noyce landed a job at Shockley Semiconductor, the nation's first semiconductor company, founded by William Shockley, co-inventor of the transistor. In 1957, Noyce and a group of Shockley employees formed the Fairchild Semiconductor Company. It was here, in 1959, that Noyce developed the integrated circuit. That same year, Jack Kilby of Texas Instruments also devised his integrated circuit. Although the materials and method of making interconnections varied in the two discoveries, the U.S. Patent Office granted patents to both Kilby and Noyce, recognizing both as co-inventors of the integrated circuit.

11 - Home Site of Sarah Wallis SHL 969
South side of La Selva Drive, between Military Way and Magnolia Drive, Palo Alto

It was at this site in the early 1860s that Sarah Wallis dedicated the remaining years of her life to the suffrage movement. Her Mayfield Farm home became the center for woman's rights activity in this region. State and national leaders met here and made plans to further the cause. Wallis was elected the first president of the California State Suffrage Education Association. In 1877 she represented the association in petitioning the state legislature to pass the "Woman Lawyer Bill," which admitted women to practice before the bar in California.

12 - Our Lady of the Wayside SHL 909
930 Portola Road, Portola Valley

The first design by architect Timothy Pflueger, to be constructed was "Our Lady of the Wayside Roman Catholic Church," which was erected in 1912. Pflueger later became a well-known designer of commercial buildings and art deco theaters, a radical departure from this early mission-style building.

13 - Lou Henry Hoover House SHL 913
623 Mirada Road, Stanford

Herbert Hoover learned of his election as thirty-first President of the United States while living here in 1928. This 21-room home was named in honor of Mrs. Lou Hoover who had a major hand in its design. It remained the Hoover family home from 1920 to 1944 and was given to Stanford University, the President's alma mater, upon her death.

13 - Birthplace of Motion Pictures SHL 834
Stanford University, Campus Drive off Junipero Serra Boulevard, Stanford

Leland Stanford and Eadweard Muybridge conducted an experiment from 1878-1879 to prove that a horse, when running, can have all four feet on the ground at the same time. A battery of 24 cameras were rigged to take instantaneous pictures as the horse ran. These historic photographs triggered the idea of motion pictures.

13 - Stanford University Museum
Lomita Drive and Museum Way, Stanford (415) 497-4177

This is the oldest museum west of the Mississippi, and the first to use reinforced concrete in its construction. Among the historic items on display are Stanford family memorabilia, coins, medals, and the "gold spike" that joined the Central Pacific and Union Pacific Railroads, to complete the first transcontinental railroad, in 1869.

14 - Foothill College Electronics Museum
12345 El Monte Road, Los Altos Hills (415) 948-8590

Pioneer electronic material from the 1890s is displayed in this unique museum, including personal memorabilia of the "Father of Radio," Lee de Forest, and relics from the first broadcast station, KQW. A visual history of electronics through the development of the silicon chip is also presented.

14 - Juana Briones de Miranda Adobe SHL 524
Old Trace Road east of West Fremont Avenue near junction with Arastradero Road, Los Altos

Juana Briones de Miranda purchased the Mexican land grant, known as Rancho La Purisima Concepcion, in 1844, where she lived with her family in this adobe. Standing here today is the original adobe on which additional rooms were added by later owners.

14 - Los Altos History House Museum
51 South San Antonio Road, Los Altos (415) 948-9427

Local historical artifacts and photographs depicting Los Altos history is displayed in this 1905 Craftsman-style home. Redwood from nearby mountains was used in the interior and exterior construction of this turn-of-the-century farmhouse.

15 - Moffett Field
North of U.S. 101, Mountain View (415) 404-4000

Dedicated in April 1933, Moffett Field was built as a base for the Navy's dirigibles. A week before the dedication, the dirigible *Akron*, which was to be stationed here, crashed. Seventy-three lives were lost, including that of Rear Admiral William A. Moffett, for whom this field was named. The crash of another dirigible, less than two years later, soon brought an end to the Navy's dirigible program.

15 - N.A.S.A./Ames Research Center
Moffett Field, Mountain View, reservations must placed for all tours (415) 604-6274 or (415) 604-649,

Highlights include space program history and the world's largest wind tunnel.

16 - Sunnyvale Historical Museum
Martin Murphy Jr. Historical Park, North Sunnyvale at California, Sunnyvale (408) 749-0220

Located on the site of the 30-room home of Martin Murphy Jr., pioneer settler and founder of the city of Sunnyvale, this museum features furnishings from the Murphy home, and personal items from the collection of Sunnyvale's first city clerk.

16 - Site of Martin Murphy Home   SHL 644
252 North Sunnyvale Avenue, between California and Arques, Sunnyvale

One of the first frame houses in California was erected from prefabricated material shipped around the Horn from Bangor, Maine. Murphy, one of California's pioneer settlers, emigrated here in 1844. He brought the first farm machinery from the East, planted the first orchards in the Santa Clara Valley, and let Southern Pacific Railroad build a station and lay tracks on his land. Murphy's 30-room house included a room with an altar for the Mission Santa Clara priests, who would use it to say Mass, and conduct baptism and marriage ceremonies. His original home was demolished in 1961. Sunnyvale Historic Museum, with Murphy's furnishings, is located on this site.

17 - Cupertino Historical Museum
Quinlan Community Center, 10185 North Stelling Road, Cupertino (408) 973-1495

The history and culture of the people who lived here, and founded the city of Cupertino, is captured in the hundreds of household objects, furniture, clothing, photographs and documents displayed in the city's first museum of history.

17 - Arroyo de San Joseph Cupertino SHL 800
Monta Vista High School parking lot, McClellan Road and Byrne Avenue, Cupertino

Juan Bautista de Anza camped here in 1776, where he named this creek, Arroyo de San Joseph Cupertino. It was renamed Stevens Creek for Captain Elisha P. Stevens who led the Murphy Party over the Sierra Nevada in 1844. Stevens built his home on the banks of this creek in the mid-1800s. His home was destroyed in the earthquake of 1906.

18 - Battle of Santa Clara SHL 260
El Camino Real and Lawrence Expressway, Santa Clara

Several encounters between Mexicans and Americans followed the raising of the American flag over Monterey in July 1846, and the declaration that California was a possession of the United States. One of those battles took place near here in January 1847, with the loss of several lives. It was at this site that a treaty was signed ending the conflict in this valley.

18 - Santa Clara Historic Homes
Chamber of Commerce, 2200 Laurelwood Road (408) 970-9825

Nine homes are listed by the Chamber of Commerce as having historical importance in the Santa Clara area. A list of these homes is available from the Chamber. Included are the homes of physicians, authors and political figures from Santa Clara's early history.

18 - Third Santa Clara Mission Site
490 Lincoln Street, Santa Clara

Three months before his death in 1784, Father Junipero Serra dedicated the third Santa Clara Mission at this site. The earthquakes of 1812 and 1818 caused extensive damage to the mission buildings and in 1819, the mission was moved again.

18 - Mission Santa Clara de Asis SHL 338
De Saisset Museum
University of Santa Clara, 820 Alviso Street, Santa Clara (408) 554-4023

Floods and earthquakes caused the original Santa Clara Mission to be relocated five times between 1777 and 1822. After secularization of the California missions in 1836, Santa Clara Mission fell into a state of ruins. Santa Clara College acquired the mission in 1851 and restored its buildings, which the college used for classrooms and dormitories. A fire in 1926 destroyed the church. A cement replica of the original mission church was erected in its place. The University of Santa Clara has built many new structures around the old mission site and preserves the history of the mission in an early California history collection at De Saisset Museum.

18 - Charles Copeland Morse Home SHL 904
981 Fremont Street, Santa Clara

This 12-room, Queen Anne style, Victorian home was built in 1892 for Charles Copeland Morse and his wife Maria. Morse and a partner bought 50-acres of land, and the two-year-old seed company of O. W. Wilson, in 1877. By 1888, their successful seed operation comprised 1,400 acres. After Charles Morse died in 1900, his son Lester continued the business and merged with D. M. Ferry to form the Ferry-Morse Seed Company.

18 - Old Adobe Woman's Club SHL 249
1067 The Alameda, between Franklin and Benton Streets, Santa Clara (408) 296-9830

Built in the early 1790s, this single-story adobe was an Indian dwelling for married mission Indians. It is among the oldest adobes in the state, and is being preserved by the Santa Clara Woman's Club, who occupy this building as their headquarters.

18 - Original Santa Clara Mission Site SHL 250
Plaque at Kifer Road and De la Cruz Boulevard, Santa Clara

The first location of Mission Santa Clara de Asis was established at this site in January 1777. Heavy rain and flooding of the nearby

Guadalupe River, forced the Padres to relocate the mission two years later, to a second site just south of the original location.

18 - Second Santa Clara Mission Site
Martin Avenue and De la Cruz Boulevard, Santa Clara

Santa Clara Mission was moved to this second site after the original mission was twice flooded by the Guadalupe River. A memorial cross marks the site of the temporary mission that stood here from 1779 to 1784.

Mission Santa Clara de Asis. Courtesy of Santa Clara Chamber of Commerce and Convention and Visitors Bureau.

18 - Harris-Lass Historic Preserve/Museum
1889 Market Street, Santa Clara (408) 248-2787

In 1987, the city of Santa Clara purchased the Harris-Lass house, and an acre of surrounding farm property for development as a living history museum. Santa Clara's agricultural heritage is preserved with original structures from the Harris-Lass farm, including: a barn, tank house, summer kitchen, and the Italianate-style house built by Henry Harris in 1865.

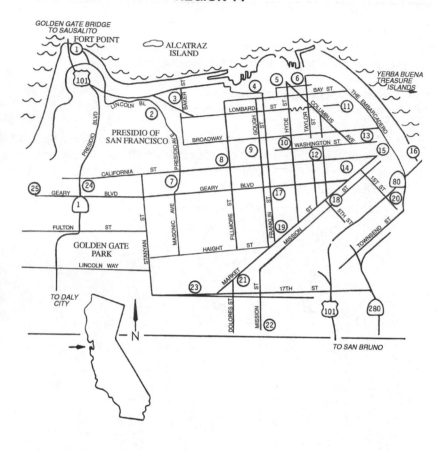

---

1 - Golden Gate Bridge   SHL 974

Spanning San Francisco Bay, between Sausalito and San Francisco, is one of the longest bridges in the world, the internationally-known Golden Gate Bridge. Joseph B. Strauss, the bridge's designer and chief engineer, began building the "bridge-called-impossible" in 1933, after 20 years of lobbying for its construction. After four years of fighting the elements, the 9,266-foot span was completed. Its two, 746-foot-high towers, the largest ever built, were permanently illuminated in 1987, on the bridge's golden anniversary.

World famous Golden Gate Bridge and Fort Point National Historic Site. Courtesy of U.S. Dept. of the Interior, National Park Service, photo by Richard Frear.

Fort Point National Historic Site. Courtesy of U.S. Dept. of the Interior, National Park Service, photo by Richard Frear.

1 - Fort Point National Historic Site   SHL 82

Long Avenue, north of Lincoln Boulevard, underneath the Golden Gate Bridge, Fort Point, San Francisco (415) 566-2857, (415) 556-1693, or T.D.D. accessible line (415) 556-0505

It was at this site, in 1794, that the Spanish built Castillo de San Joaquin to protect the Presidio of San Francisco. That first adobe fort was replaced by this brick and granite structure constructed by the U.S. Army Engineers between 1853-1861, and renamed Fort Point. It is the most massive brick fort erected on the West Coast. Its 120 cannons and garrison of 150 soldiers guarded the entrance into San

Francisco Bay. Point's museum features a collection of historic military artifacts, including Civil War relics.

1 - San Carlos Entrance Into San Francisco Bay   SHL 236
Long Avenue, north of Lincoln Boulevard, Fort Point, San Francisco

Juan de Ayala made the first recorded entrance into San Francisco Bay in August 1775, when he sailed the ship, *San Carlos*, into the bay through the Golden Gate. Ayala and his crew spent six weeks exploring the bay, surveying its tributaries and mapping the area.

1 - Fort Point Lighthouse
Fort Point, Long Avenue north of Lincoln Boulevard, San Francisco

This 1852 lighthouse was moved twice before being located, in 1864, at this final location. Completion of the Golden Gate Bridge in 1937, eliminated the need for this lighthouse station. This old iron-sided lighthouse has been preserved and renovated by the National Park Service, as part of historic Fort Point, and is open to the public.

2 - Presidio of San Francisco   SHL 79
Presidio Army Museum
Lincoln Boulevard and Funston Avenue, Presidio San Francisco
(415) 556-0856

Jose Joaquin Moraga, a member of the Anza expedition who led the first party of settlers to San Francisco, dedicated the Presidio of San Francisco on September 17, 1776. This Spanish fort was occupied by American forces in July 1846, when California was declared a possession of the United States. It became a major military installation and is headquarters of the U.S. Sixth Army. The adobe building used as the commandant's headquarters in the early 1800s, and an 1863 hospital, which houses the Presidio Army Museum, can be seen on tours of this military reservation. Military artifacts and items from the 1895, 1915 and 1939 World's Fairs are exhibited.

3 - Palace of Fine Arts
3601 Lyon Street, San Francisco (415) 567-6642

Built for the Panama-Pacific Exposition in 1915, this colossal Greco-Roman colonnaded rotunda and its adjoining lagoon is among the most impressive structures in San Francisco. The Exploratorium is housed inside this structure and features a collection of 500 participatory exhibits and art works.

4 - Fort Mason Historic District
North and east of Franklin Street and McArthur Avenue, San Francisco
(415) 441-0640

This was originally the site of a 1797 Spanish fortification. During the Civil War, the U.S. Army occupied and fortified this area, converting homes into military quarters. Many of those original 1855 homes remain today in this historic district.

4 - San Francisco African-American Historical and Cultural Society
Fort Mason, Building C, Marina Boulevard and Laguna Street Gate, San Francisco (415) 441-0640

History of black Californians, and a collection of artifacts depicting their involvement in the Civil War, are on permanent display.

4 - SS.*Jeremiah O'Brien*
Fort Mason, Marina Boulevard and Laguna Street Gate, San Francisco
(415) 441-3101

U. S. soldiers, by the hundreds of thousands, boarded Liberty Ships from Fort Mason's piers during the early 1940s, for duty in the Pacific. The last operating Liberty Ship, the SS *Jeremiah O'Brien*, which carried cargo across both the Atlantic and Pacific during World War II, is moored at Pier 3, and is open to the public. The ship's engines still power this historic vessel on occasional voyages around San Francisco Bay.

Buildings that were once part of Fort Mason's military complex now house the: Mexican Museum, San Francisco Craft and Folk Art Museum, *Museo Italo Americano*, and collections of the African-American Historical and Cultural Society.

5 - San Francisco Maritime State Historical Park
2905 Hyde Street, between Fisherman's Wharf and Aquatic Park, San Francisco (415) 556-3002

Eight restored historic ships, administered by the National Maritime Museum, are open to the public and include: *Eureka*, an 1890 sidewheel ferry used to carry railroad cars; *C. A. Thayer*, an 1895 three-masted schooner; *Wapama*, a 1915 wooden hull vessel; *Hercules*, an ocean-going tug; *Eppleton Hall*, a river tug; *Balclutha*, an 1886 square-rigger which made 17 trips around the Horn and the USS *Pampanito*, a World War II fleet submarine.

Historic square-rigged sailing ship Balclutha. *Courtesy of National Maritime Museum.*

1890 wooden paddle wheel ferry boat Eureka. *Courtesy of U.S. Dept. of the Interior, National Park Service, photo by Richard Frear.*

5 - National Maritime Museum, San Francisco
At the foot of Polk Street, in Aquatic Park, San Francisco (415) 556-8177

Inside this museum are 100,000 photographs, artifacts from historic vessels, small crafts, harpoons, anchors, displays of full-scale portions of vessels and detailed ship models.

Historic building, structure and lighthouse on Alcatraz Island in San Francisco Bay. Courtesy of National Park Service.

5 - Alcatraz Island/Museum
San Francisco Bay (415) 546-2805. Transportation from Pier 44 near Fisherman's Wharf via the Red and White Fleet (415) 546-2896

Alcatraz is best known for its Federal penitentiary which closed in 1960 after nearly a century of operation. First used as a prison during the Civil War, it was the "escape proof" home of some the country's most dangerous criminals. The National Park Service now operates Alcatraz as a museum.

In 1854, the first lighthouse on the California coast was put into operation on Alcatraz Island. Within a few months a foghorn was installed because of the region's constant fog.

5 - Ghirardelli Square
900 North Point Street, San Francisco (415) 775-5500

Ghirardelli Square was the country's first manufacturing complex that was renovated into shops and restaurants. The square's oldest building, The Woolen Mill, made Civil War uniforms in 1864. The original vats and ovens where chocolate was produced between 1893 and 1960 were renovated and are operating today. Ghirardelli Square is a registered National Historic Landmark.

6 - Museum of Opthamology/Historical Library
American Academy of Opthamology, 655 Beach Street, Suite 300, San Francisco (415) 561-8500

A collection of more than 6,000 artifacts, with ophthalmic-related objects from around the world, dating from as late as the third century B.C., is exhibited. Displays include: period reproductions of ophthalmologists' offices; pharmaceuticals; nostrums and sundries; diagnostic and surgical instruments dating back to the 1800s; spectacles, lorgnettes and monocles; memorabilia; and literature tracing the development of ophthalmology.

7 - San Francisco Fire Department Museum
655 Presidio Avenue, at Bush Street, San Francisco (415) 861-8000

Antique fire-fighting equipment, fire horns, helmets, photographs and other memorabilia from San Francisco's fire companies are displayed here. An 1849 hand pumper, chief's buggy, and Lillie Hitchcock Coit exhibit are some of the unusual items featured in this museum.

7 - Site of Laurel Hill Cemetery   SHL 760
Marker at 3333 California Street, San Francisco

Established in 1854, Laurel Hill Cemetery was the burial place for many of California's distinguished pioneers. Burials are no longer permitted within the city of San Francisco, except in the National Cemetery at the Presidio.

8 - Museum of Russian Culture
2450 Sutter Street, San Francisco (415) 921-4082

Russian artifacts from pre-revolutionary days in Russia are displayed with military items, coins and medals. Personal items from the Czars, letters from Tolstoy and photographs are part of this museum's special collections.

9 - Schubert Hall
2099 Pacific Avenue, San Francisco (415) 567-1848

This 1905 structure is noted for its ornate grille work. The California Historical Society maintains this historic structure, which houses the society's library and genealogical collection.

9 - Octagon House
2645 Gough Street, San Francisco (415) 441-7512

One of five such houses in early San Francisco, this octagonal house was built by William McElroy in 1861. It was moved to its present site in 1951 and was completely restored by the Colonial Dames of America. They now operate the house as a museum of Colonial and Federal period decorative arts. Furniture, samplers, ceramics, silver and lacquer-ware are on exhibit, along with documents signed by 54 of the 56 men who signed the Declaration of Independence.

9 - Haas-Lilienthal House
2007 Franklin Street, San Francisco (415) 441-3004

This 24-room, Queen Anne style, Victorian House was constructed in 1886 by William Haas. It was donated to the Foundation for San Francisco's Architectural Heritage in 1973. The foundation now uses the house as its headquarters. Many original antiques, furnishings, accessories and paintings are on display inside this home.

10 - Whittier Mansion
2090 Jackson Street, San Francisco (415) 567-1848

Constructed of red sandstone in 1895, this mansion was the home of William F. Whittier, a founder of Fuller-O'Brien Paints. Used as the German Consulate before World War II, it is now the home of the

California Historical Society. Paintings, sculpture and furnishings of the period accent the elegant interior of this structure.

11 - Telegraph Hill   SHL 91
#1 Telegraph Hill Boulevard at the end of Lombard, San Francisco
(415) 362-0808, Coit Tower

A two-story signal station was built at the top of this hill in 1849. Observers were stationed here to report ships entering the Golden Gate. A semaphore system was used to signal the type of ship to the city below the hill. The first telegraph in California was stationed here in 1853. Mark Twain, Joaquin Miller and Bret Harte are among the famous writers who once lived on Telegraph Hill. The 210-foot Coit Tower, which is open to the public, was erected in 1933 to commemorate volunteer firemen of the 19th century. Twenty-five murals of "Life in California, 1934," were painted by WPA (Work Projects Administration) artists on the first floor walls.

11 - St. Francis Church
610 Vallejo Street, San Francisco (415) 421-4095

St. Francis Church is the second oldest Roman Catholic church in San Francisco. This structure was erected in 1859 and fully restored following the 1906 fire that destroyed the interior of the church.

12 - Fairmont Hotel
950 Mason Street, San Francisco (415) 772-5000

For an eleven-week period in 1945, the Fairmont Hotel was the center of world-wide attention. In its eight-room, penthouse suite, the U. S. Secretary of State, Edward R. Stettinius, and his delegation, met to form the United Nations. They drafted the United Nations Charter in the penthouse's two-story, circular library.

12 - Cable Car Museum, Powerhouse and Barn
1201 Mason Street, San Francisco (415) 474-1887

Built in 1887, to house machinery to power the original cable cars, this building was rebuilt following the 1906 earthquake, and has been renovated. The working machinery of the power-house can be viewed as cables enter and leave the barn. The first cable car put in service, in San Francisco, is on display with photographs and artifacts from the early history of this National Historic Landmark.

12 - Site of the Mark Hopkins Institute of Art   SHL 754
1 Nob Hill, California at Mason Street, San Francisco (415) 392-3434

Mark Hopkins, one of the "Big Four" who built the Central Pacific Railroad, had a mansion on Nob Hill. It was donated to the University of California, for the San Francisco Art Institute, in 1893. The institute was later moved to Chestnut and Jones streets and the Mark Hopkins Hotel was erected on this site. Across the street is the only Nob Hill mansion that survived the 1906 earthquake and fire, the former home of Comstock millionaire, James Flood. That mansion is now the Pacific Union Club.

13 - Jackson Square Historic District
Sansome, Washington, Kearny, Columbus and Broadway Streets, San Francisco

Located within this historic district are the only surviving buildings from the gold rush period in San Francisco.

13 - El Dorado and Parker House   SHL 192
Merchant and Kearny Streets, San Francisco

During the early gold rush days, the El Dorado and Parker House, were among the most famous saloons and gambling spots in San Francisco. Both were destroyed by fire several times and rebuilt at their original locations. The Jenny Lind Theater replaced the Parker House in 1850. It was then purchased by the city in 1852, for use as a city hall. That acquisition was widely protested, and was the subject of a public indignation meeting, held at Portsmouth Plaza.

13 - Farnsworth's Laboratory   SHL 941
202 Green Street, San Francisco

Philo T. Farnsworth demonstrated the first working model of a television system he invented here in 1927. This 21-year-old inventor made a major discovery with this practical transmission of a television signal. He went on to patent many discoveries, including the 1956 cathode-ray tube of the "storage" type for televisions of the future.

14 - Lucas, Turner and Company Bank   SHL 453
Montgomery and Jackson Streets, San Francisco

After resigning from the army in 1853, William Tecumseh Sherman became a San Francisco banker. In 1854 he moved the branch of Lucas, Turner and Company Bank to this building, and headed its operation until 1857. Sherman rejoined the army in 1861, after Louisiana seceded from the Union, and by 1869 was General of the U. S. Army.

14 - Site of First Jewish Religious Services   SHL 462
Montgomery between Washington and Jackson Streets, San Francisco

Forty pioneers met at the building that stood on this site September 26, 1849, and celebrated Yom Kippur. This was the beginning of Jewish religious services in San Francisco.

14 - Site of the First Meeting of Masons   SHL 408
728 Montgomery Street, San Francisco

The first recorded meeting of the Free and Accepted Masons, in California, was held at this site in November 1849. It was originally chartered as California Lodge No. 13 by the Grand Lodge of the District of Columbia. The buildings now standing at this location were erected in the 1850s.

14 - Pony Express—Western Business Headquarters   SHL 696
617 Montgomery Street, San Francisco

The Leavenworth, Kansas firm of Russell, Majors and Waddell, that operated the Pony Express, had their western business headquarters at this site. The first westbound express rider arrived here on April 14, 1860. Completion of the transcontinental telegraph, in 1861, brought an end to the Pony Express after operating for just 18 months.

14 - Site of First U. S. Branch Mint in California   SHL 87
Pacific Heritage Museum, 608 Commercial Street, San Francisco
(415) 399-1124

From 1849 to 1850, fifteen different organizations in California were minting private gold coins. The first government branch mint was established in California in April 1854, and began operating at this site. Privately minted coins remained legal tender for two more years. The Pacific Heritage Museum is housed in this restored historic building and features the history and culture of Pacific Basin immigrants. Rare artifacts, models and the history of this landmark building are exhibited.

14 - Montgomery Block   SHL 80
Plaque in building at 600 Montgomery Street, San Francisco

One of San Francisco's first fire proof buildings was erected in 1853, in what was then known as the Washington Block. This four-story brick building survived the 1906 earthquake and fire, and stood for more than a century until it was demolished in 1959.

14 - Wells Fargo History Museum
420 Montgomery Street, San Francisco (415) 396-2619

This museum's collection includes well-preserved and protected relics of the gold rush period and early Wells Fargo operations. Authentic Concord stage, gold ore, stage strongboxes, Pony Express artifacts, guns, miners' equipment and old photographs are among the many interesting items on display.

14 - Landing Place of Captain Montgomery   SHL 81
Montgomery and Clay Streets, San Francisco

Commander of the USS *Portsmouth*, Captain John Montgomery, landed near this spot on July 9, 1846 (San Francisco Bay's water extended this far inland at that time). He raised the American flag that day, where the old Custom House stood in Portsmouth Square, and proclaimed California as part of the United States. Bank of America built its first head office at this site in 1904, and uses the USS *Portsmouth* on its seal.

14 - Site of Mellus and Howard Warehouse   SHL 459
Montgomery and Clay Streets, San Francisco

The oldest historical society in California was organized here in 1850 under the name, Society of California Pioneers. W. D. W. Howard, the Society's first president, was an owner of the Mellus and Howard warehouse which once stood here.

14 - Niantic Hotel   SHL 88
Clay and Sansome Streets, San Francisco

Two hundred and fifty immigrants from Panama arrived here aboard the ship *Niantic* in 1849. Unable to get a crew for the return voyage, because of the lure of the gold fields, the *Niantic* stayed at its anchorage and was converted into offices, stores and a warehouse. The ship burned in 1851. The new Niantic Hotel was built at the same location on top of the hulk of the old ship.

14 - Office of *The Star* Newspaper   SHL 85
Washington and Brenham Streets, San Francisco

San Francisco's first newspaper was established in the building that stood behind the home of its editor, Samuel Brannan. First published on January 9, 1847, as *The Star*, its name was later changed to *The California Star*, and then *The Alta Californian*. The building that now stands here was erected in 1909 as the Chinese Telephone Exchange.

14 - Fort Gunnybags   SHL 90
Sacramento Street between Davis and Front Streets, San Francisco

Headquarters of the San Francisco Vigilance Committee was established at this site in 1856. "Fort Gunnybags" derived its name from the sand-filled gunnysacks placed as a barricade around the building. The Vigilance Committee was formed after the murder of James King of William, the editor of the *San Francisco Bulletin*, by James P. Casey, whom King exposed for his political corruption. Casey was executed in front of Fort Gunnybags and the Vigilance Committee went on to clean-up the city.

14 - What Cheer House   SHL   650
Sacramento and Leidesdorff Streets, San Francisco

This was the site of the famous "What Cheer House," erected in 1852, by Robert Woodward, who would later build Woodward's Gardens, a pioneer amusement park. San Francisco's first free library and museum were housed in this all-male hotel.

14 - Long Wharf (Central Wharf)   SHL 328
Commercial Street, west of Montgomery Street, San Francisco

In 1848, Central Wharf (called Long Wharf) was built 800 feet into the bay from what is now Leidesdorff Street. It was extended an additional 2,000 feet after 1850 and became a popular promenade, with buildings erected on piles along both sides of the wharf. The success of this wharf resulted in additional wharves being built in the same area until the entire cove between California and Broadway Streets was filled-in with sand.

14 - Hudson Bay Company Headquarters   SHL 819
Montgomery, between Sacramento and Commercial Streets, San Francisco

In the 1820s, trappers from the Hudson Bay Company first came to California from Canada, following trails blazed by early explorers such as Jedediah Smith. They established their headquarters at this location in 1841, but insufficient profits, and a dwindling fur trade, led to its closing five years later. Hudson Bay Company sold their building. It later became the United States Hotel.

14 - Chinese Historical Society of America Museum
650 Commercial Street, San Francisco (415) 391-1188

The first Chinese-American museum in America devoted to the preservation of Chinese-American artifacts and material was established at this site in the city's Chinatown district. Exhibits include: a 14-foot California Redwood sampan; an 1880 Chinese Buddhist altar; clothing and slippers of 19th century Chinese-American pioneers; a three-pronged fighting spear made in Weaverville for the Chinese Tong War; historical photographs and other artifacts.

14 - Site of Parrott Granite Block SHL 89
Northwest corner of California and Montgomery Streets, San Francisco

San Francisco's first fireproof building was built here in 1852 of granite blocks shipped from China. It was demolished in 1926 after surviving the 1906 earthquake and fire.

14 - California First State Fair SHL 861
Bush and Montgomery Streets, San Francisco

California's first state fair was held at this site in October 1854. The fair was hosted by different cities each year until 1861, when Sacramento became the state fair's permanent home.

14 - Site of The California Theatre SHL 86
North side of Bush between Kearny and Grant Avenue, San Francisco

The 1600-seat California Theatre was built on this site in the late 1860s. A distinguished cast performed the comedy *Money* on the theatre's opening night, January 15, 1869. Important artists of the period, including Lotta Crabtree, played here before the theatre closed in 1888.

14 - Portsmouth Plaza SHL 119
Kearny between Clay and Washington Streets, San Francisco

Known as La Plaza to the first Spanish settlers, this was the site of the old adobe Custom House, where Captain John Montgomery, commander of the USS *Portsmouth*, raised the American flag on July 9, 1846, and declared California a possession of the United States. Renamed Portsmouth Plaza, it was the center of San Francisco and the site of several historic events. Robert Lewis Stevenson, who spent many hours here, was honored by a statue erected in 1897. It was the first monument to be erected to honor Stevenson's memory.

14 - Site of First Public School SHL 587
Portsmouth Plaza, Clay and Brenham Streets, San Francisco

California's first public school opened at this site in April 1848, at what was then the center of San Francisco. The original building was used as a town hall, courthouse, church and school.

14 - Clay Street Hill Railroad Company SHL 500
Portsmouth Plaza, Clay and Kearny Streets, San Francisco

Andrew Hallidie, an English builder of aerial cable cars, invented the world famous San Francisco cable car and started the first line here in 1873. San Francisco's cable car system grew to eight lines, with this original line operating until 1942. Today it is a registered National Historic Landmark.

14 - Old St. Mary's Church SHL 810
660 California Street, San Francisco (415) 986-4388

San Francisco's first Catholic cathedral, the first building erected as a cathedral in California, was built here in 1854. Bricks used in the construction of the original building came around the Horn, and some of the stone was quarried in China. All but the walls were destroyed in the fire that followed the 1906 earthquake. St. Mary's Church was rebuilt within its original walls, and rededicated in 1909.

14 - Original Site of the Third Baptist Church SHL 1010
1642 - 44 Grant Avenue, San Francisco (415) 346-4426

The first African-American Baptist Church west of the Rocky Mountains was established at this site in 1852. It was named the First Colored Baptist Church. It was then relocated to Bush and Powell, and in 1855, the name changed to the Third Baptist Church. The fire that followed the 1906 earthquake destroyed that building, but the church was rebuilt at a new site, on Nob Hill, at Hyde and Clay Streets. During its distinguished history, the Third Baptist Church made outstanding contributions to the religious, social, political and physical well-being of the community through innovative programs and the dynamic leadership of its leaders.

14 - Museum of Money of the American West
Bank of California, 400 California Street, San Francisco (415) 765-0400

Privately minted coins from the gold rush period, and gold nuggets, are featured in this bank's collection of currency from the early days of California.

14 - Chevron World of Oil Museum
555 Market Street, San Francisco   (415) 894-7700

A series of exhibits tell the story of: the origin of oil, tools used to search for and extract petroleum, scaled down models of a tanker and drilling rig, and the refinery process that transforms oil into different products. Life-sized dioramas recreate Chevron history around the turn-of-the-century, displaying: the first West Coast gasoline station; an old-fashioned kitchen with kerosene lamps, oil stove and heater; and a bulk plant that's used to store and distribute petroleum products.

14 - Site of Invention of the Slot Machine
406 Market Street, San Francisco

In 1895, Charles Fey invented the famous three-wheel slot machine and manufactured them at this location. From here they were shipped to gambling houses around the world.

14 - City of Paris Building   SHL 876
Geary and Stockton Streets, San Francisco

One of the finest commercial buildings of the beaux-arts style was constructed here in 1896. It was built to house the Verdier family business, which first started as a store aboard the ship *La Ville de Paris*, in 1850. Renovation was made following the 1906 earthquake.

14 - Union Square   SHL 623
Geary and Powell Streets, San Francisco

On January 3, 1850, San Francisco's first Mayor, John W. Geary, made this area to a public square. Geary was appointed Governor of Kansas by President Pierce in 1856, and served in the Civil War as a Union General. In 1860, this area was named "Union Square," when meetings in support of the Union cause were held here.

15 - Union Ferry Depot Building
Embarcadero at Market Street, San Francisco

Before the Golden Gate Bridge was completed in 1937, one hundred thousand passengers were transported daily across the bay, by eight ferry boats that operated from this 1903 building. Moored nearby is the Santa Rosa Ferryboat that once operated between San Francisco and Sausalito.

15 - Shoreline Markers   SHL 83
Battery, Bush and Market Streets, San Francisco

Two markers, opposite the street from each other, show San Francisco Bay's shoreline, from the time gold was discovered in 1848, to the time these markers were placed in 1921. Years of unregulated earth filling projects gradually increased the Bay's shoreline, while, at the same time, decreased the number of square miles of surface area in the Bay.

16 - Yerba Buena Island Lighthouse
Northeast of San Francisco via I-80 on Yerba Buena Island

Yerba Buena Island Lighthouse was established on this San Francisco Bay island, in 1875. The island was first used by the military and is now a Coast Guard repair depot. In 1936, the island was tunneled through as a mid-bay bridge support for the San Francisco-Oakland Bay Bridge. The lighthouse is not accessible to the public.

16 - Treasure Island   SHL 987
Treasure Island Museum, Avenue of the Californians at California Avenue, Building Number 1, Naval Station Treasure Island, San Francisco
(415) 395-5067

During an 18-month period, from 1936-1937, the Army Corps of Engineers constructed 400-acre Treasure Island, from mud dredged off the bottom of San Francisco Bay. It is one of the world's largest artificial islands. From 1938-1945, it became the home port of Pan American Airways "China Clippers," America's first regularly scheduled transpacific passenger flights. Two years before the outbreak of World War II, buildings of "Pacific Basin" design were erected on the island for the Golden Gate International Exposition, "Pageant of the Pacific," California's last world's fair. The largest military museum in the Western United States is housed in one of the three remaining airport buildings. Exhibits interpret the history of the Navy, Marine corps and Coast Guard from 1813 to the present.

17 - Tomb of Thomas Starr King SHL 691
Franklin between Starr King and Geary Streets, San Francisco

Pastor of the First Unitarian Church, from 1860-1864, Thomas King conducted an extensive state-wide campaign to arouse the spirit of loyalty for the Union during the Civil War. His efforts for the Sanitary Commission (the forerunner of the Red Cross) helped save it from financial ruin. His memory is honored in many locations: with a portrait of him hung in the state capitol; a statue of him erected in Golden Gate Park; and a mountain peak, in Yosemite, named after him. In Statuary Hall, in the Nation's Capitol Building, King's statue stands alongside that of Father Junipero Serra. His final resting place is commemorated here at his marble tomb.

18 - Old Mint Museum SHL 875
5th and Mission Streets, San Francisco (415) 974-0788

The only Federal Greek Revival structure in California was constructed in 1870, as the second U.S. Branch Mint. It became the principal mint in the United States, and the chief Federal depository for gold and silver produced in the West. Today, it is operated as a museum where gold bars and a $3 million gold coin collection are displayed. Restored period rooms, an 1860 stagecoach, and an 1898-1925 Victrola exhibit are preserved in this historic museum.

19 - Society of California Pioneers Museum and Library
456 McAllister Street, San Francisco (415) 861-5278

Displays of early California history are the primary exhibits of this museum. An original Concord stagecoach and the Vigilance Committee Bell, that once called the committee to Fort Gunnybags, are two of the museum's featured items.

19 - Birthplace of the United Nations SHL 964
War Memorial Complex, 301 Van Ness, San Francisco

Opened in 1932, as a memorial to World War I veterans, this was the birthplace of the United Nations. Representatives from 46 countries met here, and on June 26, 1945, signed the United Nations Charter. The treaty of peace was signed with Japan in September 1951, at this historic building.

20 - Rincon Hill SHL 84
First Street, between Harrison and Bryant, San Francisco

St. Mary's Hospital, the first Catholic hospital on the Pacific Coast, and the U.S. Marine Hospital, were built here in the 1850s. Some of San Francisco's well-known families had their homes on this hill during the 1860s and 1870s. Many homes were lost in the 1906 fire; and most of Rincon Hill was leveled when the San Francisco-Oakland Bay Bridge was constructed.

20 - Cartoon Art Museum
665 - 3rd Street, San Francisco (415) 546-9481

Our social, economic and cultural history has been recorded in the truly original American art form of cartooning. That history is preserved in this unique museum in two and three dimensional art forms. Included in the collections are: newspaper strips, sports and editorial cartoons, comic book illustrations, magazine cartoons, animation, advertising, greeting cards, and videos.

21 - First Bancroft Library Site SHL 791
1538 Valencia Street, San Francisco

The largest book and stationery business west of Chicago was operated by Hubert Bancroft in the 1850s. It was here that Bancroft established a library of historical items relating to Central America, Mexico and the Western United States. This library was used by Bancroft's staff to publish a 39-volume history of Western North America. In 1905, the complete library of 60,000 items were presented to the University of California, at Berkeley, where it is housed today.

21 - Woodward's Gardens SHL 454
Mission and Duboce Streets, San Francisco

Robert Woodward, owner of San Francisco's unusual "What Cheer House," built his home on this site in 1866. He filled his home with art objects and opened his gardens to the public who showed an appreciation for his collections. Woodward added attractions to his property, including a 5000-seat octagonal pavilion. Across the street he established a wild animal collection and aquarium that he connected to his other property with a tunnel. Woodward's gardens were San Francisco's most popular attraction before it closed in 1892.

21 - The Golden Hydrant
20th and Church Streets, San Francisco

A valiant battle against the fire that ravaged San Francisco following the 1906 earthquake was fought, and won, from this obscure location. Water from the fire plug at this intersection was used to stop the fire before it destroyed the famous Mission District. For many years, on the quake's anniversary, April 18th, survivors of this infamous event met here to paint the fire plug "gold."

21 - Mission San Francisco de Asis (Mission Dolores)   SHL 327
16th and Dolores Streets, San Francisco (415) 621-8203

The sixth mission founded by the Franciscan Padres was dedicated by Father Junipero Serra, in 1776, at the site selected by Juan Bautista de Anza. Its four foot-thick adobe walls were so well constructed that the mission suffered no major damage in the 1906 earthquake. This mission features an ornate Spanish altar and a cemetery with the graves of early Californians. The grave of Don Luis Antonio Arguello, the first appointed Mexican Governor of California, is in one corner of the cemetery. Jose Joaquin Moraga, who founded the Presidio of San Francisco in 1776, is buried within the church.

21 - El Camino Real - Northern Terminus   SHL 784
Mission Dolores, 16th and Dolores Streets, San Francisco

On the 250th anniversary of the birth of Father Junipero Serra, a plaque was placed to mark the northern terminus of the trail he helped blaze between the nine missions he established. This trail was called "El Camino Real" the king's highway and was the major north-south route through California along the coast. Even today our highways follow much of the original trail.

21 - Site of the Giant Powder Company   SHL 1002
Glen Canyon Park, east of O'Shaughnessy Blvd., San Francisco

In August 1867, the Giant Powder Company was established in San Francisco to produce Alfred Nobel's new dynamite for the state's gold miners and railroads. On March 19, 1868, the first commercial manufacture of dynamite in the United States was produced at this site. A year later the plant, and every building at the site, would be destroyed in an explosion, but the company would rebuild. Eventually, more than a dozen companies produced explosives in the San Francisco area, making it the dynamite capitol of the world.

22 - Site of St. Mary's College   SHL 772
Mission and Crescent, San Francisco

St. Mary's College was established at this location in 1863, by Archbishop Joseph Alemany. In 1889 the college was moved to Oakland, where it remained until it was relocated to its present campus at Moraga, in 1928.

23 - Josephine D. Randall Junior Museum
199 Museum Way, San Francisco (415) 554-9600

This children's museum features Indian artifacts, natural history, geology and other areas of interest to youngsters such as model railroading and live animals.

24 - The Conservatory   SHL 841
Golden Gate Park, J. F. Kennedy Drive, San Francisco (415) 666-7017

California's first municipal greenhouse, and the oldest building in Golden Gate Park, was erected from prefabricated glass sections shipped around the Horn in 1875. This enormous victorian glass structure, which took four years to construct, was rebuilt after a fire in 1883, and has remained standing since.

25 - Cliff House/Musee Mechanique
1090 Point Lobos Avenue, San Francisco (415) 386-3330 or (415) 386-1170

The city's 24th mayor, Adolph Sutro, erected Cliff House, an elaborate gingerbread resort, at this site in 1896. The present Cliff House is the fourth built on the site since the first one was destroyed by fire in 1907. Musee Mechanique, an old-fashioned penny arcade, is housed here and features 140 ancient amusement devices. Just north of Cliff House are ruins of the 1896 Sutro Baths, once the largest indoor swimming pools in the world.

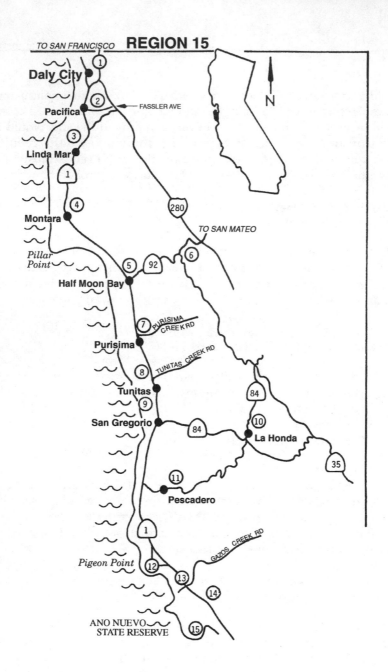

TO SAN FRANCISCO

Daly City

Pacifica

FASSLER AVE

Linda Mar

Montara

Pillar
Point

Half Moon Bay

Purisima

PURISIMA
CREEK RD

Tunitas

TUNITAS CREEK RD

San Gregorio

84

84

La Honda

35

Pescadero

Pigeon Point

GAZOS CREEK RD

ANO NUEVO
STATE RESERVE

280

TO SAN MATEO

92

N

1 - Site of Broderick-Terry Duel   SHL 19
1100 Lake Merced Boulevard, Daly City

The last of the great duels in California was fought at this site on September 13, 1859, between U.S. Senator David Broderick, and Chief Justice of the California Supreme Court, David Terry. Terry was a Southerner and Broderick's sympathies were with the North. Terry challenged Broderick to a duel for statements the Senator made that Terry felt "impugned his honor." Broderick was fatally wounded in the duel and died three days later. The places where these men stood that day are marked by two granite shafts. Terry, who became a brigadier general in the Confederate Army, returned to Stockton after the Civil War ended. He was later shot at a railway station by the bodyguard of U.S. Supreme Court Justice Stephen Field, whom he had threatened.

2 - Site of Discovery of San Francisco Bay   SHL 394
Plaque located southeast corner of Crespi Drive and Hwy 1, Pacifica

Portola's expedition crossed Sweeney Ridge on November 4, 1769, and discovered San Francisco Bay. This discovery site has been designated a National Historic Landmark.

2 - Ocean Shore Railroad (Pacifica)
Pedro Point, Pacifica

Ocean Shore Railroad was built to run along the coast between San Francisco and Santa Cruz in the early 1900s. Before the first run was made, the San Francisco earthquake of 1906 cost the company thousands in lost equipment. Additional losses caused by the eroding coastline brought an end to the line in 1921. Tobin Station still stands on Pedro Point in Pacifica. Half Moon Bay's, Arleta Park Station, is now a private residence at Poplar and Railroad Avenues.

3 - Portola Expedition Camp (Pedro Valley)   SHL 24
Hwy 1, at San Pedro Beach, Linda Mar

Sergeant Ortega departed Portola's base camp on October 21, 1769, to find the site of Monterey Bay. A hunting party from this same base camp reported their sighting of San Francisco Bay on November 2, 1769.

3 - Sanchez Adobe Historic Site   SHL 391
1000 Linda Mar Boulevard at Adobe Drive, Linda Mar   (415) 359-1462

The Sanchez Adobe, ethnographic village, and mission outpost location have been preserved on this five-acre historic site. Mission Dolores (San Francisco de Asis) established an agricultural outpost, in 1786, on the site of what was an ancient Costanoan Indian Village. In 1842, Francisco Sanchez, commandant of the presidio, and several times mayor of San Francisco (during the Mexican rule of Alta California), built a two-story adobe on this part of his 8,900-acre rancho. Today, the museum operates in part of this completely restored adobe. On display are: artifacts found from archaeological digs on the site, 19th century furnishings, and exhibits of the area's history.

Sanchez Adobe. Courtesy of San Mateo Historical Association.

4 - Portola Expedition Camp (Martini's Creek)   SHL 25
Northeast of Montara at Martini Creek and Montara State Beach

Portola's expedition camped at the base of Pedro (Montara) Mountain where a member of the party was sent ahead to blaze a trail over the mountain. On October 31, 1769, they crossed Pedro Mountain.

4 - Point Montara Lighthouse
16th Street at Hwy 1, Montara (415) 728-7177

Offshore hazards near this point brought about the construction of a fog signal in 1875. In 1900, a light was installed to improve navigation safety along this dangerous shoreline. A thirty-foot conical tower was erected in 1928, on a seventy-foot cliff, to provide better visibility for this lighthouse's warning signal. This historic lighthouse station has now been restored and converted into a hostel for overnight stays.

5 - Portola Expedition Camp (Half Moon Bay)   SHL 21
Arroyo Canada Verde Creek and Hwy 1, Half Moon Bay

Portola's expedition stayed here two days and first saw Pillar Point to the northwest of their camp. They next traveled on October 30, 1769.

5 - Half Moon Bay Walking Tour
Spanishtown Historical Society (415) 726-5202

Spanish influence is evident in Half Moon Bay's historical landmarks, which date back to the Spanish and Portuguese settlers of the 18th century. Some of the town's landmarks include: the 1853 Johnston House, built using wooden pegs; Half Moon Bay Community Methodist Church, built in 1872, one of the oldest Protestant churches in the country; and Pilarcitos Cemetery, established in 1820 by the Catholic church.

5 - Ocean Shore Railroad (Half Moon Bay)
Poplar Avenue and Railroad Avenue, Half Moon Bay

Ocean Shore Railroad was built to run along the coast between San Francisco and Santa Cruz in the early 1900s. Before the first run was made, the San Francisco earthquake of 1906 cost the company thousands in lost equipment. Additional losses caused by the eroding coastline brought an end to the line in 1921. Tobin Station still stands on Pedro Point, in Pacifica. Half Moon Bay's, Arleta Park Station, is now a private residence.

6 - Portola Expedition Camp (Crystal Springs Lake) SHL 94
Junction of I-280 and Hwy 92, south of Hillsborough

The November 5, 1769, camp of the Portola expedition, and the trail they followed south along San Francisco Bay, is now covered by Crystal Springs reservoir.

7 - Portola Expedition Camp (Purisima Creek) SHL 22
Hwy 1 on south side of Purisima Creek

Portola's expedition camped here on October 27, 1769, across the creek from an Indian Village. Some of Portola's men used the village's abandoned huts that night.

8 - Tunitas Beach, Indian Village Site on Portola Route SHL 375
West ot Hwy 1 on the north side of Tunitas Creek

After their failed attempt to locate Monterey Bay, Portola's Expedition camped at many of their original campgrounds on their return trip to San Diego. En route, they discovered the Indian Village, at Tunitas Creek, about the middle of November 1769.

9 - Portola Expedition Camp (San Gregorio Creek) SHL 26
San Gregorio State Beach, Hwy 1, San Gregorio

Portola's expedition spent two days here in October 1769, to rest his men. Father Crespi, a member of the expedition, was impressed by the Indian settlements and proposed this as a possible mission site.

10 - Site of John L. Sears Store SHL 343
Northwest corner of La Honda (Hwy 84) and Sears Ranch Roads, La Honda

John L. Sears had this store built in 1861-1862, at a place he named "La Honda." His store became known as the "Bandit-Built Store" because Sears employed two newcomers to the area who were later believed to be Bob and Jim Younger, members of the Jesse James Gang. Sears' store stood almost a century before it was torn down in 1960.

11 - First Congregational Church of Pescadero   SHL 949
San Gregorio Street, Pescadero

The oldest surviving Protestant church building on the San Francisco Peninsula, and in the Santa Clara Valley, is the First Congregational Church, erected here in 1867.

12 - Pigeon Point Lighthouse   SHL 930
Pigeon Point Road, Hwy 1, Pigeon Point (Pescadero)   (415) 879-0633

This lighthouse became operational in 1872. It was named for the American clipper ship, *Carrier Pigeon,* that was lost 500 feet offshore, on a stormy night in 1853. This lighthouse became operational in 1872. At 115 feet, it is among the tallest lighthouse structures on the Pacific Coast. Tours can be made of this fully automated lighthouse, which has been in continuous operation for more than a century and is now open to the public as a hostelry.

13 - Portola Expedition Camp (Gazos Creek)   SHL 23
Hwy 1 at Gazos Creek, south of Pigeon Point

Portola's expedition spent the night of October 23, 1769, at this Indian village, where they heard rumors of a port and ship, to the north. It was those rumors that encouraged them to continue north in search of Monterey Bay.

14 - Steele Brothers Dairy Ranches   SHL 906
Green Oaks Ranch, east of Hwy 1, 13 miles south of Pescadero

Between 1854-1857, the three Steele brothers came to California. From their dairy, north of San Francisco, they began producing a high quality cheese. They later leased land here and built an extensive cheese business that included several dairies on 7,000 acres of land. Headquarters of the Steele's business was located here, at Green Oaks Ranch, in this original ranch house. Cheese production continued until the 1930s.

15 - Dickerman Barn
Interpretive Center, Ano Nuevo State Reserve, New Years Creek Road, west of Hwy 1, south of Pescadero (415) 879-0595

Shipwreck artifacts, early farm equipment, Indian boats and early photographs are on display inside the 1880 Dickerman Dairy Barn Museum. The park is a state wildlife reserve where elephant seals, once hunted to near extinction, are protected in a natural environment.

15 - Site of Ano Nuevo Lighthouse
Point Ano Nuevo, west of Hwy 1

Erected in 1890, this station was converted into a day-beacon, in 1948, because of changing marine traffic. The station's islet has become a popular place for sea lions from the nearby Point Ano Nuevo State Reserve. Only skeletal remains of the tower and keeper's house are visible.

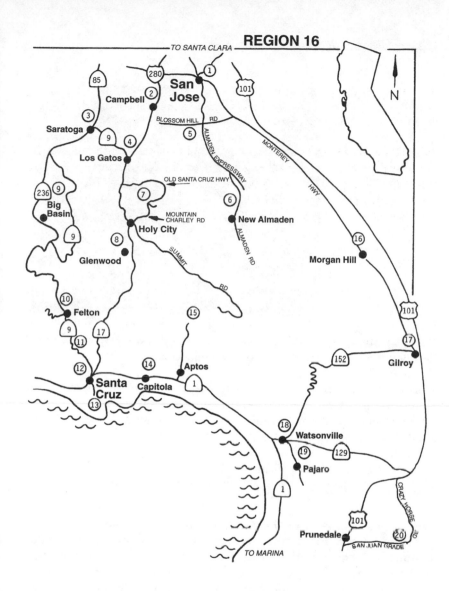

REGION 16

*Winchester
Mystery House
Gardens and
Historical
Museum. Courtesy
of Winchester
Mystery House
Gardens and
Historical
Museum.*

1 - First Successful Introduction of the Honeybee   SHL 945
San Jose Municipal Airport, 1661 Airport Boulevard, San Jose

Christopher A. Shelton successfully introduced the honeybee to California in 1853. Shelton purchased the beehives in Panama and brought them north to this region of California, where he established California's beekeeping industry.

1 - Winchester Mystery House   SHL 868
525 South Winchester Boulevard at I-280 and Hwy 17, San Jose
(408) 247-2101

The largest home, and the strangest in the United States, was constructed here for Sarah L. Winchester, widow of the heir to the famous Winchester Rifle fortune. Following the death of her husband, Sarah was convinced by a Boston spiritualist, that only by moving West, buying a house and continuously building on it, could she appease the evil spirits of those killed by the Winchester rifle. Thirty-eight years of around-the-clock construction changed the original 8-room farmhouse into a 160-room mansion with 47 fireplaces and 10,000 windows. Doors that open into blank walls, stairways that lead nowhere, and secret passageways reflect the many changes that Sarah made during its construction. More than a hundred of the mansion's rooms are open the public. Also on the grounds of this historic house is a museum of antique firearms.

134

1 - El Pueblo San Jose de Guadalupe   SHL 433
Hobson and Vendome Streets, San Jose

California's oldest civil settlement was established at this site in 1777, as an agricultural community to supply the needs of the missions and military in Alta California. El Pueblo San Jose de Guadalupe eventually became the city of San Jose.

1 - Roberto-Sunol Adobe   SHL 898
770 Lincoln Avenue, San Jose

One of the few Indians to be awarded a Mexican land grant was known as Roberto. Here, he made his home and built this adobe, in 1839. In 1847, he sold his ranchero and adobe to Antonio Sunol, who lived here until 1853. Sunol then sold the adobe to a sea captain, who added the second story. This well-preserved example of 1840s and 1850s construction has been completely restored.

1 - Edwin Markham Home   SHL 416
432 South 8th Street, San Jose

California poet, Edwin Markham, lived here from 1869 to 1889 where he wrote, *The Man with the Hoe*, as a protest against the degradation and exploitation of labor. He taught school in Evergreen after graduating from the normal school at San Jose.

1 - First Normal School in California
(San Jose State College)   SHL 417
125 South 7th Street, San Jose (408) 924-1000

The first teachers' college in California was a private school started in San Francisco as the Minns' Evening Normal School in 1857. It became a public institution of higher learning in 1862, and was permanently located in San Jose in 1870. Its original buildings were damaged by fire in 1880 and by the 1906 earthquake. The college was rebuilt, and in 1935 became San Jose State College.

1 - California's First State Capitol SHL 461
Monument at 100 South Market Street, San Jose

California's first seat of government was established in the building that once stood on this site. General M. G. Vallejo, John Bidwell and David C. Broderick were among the members of the first Legislature who met here and chose, John C. Fremont, and William Gwin, to be California's first two U.S. Senators. California's capitol remained in San Jose from 1849 until 1851.

1 - Old Post Office SHL 854
110 Market Street, San Jose

San Jose's first federal building was established in this sandstone structure in 1892. In 1933, the building was used as a library, and today it houses the San Jose Museum of Art.

1 - St. Joseph's Catholic Church SHL 910
Market and San Fernando Streets, San Jose (408) 283-8100

St. Joseph's church was established here in 1803, by padres from the Santa Clara Mission. The original small adobe structure was replaced by this stone building in 1877. It stands on San Jose's first plaza.

1 - First Radio Broadcasting Station Site
First and San Fernando Streets, San Jose

The first radio station in the world was erected here in 1909 by Dr. Charles Herrold. It was first known as KQW, and is now KCBS in San Francisco.

1 - American Museum of Quilts and Textiles of San Jose
766 South 2nd Street, San Jose (408) 971-0323

Fine examples of quilts and coverlets from the ninteenth century are exhibited with twentieth century quilts and textiles from around the world. Changing exhibits throughout the year feature various themes, textiles and quilt art.

1 - First Unitarian Church of San Jose   SHL 902
160 North Third Street, opposite St. James Park, San Jose (408) 292-3858

This distinctive, Richardsonian, Romanesque-style building has been in continual use as the First Unitarian Church of San Jose since its construction in 1891-1892.

1 - Luis Maria Peralta Adobe   SHL 866
184 West St. John Street, San Jose (408) 287-2290

The oldest structure in San Jose and the last remaining original building of El Pueblo San Jose de Guadalupe is the adobe home of Luis Maria Peralta. Built around 1800, it is being preserved as part of the San Jose Historical Museum.

1 - Hayes Mansion   SHL 888
200 Edenvale Avenue, San Jose

This Spanish Mission style mansion was constructed in 1904 as the home of the Hayes family. This family was active in establishing Santa Clara's fruit industry. They were also important leaders in San Jose's newspaper publishing business.

1 - Site of Louis Pellier Nursery   SHL 434
Northwest corner of North San Pedro Street at Pellier Park, San Jose

In 1850, Louis Pellier established the nursery he called "City Gardens." He and his two brothers introduced the French prune to California in the winter of 1856-1857, for which Santa Clara Valley became famous. Pellier's nursery no longer remains.

1 - Montgomery Hill   SHL 813
Evergreen Valley College, 3095 Yerba Buena Road, San Jose

Professor John J. Montgomery, of Santa Clara College, performed 55 successful glider flights from nearby "Montgomery Hill," to demonstrate aerodynamic developments he made after he flew the world's first successful heavier-than-air craft in 1883. He was killed in a glider crash at this site in 1911.

1 - San Jose Historical Museum
1600 Senter Road, at the south end of Kelley Park, San Jose (408) 277-4017

Original and authentic replicas of Victorian homes, businesses, and other historical landmarks that existed in San Jose, from 1870 to 1930, occupy 25 acres of Kelley Park, in a turn-of-the-century setting. Among the 26 historic structures in this large outdoor exhibit are: an imposing 115-foot electric light tower; a blacksmith shop, with antique carriages and buggies; an Empire firehouse; a 1927 Associated Oil Company gas station; Coyote post office; a trolley barn, with restored trolleys; and a Bank of Italy building, with a turn-of-the-century banking display. The master plan of this ambitious project calls for a total of 74 exhibit structures. Museum displays of: furniture, household items, business accessories, local historic artifacts and memorabilia, trace the history of Santa Clara County from the time of the Ohlone Indians.

Empire Firehouse. Courtesy of San Jose Historical Museum.

2 - Moreland School   SHL 489
Payne and Saratoga Avenues, Campbell

The oldest rural school district in California was established here in 1851. The following year, Zechariah Moreland's home was obtained as the first public school building. The school was renamed in Moreland's honor in 1862.

2 - Campbell Historical Museum
51 North Central Avenue, Campbell (408) 866-2119

This fire station was the first city office. It now houses the Campbell Historical Museum. Historical objects from 1846, to the recent past, are the featured items exhibited. Also on display are old photographs and agricultural equipment from this region.

3 - Saratoga SHL 435
Junction of Hwy 9 and Hwy 85

Saratoga was a pioneer lumbering region, but its fame came from its medicinal springs, which made it a popular resort between 1866 and 1942. Saratoga's pioneer cemetery includes the graves of: A. T. Dowd, discoverer of the Calaveras Big Trees; Riley Moutrey, a rescuer of the Donner party; and Mrs. Mary Brown, widow of John Brown (famous abolitionist of Harper's Ferry).

3 - Saratoga Historical Park
Saratoga-Los Gatos Road (Hwy 9) at Oak Street, Saratoga (408) 867-4311

This one-acre park includes: the Saratoga Historical Museum; the 1865 McWilliams House; and Saratoga's first library, built in 1927. Historical artifacts, turn-of-the-century furnishings and memorabilia relating to local history is displayed within these buildings.

3 - Paul Masson Winery SHL 733
13150 Saratoga Avenue, Saratoga (408) 741-0763 or (408) 741-5182

Built of sandstone in 1852, the Paul Masson Winery was one of California's pioneer wineries. Damaged twice by fire, it was rebuilt both times and continues to operate at its original location.

3 - Gubserville SHL 447
Saratoga Avenue and Los Felice Drive, Saratoga

Frank Gubser's Half-Way House was the first mail stop on the stage road out of Santa Clara. Gubserville was an important settlement along this route until the end of the nineteenth century. Today, none of the town's original buildings remain.

3 - Villa Montalvo Center for the Arts
15400 Montalvo Road, Saratoga (408) 741-3421

Senator James Phelan named his 1912 home, Villa Montalvo, which he willed to the San Francisco Art Association. This 19-room mansion, and its carriage house, contains furnishings of the original Phelan estate, including its original art objects.

4 - Kotani-En SHL 903
15891 Ravine Road, Los Gatos

Construction of this classical Japanese home began in 1918. Its formal landscaped gardens include a Buddhist Temple.

4 - Los Gatos Museum
4 Tait Avenue, Los Gatos (408) 354-2646

Art, cultural exhibits and historical items from the Los Gatos area are on display in the city's former firehouse.

4 - Forbes Flour Mill SHL 458
75 Church Street, south of Main, Los Gatos (408) 395-7375

The town which became Los Gatos, had its beginnings when James Forbes built a four-story mill here in the early 1850s. Two stories of the original mill, constructed of stone from the nearby canyon, remain and now house historic photographs and artifacts.

4 - Los Gatos Old Town
50 University Avenue, Los Gatos (408) 354-6596

Restored Spanish and Victorian buildings house numerous retail stores and businesses in this historic section of Los Gatos.

5 - Almaden Vineyards SHL 505
1530 Blossom Hill Road, San Jose (408) 637-7775

Charles LeFranc planted cuttings from France in 1852 and began the famous Almaden Vineyards. LeFranc's home and the present winery were built in 1876. His original wine cellar is still in use at this historic pioneer vineyard.

6 - New Almaden Mine   SHL 339 and SHL 339.1
Almaden Quicksilver County Park, 21570 Almaden Road, New Almaden
(408) 268-7869

The need for mercury, in the gold mining process, increased the importance of this mine to Californians during the mid-1800s. Between 1845 and 1975, more than $50 million, in mercury, came from 18 shafts that were cut into these hills. The mine superintendent's mansion (the Casa Grande), opera house and Wells Fargo building can still be seen in town along with other early 1850s homes. Warm weather tours of the mine shaft region are available.

7 - Patchen   SHL 448
Junction of Mountain Charley Road and Old Santa Cruz Highway, east of Hwy 17, Holy City

One of the first settlers in the Santa Cruz Mountains was Charles Henry McKiernan, who became a local folk hero after his encounter with a grizzly bear. "Mountain Charley" lived near here from the early 1850s, until 1884, during which time he built and operated a toll road, had interest in a stage line, and operated a sawmill on 3,000 acres of redwoods that he controlled.

8 - Glenwood   SHL 449
West ot Hwy 17 at Glenwood cut-off, Glenwood

Immigrating from Nova Scotia in the late 1840s, Charles Martin homesteaded this property, where he operated a stage stop and tollgate. Martin built a store in 1873. In 1880 he became Glenwood's first postmaster. Construction of the South Pacific Coast Railroad in the late 1870s brought an influx of tourist travel to the area. In 1890, the Glenwood Resort Hotel was built by Martin. Remains of the railroad tunnel and a few of the historic buildings, including the old hotel, can be seen here.

9 - Big Basin Redwoods State Park   SHL 827
Hwy 236, west of Hwy 9, Big Basin (408) 338-6132

The Sempervirens Club was the name selected by a group of individuals, in 1900, who were concerned with the preservation of these California redwoods. The efforts of this organization resulted in the acquisition of 3,800 acres of redwoods, by the state, in 1902.

This acquisition marked the beginning of the State Park system in California. The individual efforts of A. P. Hill to preserve this area's redwoods as a park, were honored by the Club with the dedication of a fountain in the center of the park, in 1923. An exhibit of the park's natural history is maintained at park headquarters.

10 - Roaring Camp and Big Trees Narrow-Gauge Railroad
Graham Hill Road, south of Mt. Hermon Road, Felton (408) 335-4400

Six steam locomotives, half of them built before the turn-of-the-century, operate along a 6-mile, narrow-gauge track through the redwoods. An 1880 general store, covered bridge and other interesting historic buildings are featured here.

10 - Felton Covered Bridge   SHL 583
Graham Hill, west of Hwy 9, Felton

Built in 1892, across the San Lorenzo River, Felton's covered redwood bridge is the tallest covered bridge in the country. Including its wooden approaches, the span is 180 feet long. This well-preserved structure is one of eleven covered bridges remaining in California. It is now incorporated within the Santa Cruz County Park system and can be crossed by foot, or on bicycle.

11 - Henry Cowell Redwoods State Park
1 mile south of Felton (main entrance) (408) 335-4598

This was the Santa Cruz Big Trees County Park, but it is now part of the State Park system. General Fremont was said to have camped here, in 1846, with his men during a march through this region.

12 - Mission Santa Cruz   SHL 342
126 High Street, Santa Cruz (408) 426-5686

Construction of the twelfth mission in California, Mission la Exaltacion de la Santa Cruz, was begun in September 1791, at a site near the San Lorenzo River. In 1793, a new mission was constructed on higher ground, as the original mission location proved to be too close to the river. An 1840 earthquake weakened the mission, and another quake in 1857 caused total destruction. In 1931, a half-sized replica of the first mission was constructed. Inside this structure is a museum containing books, vestments and art from the early 1800s.

12 - Santa Cruz Mission State Historical Monument
134 School Street, Santa Cruz (408) 425-5849

Santa Cruz's oldest building was constructed here in 1791-1793 as headquarters for the mission guard. This building has been in continuous use since it was built and is called the Neary-Hopcroft adobe. In 1959 it was designated as a State Historical Monument.

12 - Santa Cruz County Historical Museum
118 Cooper Street, Santa Cruz (408) 425-7278

The museum is housed in this one-story brick octagonal-shaped structure, erected in 1882. Local historical items are on display.

12 - Villa de Branciforte SHL 469
Water and Branciforte Drive, Santa Cruz

The third, and final, pueblo established in California was at this site, across the river from the Mission Santa Cruz, in 1797. Villa de Branciforte was a planned settlement that became part of the city of Santa Cruz in 1907. Branciforte Avenue was originally a mile-long race track when the town was laid out in 1797.

12 - Santa Cruz City Museum
1305 East Cliff Drive, Santa Cruz (408) 429-3773

Local historical and California Indian artifacts are featured by this museum. An interesting exhibit of local historical art is displayed.

13 - Santa Cruz Lighthouse (Mark Abbott Memorial Lighthouse)
Santa Cruz Surfing Museum, West Cliff Drive near Pelton Avenue, north of Santa Cruz Pier, Santa Cruz (408) 429-3429

The Mark Abbott Memorial Lighthouse was built in 1967 to replace the Santa Cruz Lighthouse that was being undermined by three large sea caverns. The first light keeper was Adna Hecox, who began manning the light in 1870. After his death in 1883, his daughter, Laura, took over the duties and remained light keeper for the next 33 years. Displayed inside are the collections of the Santa Cruz Surfing

Museum, featuring 120-pound redwood surfboards, and surfing memorabilia from the 1920s and 1930s.

13 - Santa Cruz Beach Boardwalk SHL 983
400 Beach Street, Santa Cruz (408) 426-7433

The Boardwalk at Santa Cruz Beach is one of the state's oldest amusement parks, and the last major operating seaside park on the Pacific Coast. Fred Swanton, Santa Cruz's imaginative promoter, opened the Boardwalk casino in 1904, but it was destroyed by fire two years later. The park reopened in 1907, with a larger casino, extended boardwalk and giant indoor swimming pool. In 1911, a new Looff Carousel, with 74 hand-carved horses, was delivered to the Boardwalk. In 1924, the Giant Dipper roller coaster, which would become the park's most popular ride, was built by Charles Looff's son, Arthur. Both rides have been named National Historic Landmarks. Swanton's other contributions to Santa Cruz include: securing the rights from Alexander Graham Bell for the first commercial telephone system in California, opening the state's first hydroelectric generating plant, and establishing an electric streetcar system for the city.

14 - Capitola Historic Walking Tour
Capitola Historical Museum, 410 Capitola Avenue, Capitola

More than 20 local historic sites are included in the walking tour of Capitola. A guide to these points of interest is available from the Capitola Historical Museum.

14 - Camp Capitola Headquarters SHL 860
201 Monterey Avenue, Capitola

Frederick Hihn developed the town of Capitola in 1869 as a summer resort. This building, the oldest commercial structure in town, was the headquarters for his resort, which he named "Camp Capitola." A wealthy lumberman, Hihn built a 150-room hotel, bathhouses and a rail line to Watsonville. He then promoted home sites in the city of Capitola, which he laid out around his resort.

15 - Forest of Nisene Marks State Park
4 miles north of Aptos on Aptos Creek Road (408) 335-5858

Inside this hike-in camp are the decimated remains of China Camp, an early pioneer logging camp.

16 - Hill Country Museum
15060 Foothill Road, Morgan Hill (408) 227-4607

Formerly known as the Wagons to Wings Museum, this museum features many early and modern transportation vehicles. Wagons, stages, aircraft and unusual exhibits are featured in this display.

16 - Site of Vasquez Tree and 21 -Mile House   SHL 259
1 and 1/4 miles south of Morgan Hill on U.S. 101

The old 21-Mile House was a stage station along El Camino Real, between San Jose and Monterey, during the mid-1800s. The oak tree that stood here until 1970 was known as the "Vasquez" tree and was said to be a stopping place for the infamous bandit Tiburcio Vasquez. Neither the tree, or the 21-Mile House, remains standing.

17 - Gilroy Historical Museum
195 Fifth Street, Gilroy (408) 847-2685

Gilroy's 1910 Carnegie Library building now houses the collections of the Gilroy Museum. More than 10,000 historical items, that relate to the history of the city and surrounding area, are on display in this two-story museum. Displays include: farm implements, greeting cards, post cards, household items, musical instruments, sheet music, office furnishings and science laboratory equipment. A guide to 26 historic buildings in the Fifth Street area of Gilroy is also available from the museum.

18 - Watsonville Historic Tour
Watsonville Chamber of Commerce, 318 Main Street, Watsonville
(408) 724-3900

More than 30 historical points of interest, from the 1850s through the turn-of-the-century, are listed in the Watsonville Historical Tour available from the Chamber of Commerce. Many of the historic homes in town were designed by William H. Weeks, one of the most prolific architects of his time in Northern and Central California.

18 - William Volck Memorial Museum
261 East Beach Street, Watsonville (408) 722-0305

This 1901 home of Richard Pearson, a local farmer, houses the collection of the William Volck Memorial Museum. Period costumes, old photographs and slides of Watsonville's historic buildings are exhibited.

18 - The Castro Adobe at Rancho San Andres SHL 998
184 Old Adobe Road, Watsonville

During the early 1800s, the business, political, and social activities for this region were held at the home of Jose Joaquin Castro, headquarters for the sprawling 250,000-acre family empire. This Monterey Colonial-style Castro adobe, a virtual copy of the Monterey home built by U.S. Consul Thomas O. Larkin, is the only rancho hacienda in the Monterey Bay area.

19 - Site of The Glass House SHL 387
East of Hwy 1 at the junction of Salinas and Hillcrest Roads, Pajaro

In the 1820s Ignacio Vallejo built a two-story adobe home on this site. It was called the glass house because of the many glass windows that enclosed the upper porch. One of the Vallejo children who lived here was Mariano Guadalupe, who would become a General in the Mexican Army and a member of the convention that drafted the Constitution of California, in 1849. Nothing remains of the adobe.

20 - Battle of Natividad SHL 651
Marker near the junction of San Juan Grade Road and Crazy Horse Roads, east of Prunedale

The only major conflict to take place in Northern California after American military occupation in 1846, was at this site on November 16, 1846. A party of Americans were driving horses to San Juan Bautista, to join with Fremont, when they were attacked by a group of native Californians. Both sides suffered losses, but the Americans were eventually successful in reaching Fremont's position.

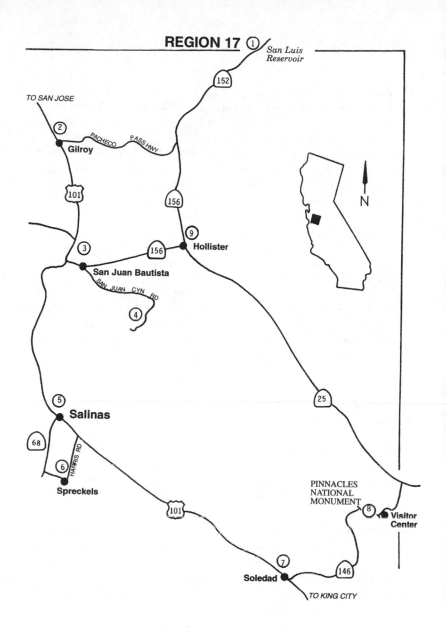

1 - Pacheco Pass   SHL 829
Off Hwy 152 near San Luis Dam, west side of San Luis Reservoir

The first recorded crossing of Pacheco Pass was by Lt. Gabriel Moraga and his men, when they explored the San Joaquin Valley, in 1806. It has since been traveled by forty-niner prospectors, by cowboys driving their cattle to San Francisco, and by the stages of the famous Butterfield Overland Stage Company.

2 - Gilroy Historical Museum
195 Fifth Street at Church Street, Gilroy (408) 847-2685

Gilroy's 1910 Carnegie Library building now houses the collections of the Gilroy Museum. More than 10,000 historical items, that relate to the history of the area are on display. Displays include: farm implements, greeting cards, post cards, household items, musical instruments, sheet music, office furnishings and science laboratory equipment. A guide to 26 historic buildings, in the Fifth Street area of Gilroy, is also available from the museum.

3 - San Juan Bautista State Historic Park
200 Second Street, San Juan Bautista (408) 623-4881

In 1934, the State of California purchased the historic buildings, surrounding the plaza by San Juan Bautista Mission, in order to preserve them. These buildings have been restored and include furnishings of the period between 1840-1870.

In addition to the Castro adobe and the Plaza Hotel, which are State Historic Landmarks in their own right, the park includes: San Juan Bautista's jail; a sheepherder's cabin, relocated here from the surrounding hills; Plaza Hall (Zanetta House), built from adobe bricks that were once the mission nunnery; and the Plaza Stable, with its collection of buggies and wagons. A section of the original El Camino Real can also be seen in this park.

3 - Castro Adobe   SHL 179
San Juan Bautista State Historic Park, San Juan Bautista

During 1840-1841, General Jose Castro built this two-story adobe after his appointment as prefect of Northern California. This was to be his headquarters and administrative office for the region, which was then known as San Juan de Castro. In 1848, General Castro sold this adobe and 400 acres of land to Patrick and Margaret Breen, who, with their seven children, were survivors of the ill-fated Donner Party. Members of the Breen family lived here until this adobe became part of the San Juan Bautista State Historic Park in 1933. Furnishings from the 1870s are on display in this restored adobe.

3 - Plaza Hotel SHL 180
San Juan Bautista State Historic Park, San Juan Bautista

Angelo Zanetta purchased the adobe barracks that were constructed here in 1813-1814 for the mission's Spanish guard. Zanetta then added a second story and, in 1859, opened the Plaza Hotel. This hotel became a main stop on the stage road between Los Angeles and San Francisco.

3 - El Camino Real "Earthquake Walk"
San Juan Bautista State Historic Park, San Juan Bautista

Activity along the well-known "San Andreas Earthquake Fault" can be seen in a seismograph display along this boundary of the American and Pacific plates.

3 - Mission San Juan Bautista SHL 195
2nd and Mariposa Streets, San Juan Bautista (408) 623-4528

Franciscan Padres founded the fifteenth of the 21 missions in San Juan Bautista in 1797. Construction of the mission church began in 1803. This church, the largest of its kind in the state, has been completely restored. Church services have continually been held since the building was originally constructed. Historical artifacts are displayed by the Catholic church, who still own and run the mission.

3 - San Juan Bautista Historic Walking Tour
Chamber of Commerce, 402-A Third Street, San Juan Bautista
(408) 623-2454

Next to San Juan Bautista State Historic Park and Mission are three dozen historic structures that can be seen on a twelve-block walking tour. A guide to this area, which includes buildings erected as early as 1835, is available from the Chamber of Commerce and park office.

4 - Fremont Peak SHL 181
Fremont Peak State Park, San Juan Canyon Road, 11 miles south of San Juan Bautista. Plaque located at park, southeast corner of 4th and Muckelem Streets (408) 623-4255

Captain John Fremont was ordered to leave California in March 1846, by General Jose Castro, Mexican military commander of this region. Instead, Fremont and his men marched to this peak, then known as Gavilan Peak, built a log fort, and on March 4, 1846, raised the first American flag to fly over California. After less than a week, Fremont retreated and marched to Sutter's Fort. The site where the American flag was raised is marked at this state park but nothing remains of the log fort.

5 - Temporary Detention Camps for Japanese-Americans SHL 934
California Rodeo Grounds, 1034 North Main Street, Salinas

After the Japanese attack on Pearl Harbor in 1941, and Japan's declaration of war against the United States, all Japanese and Japanese-Americans in California were ordered to report to temporary detention camps for relocation to permanent settlements across the United States. They were held in these settlements until the end of World War II. Japanese population reached a maximum of 3,586 in the three months that this facility served as an assembly center.

5 - Jose Eusebio Boronda Adobe SHL 870
Boronda History Center, 333 Boronda Road at Calle del Adobe, Salinas
(408) 757-8085

The oldest structure in Salinas is this Monterey, Colonial style adobe, built by Jose Boronda in 1844-1848. It was restored in 1975 by the Monterey County Historical Society to its original condition using handmade materials.

5 - John Steinbeck House
132 Central Avenue, Salinas (408) 424-2735

John Steinbeck was born February 27, 1902, in this 1897 Victorian home. He became one of the most famous and popular authors in America. Steinbeck won the 1939 Pulitzer prize for *The Grapes of Wrath*, and the 1962 Nobel Prize for literature for *Travels With Charlie in Search of America*. In 1964, he received the Presidential Medal of Freedom. John Steinbeck memorabilia is on display in his home that was purchased in 1973 by the Valley Guild. Today, a luncheon restaurant is operated in this historic home.

Interior John Steinbeck House. Courtesy of the Valley Guild, photo by E. A. Grensted.

John Steinbeck House, Salinas. Courtesy of the Valley Guild, photo by E. A. Grensted.

5 - Harvey-Baker House
238 East Romie Lane, Salinas (408) 757-8085

Salinas' first mayor, Issac Harvey, built this house in 1868, from redwood planks that he hauled from the early port of Moss Landing. It has been completely restored by the Monterey County Historical Society, which operates the house as a museum of local history.

5 - Steinbeck Country Self-guided Tours
Chamber of Commerce, 119 E. Alisal Street, Salinas (408) 372-3214

Places that served as settings for John Steinbeck's prize-winning novels have been identified by the Chamber of Commerce and are listed as self-guided tours in their Steinbeck Country booklet.

6 - Hill Town Ferry   SHL 560
Spreckels Boulevard and Hwy 68, south of Salinas

During the 1870s, and until a bridge was erected here in 1889, Hiram Cory operated one of the first ferries to cross the Salinas River. The importance of that pioneer transportation system is commemorated by this plaque.

7 - Mission Nuestra Senora de La Soledad   SHL 233
36641 Fort Romie Road, off Arroyo Seco Road, west of Soledad on U.S. 101
(408) 678-2586

Established as the thirteenth mission in 1791, Soledad Mission was the last of California's missions to be restored. Restoration began in 1954, when little more than ruins of the original mission remained. Open to the public are: the mission museum; its gardens; and the smaller chapel, which replaced the church destroyed in the 1824 flood.

7 - Richardson Adobe   SHL 494
1 mile south of Soledad on U.S. 101

William Richardson built this adobe in 1843 on Los Coches Rancho, which was granted to his wife, Maria Josefa Soberanes, by the Mexican government in 1841. It served as a stage stop, post office, and a house for tenant farmers. Richardson's adobe has been acquired by the state and restored as part of the Los Coches State Wayside Camp and Los Coches Adobe State Historical Monument.

8 - Pinnacles National Monument
Hwy 146, exit west off Hwy 25 (408) 389-4485

Proclaimed a National Monument in 1908, by President Theodore Roosevelt, Pinnacles National Monument embraces more than 15,000 acres and contains: spire-like rock formations, 500 to 1,200 feet high; caves and a variety of volcanic features. A natural history museum is maintained at the visitor center, on the park road, from the east entrance to the park. There is no through road across the monument.

9 - San Benito County Historical Society Museum
West Street, between 4th and 5th Streets, downtown Hollister (408) 637-4747

Historic photographs, costumes, and a collection of San Benito County artifacts are exhibited in the society's museum. The society also maintains a historical village, at the San Benito County Historical and Recreational Park, one mile south of Tres Pinos on Airline Highway. Included in the park are a restored settler's home, farmhouse, schoolhouse, barn and agricultural equipment.

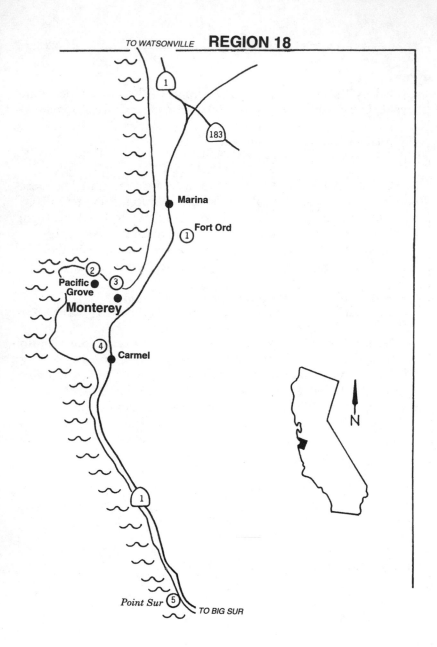

TO WATSONVILLE

1

183

Marina

Fort Ord
1

2
Pacific
Grove
3
Monterey

4
Carmel

1

Point Sur 5
TO BIG SUR

N

1 - Fort Ord and 7th Infantry Division Museum
Building 1040 and 1042, Fort Ord, main gate entrance off Hwy 1, south of
Marina (408) 242-4905

History of Fort Ord and the 7th Infantry is displayed in these
buildings from World War II. Artifacts of the post, and foreign art
work presented to the 7th Infantry, are featured displays.

2 - Chautauqua Hall   SHL 839
16th and Central Avenue, Pacific Grove (408) 648-3130

Construction of Chautauqua Hall in 1879 changed Pacific Grove
from a tent city to an unequaled cultural center. "Chautauqua-by-
the-Sea" presented the highest quality entertainment and concerts.
Chautauqua Hall, Pacific Grove's oldest building, is in use today as a
city recreation hall.

2 - John Steinbeck Memorial Museum
222 Central Avenue, Pacific Grove (408) 373-6976

During the depression, John Steinbeck built a small cottage and
studio on the grounds near his grandparents' small Victorian home.
The house and cottage are now a museum dedicated to the memory
of this famous California author. Period furnishings, family photographs, Steinbeck memorabilia, and first editions are exhibited in the
house museum. His personal desk and typewriter are featured in
the adjacent cottage.

2 - Pacific Grove Walking Tour
The Heritage Society of Pacific Grove (408) 372-2898

Fifteen historic homes are listed by the Heritage Society of Pacific
Grove in their walking tour guide. "The Barn," at 607 Laurel Street,
in Pacific Grove, exhibits local history.

2 - Point Pinos Lighthouse
Pacific Grove Museum of Natural History, Lighthouse Avenue, between
Sunset Drive and Asilomar Avenue (408) 372-4212

Point Pinos was the second lighthouse illuminated on the Pacific
Coast. Since 1855, a light has continuously operated here, using
various light sources, from lard oil lanterns to its present 50,000

candlepower beam. It has been converted into a museum and is operated by the Pacific Grove Museum of Natural History.

3 - Monterey "Path of History"
Monterey State Historic Park (408) 649-7118

A self-guided, "Path of History," tour of Monterey includes forty-five historic homes, and the buildings that are part of Monterey State Historic Park. An orange-red line is painted down the center of all streets that lead to these buildings and plaques explain the history of each structure.

Mayo Hayes O'Donnell Library (originally St. James Episcopal Church). Monterey Path of History. Courtesy of Monterey History and Art Association.

Fremont Headquarters, Monterey Path of History. Courtesy of Monterey History and Art Association.

3 - Historical Wax Museum
700 Cannery Row, Monterey (408) 375-3770

This museum features famous individuals from California's past. They have been recreated in wax and are exhibited in historic settings. Among the thirty-nine figures featured are: John Fremont, Father Junipero Serra, Juan Bautista and Jedediah Smith.

3 - Presidio of Monterey
Pacific Street, north of Decatur Street, Presidio of Monterey (408) 242-5847

The original Presidio of Monterey, near the Park of El Estero, was founded in 1770, by Gaspar de Portola. It was abandoned in favor of this present location. From this fortification, the Monterey Garrison defended the city against the pirateer, Hippolyte Bouchard, in 1818. U.S. forces built Fort Mervine in 1846, after declaring California a possession of the United States. Ten historic sites and monuments are now on this large Presidio, including the Sloat Monument, and the U.S. Army Museum with its miniatures of early forts, cavalry uniforms and weapons.

3 - Landing Place of Sebastian Vizcaino SHL 128
Just south of Monterey Presidio on Pacific Street, Monterey

The first European to land on the shores of Monterey Bay was Sebastian Vizcaino, in December 1602. In a ceremony, under a large oak tree that stood here, Vizcaino took possession of California in the name of the King of Spain. The oak died in 1905, but its trunk is preserved in the rear garden of the San Carlos Church. Also commemorated at this site is the landing of Father Junipero Serra in 1770, and his meeting with Captain Gaspar de Portola to establish the second mission.

3 - Monterey Custom House SHL 1
Alvarado and Waterfront Streets (Custom House Plaza), Monterey

Built by Spaniards in the early 1880s, Custom House is the oldest government building in California. During the period of Spanish and Mexican rule, all ships that wanted to trade along the California coast were required to first register their cargo at this custom house. It was here on July 7, 1846, that Commodore John Drake Sloat first raised the American Flag and declared California a possession of the United States. Custom House is restored and part of Monterey State Historic Park.

3 - First Theatre in California SHL 136
Scott and Pacific Streets, Monterey

Jack Swan, a Scottish sailor, built this adobe structure as a seaman's lodging house in 1843-1844. He added a frame building to the original structure for use as a barroom. In 1848, a group of mustered-out soldiers of Colonel Stevenson's New York volunteers, used part of the building to present melodramas. The first American theater in California is now restored and contains relics of the theater's early history.

California's first theatre, Monterey Path of History. Photo courtesy of Jennifer Roberts.

3 - Casa de Oro (Boston Store) SHL 532
Scott and Olivier Streets, Monterey

Joseph Boston and Company operated a general store in this building, in the 1850s. It has been preserved as part of Monterey State Historic Park and features trade items from the days of the gold rush.

3 - Pacific House SHL 354
Scott Street and Calle Principal, Monterey

This large two-story adobe was built around 1847 and has served a variety of purposes. It was a hotel, tavern, storehouse, newspaper office, courtroom and ballroom. It is now used as a museum of California history and houses a major collection of Indian artifacts. The building is preserved by the state as part of Monterey State Historic Park.

3 - Soberanes Adobe SHL 712
336 Pacific Street, Monterey (408) 649-2836

Built in the 1830s, this restored adobe has never been altered, but is well-preserved and maintained. Furnishings in the house were donated to the state along with the building in 1922. Old photographs of the Soberanes family, who lived here from 1860 to 1922, are displayed in one room of this adobe home.

3 - Casa Vasquez SHL 351
546 Dutra Street, Monterey

Originally a one-story adobe, this was the home of Dolores Vasquez, sister of the notorious stage bandit of the 1870s, Tiburcio Vasquez.

3 - Old Monterey Jail
Dutra Street, Civic Center, Monterey (408) 375-9944

Jail artifacts and records are housed in this 1854 jail from Old Monterey. The jail is maintained as a branch museum of Colton Hall and is open for tours.

3 - Colton Hall SHL 126
522 Pacific Street, Monterey Civic Center, Monterey (408) 646-3851

Colton Hall was erected by Reverend Walter Colton, in 1847-1849, after he was appointed mayor of Monterey by Commodore Stockton. It was in this public hall that 48 delegates met, in the fall of 1849, to draft the constitution under which California would be admitted to the Union. Robert Semple, who established California's first newspaper with Reverend Colton, was chairman of the convention.

Among the delegates were some of the great names in California's early history: John A. Sutter, General M. G. Vallejo, William M. Gwin and Thomas O. Larkin.

3 - Larkin House   SHL 106
510 Calle Principal, Monterey

Thomas O. Larkin built this wood and adobe home after arriving in California in the early 1830s. Its New England type of architecture was a radical departure from the Spanish-style homes generally constructed in this area. His home became the American Consulate after he was appointed U.S. consul to Mexican California, in 1843. He was the only person to hold that post. Many original items from the Larkin family are among the furnishings in this restored home.

3 - House of Four Winds   SHL 353
540 Calle Principal, Monterey

This 1834 structure was one of the first houses built by Thomas O. Larkin, the Yankee merchant who became the first U.S. consul to Mexican California. Used as a residence and store, it later became California's first Hall of Records. The first weather vane in Monterey was installed on this house, which gave the building its name.

3 - Maritime Museum of Monterey
550 Calle Principal, Monterey (408) 375-2553

Local naval history, and the whaling industry in Monterey, are displayed in this maritime museum. Marine artifacts, ship models, photographs and the 1880 light from the Point Sur Lighthouse are also featured exhibits.

3 - Gutierrez Adobe   SHL 713
590 Calle Principal, Monterey

In 1841, when Monterey was still under Mexican rule, Joaquin Gutierrez received a grant to build an adobe home on this site. His adobe is typical of the average home built during that period and is now part of Monterey State Historic Park.

3 - Casa Amesti
516 Polk Street, Monterey (408) 373-8173

Don Jose Amesti built a single-story, two-room adobe here in 1834. He added a second story in 1853. This restored house was given to the National Trust for Historic Preservation and is now operated as a private men's luncheon club. Antique furnishings can be seen throughout this preserved structure. Tours of this historic house can be arranged by calling the current occupants, the Old Capitol Club.

3 - Home of Governor Alvarado SHL 348
494-498 Alvarado Street, Monterey

As provisional governor of California, under Mexican rule, Juan Bautista Alvarado lived here while he held office from 1836 to 1842.

3 - Robert Louis Stevenson House SHL 352
530 Houston Street, Monterey (408) 373-2103

This two-story adobe was built in 1841. It was used as a rooming house, known as the "French Hotel," when Robert Louis Stevenson stayed here for three months in 1879. Stevenson, who came to California to seek the hand of Mrs. Fanny Van de Grift Osbourne, wrote a series of articles for the *Californian* newspaper in Monterey. It was after leaving with his new bride and returning to Europe that he wrote his classics, *Treasure Island* and *Kidnapped*. The French Hotel has been restored and appears today as it did when Stevenson lived here. Several rooms are devoted to Stevenson memorabilia.

3 - Royal Presidio Chapel SHL 105
550 Church Street, Monterey (408) 373-2628

Father Junipero Serra originally established this as a mission in 1770, but the mission site was moved to Carmel the following year. This church became the Presidio Chapel and is the only surviving building of the original Presidio complex. The adobe church, which Father Serra founded on this site, was replaced by the present stone building, in 1795. This well-preserved landmark houses many of the original furnishings from the mission in Carmel, which were brought here in 1836.

Monterey Bay Aquarium. Courtesy of Monterey Bay Aquarium.

3 - Cannery Row
Monterey Bay Aquarium, Cannery Row Information Center, 886 Cannery Row, Monterey   (408) 373-1902

Monterey's fishing port was once the busiest in the country with flourishing canneries processing daily shiploads of once-abundant sardines. As the overfished sardines vanished, so did many of the canneries and packing houses. Today, most of Cannery Row's original structures have been restored or converted to house restaurants, shops and hotels. Many of the businesses immortalized in John Steinbeck's novel, *Cannery Row*, remain in this 40-square block area. Hovden Cannery, the largest, and the last to close on Cannery Row, now houses the world-famous, $55 million, Monterey Bay Aquarium. The Aquarium's Boiler House exhibit displays the restored boilers from the old Hovden Cannery and details, in graphics, the entire canning process. Cannery Row artifacts and a historical film recall the history of this well-known street.

4 - Mission San Carlos Borromeo de Carmelo   SHL 135
3080 Rio Road and Lausen Drive, Carmel (408) 624-3600

Father Junipero Serra founded California's second mission in 1770, at Monterey, on what is now Church Street. The following year, the mission's location was moved to Carmel because of the original site's poor soil, and its close proximity to the military barracks of the Presidio. Father Serra used this mission as his headquarters. It was from here that he established the next seven missions in California. Restoration of the mission began in the 1800s and took more than 60 years to complete. A small museum, and the tomb of Father Serra, is maintained inside the sandstone walls of the mission church.

5 - Point Sur Lighthouse
7 miles north of Big Sur off Hwy 1 in Point Sur State Historic Park
(408) 667-2315

Established in the center of Big Sur country in 1889, Point Sur Lighthouse stands atop a fog signal building, more than 300 feet above sea level. A cause-way connects the lighthouse location with the mainland. Tours are being planned by the State Department of Parks.

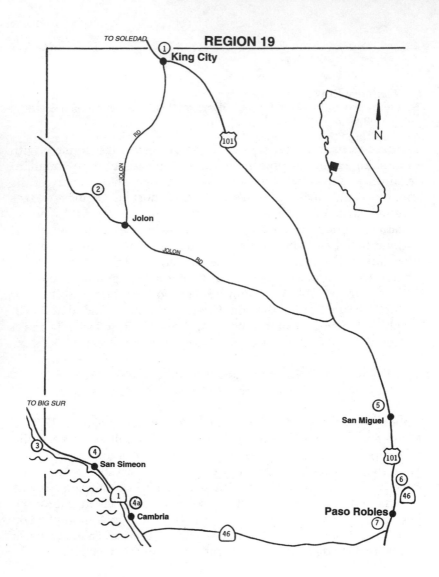

1 - San Lorenzo Agricultural Museum
San Lorenzo Recreation Area, off U.S. 101, west of King City (408) 385-1484

Agricultural practices during mission times, antique farm equipment and tools are displayed in the main exhibit barn at this park. Also exhibited are: the Olson Farm working blacksmith shop, Spreckels Farmhouse, La Gloria one-room schoolhouse and "The Great Machine" (a large harvester).

2 - Mission San Antonio de Padua   SHL 232
Hunter Leggitt Military Reservation, via Jolon Road, northwest of Jolon (408) 385-4478

Father Junipero Serra founded California's third mission in 1771, at a site along the San Antonio River, in the Los Robles Valley. When the San Antonio River ran dry the following summer, the mission was relocated to this area where there was a constant water supply. The present church was constructed in 1810 and completely restored in 1948-1949. The mission's gristmill, water wheel, tannery and soldier's barracks have also been carefully restored and preserved.

3 - Piedras Blancas Lighthouse
Hwy 1, north of San Simeon

Completed in 1875, its original light was on top of this 74-foot tower. Its iron lantern house was removed when the present aero-marine beacon was installed. This area is not presently open to the public.

4 - Hearst-San Simeon State Historical Monument   SHL 640
Hwy 1, San Simeon, tours by reservation only at (800) 444-7275, or call any Ticketron outlet

No other building in the state matches the grandeur of Hearst Castle. Built between 1919 and 1947, at a cost of $20 million, by William Randolph Hearst and his architect, Julia Morgan, this 123-acre estate was the Hearst home. Presidents and heads of state were frequent guests. The main house, "La Casa Grande," has 115 rooms, an indoor and outdoor pool, a movie theater and furnishings from around the world. In addition, the grounds of this massive estate include: three guest houses, with 46 rooms; a private zoo; and elaborate gardens. "La Cuesta Encantada," (the enchanted hill) is adorned throughout with marble statuary, valuable art objects, paintings and tapestries.

The Hearst Corporation presented this property to the state in 1958, as a memorial to William Randolph Hearst, and his mother, Phoebe Apperson Hearst.

4 - The Sebastian Store SHL 726
Hwy 1, San Simeon Road, San Simeon (805) 927-4217

The Sebastian Store was built about a half-mile west of here, in the 1860s, when San Simeon was the center of an extensive whaling industry. The store was relocated to this site in 1878. It is among the oldest buildings along the Northern Coast of San Luis Obispo County.

4A - Nit Wit Ridge SHL 939
881 Hillcrest (Bedford) Street, West Cambria

Thousands of once-plentiful abalone shells, river rock from Santa Rosa Creek, and salvaged material from demolished buildings, were cemented together by Arthur Beal to form "Nit Wit Ridge." His fifty-year effort turned the steep hillside into a multi-leveled, delicate looking, sand castle-like structure that would become one of California's intriguing, twentieth century folk art environments.

5 - Rios-Caledonia Adobe SHL 936
700 Mission Street, on the grounds of Mission San Miguel, San Miguel

In 1846, Petronilo Rios built this two-story adobe residence using Indian labor. It served as an inn and stage stop on the San Francisco-Los Angeles Road from 1860 to 1886. The county purchased this property in 1964 and, with help from the "Friends of the Adobes," completed restoration in 1972. In 1978, a museum was opened.

5 - Mission San Miguel Arcangel SHL 326
700 Mission Street, San Miguel (805) 467-3256

The sixteenth mission in California was founded in 1797, in temporary wooden buildings. Permanent adobe buildings were constructed, and the mission completed, in 1804. Fire in 1806 destroyed most of the mission, but an even larger church was constructed on the same site in 1816-1818. Mission San Miguel has one of the best preserved interiors of any of the missions and includes the original decorations made by mission Indians. It is now operated by the Franciscan Order as a parish church and museum.

6 - Estrella Adobe Church   SHL 542
Airport Road, 4 miles northeast of Paso Robles off Hwy 46

The first Protestant church in Northern San Luis Obispo County was this one-story adobe, built in 1877-1878, by the area's early pioneers. Restoration was completed in 1952, with the assistance of boys from the State Department of the Youth Authority. It is now maintained by the "Friends of the Adobes."

6 - Helen Moe's Antique Doll Museum
U.S. 101 and Wellsona Road, 4 miles north of Paso Robles (805) 238-2740

More than 800 antique and collectible dolls and toys are exhibited in the museum's Ethan Allen style building. Dollhouses, period settings depicting life at the turn-of-the-century, mechanical dancing dolls and the Schoenhut Circus are among the interesting displays.

7 - El Paso de Robles Area Pioneer Museum
2010 Riverside Avenue, Paso Robles (805) 239-4556

A number of interesting collections are featured inside this museum of history, including: the Clark Smith Collection of rifles used by the region's first settlers; early taxidermy work; antique fishing equipment dating back to 1902; the largest collection of barbed wire in California; the Emma Linn Hoffman bedroom suite, shipped around the Horn in 1850; a turn-of-the-century opera carriage; and a number of pioneer recipes, some dating back to 1849. In the museum's outdoor exhibit, visitors can see a Jeanseville Pump, used in the early petroleum industry, and many pieces of restored vintage farm and ranch equipment.

7 - Call-Booth House Gallery/Paso Robles Art Association
1315 Vine Street, Paso Robles (805) 238-5473

Victorian heritage has been preserved in this beautifully restored, circa 1893, Queen Anne style cottage. It was built by Dr. Samuel Call, resident physician at the nearby Hotel El Paso de Robles, which was also known as the Paso Robles Hot Springs. Dr. Call sold the house in 1904 to his sister Susie Booth, whose husband, Alfred, established the town's first pharmacy. Alfred Booth later became the town's postmaster. Susie Booth was appointed postmaster after her husband's death in 1906. The Call-Booth home is now operated as a museum of contemporary art.

REGION 20

TO PASO ROBLES

TO SAN SIMEON

① Templeton

② Atascadero

46

41

① ⑧ Cayucos

41

③ ⑤⑧ Santa Margarita

④ Morro Bay

①

⑤ San Luis Obispo

N

Avila Beach ⑥

⑦ Arroyo Grande

⑨ Nipomo

101

---

1 - Templeton Historic Tour
Templeton Chamber of Commerce, 5th and Crocker Streets, Templeton
(805) 434-1414

The 1888 Presbyterian and 1891 Lutheran churches are among the town's original buildings still in use today. Restaurants, stores and inns now occupy some of Templeton's turn-of-the-century structures.

2 - Atascadero City Administration Building   SHL 958
Atascadero Historical Society Museum, 6500 Palma Avenue, Atascadero
(805) 466-8341

Edward G. Lewis, a successful magazine publisher, founded the colony of Atascadero in the summer of 1913. The following year he laid the cornerstone for the Administration building that became the landmark of this city. Atascadero Historical Society operates their museum, the "Treasure of El Camino Real," in the first floor rotunda of this impressive building. Local historical artifacts, photographs, and private collections from early Atascadero families are exhibited. Other floors of the building house city administration offices.

3 - Asistencia of Santa Margarita   SHL 364
1/4 mile west of Santa Margarita off U.S. 101 and Hwy 58

An outpost of the Mission San Luis Obispo was established at this site to serve the Indians who lived north of the mission, across Cuesta Pass. Ruins of the chapel and storehouse are all that remain today.

4 - Morro Bay State Park Museum of Natural History
State Park Road, on the coast south of Morro Bay (805) 772-2434

This natural history museum features a Chumash Indian collection and natural history of the Central California coast.

4 - Morro Rock   SHL 821
Off the coast of Morro Bay, west of Hwy 1 on Coleman Drive

Morro Rock, a 576-foot volcanic rock, at Morro Bay's harbor entrance, has long been an important navigational landmark. Gaspar de Portola's expedition camped here in 1769 while in search of Monterey Bay to the north. Morro Rock is an environmentally protected home of the Peregrine Falcon.

5 - Hollister Adobe Museum
3 miles north of San Luis Obispo off Hwy 1, on the campus of Cuesta College (805) 543-7831

Built in the 1880s, this preserved adobe now houses the museum's exhibits of Chumash Indian artifacts and antique farm implements.

5 - Mission San Luis Obispo de Tolosa   SHL 325
782 Monterey, between Charro and Broad Streets, San Luis Obispo
(805) 543-6850

Father Junipero Serra founded his fifth California Mission, in San Luis Obispo, on September 1, 1772. After hostile Indians set the roof of the mission on fire three times, mission padres developed a clay tile roofing material which became the standard for every mission after 1784. During the 1930s the church, and its adjoining adobe buildings, were extensively restored and are now in use as the parish church and museum.

5 - San Luis Obispo County Historical Society Museum
696 Monterey Street, San Luis Obispo   (805) 543-0638

Housed in the 1904 Carnegie Library Building, the San Luis Obispo Historical Society Museum includes: a mid-Victorian era parlor, with costumes of the late 1800s; a Fresnel lens from the Port San Luis Obispo Lighthouse; a model of the Hearst Castle; a century-old hurdy-gurdy; Chumash and Salinan Indian artifacts; and local historical items.

5 - Apple Farm Mill House
2015 Monterey Street, San Luis Obispo   (805) 544-2040

An operating replica of a 19th century mill house was erected at the Apple Farm Inn to demonstrate how pioneers harnessed water to power the mill's equipment. A 14-foot overshot water wheel drives the mill's authentic, circa 1873 gristmill, restored 1850 cider press and ice cream maker. The adjacent Victorian-style inn, and beautifully landscaped grounds, add to the country atmosphere.

5 - San Luis Obispo Heritage Walks
Guide available from Chamber of Commerce, Chorro and Monterey Streets
(805) 543-1323

Heritage walking tours to more than 70 historic and interesting structures of different architectural styles are described in the city's guide. The downtown walk begins at the circa 1850 Murray Adobe, the home of Judge Walter Murray. Murray was a co-founder of the *Tribune*, a newspaper that was published in San Luis Obispo. The house is a fine example of the Chumash Indians' adobe craftsmanship. Structures along the original business district range from an 1830 adobe, to a 1941 Art Deco theatre, and include the 1884 Sinsheimer building, the only "iron front" structure on the Central Coast. The residential tour includes homes built from locally quarried rock, and various examples of Victorian-style construction.

5 - Ah Louis Store   SHL 802
800 Palm Street, San Luis Obispo (805) 543-4332

Constructed of brick in 1874, the Ah Louis store was the first Chinese store in the county. Ah Louis became a labor contractor, and put together the Chinese crews that built the railroad tunnels through the Cuesta grade for the Southern Pacific Railroad in 1884-1894. His store is still being run by the Louis family, practically unchanged from when it opened more than a century ago.

5 - Dallidet Adobe   SHL 720
1185 Pacific Street, San Luis Obispo (805) 543-0638

Pierre Hyppolite Dallidet, a Frenchman, settled here and planted a vineyard in 1853. He built this single-story adobe that same year, and added the wooden section as his family grew. A family residence for more than a century, it was deeded to the San Luis Obispo Historical Society by Pierre's youngest son, Paul in 1953. Original furnishings and possessions of the Dallidet family are now on display along with a collection of antique vehicles.

6 - San Luis Obispo Lighthouse
Harford Drive, at Point San Luis, west of Avila Beach (not open to the public)

A frame lighthouse was put into operation in 1890 with four additional buildings erected between 1948 and 1960 to house families of the Coast Guard crew that were stationed here. An automated navigation light and fog signal were installed near the original station which is no longer in use. The old lighthouse stands on the outer grounds of the Diablo Canyon Nuclear Power Plant.

7 - Arroyo Grande Old Village Walking Tour
Arroyo Grande Chamber of Commerce, 800 West Branch, Arroyo Grande
(805) 489-1488

The community of Arroyo Grande had its beginnings when Francisco Zeba Branch started selling parcels of his 17,000-acre cattle ranch in 1864. City landmarks, from the 1860s to the early 1900s, are described in a guide from the Chamber of Commerce. Among the 23 listed sites are: Santa Manuela School House, the last remaining one-room school in San Luis Obispo County; the 1889 Paulding Home, residence of the community's first doctor; Trestle Bridge, site of the 1886 "Terrible Tragedy," where a local farmer was lynched in a land dispute; a cottage hotel for passengers of the Pacific Coast Railroad Line; a block of vintage commercial buildings dating from the late 1890s; and Swinging Bridge, first built from rope in the 1880s.

8 - Cayucos Historical Tour
Chamber of Commerce, Candy Counter in The Way Station, 80 North Ocean, Cayucos (805) 995-1200

Captain James Cass settled here in 1867, after sailing around the Horn, from his New England home. Cass and his partner, Captain Ingalls, built a wharf, store and warehouse, and established Cayucos as a Central Coast seaport. The Way Station, built in 1876, as a hotel and restaurant for stagecoach travelers, is operated today as a restaurant, bar and a number of small retail shops. A guide to Cayucos' turn-of-the-century buildings is available from the Chamber of Commerce.

9 - Dana Adobe
671 South Oak Glen Road, Nipomo (805) 543-0638

Captain William Dana, a native of Boston, was awarded a Mexican Land Grant of 37,000 acres, at Nipomo in 1835. He began building this large adobe home in 1839, for Marin Carrillo, his wife of eleven years, and their children. As his family grew, Dana added a second story, and wings to the main building. His rancho was the center of trade for the region, and later became a stage stop and relay station for Pony Express riders. This landmark on El Camino Real is being preserved by the San Luis Obispo County Historical Society.

REGION 21

1 - Santa Maria Historical Museum
616 South Broadway, Santa Maria (805) 922-3130

Chumash Indian relics, period rooms from early rancheros, and items of historical importance, are displayed in this museum. The Historical Society has also restored the 1878 Ruben Hart Home, Santa Maria's oldest residence.

2 - Chapel of San Ramon SHL 877
Foxen Memorial Chapel, Tepusquet and Foxen Canyon Roads, Sisquoc

Benjamin Foxen, Colonel John Fremont's guide over San Marcos pass, was buried here in the family's cemetery. His daughter, Ramona Wickenden, erected this frame redwood chapel in 1875-1876 as a memorial to her father.

3A - Union Hotel
362 Bell Street, Los Alamos (805) 344-2744

Restoration of the 1880 Union Hotel was completed using materials salvaged from local turn-of-the-century buildings. The entire hotel is furnished with period furniture, antiques, and memorabilia from the era when stagecoach passengers stayed here. A 1918 White touring car, one of the 175 touring cars originally built for use in Yellowstone, takes hotel guests on a tour of the small western town of Los Alamos. The neighboring 1864 Victorian has been restored as the hotel's annex with six unique theme rooms for overnight guests.

3 - Hill 4 Oil Well SHL 582
Plaque located 1 1/2 miles north of Union Oil Company off Rucker Road, north of Lompoc

It was here in the early 1900s that a technique was pioneered to improve the productive life of oil wells by use of a water shutoff. This well, which was drilled to a depth of over 2,500 feet, produced oil for more than 45 years using the cementing technique that was developed here.

4 - Mission La Purisima Concepcion SHL 340
La Purisima Mission State Park, 2295 Purisma Road, east of Lompoc
(805) 733-3713

Padre Lasuen established Mission La Purisima in 1787, at a site about four miles southwest of here. That first mission was completely destroyed by an earthquake in 1812, and rebuilt here in 1813-1818. After secularization in 1833, the mission was neglected, and had become almost a total ruin when the state acquired it in the 1930s. Through the efforts of the Civilian Conservation Corps, and the National Park Service, the mission buildings were restored in what was to be the most extensive and complete restoration of any of the missions. Today, it is preserved as La Purisima Mission State Historic Park. It is one, of only two, missions owned by the state. Authentic furnishings are found in nine of the nineteen restored buildings of this mission.

5 - Site of First Mission de La Purisima   SHL 928
500 block of South "F" Street, Lompoc

Father Fermin de Lasuen established his second mission, and the eleventh in the chain, at this site in 1787. In 1812 it was destroyed by an earthquake, and a new mission was rebuilt four miles northeast of this site, at what is now La Purisima Mission State Historic Park. Ruins of the original mission are all that remain at this site.

5 - Lompoc Museum
200 South "H" Street, Lompoc (805) 736-3888

The donation of almost 2,500 Indian artifacts by Clarence and Jennie Ruth gave this museum its start in 1969. Lompoc's 1910 Carnegie Library, one of 26 remaining of the almost 2,000 built in the United States, houses the museum's collection of aerospace exhibits and historical items of the region. This museum also has several interesting exhibits that change throughout the year.

Lompoc Museum. Photo by Bruce Fall Photography.

5 - Lompoc Valley Historical Society
Fabing-McKay-Spanne House, 207 North "L" Street, Lompoc
(805) 736-5044

The 1875 Fabing-McKay-Spanne House serves as the Lompoc Valley Historical Museum. This redwood building was the first two-story home built in the Lompoc Valley. It has been preserved by the Historical Society, along with antique furnishings of the original owners, farm implements, vehicles and the carriage house.

6 - Mattei's Tavern
Railway Avenue (Frontage Road to Hwy 154), west of Grand Avenue, Los Olivos (805) 688-4820

Felix Mattei built this tavern in 1886 to serve the stage and railroad traffic that came here. Mattei's Tavern became a major stage stop, and the town of Los Olivos was the southern terminus of the Pacific Coast Railroad. The narrow-gauge line ran until 1934. The town has continued to grow and Mattei's pioneer business is still operating as a dinner house.

7 - Ballard's One-Room Schoolhouse
2425 School Street by Cottonwood, Ballard (805) 688-4812

Ballard's 1883, one-room schoolhouse is still in use today, where students attend through the third grade. The schoolhouse was founded three years after the town of Ballard (the first town established in the Santa Ynez Valley) and has remained in continuous operation.

8 - Solvang
On Hwy 246 east of Buellton

Founded in 1912 by a group of Danish educators, Solvang is known today as the "Danish Capitol of America." Danes were attracted here by the valley's fertile soil and the region's moderate climate. Most of Solvang's buildings were the traditional Spanish-style until the 1950s when new construction began going "all Danish." Authentic Danish designs are seen in both the commercial and residential sections of this unique city.

8 - Elverhoy Museum
1624 Elverhoy Way, Solvang (805) 686-1211

The former 1950 Brandt-Erichsen residence, built in the traditional style of large eighteenth century Danish farmhouses, has been completely restored and is now Solvang's museum of Danish-American history. Old photographs, documents and pioneer artifacts from the period 1911-1940, that trace the history of Solvang are exhibited in the former living room of Elverhoy. Period rooms depict the life-style and culture of this Danish colony.

8 - Mission Santa Ines   SHL 305
1760 Mission Drive, Solvang (805) 688-4815

Mission Santa Ines was the first mission founded by Father Estevan Tapis, who succeeded Father Lasuen as Padre Presidente in 1803. The mission church was rebuilt after the 1812 earthquake and remains today in an excellent state of restoration. In 1844, Pope Gregory XVI appointed Francisco Garcia Diego y Moreno as Bishop of Baja and Alta California. Bishop Moreno established the first seminary for training priests in California at Mission Santa Ines. This mission has an outstanding museum with an impressive collection of paintings, sculptures and artifacts.

9 - Santa Ynez Historical Museum
3596 Sagunto Street, Santa Ynez (805) 688-7889

Chumash Indian artifacts, pioneer clothing and period rooms are exhibited in the main museum building. A restored carriage house contains a large collection of horse-drawn carriages. An English hunt wagon, covered wagon and a 1910 Yosemite Stage are among some of the historic vehicles exhibited.

10 - Point Arguello Lighthouse
Point Arguello, southwest of Lompoc

This 1901 lighthouse marks the section of California's coast considered to be one of the most dangerous navigation areas along the West Coast. A side-wheel steamer was wrecked here in 1854 and seven U.S. Navy destroyers were torn open in 1923. The original station was replaced with a 48-foot lighthouse in 1934, and today a pole light signals the dangers of this area. There is no public access.

11 - Point Conception Lighthouse
Santa Barbara Channel at Point Conception

The location of the original lighthouse, built in 1856, was so often shrouded in fog that the station was rebuilt at a lower elevation in 1882. Its light and fog signal still operate on this well-known point along Southern California's coast. There is no public access.

12 - Gaviota Pass   SHL 248
4 miles northeast of Gaviota on U.S. 101

Colonel John Fremont and his American forces were originally planning to use Gaviota Pass in their march to occupy Santa Barbara in December 1846. It is said that Mexican soldiers from the presidio had left Santa Barbara to wait for Fremont's attempted crossing here. Fremont by-passed Gaviota Pass on El Camino Real and used San Marcos Pass to take Santa Barbara without bloodshed.

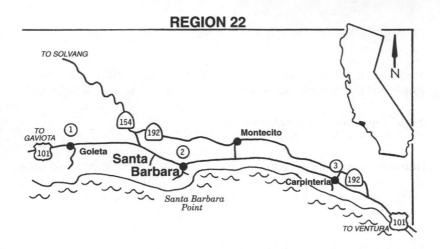

---

1 - South Coast Railroad Museum at Goleta Depot
300 North Los Carneros Road, Goleta   (805) 964-3540

Goleta's 1901 Victorian style railroad depot is preserved as part of Lake Los Carneros County Park. Housed in this historic building is a railroad museum with informative displays, "hands-on" exhibits, rare railroad artifacts and memorabilia. This depot also maintains working railroad communication and signaling equipment.

1 - Stow House/Sexton Museum
304 North Los Carneros Road, Goleta   (805) 964-4407

One of the oldest landmarks in the Goleta Valley is this 1873 ranch house built by Sherman Stow. In the early 1870s, the Stows planted one of California's pioneer commercial lemon orchards. In 1967, the last Stow descendant donated this house and its furnishings to the Goleta Valley Historical Society. The Historical Society operates a museum, restored blacksmith shop and bunkhouse on this old ranch property.

2 - Santa Barbara Botanic Garden
1212 Mission Canyon Road, Santa Barbara   (805) 682-4726

In 1806, on this site just north of the Santa Barbara Mission, Chumash Indians built a dam and an aqueduct to provide irrigation for mission crops. This historic site has been preserved as part of the 60-acre Botanic Gardens.

2 - Mission Santa Barbara   SHL 309
2201 Laguna Street, Santa Barbara (805) 682-4713

Father Serra planned Mission Santa Barbara, but it wasn't built until after his death. It was dedicated December 16, 1786, by Padre Lasuen. Called the "Queen of the Missions," because of its architectural beauty, it was the only mission that was not secularized by the Mexican decree of 1833. This beautiful mission church, completed in 1820, was completely restored following the 1925 earthquake that destroyed much of Santa Barbara. Remains of the aqueduct that was constructed to bring mountain water to the mission can still be seen. Early mission period artifacts are exhibited in the mission museum.

Mission Santa Barbara. Courtesy of Patrick Roberts and Emily Hawkins.

2 - Santa Barbara Red Tile Tour
Chamber of Commerce, 504 State Street, Suite 200, Santa Barbara
(805) 965-3023, Tourist Information, 1 Santa Barbara Street (805) 965-3021

Santa Barbara's "Red Tile Tour" covers a twelve-block route through its historic downtown district. Adobes, Presidio Gardens and museums are part of the interesting sites along this popular tour. A guide can be obtained from the information desk at the County Courthouse at Santa Barbara and Anapamu Streets.

Santa Barbara County Courthouse. Courtesy of Patrick Roberts and Emily Hawkins.

2 - Santa Barbara County Courthouse
1100 Anacapa Street, Santa Barbara (805) 962-6464

This Spanish-Moorish style building was erected in 1929 and is considered one of the most beautiful public buildings in the West. The interior of this building has winding staircases, imported tile floors, heavy carved doors, wrought iron chandeliers, a 70-foot high observation tower and historic murals of Santa Barbara.

2 - Hill-Carrillo Adobe SHL 721
11 East Carrillo Street, Santa Barbara

Rafaela Ortega, granddaughter of Jose Francisco Ortega, founder and first commandante of the Santa Barbara Presidio, lived here with her husband, Daniel Hill, who built this adobe in 1826. Isobel Larkin, the daughter of the first American consul in California, Thomas O. Larkin, was born in this adobe in 1833. She was the first child born to American parents in Santa Barbara. Later, this adobe became the home of the Carrillo family.

2 - Lobero Theatre SHL 361
33 East Canon Perdido Street, Santa Barbara (805) 963-0761

On this site in 1873, Giuseppi "Jose" Lobero built one of the largest adobe structures in California as an opera house and theatre. The original building was torn down in the 1920s and the existing structure erected in its place. In 1984, a three-year restoration project was completed and the theatre, which once saw such masters as

Lionel Barrymore, Clark Gable, Rachmaninoff and Stravinsky on its stage, was once again open to the public.

2 - Santa Barbara Presidio SHL 636
El Presidio de Santa Barbara State Historic Park
123 East Canon Perdido, Santa Barbara (805) 965-0093 or (805) 966-9719

The Santa Barbara Presidio was the last of four royal fortresses established by Spain, in Alta California, in April 1782. The military barracks of the presidio, "El Cuartel," is the oldest building in Santa Barbara and is part of El Presidio de Santa Barbara State Park. A second building of the original presidio, "La Caneda Adobe," has been restored. Excavation of the original chapel site is underway, with plans to reconstruct the building using its original adobe bricks. Historical exhibits are on display including a scale model of the presidio.

2 - Casa de La Guerra SHL 307
15 East De la Guerra Street, Santa Barbara

Commandant of the Presidio at Santa Barbara, Jose Antonio Julian de la Guerra y Noriega, built this adobe house in 1818-1826, with the aid of Indian laborers. His home was the center of Santa Barbara's social activity and a stopping place for many distinguished visitors to the city. Richard Henry Dana was a wedding guest here and described the events in his book, *Two Years Before The Mast*. This restored adobe is the center of "El Paseo—The Street in Spain, " a shopping arcade with stone walkways, courtyards and passageways resembling old Spain. The Plaza de la Guerra is the site of Santa Barbara's first city hall and the meeting place of its first city council.

2 - Santa Barbara Historical Society Museum
136 East De la Guerra Street, Santa Barbara (805) 966-1601

Four historical homes are preserved by the Historical Society along with genealogical material, old photographs and clipping books. Rare mementos, costumes and historic items from Indian, Spanish, Mexican and American cultures that lived in this region are exhibited.

Casa de La Guerra. El Presidio de Santa Barbara SHP. Courtesy of Santa Barbara Trust for Historic Preservation, photo by William B. Dewey Photography.

2 - Covarrubias Adobe SHL 308
715 Santa Barbara Street, Santa Barbara (805) 966-1601

This restored adobe was built in 1817 by Domingo Carrillo. Carrillo's daughter, Maria, lived here after marrying Jose Covarrubias in 1832. Descendants of the Carrillo and Covarrubias families lived here for more than a century. In July 1846, the last Mexican territorial assembly met here. In December 1846, Colonel John Fremont had his headquarters in the adobe, which was relocated here, and now adjoins this building.

2 - Burton Mound SHL 306
129 West Mason Street, Santa Barbara

Remains of various Indian cultures were discovered here, in 1923, when this site was excavated by the Museum of the American Indians. The first written record of these Indians, and their village that stood on this knoll was made by Cabrillo during his expedition of 1542.

2 - Trussell-Winchester Adobe SHL 559
414 West Montecito Street, Santa Barbara (805) 966-1601

Captain Horatio Gates Trussell salvaged timbers and brass from the steamer, the *Winfield Scott*, which was wrecked off Anacapa Island, in 1853. They were used in building this wood and adobe house. For the next 15 years he lived here with his wife, Ramona Burke, who was said to be a great-granddaughter of one of the mutineers on the *Bounty*. This house, its furnishings and the neighboring "Fernald House" are owned and maintained by the Santa Barbara Historical Society.

2 - Moreton Bay Fig Tree
Chapala and Montecito Streets, Santa Barbara (805) 965-3021

This century-old Moreton Bay Fig Tree, from Australia, is the largest tree of its type in the nation. Planted here by a Santa Barbara family in 1877, this massive tree could provide shade for 10,000 people standing under its branches at high noon.

2 - Santa Barbara Lighthouse
1 mile east of Santa Barbara Point near the harbor

Santa Barbara Lighthouse was one of eight original lighthouses built on the Pacific Coast. Established in 1856, its first principal keeper, Albert Williams, turned the station over to his wife, who operated it for forty years. The light station is not accessible to the public.

2 - Stearns Wharf
Foot of State Street, at the harbor, Santa Barbara (805) 966-6624

Built in 1872, Stearns Wharf is the oldest remaining open-ocean pier on the California coast.

3 - Site of Chumash Indian Village of Mishopshnow   SHL 535
Carpinteria Valley Historical Society Museum, 956 Maple Avenue, Carpinteria (805) 684-3112

The Cabrillo Expedition of 1542 discovered a village of Chumash Indians, near this location, on the bank of Carpinteria Creek. Asphalt, naturally occurring near the mouth of this creek, was used by the Chumash to seal the boats they constructed in the mid-1800s. Wharves were built and asphalt was shipped to northern towns. Later excavations of these pits revealed the presence of ancient Indian cultures and prehistoric animals similar to those found in the La Brea Tar Pits, in Los Angeles.

3 - Carpinteria Valley Historical Society and Museum
956 Maple Avenue, Carpinteria (805) 684-3112

Hand-made agricultural tools, period rooms, and artifacts from the Chumash Indians that lived on this site are part of this museum's permanent collection. Information, about historical points of interest in this area, is offered by the museum staff.

3 - Tar Pits
Carpinteria Beach State Park, at end of Calle Ocho, Carpinteria

Asphalt from this ancient tar pit was used by the Chumash Indians as caulking for their boats and to make water-tight containers. Seepage can still be seen in the bluff where these Indians lived.

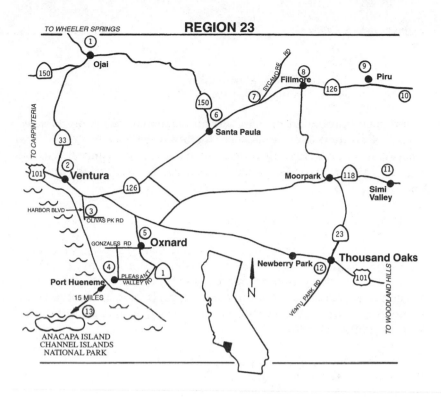
1 - Ojai Valley Museum and Historical Society
109 South Montgomery Street, Ojai (805) 646-2290

Exhibits depicting the evolution of Ojai from early pioneer days to the present are featured in the city's old fire station museum. Chumash Indian artifacts and relics of the reigons first settlers are also displayed.

1 - Gallery of Historical Figures
McNell and Reeves Road, Ojai (805) 646-6574

More than 100 hand-carved, historic figures are authentically presented in realistic detail by this unusual studio. Costumed dolls representing famous Americans from the eighteenth and nineteenth centuries are the featured works exhibited by artist and historian George Stuart.

2 - Ventura County Historical Museum
100 East Main Street, Ventura (805) 653-0323

This museum, founded in 1913, has an extensive collection of early Ventura County photographs, local history displays and the George Stuart Collection of historical figures. Early farm equipment; tools; and art of the Indian, Mexican and American settler periods are also featured.

2 - Albinger Archaeological Museum
113 East Main Street, Ventura (805) 648-5823

More than 3,500 years of history have been unearthed at this archaeological dig. Foundations of the first church of Ventura's mission were uncovered along with remains of ancient Indian villages. Exhibits of the items found in this dig are displayed in the museum building.

2 - Mission San Buenaventura   SHL 310
211 East Main Street, Ventura (805) 643-4318

Mission San Buenaventura was established by Father Junipero Serra, on Easter Sunday 1782. It was the ninth of the twenty-one missions to be founded in California, and the last by Father Serra. The adobe chapel was completed in 1809 and has had two major restorations. Preserved in the mission museum are: the original wooden pulpit that was carved and painted by mission Indians; a pair of wooden bells (the only ones known to be used in the mission chain); statues; Indian artifacts; mission vestments and religious artifacts.

Mission San Buenaventura. Courtesy of Patrick Roberts and Emily Hawkins.

2 - Ortega Adobe
215 West Main Street, Ventura (805) 644-4346

The last remaining single-story adobe in Ventura is this restored 1857 adobe. Furnishings from the 1850s are preserved inside this historic house.

2 - Ventura County Courthouse   SHL 847
San Buenaventura City Hall, 501 North Poli Street, Ventura (805) 654-7800

Ventura's City Hall now occupies this impressive structure. It was erected in 1913 to serve as the Ventura County Courthouse. This neoclassic style of architecture was popular for public buildings erected during that period.

2 - Junipero Serra's Cross   SHL 113
Grant Park, east of Ventura Avenue off Cedar Street on Ferro Drive, Ventura

Father Junipero Serra erected a large wooden cross on the hill behind the Mission San Buenaventura when he founded the mission in March 1782. His original cross, which stood here for 50 years, has been replaced several times in the past two hundred years.

2 - Mission Reservoir   SHL 114
Eastwood Park, at the top of Valdez Alley just west of 107 East Main Street, also accessible from west end of Poli Street, Ventura

Mission padres constructed a seven-mile aqueduct to bring water to this reservoir for their gardens. This remaining adobe structure was the mission's filtration tank. Water was redistributed from here to the mission and homes of neighboring Spanish families.

2 - Channel Islands National Park Visitor Center
1901 Spinnaker Drive, off Harbor Boulevard, Ventura (805) 658-5730

Channel Islands National Park maintains a visitor center on shore where historical exhibits and other displays are featured. Information about park tours and the park's history can be obtained at the center.

Mission Reservoir. Courtesy of Patrick Roberts and Emily Hawkins.

Channel Islands National Park Visitor Center. Courtesy of Roberts and Hawkins.

3 - Olivas Adobe   SHL 115
4200 Olivas Park Drive, east of Harbor Boulevard, Ventura   (805) 644-4346

In 1837, Raimundo Olivas, a wealthy cattle rancher, built a one-story adobe home on this 4,700-acre property which would be granted to him in 1841. He added an additional story to his home in 1849 to help house his family which then numbered 21 children. His adobe has undergone extensive restoration and is now preserved by the State Division of Parks and Recreation. A small museum has been erected on the grounds.

4 - Point Hueneme Lighthouse
Hueneme Road, Port Hueneme

Initially only a fog signal was constructed here in 1874, but later a 48-foot tower was erected on top of a one-story building.   An earthquake in 1925 demolished the station. It was then replaced by a small light about a mile east of this point.

4 - Civil Engineer Corps/Seabee Museum
Naval Construction Battalion Center, Building 99, Cutting and Dodson Streets off Ventura Road, Port Hueneme (805) 982-5163

This museum was established in 1947 as a monument to the history of the Seabees and Naval Civil Engineer Corps. Artifacts include: military weapons, swords, personal memorabilia, uniforms, handmade tools from many countries, and displays of some of the Seabee's major construction projects.

5 - Ventura County Maritime Museum
Fisherman's Wharf, 2731 South Victoria Avenue, Oxnard (805) 984-6260

Ship models are the cornerstone of this intriguing nautical museum. The world's largest half-model, a full-sized Catalina 22 sailboat, is displayed on a 7-foot by 25-foot plaque. It can be viewed from the back side to reveal how it is fitted-out below decks. Models of 24 historic ships illustrate evolution of the sailing ship, from 2000 B.C. to the early 1900s. Two hundred year old ship models, made by French prisoners of war, from bones salvaged from their meals are among the unique antiques in this collection. Other models tell the history of the Channel Islands Harbor and development of the 2600-boat marina.

5 - Oxnard Historic Tour
Oxnard Convention and Visitor's Bureau, 400 Esplanade Drive, Oxnard (805) 648-2075

A guide to Oxnard's local historical points of interest is available from the Visitor's Bureau and the Historical Society Museum. Among the sites listed are the Chinese Pagoda (one of the last remaining park land pavilions in California) and the Carnegie Library, which houses the Cultural Arts Center.

6 - Union Oil Company Building   SHL 996
UNOCAL Oil Museum, 1003 East Main Street, Santa Paula (805) 933-0076

The building housing the UNOCAL Oil Museum was constructed in 1888-1889, using locally quarried brownstone and hand-molded bricks. Imported hand-made tiles, and oak, shipped around the Horn, can be seen in the interior of this well-preserved building. The Union Oil Company was formed here in 1890 and had their headquarters on the second floor of this building until 1900. A wooden derrick is displayed and shows how pioneer oil drilling began in California before the invention of rotary drilling equipment. A large collection of antique oil field tools, old company documents and a 1933 model service station is also exhibited. Information on the location of the "first" oil well drilled in California that yielded extensive commercial production, "Ojai #6," can be obtained from museum staff.

6 - Portola Expedition Campsite   SHL 727
Near Recreation Center, Harvard Boulevard, eastern edge of Santa Paula

Gaspar de Portola and his expedition camped here in August 1769, on their journey north to find the Bay of Monterey. They encountered friendly Indians and exchanged beads for the Indian's gifts of seeds and nuts.

6 - Santa Paula's Historic Homes
Chamber of Commerce, 200 North Tenth Street, Santa Paula
(805) 525-5561

A driving tour guide of Santa Paula's historic homes is published by the Historical Society. It lists 28 homes of historical importance and nine historic points of interest in the city. The Chamber of Commerce can be contacted to obtain a copy of this tour guide.

7 - Old Sycamore Tree   SHL 756
Hwy 126, 4 miles east of Santa Paula at Sycamore Road

This old sycamore tree was a landmark passed by General Fremont and his men on their march south, to Los Angeles, in 1846. This tree has served the community as a meeting place, an outdoor chapel and even as a post office.

8 - Fillmore Historical Museum
447 Main Street, Fillmore (805) 524-0948

Fillmore's museum of local history is housed in the 1888 Southern Pacific Railroad Depot which once served the city from its original site across the street. A guide to twenty-five historic buildings in the Fillmore area is available from this museum, or through the Chamber of Commerce.

9 - Warring Park   SHL 624
Marked at edge of park, 802 Orchard Street, Piru

Spanish explorer Gaspar de Portola discovered a village of Piru Indians at this site on his northward trek to find the Bay of Monterey in August 1769.

9 - Lechler Museum
3886 East Market Street, Piru (805) 521-1595

Local historian, Harry Lechler, operates this private museum which contains his personal collection of historical items, an antique gun collection and various stuffed birds and animals. Tours are offered at no charge to individuals, or groups, and can be arranged by calling in advance.

10 - Rancho Camulos   SHL 553
Hwy 126 (Telegraph Road) east of Piru

In the 1860s, Antonio del Valle built his adobe home on Rancho Camulos. It became a favorite stop for travelers between the missions in Ventura and San Fernando. It was here that Helen Hunt Jackson learned about early California life for her romantic tale *Ramona*. The Del Valle family also erected a chapel on the grounds for the family, employees and local Indians. A monument outside the ranch property identifies this place of historical interest, which is not open to the public.

11 - Ronald Reagan Presidential Library
40 Presidential Drive, Simi Valley (805) 522-8444

Among the interesting displays at the 153,000 square foot, Spanish-Colonial style library and museum are: a replica of the Oval Office, as it appeared during the Reagan Administration; a section of the Berlin Wall; and some of the gifts received by the President while he was in office. Reagan's patriotism and events that shaped his presidency, are featured in the museum's gallery exhibits. The Hall of Presidents, Peace and Freedom, Life in the White House, Voices of Freedom and the First Lady's Gallery are among the permanent exhibits.

11 - Grandma Prisbrey's Bottle Village   SHL 939
4595 Cochran Street, Simi Valley

Tressa Prisbrey started this mammoth project at the age of sixty by building her first structure as an addition to her Simi Valley trailer home. In the twenty-five years that followed, she turned a million old bottles and a wide assortment of material salvaged from a local landfill into a bottle village of two dozen buildings, shrines and sculptures. Her work, an example of this state's twentieth century folk art environments, has received world-wide recognition. The village is currently closed to the public.

11 - Rancho Simi   SHL 979
R. P. Strathearn Historical Park, 137 Strathearn Place, Simi (805) 526-6453

Two historic houses are preserved in this historic park. One is an 1893 Victorian house, which was built around an adobe building, that was first constructed about 1795. The second is an 1888 prefabricated cottage that was built by land developers to "sell" Simi property to out-of-state buyers. Furnishings of the period, artifacts and other items from the late 1800s are exhibited by the Simi Valley Historical Society. Guided tours and group field trips can be arranged.

Victorian section of R. P. Strathearn House, built in 1892-1893. It was added to the Simi Adobe. Courtesy of R. P. Strathearn Historical Park, Simi Valley Historical Society.

Simi Adobe, built around 1800, as the headquarters of El Rancho Simi. Courtesy of R. P. Strathearn Historical Park, Simi Valley Historical Society.

11 - Old Trappers Lodge   SHL 939
Original location: 10340 Keswick Avenue, Sun Valley
New location: Pierce College, Cleveland Park, 6201 Winnetka Avenue, Sun Valley

John Ehn, a former government trapper, decorated the motel he built in the 1940s with western memorabilia. He constructed a mock graveyard, totem poles, and larger-than-life-sized figures to memorialize the Old West. The way events were depicted in the western-like setting is a good example of California's twentieth century environmental folk art.

12 - Stagecoach Inn   SHL 659
51 South Ventu Park Road, Thousand Oaks (805) 498-9441

The original redwood frame building erected here in 1876 was known as the Grand Union Hotel and was an important stop on the stage route between Los Angeles and Santa Barbara. The building was moved out of the path of the Ventura Freeway, which was being constructed through the area in 1964, and became a museum of the Conejo Valley Historical Society. Fire in 1970 completely destroyed the building and most of its historic collection. An exact replica of the original inn was rebuilt and 400 artifacts, saved from the ashes of the fire, were restored for use at the new museum.

13 - Anacapa Island Lighthouse
Channel Islands National Park, for tour information contact the Visitor Center, 1901 Spinnaker Drive, Ventura (805) 644-8262

Marking the south side of Santa Barbara channel's east entrance is this Spanish-style lighthouse, which stands 277 feet above sea level. When constructed in 1932, it was one of the last lighthouses built in the United States. The first beacon established on this island was a pyramid-shaped tower erected in 1912. Public access is by boat only.

REGION 24

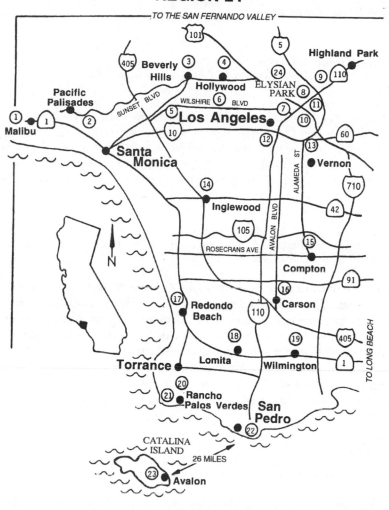

Route 66

About 80% of the original U.S. Route 66 that stretched 2,300 miles from Chicago, to Santa Monica, remains intact, but without the official highway signs that once marked America's most famous roadway. Historical groups across the country have preserved the memory of "America's Main Street" with "Historic Route 66" signs, and markers on the Interstate directing travelers to sections of the old highway. Some of the unique motels, cafes and roadside businesses that catered to travelers can still be seen today.

1 - Point Dume   SHL 965
Point Dume State Beach, corner of Cliffside Drive and Birdview Avenue, Malibu

On November 24, 1793, while on his second voyage to California, English explorer, Captain George Vancouver, named this rocky promontory, Point Dume, in honor of Padre Francisco Dumetz of Mission San Buenaventura. Point Dume was one of several navigational landmarks named by Vancouver along the California Coast.

1 - Adamson Beach Home   SHL 966
Malibu Lagoon Museum, Malibu Lagoon State Beach, 23200 Pacific Coast Highway, Malibu   (310) 456-8432

Rhonda Adamson built this Spanish-Moorish style beach home in 1929, while she was president of the Marblehead Land Company. Her parents, Frederick and May Rindge, acquired the Malibu ranchero in 1881. Hand-carved teakwood doors, Malibu tile and hand-wrought filigree ironwork are featured throughout this exquisite 10-room home. An adjoining museum contains artifacts, photographs and historical items that trace the history from the time Indians lived along this part of the coast to the Rindge and Adamson family era.

1 - Malibu Pier
Between Sweetwater Canyon and Serra Roads at Malibu Lagoon State Beach, Malibu

Malibu Pier was constructed in the early 1900s. It served as a small port for the Rindge Ranch and for an off loading site for materials to build the rail line that ran the 20 miles between Las Flores Canyon and the Ventura County line. It was opened to the public in 1934, and enlarged in 1946, to house commercial businesses. In 1980 this Malibu landmark was acquired by the state.

2 - Will Rogers State Historic Park
14253 Sunset Boulevard, Pacific Palisades   (310) 454-8212

Will Rogers, the famous performer and philosopher, lived on this 186-acre estate, from 1924 until his death in 1935. He converted the original small cottage into a sprawling two-story home and built a stable, corrals and polo field. Original furnishings, personal memorabilia, cowboy souvenirs, Indian artifacts and unusual gifts given to this well-liked entertainer are maintained throughout his home.

2 - Site of Santa Monica Forestry Station   SHL 840
701 Latimer Road, Pacific Palisades

The nation's first experimental forest area was established by the California State Board of Forestry, at this site, in 1887. Studies were made of various types of trees, by the state, and later by the University of California. The grove of trees that developed as part of this project are now part of Rustic Canyon Park

2 - Site of Port of Los Angeles   SHL 881
15100 West Pacific Coast Highway, Will Rogers State Beach Lifeguard headquarters, Pacific Palisades

Pioneer railroad builder, Collis P. Huntington, President of the Southern Pacific Railroad, built a 4,700-foot wooden wharf in Santa Monica, in 1893. His intent was to make Santa Monica, instead of San Pedro, the main deep water harbor for Los Angeles. Southern Pacific dropped Huntington's plan for this harbor after his death in 1900. In 1920, the wharf was dismantled. Today, nothing remains of what was once the world's largest wooden pier.

2 - The Museum of Flying
2772 Donald Douglas Loop North, Santa Monica (310) 390-3339

Aircraft, models, artifacts and memorabilia of the aviation industry are displayed in this museum. Historic photographs of Donald Douglas and other aviation pioneers are also on exhibit.

2 - Angels Attic
516 Colorado Avenue, Santa Monica (310) 394-8331

Santa Monica's last remaining Queen Anne style Victorian was built in 1895, by Dr. and Mrs. Nathaniel Kuns. It was moved to this site in 1924, and acquired by Angels Attic in 1981, to house their extensive collection of antique dolls and vintage toys. This completely restored Victorian is a perfect setting for the museum's collection of century-old toys, dollhouses, model trains and miniatures.

2 - Santa Monica Heritage Museum
2612 Main Street, Santa Monica (310) 392-8537

In 1977, two historic Santa Monica homes were moved to this site for restoration and preservation. The first restored house is now a restaurant. The second house, the 1891 home of Santa Monica's founder, Roy Jones, has been restored as a museum of local history. Several rooms have been refurnished with original family pieces. Other rooms are devoted to a sports exhibit that includes redwood surfboards from the 1930s, bathing suits from the 1940s and old photographs of water and beach sports.

Santa Monica Heritage Museum. Courtesy of Santa Monica Heritage Museum.

3 - Harold Lloyd Estate - "Greenacres" SHL 961
1740 Green Acres Drive, Beverly Hills

At the peak of his career in 1928, actor Harold Lloyd began construction of a lavish 44-room mansion on the estate he named "Greenacres." Lloyd's mansion featured a 160-foot long entry hall, theater, exquisite furnishings, and a year-round Christmas tree decorated with 5,000 hand-made ornaments. The grounds were landscaped with gardens, fountains and waterfalls. Greenacres was left to the city when he passed away in 1971.

3 - Portola Trail Campsite No. 2   SHL 665
Plaque located on La Cienega Boulevard, between Olympic Boulevard and Gregory Way, Beverly Hills

It was here that Portola and his expedition camped on their journey northward to find Monterey Bay in 1769. Scouts for the expedition discovered the existence of the famous La Brea tar pits near here.

4 - Frank Lloyd Wright Hollyhock House
4809 Hollywood Boulevard, Hollywood (213) 662-7272

Los Angeles Municipal Art Gallery maintains this home of the famous architect, Frank Lloyd Wright. Included in the home are some of Wright's drawings and his original furniture.

4 - Frederick's of Hollywood Lingerie Museum
6608 Hollywood Boulevard, Hollywood (213) 466-8506

This unique museum features a retrospective exhibition of vintage, Frederick's under-fashions, dating back to 1946. Lingerie, worn by some the most famous names in Hollywood, are displayed. The fashions of Mae West, Lana Turner, Cybil Shepherd, Loretta Young, Cher and Madonna are among those featured in the celebrity lingerie hall of fame. Bras worn by Tony Curtis in *Some Like It Hot*, and by comedian Milton Berle, are also exhibited.

4 - Hollywood Bowl Museum
2301 North Highland Avenue, Hollywood (213) 850-2058

The history of this famous landmark is on display in the museum located next to the Bowl Patio Restaurant. Architectural models, costumes and posters of some of the well-known conductors who performed here are on display. A program featuring the beginning of the Hollywood Bowl, and its development over the years, is presented in a short video.

4 - Max Factor Museum of Beauty
1666 North Highland Avenue, Hollywood (213) 463-6668

In 1935 the Max Factor Hollywood Makeup Salon was opened here with the fanfare of a typical Hollywood movie premiere. Famous stars, who were among the 8,000 invited guests, signed the Scroll of Fame . . . one of the largest and most complete collections of screen star autographs in existence. The "Scroll" is one of the featured exhibits of this museum. Movie memorabilia, makeup artifacts, rare and autographed photos and vintage Max Factor advertisements are displayed. Fascinating devices such as the "Kissing Machine," which once tested the indelibility of lipstick, and the "Beauty Calibrator," which measured faces for perfection, are among the unique items inside this renovated Art Deco style building.

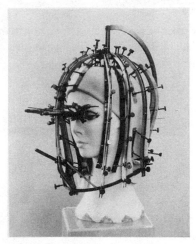

"Beauty Calibrator." Courtesy of Max Factor Museum of Beauty.

4 - Cecil B. DeMille Studio Barn   SHL 554
Hollywood Studio Museum, 2100 North Highland, across from the Hollywood Bowl, Hollywood (213) 874-2276

Hollywood's first full-length motion picture, _The Squaw Man_, was made in this barn erected by Cecil B. De Mill, in 1913. It was originally at Selma and Vine Streets, moved to Paramount Studios in 1927, and then to this location in 1983. The early history of the motion picture industry is exhibited in what in is now the Hollywood Studio Museum. Also preserved are DeMille's refurnished office and many original DeMille artifacts.

5 - Serra Springs Site SHL 522
University High School, 11800 Texas Avenue, Los Angeles (213) 478-9833

These springs were named for Father Junipero Serra, who said mass at this site, in 1770. It is also believed that Portola's expedition camped here the year before Father Serra's visit.

Grier-Musser Museum. Courtesy of Grier-Musser Museum.

6 - Grier-Musser Museum
403 South Bonnie Bray Street, Los Angeles (213) 413-1814

Family keepsakes, antiques, original furniture and household items from the 1920s decorate this restored turn-of-the-century, Queen Anne and Colonial Revival style, Victorian home. A collection of dolls including mint condition paper dolls, is displayed in the children's room.   The dining room table is set with grandma's Haviland China. Every room is thoroughly Victorian, from Douglas fir floors to ornate chandeliers.

6 - Museum of Tolerance
Simon Wiesenthal Center, 9786 West Pico Boulevard, Los Angeles
(310) 533-8403

An interactive, high tech workshop takes visitors on a unique and unforgettable voyage into the world of intolerance. The impact of racism and prejudice in America today, the struggle for civil rights, and the history of the Holocaust of World War II, are dramatically revealed in 35 hands-on exhibits and realistic settings, from 1930s to 1940s Germany. Original documents and artifacts of the Holocaust are featured, including: letters of Anne Frank, relics from Auschwitz, and highlights of Simon Wiesenthal's work.

6 - Petite Elite Miniature Museum & Gallery
1901 Avenue of the Stars, Suite 500, Los Angeles (310) 277-8108

Priceless, hand-crafted, contemporary miniatures are exhibited in true-to-scale settings in this unique museum. Master craftsmanship is evident in the intricate detail of every miniature setting. Fine silk dresses, real oil paintings, monogrammed sterling silver place settings, the world's smallest smoking pipe, and elegant furnishings add to the realism of each scene. One of the miniature settings features America's 44 First Ladies, with each of the 5" to 5 and 3/4" tall figures, adorned in an exact replica of their original inaugural gown.

6 - La Brea Tar Pits - Hancock Park   SHL 170
5801 Wilshire Boulevard, Los Angeles (213) 936-2230

Scouts for the Portola expedition of 1769 discovered these tar pits while searching for camping sites, but it was Major Hancock who discovered prehistoric bones, in this heavy crude oil, during the 1870s. The importance of his discovery was not realized until further investigation was made in 1906 by the University of California. More than one hundred tons of preserved fossil bones have been removed from this 40,000-year-old, "Death Trap of the Ages." Displays featuring prehistoric bird, insect and animal fossils are found here; and a viewing station at an active excavation pit are included in the George C. Page Museum of La Brea Discoveries, located on these grounds.

7 - American Society of Military History
Patriotic Hall, 1816 South Figueroa Street, Los Angeles (213) 746-1776

American, and foreign, military artifacts dating back to the period of the Spanish-American War are exhibited in the main lobby of this building and in its meeting rooms. Personal memorabilia of famous American military leaders are also displayed.

7 - Wells Fargo History Museum
333 S. Grand Avenue, Los Angeles (213) 253-7166

The history of the American West is authentically displayed in this museum of artifacts, relics and memorabilia from the mid-1800s. A completely restored Concord stagecoach is displayed on a section of corduroy road. An old Wells Fargo office, miner's equipment, gold nuggets, old currency and stagecoach strongboxes are part of this museum's 1,000-item collection.

8 - First Jewish Community Cemetery Site SHL 822
Near Lilac Terrace and Lookout Drive, off Stadium Way, Chavez Ravine, Los Angeles

The first organized effort by Los Angeles' pioneer Jewish community was the purchase of this property for a sacred burial ground in 1855.

8 - Navy and Marine Corps Reserve Center SHL 972
Elysian Park, 1700 Stadium Way, Los Angeles (213) 627-2891

Designed as the largest enclosed structure without walls in the world, by noted California architects, Robert Clements & Associates, this Art Deco building was constructed between 1938-1941 as a WPA project. It is the largest, and second-oldest, Navy Reserve Center in the United States. It has served as the induction, separation and training center for more than 100,000 sailors since World War II.

8 - Elysian Park Monument SHL 655
Plaque in Elysian Park, Los Angeles (213) 225-2044

Gaspar de Portola's expedition of 1769 left San Diego and traveled through this region en route north to find Monterey Bay. Several of Portola's campsites have been commemorated along his trail. Portola's first campsite in the Los Angeles City area was in the general vicinity of North Broadway and the Los Angeles River. A monument was dedicated to Portola and his expedition and placed in this park.

9 - Southwest Museum
234 Museum Drive, Highland Park (213) 221-2164

Founded by Charles Lummis in 1907, this museum features Indian collections that are among the finest in the state. An Indian village, painted ceramics, and private collections donated to the museum, illustrate the life of the American Indian.

Heritage Square Museum, Highland Park. Courtesy of Heritage Square Museum.

9 - The Heritage Square Museum
3800 North Homer Street, Highland Park (818) 449-0193

This area has been set aside by the Los Angeles Department of Recreation and Parks as a sanctuary for historic buildings that have been threatened with destruction at their original locations. Several buildings have been moved to this site. Space is allocated for a total of fifteen structures. Several architectural styles are reflected in these houses which were constructed from 1860-1910. The houses are in various stages of restoration. Some are open for tours.

9 - Lummis Home (El Alisal) SHL 531
200 East Avenue 43, Los Angeles (213) 222-0546

Founder of the Southwest Museum, Charles Lummis, built this house of boulders, telephone poles, timbers and other "found" material. A feature of this unusual 13-room house is the fireplace designed by Gutson Borglum, sculptor of Mt. Rushmore. Exhibits of the Historical Society of Southern California are displayed in the museum located within this turn-of-the-century structure.

9 - Ramona Museum of California History
4580 North Figueroa Street, Los Angeles (213) 222-0012

Founded in 1910, this historical museum features artifacts relating to the early history of California. Admission to the museum is by appointment only.

9 - Casa de Adobe
4605 North Figueroa Street, Highland Park (213) 225-8653

In 1914 this building was erected as a replica of the type of Spanish Colonial houses built in the early 1800s. Each room is furnished and includes artifacts that were typically found in most homes during that period.

10 - Site of The *Los Angeles Star* SHL 789
Commercial and North Main Streets, Los Angeles

Southern California's first newspaper, the *Los Angeles Star*, was founded near this site, in May 1851, by John Lewis and E. G. Buffum. The *Star* condemned President Lincoln for starting the Civil War. Its editor, Englishman Henry Hamilton, was ultimately imprisoned. The newspaper's mailing rights were suspended during the war and the *Star* ceased publication until 1866. The paper closed in 1879.

10 - Los Angeles Children's Museum
310 North Main Street, Los Angeles (213) 687-8800

This museum features hands-on exhibits designed primarily for elementary school-aged children. Included in the many participatory displays presented by this museum are activities associated with turn-of-the-century life in California.

10 - Site of The Bella Union Hotel SHL 656
314 North Main Street, Los Angeles

The first stage of the Butterfield Overland Mail Company arrived at this pioneer hotel on its maiden journey from St. Louis, Missouri, on October 7, 1858. The Bella Union Hotel was a center of social and political activity in Southern California. It was here that southern sympathizers hung a portrait of Confederate General P. T. G.

Beauregard and flew Confederate flags at the outbreak of the Civil War.

10 - Site of Butterfield Stage Station   SHL 744
145 South Spring Street, Los Angeles

In December 1859, the Butterfield Overland Mail Company built its Los Angeles Station on this site. It was one of the largest, and best equipped, of all the stations on the 2,800-mile line between St. Louis and San Francisco. Service was stopped when the Civil War began in 1861, and never resumed.

10 - *Herald Examiner* Building
111 South Broadway, Los Angeles

Julia Morgan, famed architect of Hearst Castle, the 123-acre San Simeon home of William Randolph Hearst, designed this 1915 building for Hearst's *Los Angeles Herald Examiner* newspaper. One of the building's outstanding features is the ornate, two-story lobby. Designs are similar to those used by Morgan at the San Simeon estate. The building was designated a Los Angeles historic landmark after the *Examiner* ceased publication in 1989.

10 - Bradbury Building
304 South Broadway, Los Angeles (213) 626-1893

This restored 1893 five-story office building features an unusual open court, central skylight, exposed elevator cages, iron ornamental rails and banisters. This interesting old office building is a Registered National Historic Landmark.

10 - St. Vincent's College Site   SHL 567
St. Vincent Court off Seventh Street between Broadway and Hill Streets, Los Angeles

Southern California's first college was moved to this site in 1868, three years after its founding, where it remained until 1887. St. Vincent's College existed for almost 50 years and was the forerunner of Loyola University.

11 - El Pueblo de Los Angeles State Historic Park
622 North Main, Los Angeles (213) 628-1274 or (213) 625-5045

The second of three pueblos to be established in Alta California was founded here September 4, 1781, by California's Governor Felipe de Neve. Pueblo de Los Angeles' first residents were eleven families who were assigned land to farm in support of the Spanish soldiers stationed in Southern California. Preserved in and around the site of the old pueblo, where Los Angeles had its beginnings, are several points of historical interest.

11 - Los Angeles Plaza SHL 156
Main and Los Angeles Streets, Los Angeles

This plaza, the second established in Los Angeles, was laid out in the early 1800s, during construction of the Plaza Church. It was the town's main meeting place and center of social activity. Sunday bullfights were held here. Homes of the town's important residents were constructed around the plaza.

11 - Old Plaza Firehouse SHL 730
134 Paseo de la Plaza, Los Angeles

This two-story brick building was constructed in 1884 as Los Angeles' first firehouse. Today it houses old horse-drawn fire fighting equipment, a collection of antique helmets, artifacts and fire station memorabilia.

11 - Site of Lugo Adobe SHL 301
Los Angeles Street, east of Los Angeles Plaza, Los Angeles

One of the few two-story houses erected in the pueblo was the adobe home of Vicente Lugo, which he built in the 1830s. After he retiredto Rancho San Antonio in 1850 he donated his home to St. Vincent's College. Nothing remains of the original Lugo home.

11 - Avila Adobe SHL 145
10 East Olvera Street, Los Angeles

The oldest home in Los Angeles, and the only adobe residence remaining at the second plaza, is this 1818 building constructed by

Francisco Avila. During the American occupation of California in 1846-1847, Commodore Robert Stockton used this home for a brief period as his headquarters. The restored Avila adobe is one of five museums located in this historic park.

11 - Merced Theater SHL 171
420-22 North Main Street, Los Angeles

William Abbott constructed Los Angeles' first theater, and at that time, the tallest building in Los Angeles, at this site in 1870. He and his wife, Mercedes Garcia, for whom he named the theater, lived with their family on the third floor. The 400-seat theater was located on the second floor, with the first floor of the building used by other businesses.

11 - The Pico House SHL 159
430 North Main Street, Los Angeles

The last Mexican Governor of Alta California, Pio Pico, and his brother, built this three-story, eighty-room hotel in 1869-1870. This former first class hotel still stands, has been partially renovated, but remains closed to the public.

Pico House, Los Angeles' first hotel and three-story building, and Moreton Bay fig tree planted in the 1880s. Courtesy of El Pueblo de Los Angeles Historic Park, photo by Frank Thomas.

11 - Nuestra Senora La Reina de Los Angeles
(Old Plaza Church) SHL 144
535 North Main Street, Los Angeles

This parish church was built as an asistencia of the Mission San Gabriel by Franciscan Padres, and mission Indians, in 1818-1822. It was known as the Plaza Church, and was the first, and only, place of Catholic worship in Los Angeles until 1876. It is still in use today where mass has been continuously offered since its construction.

12 - University of Southern California's First Building SHL 536
University Park, Figueroa Street and Exposition Boulevard, Los Angeles, Campus Tours (213) 740-2311

Widney Hall, named in honor of Judge Robert M. Widney, a leading founder of the University of Southern California, was the first building constructed for the university. This two-story building has been moved three times, but has remained in continuous use since 1880.

12 - Hancock Memorial Museum
On the campus of USC, Figueroa Street entrance, Los Angeles
(213) 743-5213

Four rooms of the Allen Hancock mansion, built in 1890, have been restored. They can be toured by appointment. Furnishings from the Hancock family home are also exhibited.

12 - Skirball Museum
Hebrew Union College, 3077 University Avenue, Los Angeles
(213) 749-3424

This museum of the Jewish religion features many works of art as well as collections about the history of the Jewish faith in Los Angeles. Individual collections of ceremonial art, artifacts and engravings are displayed as part of the museum's collection.

12 - California Museum of Science and Industry
700 State Drive, Los Angeles (213) 744-7400

Most of the displays at this museum are related to natural resources, space, science and high technology fields. Various temporary exhibits are featured that include items of historical interest, such as the Upjohn pharmaceutical collection.

12 - Natural History Museum of Los Angeles County
900 Exposition Boulevard, Los Angeles (213) 744-3414

In addition to the natural history and science exhibits featured at this museum, galleries show the history of California since the mid-1500s. Indian artifacts, military memorabilia and antique vehicles are also displayed.

12 - Los Angeles Memorial Coliseum   SHL 960
Exposition Park, 3911 South Figueroa Street, Los Angeles (213) 747-7111

In 1919, when Los Angeles' population was just over half a million, plans were made to build a coliseum to seat 75,000 spectators. The name, "Los Angeles Memorial Coliseum," was chosen as a memorial to those who gave their lives in World War I. In 1923, the year the coliseum was completed, application was made to host the 1932 Olympic Games. When the Summer Games were held here in 1984, it became the first stadium in the world to host the Olympic Games twice. The Los Angeles Memorial Coliseum was designated a National Historic Landmark in 1984.

12 - Air Conditioning & Refrigeration Industry Museum
Air Conditioning and Refrigeration J.J.A.T.C. Training Center, 2220 South Hill Street, Los Angeles (213) 747-0291

The first, and only known, museum collection of refrigeration, heating and air conditioning equipment and machinery, was founded here in 1980, by H. T. (Hy) Jarvis, former president of the Recold Company. Fascinating, early refrigeration devices on exhibit include: the 1911 "California No Ice Refrigerator," which had no moving parts; the Crosley Icyball, that cooled by evaporating ammonia; a kerosene-operated Australian absorption unit; a 1929 "Ice Cream Keeper;" and the "Whirlwind" fan that operated by heat from a kerosene lantern. Hundreds of other "firsts" in the industry are displayed here. Tours of the museum are arranged by appointment only.

2 - Watts Towers   SHL 993
1727 East 107th Street at Willowbrook, Watts   (310) 568-8181

The largest work of art ever built by one person, without aid, was constructed here over a 33-year period, by Italian immigrant, Sabato Rodia. He erected these tremendous towers, the walls, fountains and gazebo from pieces of railway tie, chicken wire, cement, glass, seashells and other cast-off material. Watts Towers are the best-known of California's twentieth century folk art environments. They are being preserved by the Cultural Affairs Department of the City of Los Angeles.

12 - Doorknob Museum
Manchester Sash and Door Company, 1228 Manchester Avenue, Los Angeles (213) 759-0344

Thousands of doorknobs, escutcheons, pulls and handles, in designs of the Eastlake, Victorian, Craftsman, Mission and Art Deco periods are displayed in this company's museum. Arts and Crafts, Mission and Art Deco hardware made locally for 1910-1940 era Pasadena and Hollywood buildings are featured exhibits.

12 - County of Los Angeles Fire Museum
L.A. County Fire Dpeartment Headquarters, 1320 North Eastern Avenue, Los Angeles (310) 421-7713

Fire service history in Los Angeles County is exhibited in displays of fire apparatus, equipment, rare artifacts and memorabilia. An 1853 Button hand pumper is the oldest piece of equipment in the collection. A vintage 1925 Stutz engine, 1903 steamer and the more recent 1973 Dodge "Squad 51" are among the interesting units exhibited.

13 - La Mesa Battlefield Site   SHL 167
4500 Downey Road, Vernon

The last military battle of the Mexican War to take place in California occurred at this site on January 9, 1847. American forces, under the command of Commodore Robert Stockton, defeated General Jose Maria Flores and his Californians, and took Los Angeles the next day. A plaque mounted on this granite memorial depicts the official map of the battle.

14 - La Casa de la Centinela
7635 Midfield Avenue, Inglewood

The Historical Society of Centinela Valley maintains this 1834 adobe house as a memorial to Daniel Freeman, the founder of the city of Inglewood. This restored adobe, is among the best preserved in the Los Angeles area. It contains antiques and furnishings from the 1800s, and artifacts collected by the historical society.

14 - Centinela Springs SHL 363
Centinela Park, 700 Warren Lane, Inglewood (310) 412-5370

Artesian water from Centinela Springs, was the main water supply for the early settlers to this area, and for the Indians that preceded them. Today, a fountain within this city park, marks the site of these historic springs.

15 - Dominguez Adobe SHL 152
18127 South Alameda Street, Compton (310) 631-5981 or (310) 636-6030

The first Spanish land grant in California, Rancho San Pedro, was made to Juan Jose Dominguez, in 1784. Manuel Dominguez moved here in 1826 and built the present adobe ranch home on his 75,000-acre ranchero. In 1846, Rancho San Pedro was the site of a battle between the Americans, and the Californians, during the Mexican War. The Claretian Order now maintains the restored Dominguez adobe which contains furnishings and relics from the 1800s.

15 - Heritage House SHL 664
205 Willowbrook, Compton

The A. R. Loomis home, built in 1869, has been preserved by the city of Compton as that city's oldest residence. It was moved from its original location, to this site, and has been restored by the city as a tribute to the community's early settlers.

16 - Site of First Air Meet in the United States SHL 718
California State University, Dominguez Hills, 1000 East Victoria Street, Carson (310) 515-3300

The first air meet in the United States was held January 10-20, 1910, at Dominguez Field, which was located near this monument. More than 175,000 people attended this historic event and witnessed the setting of new aviation records by such greats as Glen H. Curtiss, Charles Willard, Glenn L. Martin and Louis Paulhan.

17 - Old Salt Lake Site   SHL 373
Redondo Beach between Pacific and Francisca Avenues

Two pioneers erected a salt works in the 1850s that produced tons of salt using an evaporation process from the natural salt lake that once covered this area. Peak output topped 450 tons in 1879.

18 - Lomita Railroad Museum
Woodward and 250th Streets, Lomita (310) 326-6255

This museum was built in 1966 as a replica of the Boston and Maine Greenwood Station in Massachusetts. It was donated to the city of Lomita, by Irene Lewis, in her husband's memory. A collection of old locomotives and rolling stock are on the grounds. The interior of the building has been furnished in authentic detail of an early 1900s train station. This railroad museum has many interesting and unusual collections, including: hand lanterns, number plates, old marker lights and trainmen's uniform buttons.

19 - General Banning Home   SHL 147
Banning Residence Museum, 401 East "M" Street, Wilmington
(310) 548-7777

General Phineas Banning built this three-story Greek Revival mansion in 1864, a year before his election to the California State Senate. Banning was a pioneer in the development of transportation, in Southern California. He established early commercial stage routes, promoted the construction of the first breakwater for the Los Angeles harbor, and was influential in bringing the railroad to Southern California. His 30-room redwood home was occupied by members of the Banning family until 1925. It is now completely restored as a Los Angeles City Park. Many of the Banning's original furnishings are included in this museum.

19 - Drum Barracks SHL 169
Civil War Museum, 1052 Banning Avenue, Wilmington (310) 518-1955

This completely restored, two-story structure is the last remaining building of the twenty that comprised the Union Army's Southern California headquarters during the Civil War. It was the officer's quarters from 1862-1866 and is now a museum of Civil War history.

20 - Site of Jose Sepulveda Adobe SHL 383
Foot of Palos Verdes Hills, near Hawthorne Boulevard and Rolling Hills Road, Torrance

Jose Dolores Sepulveda built an adobe home at this site in 1818, on land his father, Juan Jose, used for almost ten years to graze cattle. Jose traveled to Monterey in 1824 to secure a clear title to this land, but was killed on his return trip during an Indian uprising at the Mission La Purisima. Nothing can be seen today of the 1818 adobe.

21 - Point Vicente Lighthouse
Off Palos Verdes Drive West, Rancho Palos Verde

Several ships were wrecked, on rocks near this point along the California Coast, before this lighthouse was established in 1926. Atop this traditional cylindrical tower is a million candle-power light that is fully automated and maintained by the Coast Guard. Next to the light house is the Point Vicente Interpretive Center which features exhibits of the area's natural history, marine life and landslide activity.

21 - Site of Portuguese Bend Whaling Station SHL 381
Palos Verdes Drive, 2 and1/2 miles east of Point San Vincente, Rancho Palos Verde

One of the many whaling stations to dot the coast of California from the mid to late 1800s was located here. Portuguese whalers, engaged in shore whaling, brought their catch here to render whale blubber into oil. It was the lack of fuel, for the rendering process, that resulted in the closing of this station in 1885.

22 - Site of Diego Sepulveda Adobe   SHL 380
700 block of Channel Street, San Pedro

Nothing remains today of the two-story, Monterey-style adobe that Diego Sepulveda erected here in the 1850s. This house was the first of its type to be constructed in Southern California. Diego's father, Juan Jose Sepulveda, claimed rights to this land after grazing cattle here for more than fifteen years, but it would be another ten years before a land grant would be made.

22 - Los Angeles Maritime Museum
Berth 84, Harbor Boulevard and 6th Street, San Pedro   (310) 548-7618

Built in 1941, as a municipal ferry building, to handle cars crossing the channel from San Pedro to Terminal Island, this historic building now houses the Los Angeles Maritime Museum. Models of a variety of historic ships are displayed, from the earliest Indian craft to today's modern ocean vessels. An impressive 22-foot model of the Titanic shows the interior details of the ship and passenger compartments.   U.S. Naval ship models, ships designed for Hollywood movies, marine artifacts and a collection of maritime watercolors are among the features of this museum. Nearby is the famous Ports O' Call Village.

22 - Timm's Point   SHL 384
Southern Pacific Slip, in the Port of Los Angeles, between 14th and 16th Streets, off Sampson Way, San Pedro

Before the present Los Angeles Harbor was constructed, the first deep water landing was established at this point in the late 1840s, or early 1850s. Pilings were used by the Southern Pacific Railroad in 1881 to extend their line from Wilmington,to this point, making it possible for freight and passenger trains to reach ocean vessels.

22 - Fort MacArthur Military Museum
Angels Gate Park, 3601 South Gaffey Street, off Leavenworth Drive at Battery Osgood-Farley, San Pedro   (310) 548-7705

Construction of fortifications, and this coastal artillery battery, began in 1914, to guard the newly completed deep water harbor facilities of the city of Los Angeles. It was named in honor of Lt. General Arthur MacArthur, a Civil War Medal of Honor winner, and one of the commanding generals in the Philippines during the Spanish-American War. The history of Fort MacArthur, American coast artillery, and the Nike missile program is displayed in photographs and artifacts from the period 1914-1974. A walking guide to the restored Battery Osgood (the only battery of its type and vintage in the country) and adjoining Battery Farley, can be obtained at the gift shop.

22 - Casa de San Pedro SHL 920
Middle Reservation, Fort MacArthur, San Pedro (310) 548-7705

San Pedro's first commercial building was erected here in 1823 as a hide-drogher's warehouse. Cattle hides, from the missions in San Gabriel and San Fernando, were stored here awaiting ocean shipment. For many years, this was the only structure in the San Pedro area.

22 - Los Angeles Lighthouse
At end of breakwater, east of Cabrillo Beach, Los Angeles Harbor entrance

Erected in 1913, this 69-foot structure marks the entrance to the busy Los Angeles harbor. The slight lean to this tower is the result of severe gale force winds several years after its construction.

22 - Point Fermin Lighthouse
Point Fermin Park, Gaffey Street and Paseo del Mar, San Pedro
(310) 548-7756

Development of San Pedro as a deep water port began in 1892. Two years later, Point Fermin lighthouse was established in this Victorian style building. It was staffed until 1945 when it was replaced by an automated system. Completely restored by the City of Los Angeles, this building remains today much the same as when it was an active lighthouse. It is used as the residence of the park ranger and is presently not open to the public.

23 - Catalina Island Museum
Located on the ground floor of the Casino, at the west end of Avalon Bay, Santa Catalina Island (310) 510-2414

Historical photographs, model ships, antique souvenirs of the island, Indian artifacts and old telephone equipment are featured in this museum's collection. The museum also has exhibits of 1927-1937 Catalina pottery, the history of the SS *Catalina* (a state historical landmark), and displays of silver, zinc, and lead mining on the island.

23 - SS *Catalina*   SHL 894
Historical information at Catalina Island Museum   (310) 510-2414

SS *Catalina*, the Great White Steamer, was built by William Wrigley to bring passengers to his Catalina Island estate. Regular service between the island and Pier 96, in San Pedro, began in 1924 and continued until World War II, when this ship was used as a military troop carrier. In 1946, passenger service resumed and continued for 30 years until the vessel was sold. It no longer remains in the United States.

23 - The Tuna Club of Avalon   SHL 997
100 St. Catherine Way, Avalon   (310) 430-6603

Avalon's oldest waterfront building was erected here, in 1898, by the Tuna Club. It was built specifically for use by big game anglers, with access by boat. It includes sleeping and washroom facilities for members and access to a weighing station. The Tuna Club invented the sport of big game fishing and was the first club to establish rules, and advocate fair play and conservation in ocean angling. Many distinguished guests have visited this historic club, including Sir Winston Churchill and King Olaf of Norway.

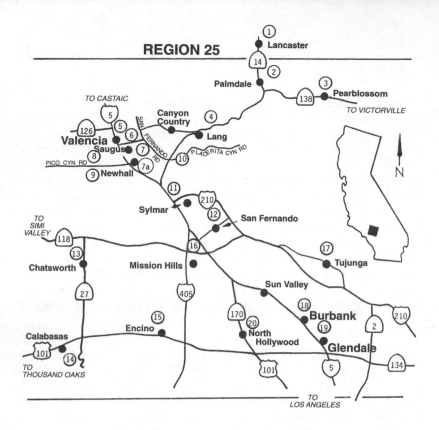

TO CASTAIC

Canyon Country ④
126 5 5 6
Valencia
Saugus 7
PICO CYN RD 8 10
9 Newhall 7a

① Lancaster
14
② Palmdale
138 ③ Pearblossom
TO VICTORVILLE

Lang
PLACERITA CYN RD

11
210
Sylmar
12 San Fernando
16
17 Tujunga

TO SIMI VALLEY
118
13
Chatsworth
Mission Hills

27
Sun Valley
405
18 **Burbank**
15
170 19
Encino
20 2 210
North Hollywood
Calabasas
101 14
TO THOUSAND OAKS
101 **Glendale**
5 134

N

TO LOS ANGELES

1 - Western Hotel   SHL 658
557 West Lancaster Boulevard, Lancaster

Erected in 1876, this hotel was the center of Lancaster's social and commercial activity. It provided housing for the construction crews building the Los Angeles-Owens River Aqueduct in 1907-1913. A restoration project has been completed and the old two-story hotel is now operated as a museum by the Western Hotel Historical Society.

2 - Antelope Valley Indian Museum
15701 East Avenue "M", Lancaster (805) 942-0662

This unusual chalet style building was built into the rocks and uses two large boulders as part of its interior walls. Artifacts from the Indians that once lived here and hunted this region's antelope are on display. Tools, rugs, blankets and other Indian items are exhibited in this museum's unusual rooms.

220

3 - Site of Llano Del Rio Colony   SHL 933
Hwy 138, Llano

The socialist movement in Los Angeles during the first part of the twentieth century was strengthened after the 1907-1908 depression. Socialist, Job Harriman, defeated in his bid to become mayor of Los Angeles in 1910, founded a utopian colony in the Antelope Valley in 1914. It thrived for almost four years, but a lack of water at this site caused them to move to another state in 1918.

4 - Lang Station   SHL 590
Lang Station Road, Soledad Canyon exit off Highway 14, Lang

Seven years after the first transcontinental railroad was completed, joining San Francisco and the Eastern United States, a golden spike was driven here—connecting San Francisco and Los Angeles. Governor Leland Stanford, Charles Crocker and Collis Huntington, (three members of the "big four" primarily responsible for completion of the first transcontinental railroad) were here when the last spike was driven on September 5, 1876. The station that stood at this site was removed in 1971, but plaques mark the spot of this historic event.

5 - Rancho San Francisco   SHL 556
Marker is 1/4 mile south of the junction of I-5 and Hwy 126, Valencia

Headquarters for the 48,000-acre Rancho San Francisco stood south of this location until 1857 when most of the buildings in this region were destroyed by an earthquake. It was here, in January 1850, that William Manly and John Rogers obtained supplies for the members of their party that were stranded in Death Valley.

6 - St. Francis Dam Disaster Site   SHL 919
32300 North San Francisquito Canyon Road, north of Saugus

The second worst disaster in California's history took place here on March 12, 1928, when the St. Francis Dam collapsed. Built in 1926 to store water brought here by the Owens River aqueduct, the 185-foot high dam was holding twelve billion gallons of water when it collapsed without warning. The wall of water that rushed down the canyon and through the valley caused millions of dollars in damage in the five hours before it reached the ocean. Thousands of people were left homeless and almost 500 lost their lives. Ruins of the dam, which was never rebuilt, can still be seen.

7A - Beale's Cut Stagecoach Pass   SHL 1006
Approximately 250 yards southeast of the intersection of Sierra Highway and Clampitt Road, Santa Clarita

Outbreak of the Civil War, in 1861, increased demand for this region's gold and oil. This put pressure on the Los Angeles County Board of Supervisors to improve the inland north-south road that Phineas Banning blazed across the San Gabriel Mountains in 1854. General Edward Beal, Surveyor-General of California and Nevada, acquired the contract for the project. In 1863, his crew created Beale's cut, a 93-foot deep, by 20-foot wide, passage through the mountain— a major technological accomplishment of its day. In the early days of motion pictures the "Cut" appeared in numerous Westerns, including John Ford's _Stagecoach_, starring John Wayne.

7 - William S. Hart County Park
24151 North Newhall Avenue, Newhall (805) 259-0855

In 1921, silent western movie star, William S. Hart, purchased the old Horseshoe Ranch, on which he filmed several western movies. The original 1910 ranch house was used in early movies. Today it houses old props and a collection of saddles. Hart's home was built in 1926-1928 and was willed to the county after his death. All his furnishings, art, Indian artifacts and personal memorabilia are well preserved in this Spanish-Mexican style hacienda.

7 - First Discovery of Gold in California   SHL 168
Placerita Canyon Park, 19152 W. Placerita Canyon Road, Newhall, plaque located at southeast corner of I-5 and Lyons Avenue (805) 259-7721

Francisco Lopez, while resting under an oak tree in 1842, discovered gold on the roots of a wild onion he pulled from the ground. The "Oak of the Golden Dream," is still preserved at this site where $80,000 in gold was found and shipped to the United States mint in Philadelphia This first discovery of gold, in commercial quantity, in California, took place six years before the more famous discovery at Sutter's Mill in Coloma.

7 - Site of Lyons Station Stage Stop SHL 688
Eternal Valley Memorial Park, 23287 North Sierra Hwy, Newhall
(805) 365-3292

Two brothers, Sanford and Cyrus Lyons, acquired the stage stop that once stood at this site. They expanded the business to include a store, tavern, post office and other services for travelers who would stop here along the route of the famous Butterfield Stage. The only remaining evidence of the stage stop, or the colony of twenty families that once lived here, is the Eternal Valley Memorial Park Pioneer Cemetery.

7 - Saugus Train Station
24107 San Fernando Road, Newhall (805) 254-1275

In 1887, Saugus Train Station was built three miles north of its present location for Southern Pacific Railroad. In 1980, the Santa Clarita Valley Historical Society acquired the station from Southern Pacific and raised money to move it to this site. Gene Autry donated the 1900 Mogul Engine No. 1629 and tender to the society for its museum. In addition to its collection of railroad artifacts, the museum has displays of Indian, Spanish, early California, and oil development artifacts.

8 - Mentryville SHL 516.2
27101 West Pico Canyon Road, west of Newhall via Lyons Avenue exit off I-5, Mentryville

In the early 1800s, pioneer oil man, Charles A. Mentry, formed this town to support the men working in the nearby oil fields and at the Star Oil Refinery. Three of the town's restored buildings remain today: an 1885 schoolhouse, a barn, and the 13-room home of the Mentry family. The Mentry house contains antiques furnished by the present residents, the Lagasse family.

9 - Pioneer Commercial Oil Well SHL 516
Pico Canyon Road, west of Newhall via Lyons Avenue exit off I-5

California's first commercially successful oil well, Pico No. 4, was drilled here in 1876, to an eventual depth of 600 feet. The success of this oil discovery led to the construction of the first oil refinery in California at a nearby site.

10 - Pioneer Oil Refinery   SHL 172
238 Pine Street off San Fernando Road, near William S. Hart Park, Newhall

The first oil refinery was constructed at this site in California, in 1876, the same year that the first successful commercial oil well was drilled near this location. Known then as the Star Oil Company, it became the predecessor of Standard Oil. In 1930 the refinery was restored to its original condition and opened to the public.

11 - The Cascades   SHL 653
North side of I-5, a short distance beyond Balboa Boulevard exit, north of Sylmar

William Mulholland, City Engineer for Los Angeles, supervised construction of a 250-mile aqueduct, in 1907-1913, to bring water from the Owens Valley to the city of Los Angeles. These cascades are the official terminus of the system that was built to supplement the Los Angeles River as the main source of the city's water.

12 - San Fernando Cemetery   SHL 753
Foothill Boulevard at Bledsoe Street, Sylmar

The burial place of many of San Fernando Valley's early pioneers is at the Morningside Cemetery, established here in the mid-1800s. This valley's first nonsectarian cemetery was used until 1939, and is now a pioneer memorial park.

12 - San Sylmar
Merle Norman Cosmetics, San Sylmar Tours, 15180 Bledsoe Street, Sylmar (818) 367-2251

Personally conducted tours (by advance reservation only) open the doors to the exquisite Merle Norman Classic Beauty Collection, a treasure house of functional fine art. Antique furnishings, classic timepieces, gold-leaf ceilings, and crystal chandeliers grace the showrooms where priceless works are exhibited. The Rolls-Royce Room is filled with Rolls-Royces from 1913 to the present. The Grand Salon has a collection of 30 antique, classic and sports cars. Other featured exhibits include: a Louis XV dining room, one of the world's largest and finest assemblages of mechanical musical instruments, and an impressive collection of grand pianos.

12 - Mission Wells
Bleeker Street and Havana Avenue, Sylmar

Mission Indians from the San Fernando Mission built this settling basin in the early 1800s for the four wells that supplied water to the mission. Water from this area is still used by the Los Angeles Department of Water and Power.

12 - Griffith Ranch   SHL 716
Foothill Boulevard and Vaughn Street, San Fernando

Silent film pioneer, David W. Griffith, built his home on former Mission San Fernando property he purchased in 1912. Many films were shot on this ranch, including the epic, *Birth of a Nation*.

12 - La Casa de Geronimo Lopez
1100 Pico Street, San Fernando (818) 365-9990

Built in 1882, the Lopez adobe was the center of social life in the San Fernando Valley. Geronimo Lopez and his wife established the first English speaking school and first post office in the valley. They operated a station for the Butterfield Overland Stage in the area now covered by the Van Norman Lakes. Their adobe, the first planned and built as a two-story structure in the valley, has been restored to its original floor plan. It can be seen today with furnishings from the late 1800s.

13 - Chatsworth Lime Kiln   SHL 911
Woolsey Canyon Road and Valley Circle Boulevard, Chatsworth

Near this site a European caldera was used to heat limestone in the manufacture of lime. It is believed that lime from this early kiln was used to make foundation cement for the Mission San Fernando. This kiln is the first evidence of European industry in the Los Angeles area.

13 - Chatsworth Historical Society Museum
Chatsworth Park South, 10385 Shadow Oak Drive, Chatsworth
(818) 882-5614

Artifacts from early Chatsworth are exhibited by the Chatsworth Historical Society in this 1886 wood-slat house, built by James Hill.

His daughter, Minnie Hill Palmer, who was born in this house in 1886, came back to live here in 1920 to care for her mother. Minnie continued to live here, pioneer style, until the age of 90, when she donated her home to the historical society.

13 - Chatsworth Community Church
Oakwood Memorial Park, 22601 Lassen Street, Chatsworth (818) 341-0344

Built in 1903 by volunteers, this Victorian style church was the first church built in the area. It served that community for more than fifty years before being relocated here. This restored church contains original furnishings. Regular Sunday services are still held here.

14 - Leonis Adobe
23537 Calabasas Road, Calabasas (818) 222-6511

Miguel Leonis, The King of Calabasas, acquired a simple adobe building at this site which he remodeled into a Monterey Colonial style house. This building, and some outbuildings on the property, have been restored and furnished to reflect how it would have appeared in the late 1800s, when the Leonis family lived here. This property is now maintained by the Leonis Adobe Association.

14 - Plummer House SHL 160
On the grounds of the Leonis Adobe, 23537 Calabasas Road, Calabasas (818) 222-6511

The Plummer family built this adobe on their 160-acre ranch in the Hollywood region of Rancho La Brea, in the 1870s. In 1937, the County of Los Angeles purchased the Plummer Ranch, which had dwindled to a 2 and 1/2-acre parcel in West Hollywood, renamed it Plummer Park, and allowed Eugenio Plummer to live there until his death in 1943. Plummer House, the oldest house in Hollywood, had deteriorated and was scheduled for demolition when it was acquired by the Leonis Adobe Association, in 1983, and moved for restoration.

15 - Los Encinos State Historic Park SHL 689
16756 Moorpark Street, Encino (818) 784-4849

It was here, in 1769, that Gaspar de Portola and his party of explorers camped on their journey north to find the Bay of Monterey. When

Alta California was under Mexican rule in 1845, Rancho El Encino, which encompassed this region, was granted to Vincente de la Ossa. The adobe house he built here in 1849 has been restored as part of this historic park. The second owners of this ranchero were French sheep ranchers, Philippe and Eugene Garnier. They built the two-story French Provincial house also preserved here.

16 - Mission San Fernando Rey de Espana SHL 157
15151 San Fernando Mission Boulevard, Mission Hills (818) 361-0186

On September 8, 1797, Father Fermin Lasuen founded the 17th mission here . In 1818, an earthquake destroyed the original church and most of the mission's buildings. The church was rebuilt but fell into ruins after secularization in 1834. It was not rebuilt until reconstruction of the mission was undertaken in 1935. In 1971, the Sylmar earthquake seriously damaged the church, and the building was demolished. An exact replica of the church was built and now stands on the original mission site. A history of the mission, artifacts and Indian relics are on display in the mission's museum.

16 - Brand Park and Memory Garden SHL 150
15100 San Fernando Mission Boulevard, Mission Hills

Two stone soap vats used by the San Fernando Mission, and two of the mission's fountains, are preserved here along with plantings from the Santa Barbara Mission. One of the fountains, a replica of a fountain in Cordova, Spain, was originally located in the courtyard.

16 - Andres Pico Adobe SHL 362
10940 Sepulveda Boulevard, at Brand Boulevard, Mission Hills
(818) 365-7810

The oldest part of this building was constructed in 1834 by former mission Indians from the San Fernando Mission. Andres Pico, brother of the last Mexican governor of California, acquired this adobe and added the second story in 1873. After the turn-of-the-century, it fell into a state of neglect, until 1930. At that time it was purchased by Dr. and Mrs. Mark Harrington, who completely restored the structure to its original condition. It is now the headquarters of the San Fernando Valley Historical Society, who maintain the adobe for the City of Los Angeles. It is San Fernando Valley's oldest house (the second oldest in Los Angeles City) and contains many Victorian furnishings from the mid-1800s.

17 - Bolton Hall
10110 Commerce Street, Tujunga (818) 352-3420

Preserved on the grounds of Los Angeles City's Little Landers Park is a single-story stone building, erected in 1913 as Tujunga's City Hall. Restored by the Little Landers Historical Society, it now houses the society's collection of local artifacts.

17 - McGroarty Cultural Arts Center
7570 McGroarty Terrace, Tujunga (818) 352-5285

The former home of State Senator and California poet, John McGroarty, was presented to the City of Los Angeles in the 1950s. It is preserved as a city monument on the grounds of McGroarty Park.

18 - Travel Town Railroad Museum
North end of Griffith Park, 5200 Zoo Drive, Los Angeles (213) 662-5874

Antique steam locomotives dating from 1867 to the early 1900s, passenger cars, trolleys and antique airplanes are in this museum's outdoor display. Antique fire-fighting equipment and early vehicles are displayed inside the museum which also features a collection of transportation memorabilia. The Los Angeles Live Steamers exhibit a scale railroad and members provide free train rides.

18 - Gene Autry Western Heritage Museum
Griffith Park, 4700 Western Heritage Way, Los Angeles (213) 667-2000

The colorful history of the Old West is brought to life for visitors to this museum in exhibits created through the magic of Walt Disney engineers. Many one-of-a-kind articles are displayed from the museum's extensive collection of western artifacts and memorabilia. Spurs worn by Clayton Moore who portrayed the Lone Ranger in the television series, Annie Oakely's gold pistol, and original works of art by Frederic Remington and Charles M. Russell are among the treasures exhibited.

18 - Gordon R. Howard Museum
1015 West Olive Avenue, Burbank (818) 841-6333

This museum complex features a completely restored and refurnished 1887 Victorian house. Two other structures contain a collection of antique vehicles and items relating to the one hundred year history of Burbank. Movie sets, artifacts from the Walt Disney Studios and the history of Lockheed Aircraft, comprise some of the museum's unique exhibits.

19 - Catalina Verdugo Adobe SHL 637
2211 Bonita Drive, Glendale

The last of five adobes constructed by the Verdugos, on Rancho San Rafael, was built for Catalina Verdugo, the blind daughter of Don Jose. This 1875 adobe house is the last remaining of the Verdugo homes built on their 36,000-acre ranchero.

19 - Casa Adobe de San Rafael SHL 235
1330 Dorothy Drive, Glendale

Retired Los Angeles Sheriff, Thomas Sanchez, purchased 100 acres of land from the San Rafael Rancho and built an adobe hacienda here in 1865. This house, where Sanchez, his wife and their nineteen children lived, is now owned by the City of Glendale. It is being preserved with original, late 19th century furnishings and antiques.

19 - Forest Lawn Museum
1712 South Glendale Avenue, Glendale (213) 254-3131

American history, from the 1770s to the present, is displayed along with a collection of old coins, gems and statues.

20 - Campo de Cahuenga SHL 151
3919 Lankershim Boulevard, North Hollywood
(818) 769-8853 or (818) 763-7651

The Mexican War in California ended with the signing of the "Treaty of Cahuenga," at this site on January 13, 1847. A replica of the adobe house, where the historic treaty was signed between John Fremont and General Andres Pico, has been reconstructed at this memorial park. Copies of documents and other historical items are displayed.

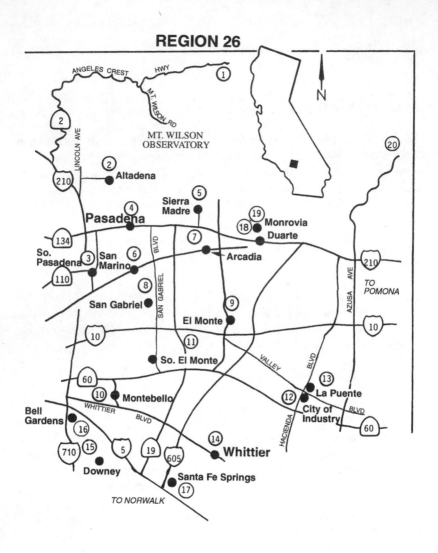

1 - First Government Ranger Station ("Old Short Cut") SHL 632
Chilao Visitor Center, off Angeles Crest Highway (Hwy 2),
27 miles northeast of La Canada Flintridge

California's first ranger station, built with government funds, was
this log building constructed off Mt. Wilson Road near the west fork
of the San Gabriel Canyon. It was staffed by the forest service until
1977. Completely restored, this log cabin has been relocated to this
visitor center and furnished with tools and utensils of the period.

2 - Zane Grey Home
396 East Mariposa Street, Altadena (818) 797-1450

Zane Grey was a well-known writer of Western novels when he moved into this Spanish style house in 1918. He added the third story, which he used as his "writer's den." In 1928, a two-story east wing was added. Zane Grey's home is listed on the National Register of Historic Places, but is not presently open to the public.

2 - Christmas Tree Lane   SHL 990
Santa Rosa Avenue, between Woodbury Avenue and Altadena Drive, Altadena (818) 794-3988

The magnificent 80-foot tall Deodar Cedar trees, that line both sides of this six-block-long residential street, were planted in 1885, from seedlings by Altadena's founders, John and Fredrick Woodbury. In 1920, thousands of lights were strung on these trees to create, "Christmas Tree Lane," the Los Angeles area's first major lighting spectacle. Every Christmas season since, except during the dark days of World War II, and the 1958 and 1974 holiday seasons, thousands of visitors have come here to view this Yuletide festival of lights.

3 - South Pasadena Heritage Tour
Cultural Heritage Commission, 1414 Mission Street, South Pasadena

Two dozen cultural heritage landmarks in the City of South Pasadena are listed in a guide published by the Cultural Heritage Commission. Waiting stations for the old "big red cars," an adobe that served as headquarters for the Mexican Army in 1847, and late 1800s homes and businesses are among the sites of historical interest.

4 - Wrigley Mansion
391 South Orange Grove Boulevard, Pasadena (818) 449-4100

The headquarters of the Tournament of Roses Association is located in this former Wrigley Mansion. Expensive and rare woods were used in the construction of this Italian Renaissance style building which took eight years to complete. Tours of the house include one room that is set aside for memorabilia from all the Rose Bowl games played in Pasadena's famous stadium.

4 - David B. Gamble House (Gamble House) SHL 871
4 Westmoreland Place, Pasadena (818) 793-3334

In 1966, this winter home of David B. Gamble, of the Proctor and Gamble Company, was presented to the City of Pasadena and the University of Southern California's School of Architecture. The firm of Charles and Henry Green designed this 1908 California bungalow style house and everything that went into it, including its furnishings and hardware. Original furnishings can still be seen throughout.

The Gamble House.
Courtesy of the
Gamble House.

4 - Pasadena Historical Society Museum (Fenyes Mansion)
470 West Walnut Street, Pasadena (818) 577-1660

This 1905 mansion was the home of the Finnish consul, Y. A. Paloheimo, after he married the granddaughter of the owner of this estate, in 1946. In 1970, this building and its furnishings were donated for use as the Pasadena Historical Museum. Early Pasadena history is preserved here, including: a Finnish folk exhibit, artifacts, antique furnishings and art objects.

4 - California's First National Forest SHL 717
Angeles National Forest, Supervisor, 701 North Santa Anita Avenue, Arcadia (818) 574-5200

In December 1892, President Benjamin Harrison designated Angeles National Forest (then known as the San Gabriel Timberland Reserve) as the first national forest in California. More than one third of Los Angeles County's timberland is protected in this national forest.

4 - Pasadena Playhouse   SHL 887
39 South El Molino Avenue, Pasadena   (818) 792-8672

Architect Elmer Grey designed this Spanish Colonial Revivial style building, in 1925, to house the Pasadena Playhouse, the oldest theatrical production organization in the West. Many famous actors received their training on the stage of this theater before it closed in 1969. It has been completely restored and is once again open with regularly scheduled performances.

4 - Pacific Asia Museum   SHL 988
46 North Los Robles Avenue, Pasadena   (818) 449-2742

Grace Nicholson built this flamboyant "Chinese" Treasure House from 1924-1929, to house her extensive collection of Native American basketry, crafts, and Asian folk art. It was one of the first art dealerships in California established in a building designed with the capacity to become a museum. Treasure House, with a lecture hall and eight specialized exhibition rooms, also served as a community fine arts center. When Nicholson deeded the building to the City of Pasadena, in 1943, it became the Pasadena Art Museum. Since 1970 it has housed the Pacific Asia Museum.

5 - Richardson House
Mt. Wilson Trail Road and Mira Monte Avenue, Sierra Madre

Sierra Madre's oldest home, was built in 1864, from lumber brought down from Mt. Wilson. It has been restored by the Sierra Madre Historical Society as a museum of local history. The seven-mile, Mt. Wilson trail, which begins near here, was originally constructed in 1864 as a logging road, under the direction of Wilson with Indian labor. Twenty-five years later this trail was used to transport equipment for the observatory constructed at Mt. Wilson.

6 - El Molino Viejo   SHL 302
1120 Old Mill Road, San Marino   (818) 449-5450

Padre Jose Marin Zalvidea, from the Mission San Gabriel, supervised construction of California's first water-operated gristmill, at this site in about 1810-1812. It served the mission until a mill closer to the mission was completed in 1823. This mill was renovated in the 1930s by an heir to the Henry E. Huntington estate and is now the office and museum of the Southern California Historical Society.

6 - Site of Governor Stoneman's Adobe   SHL 669
1912 Montrobles Place, San Marino

General of the Union Army, George Stoneman, came to California after his retirement in 1871. He was elected as the fifteenth Governor of California and served between 1883 and 1887. He built an adobe home on his 400-acre "Los Robles" estate. This monument incorporates adobe bricks from that original structure.

7 - Los Angeles State and County Arboretum (LASCA)
301 North Baldwin Avenue Arcadia (818) 821-3222

This 127-acre Arboretum has plantings from around the world. It was established on the site of a Gabrielino Indian Village. Today, the property houses four historic structures: Indian Village, the Hugo Reid Adobe, Baldwin's Queen Anne Cottage and Carriage House.

> **Indian Village** - Brush shelters, called "wickiups," have been reconstructed here at the site where Gabrielino Indians had their village before the Spanish and Mexican settlers came to Alta California.

> **Hugo Reid Adobe   SHL 368** - Rancho Santa Anita was granted to Hugo Reid in 1841, on which he constructed his three-room adobe. "Lucky" Baldwin purchased this ranch, in 1875, and made the adobe his home. Handmade furnishings and relics are displayed throughout the house and can be seen through the windows of this restored adobe.

> **Queen Anne Cottage   SHL 367** - In 1885-1886 "Lucky" Baldwin built this beautiful Queen Anne house, a combination of three architectural styles, for his fourth wife (who left him before it was completed). Today, it stands completely restored and furnished as a memorial to his third wife, Jennie Dexter.

> **Carriage House** - Built in 1879 for the carriage horses and many vehicles owned by "Lucky" Baldwin, this restored coach barn now contains many types of ranch equipment of the period.

7 - Temporary Detention Camps for Japanese-Americans SHL 934
Santa Anita Park, 285 West Huntington Drive, Arcadia (818) 574-7223

After Japan declared war on the United States in 1941, all Japanese and Japanese-Americans, on the West Coast, were ordered to report to temporary detention camps for eventual relocation to permanent camps across the United States. The Japanese people were held in these camps until the end of World War II. Population reached a maximum of 18,719 in the seven months that Santa Anita served as an assembly center.

8 - Church of Our Savior
535 West Roses Road, San Gabriel (818) 282-5147

San Gabriel Valley's oldest Protestant church, and the oldest Episcopal church, in Southern California, was founded here in 1867. Among its early members were: Benjamin "Don Benito" Wilson, charter mayor of Los Angeles; his daughter Ruth; and her son George, who became one of the most famous soldiers in World War II—General George Patton.

8 - Mission San Gabriel Archangel SHL 158
537 West Mission Drive, San Gabriel (818) 282-5191

A temporary mission church was constructed at this second mission site until the present church was built in 1791-1803. Stone, mortar and bricks were used in the construction of this unusual mission church structure. Mission San Gabriel was among the most prosperous of all the missions. Its padres controlled over a million and a half acres of land and more than 40,000-head of cattle. The former priest quarters now house the mission's museum where vestments, Indian artifacts and old tools are displayed. A most interesting exhibit is the fourteen Stations of the Cross painted by a mission Indian on sail cloth.

9 - Vigare Adobe SHL 451
616 South Ramona Street, San Gabriel

Don Juan Vigare, a soldier of the mission guard for the San Gabriel Mission, built this adobe house sometime during the late 1790s, or early 1800s. It is one of the oldest adobe structures in the county and has been the home for several generations of Vigares. It has undergone many structural changes over the years and stands today at about half its original size.

8 - San Gabriel Historical Association Museum
San Gabriel Historical District, 546 West Broadway, San Gabriel
(818) 308-3223

Reverend George Findley Bovard, President of the University of Southern California, from 1903 to 1922, lived in this home. It was built for him and his wife, Emma, in 1887, when he was a Presiding Elder of the Methodist church. Subsequent owners were: Milton Wilson, Justice of the Peace for the San Gabriel township; and Edwin Hays, one of the first members of the City Council. The Victorian home now houses a museum that features history of the Gabrielino Indians; the San Gabriel Mission; and John Steven McGroarty's _Mission Play_—the story of the California Missions, which was presented at his nearby Mission Playhouse, from 1912 to 1933.

9 - El Monte Historical Society Museum
3150 North Tyler Avenue, El Monte (818) 444-3813

Many emigrants to California who traveled the Santa Fe Trail settled here in El Monte, an area of abundant land and natural springs. The history of these early settlers is displayed in the museum, along with Native American and Mexican artifacts, tools and furnishings.

9 - El Monte: First Southern California Settlement by Emigrants from the United States   SHL 975
Pioneer Park (Santa Fe Trail Historical Park), 3535 Santa Anita Avenue
El Monte

The city of Lexington was founded at this spot on the Santa Fe Trail, by eastern and mid-western pioneers, who arrived here by covered wagon in 1851-1852. Captain Johnson, who led one of the first wagon trains, constructed his home of sticks and mud, built the first grist mill in California, and gave the town its name. The town, which would later be called El Monte, was southern California's first all English-speaking community. The first school house in the Los Angeles basin, and the first Protestant Evangelical Baptist Church, were erected here by these settlers.

El Monte's first jail, Pioneer Park (Santa Fe Trail Historical Park).

10 - Site of First Mission San Gabriel   SHL 161
North San Gabriel Boulevard and Lincoln Avenue, Montebello

On September 8, 1771, Mission San Gabriel Archangel was founded at this site as the fourth mission, in the chain of twenty-one, to be established in California. In 1775 the mission was moved five miles north, to its present site, because of frequent flooding by the San Gabriel River. The original mission site became known as "Mission Vieja" and is commemorated here.

10 - Juan Matias Sanchez Adobe
946 Adobe Avenue, Montebello (213) 722-4100

Juan Sanchez added onto this adobe when he acquired half the Rancho La Merced, in 1852. He lost most of his property in 1876 when the Workman-Temple bank failed, but was able to keep his home and 200 acres of land. His adobe was restored in the late 1960s and donated to the City of Montebello as a museum of local history. Furnishings and artifacts were contributed by the Montebello Historical Society.

10 - Rio San Gabriel Battlefield Site   SHL 385
Washington Boulevard and Bluff Road, Montebello

A battle of the Mexican War took place at this site, between the American forces, under the command of Captain Robert Stockton and General Stephen Kearny, and the Californians, commanded by General Jose Flores. General Flores and his men held this position and were able to fire down on the Americans crossing the river below. After a two-hour battle, the Americans took the hill and pushed the Californians back toward Los Angeles.

11 - American Heritage Park
1918 North Rosemead Boulevard, South El Monte   (818) 442-1776

Ninety military vehicles from World War II, and other conflicts, are on display in this outdoor exhibit. Operating equipment ranges in size from a half-ton jeep to a Sherman Tank.

12 - John A. Rowland Home and Dibble Museum
16021 Gale Avenue, City of Industry   (818) 336-7644

John Rowland and William Workman arrived in Southern California, in 1841, with the first wagon train of emigrants to settle in this part of the state. They were jointly granted the 49,000-acre Rancho La Puente, in 1845. Rowland took the eastern half and built an adobe home just north of this site. In 1855, Rowland built this 15-room house, the first brick house in the San Gabriel Valley. It is now completely renovated and furnished with items used by the three generations of the Rowland family that lived here. Rowland's granddaughter, Lilian (Lillian) Dibble, converted the water tank on this site into a museum in 1950. The museum contains Indian artifacts and was designed to appeal to school children. She willed the home and museum to the Hacienda-La Puente Unified School District.

12 - Workman and Temple Family Homestead Museum   SHL 874
15415 East Don Julian Road, City of Industry   (818) 968-8492

William Workman and John Rowland brought the first party of emigrants to Southern California in 1841. Workman and Rowland formally divided Rancho La Puente, which they received as a

Mexican land grant, in 1845. From 1869-1872, Workman remodeled his original adobe into this English-style manor house.

"El Campo Santo" was established as San Gabriel Valley's first private family cemetery in 1850. A mausoleum, erected in 1919 by Workman's grandson, contains the remains of the Workman and Temple families. The final resting place of Pio Pico, the last Mexican governor of California, was moved to this mausoleum from a Los Angeles cemetery.

South facade, the Workman and Temple family homestead. Courtesy of the Workman and Temple family homestead, photo by Julius Shulman.

13 - La Puente Valley Historical Society
15900 East Main Street, La Puente City Hall, La Puente (818) 336 2382

La Puente Valley Historical Society maintains this "Heritage Room" at the City Hall to preserve and display the history of the La Puente Valley area. Items of local historical interest are featured. The society also maintains the John A. Rowland Home and Dibble Museum in the City of Industry.

14 - Pio Pico State Historic Park   SHL 127
6003 South Pioneer Boulevard, Whittier (310) 695-1217

The last Mexican governor of Alta California, Pio Pico, lived in a thirty-room, two-story mansion erected here in 1852. The nearby San

Gabriel River flooded the area in 1883, washing away more than half of the mansion. Pico pledged his property as security to finance the mansion's reconstruction, but he couldn't make payment on the loan and lost all his property in 1892. Part of the remaining adobe was restored and furnished with pieces from the period 1850-1890. Restoration is underway again in the wake of the 1987 Whittier earthquake which caused extensive damage.

14 - Johnson-Harrison House
6554 Friends Avenue, Whittier

Founder of the Whittier National First and Savings Bank, and a Whittier College trustee, A. C. Johnson built this two-story Craftsman bungalow, in 1912. After the Johnsons' death, the house was purchased by their nephew, William Harrison, an accomplished Whittier architect. Harrison designed the former United California Bank building in Uptown Whittier and the Whittier City Hall. The house is being preserved as a city historical landmark.

14 - Grave of "Greek George" SHL 646
Founders Memorial Park, Broadway and Citrus Avenues, Whittier

In the late 1850's, camels were brought to Fort Tejon in an experiment to see if they could adapt to the deserts of Southern California. "Greek George" Caralampo, a camel driver from Asia Minor, arrived with a shipment of camels purchased by the War Department for this experiment. He settled in the Los Angeles area after the venture was abandoned, became a naturalized citizen in 1866, and took the name George Allen. He died in September 1915, at the age of 75, and was buried here. Although no headstones or markers remain, the city is planning a permanent memorial to its pioneer families at this site.

14 - Bailey Ranch House
13421 East Camilla Street, Whittier

The Quaker community of Whittier was formed in 1887, when Jonathan Bailey moved into this ranch house and held the town's first religious service on its front porch. Restored by the Whittier Historical Society, it is preserved as a local historical landmark by the City of Whittier.

14 - Whittier Museum
6755 Newlin, Whittier (213) 945-3871

This museum's McFarland Gallery features a 1900s Main Street, Queen Anne cottage, walk-through barn, and artifacts from Whittier and its residents. Historical newspapers, photographs, post cards and other documents are also exhibited. A guide to Whittier's local historical landmarks can be obtained here.

14 - Fred C. Nelles School   SHL 947
11850 East Whittier Boulevard, Whittier

California's state legislature established two correctional institutions for boys in 1888. One in Northern California, and the second at this location. It was originally known as the Whittier School for Boys, and was established to keep juvenile offenders from being sent to prison, where they could associate with hardened criminals. The Fred C. Nelles School for Boys is now operated by the Department of the Youth Authority in this historic building.

14 - Whittier Walnut Tree   SHL 681
12300 East Whittier Boulevard, Whittier

In 1907 this paradox hybrid walnut tree was planted as part of an agricultural experiment by the University of California Experiment Station. The Quaker colony of Whittier became the world's largest walnut growing area in the early 1900s. A mission bell guidepost, at this site, marks this road as part of El Camino Real—the King's Highway, which led to all the missions in California.

14 - Sheriff's Museum
11515 South Colima Road, Whittier (310) 946-7081

The history of the Los Angeles County Sheriff's Department, from 1850 to the present, is brought to life in the museum's realistic displays. Featured exhibits include: equipment used by the mounted posse; a replica 1880 sheriff's office; a refurbished 1938, four-door, Studebaker patrol car; a Hughes 300 patrol helicopter; and a Sikorski rescue helicopter. Video programs of major events in county law enforcement history, photographs, weapons and department memorabilia are also presented in this interesting museum.

15 - Downey History Center
Apollo Park, 12540 Rives Avenue, Downey (310) 904-7128

Newspapers, photographs and legal documents from the early history of Downey are some of the records preserved at the Downey History Center. Relics of the city's past, and other items representative of those used in the area, are exhibited inside the center. Downey's pioneer cottage has been relocated to the park grounds and is being restored by the Downey Historical Society.

16 - Casa de Rancho San Antonio (Henry Gage Mansion) SHL 984
7000 East Gage, Bell Gardens

Francisco Lugo began building this adobe hacienda, the second oldest structure in Southern California, in 1780. It was finished by his son Antonio, in 1810, after the 29,514-acre San Antonio Rancho was granted to him. The house, and 27 acres of land, was deeded to Henry Tiftt Gage upon his marriage in 1880, to Francesca Rains, Lugo's great-granddaughter. In 1885, Gage was appointed a State Supreme Court Justice. He was elected Governor of California in 1899. As Governor, he started the State Park System, the California Redwood Commission, and the Commission of Public Works to save waterfronts from private ownership. Gage finished his public career in 1911 as the U.S. Ambassador to Portugal.

17 - Heritage Park
12100 Mora Drive, Santa Fe Springs (310) 946-6476

Restored and reconstructed buildings, from the elegant 1880s Hawkins Ranch Estate, are the centerpiece of the city's Heritage Park. The Carpenter Gothic style Carriage Barn, which was the most expensive structure of its kind in the county, exhibits historical artifacts that chronicle life at the turn-of-the-century. Hawkins also built Southern California's first concrete fountains for his formal English-style garden, which the *Los Angeles Times* called at the time, the "showplace of the County." In 1970, archaeologists discovered the cobblestone foundation of the circa 1800-1815 Patricio Ontiveros' adobe, one of the largest of the Mexican period. Ontiveros used the adobe as his headquarters when he was mayordomo of Mission San Juan Capistrano's vast cattle enterprise.

Heritage Park, Santa Fe Springs. Courtesy of Santa Fe Springs

18 - Duarte Historical Museum
777 Encanto Parkway, Duarte (818) 357-9419

In the late 1800s, Duarte orange groves were producing some of the finest citrus in the world. History of Duarte's pioneer families and the area's orange industry are the featured exhibits displayed by the Historical Society.

19 - Monrovia Historical Museum
Recreation Park, 742 East Lemon Avenue, Monrovia (818) 357-9537

Monrovia's 1925 Municipal Plunge, the city's first public swimming pool, and now the last remaining Spanish Colonial Revival style building in the city, has been completely renovated to house a collection of city memorabilia and historical artifacts.

20 - Sedley Peck Memorial Museum
Fellows Camp exit off Hwy 39 (San Gabriel Canyon Road) north of Vehicle Recreation Area

The last original structure from the Fellows Camp mining settlement, a century-old, one-room, frame and stone building, has been dedicated as a museum of mining history in the San Gabriel Canyon. Photographs and memorabilia of life in this community during the 1800s are displayed.

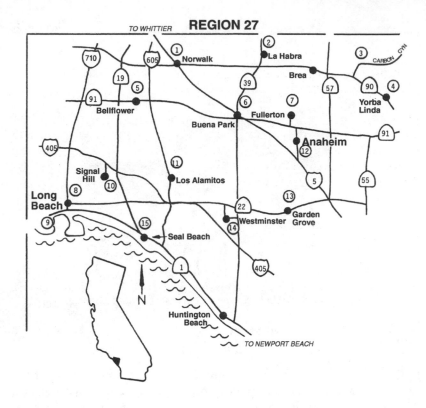

---

1 - Gilbert Sproul Museum
12237 East Sproul Street, Norwalk (310) 864-9663

Norwalk's founder, Gilbert Sproul, built this single-story redwood house in 1870. Furniture that originally belonged to the Sproul family has been preserved in this city museum. Archives of the city, early maps and old photographs are also maintained here.

1 - Hargitt House Museum
12450 Mapledale Avenue, Norwalk (310) 864-9663

In 1876, D. D. Johnson, who organized the first school system in Norwalk, built this two-story, Victorian style home. It was donated to the city as a museum in 1975 and contains original Johnson family furnishings.

2 - Children's Museum at La Habra
301 South Euclid Street, La Habra (310) 905-9793

Housed in a 1923, Mission Revival style, Union Pacific Railroad Depot this museum provides children with hands-on experience in many different areas of interest. Included in the museum are local historical artifacts and memorabilia from pioneer days in La Habra. The Pacific Electric Depot on the grounds is used as a theater.

3 - Olinda SHL 918
Carbon Canyon Regional Park, 4442 Carbon Canyon Road, Brea
(714) 996-5252

The boom town of Olinda stood for over forty years after the discovery of oil, by Edward Doheny, in 1897. Most of the town's residents left after the oil wells dried-up. Today the land is used as a county regional park.

4 - Richard Nixon Library and Birthplace
18001 Yorba Linda Boulevard, Yorba Linda (714) 993-3393

Richard Milhous Nixon, the first California native to become president, was born in this small wood-frame house that was built by his father in 1912. The Presidential Library and Museum erected around this historic site feature: a 12-foot high section of the Berlin Wall; a replica of the White House Lincoln Sitting Room, with original furniture used by Nixon; priceless gifts of State; the Domestic Affairs Gallery, reminiscent of the Capitol rotunda in Washington; First Lady gowns and Watergate Gallery. Memorabilia on display includes: an engraved copy of the "Declaration of Independence", a pistol presented to Nixon by Elvis Presley, and the telephone used by the President to talk to the *Apollo 11* astronauts while they were on the moon. In late June 1993, First Lady Pat Nixon passed away and was laid to rest at this site, next to the home where President Nixon was born.

4 - Site of Don Bernardo Yorba Adobe SHL 226
Esperanza Road at Echo Hill Drive, Yorba Linda

In 1834, Don Bernardo Yorba received a Mexican land grant here totaling more than 13,000 acres. He soon erected a large, two-story, adobe house that was one of the grandest Mexican haciendas built in California, and one of the most important homes in Orange County. After it was demolished in 1927, pieces of stone and tile from the adobe mansion were used in the creation of this monument.

5 - Carpenter House Museum
Ruth Caruthers Park, 10500 East Flora Vista, Bellflower (310) 867-2212

Built in 1928, as the residence of the Carpenter family, this is the oldest remaining dairy house in Bellflower. Donated to the city, this house is now a museum of local history. Artifacts, photographs and exhibits are maintained along with several rooms in the house that have been furnished to reflect various periods of Bellflower's past.

5 - Maizeland School SHL 729
Knott's Berry Farm, 8039 Beach Boulevard, Buena Park (714) 220-5200

Several old western buildings were relocated to Knott's Berry Farm for preservation by Walter Knott, including this one-room schoolhouse. This structure was first erected in 1868, in the Rivera School District of Los Angeles County.

6 - Buena Park Historical Society Museum
7842 Whitaker Street, Buena Park (714) 521-9900

The 1887 home of Andrew Whitaker now houses the collections of the Buena Park Historical Society. Old furnishings, and a First Lady doll collection, are among the society's featured exhibits. The home of Robert Beacon, believed to be the oldest home in the county, has been relocated here and can be seen on the grounds.

6 - International Printing Museum
8469 Kass Drive, Buena Park (714) 523-2070

Craftsman, dressed in period clothing, demonstrate more than 500 years of printing history for visitors to this 25,000 square-foot museum—the largest antique printing museum in the world. Displayed in its galleries are rare equipment collected and restored by founder Ernest Lindner. Among the many antique pieces assembled here are: an 1810 Stanhope, the oldest all-metal press in America; an 1828 Imperial Printing Press, from England; a rare

Rogers typograph; and a one-of-a-kind Columbian Press. Veteran actors portray famous "guest speakers" on the stage of the museum's 85-seat, Victorian style theatre.

7 - Heritage House
Fullerton Arboretum, Yorba Linda Boulevard and Associated Road, Fullerton (714) 773-2843

The Fullerton Arboretum is located on the grounds of the former Gilmore Ranch. The 1894 home, and office, of Dr. George Clark is preserved here with furniture and memorabilia of the family and business. The collection also includes: doctor's equipment from the 1890s, musical instruments and old pharmacy paraphernalia.

7 - Fullerton Museum Center
301 North Pomona Avenue, Fullerton (714) 738-6545

History of the region, and Indian culture, are the museum's featured exhibits. A permanent collection of textiles and costumes are displayed along with a variety of changing exhibits.

8 - Long Beach Firefighters Museum
1445 Peterson Avenue, Long Beach (310) 597-0351

Antique fire fighting apparatus and equipment fills Long Beach's 1925 Old Station #10. The city's first aerial ladder truck, a 1923 Seagrave; an 1894 Amoskeg, horse-drawn, steam fire engine; a rare 1894 Robinson hose wagon; and the Howard Hughes hose cart used for protection of the Spruce Goose, are among the pieces on display.

8 - Rancho Los Cerritos   SHL 978
4600 Virginia Road, Long Beach (310) 424-9423

Jonathan Temple, who built this two-story adobe in 1844, was appointed American alcalde of Los Angeles after Commodore Stockton took control of the city in 1846. In October 1846, Temple was captured and his adobe seized by the Californians. They used the adobe as their headquarters during the Mexican War. Furniture, household items, and other 1800s relics of historic interest are preserved in this restored two-story adobe.

8 - Rancho Los Alamitos
6400 Bixby Hill Road, Long Beach (310) 431-3541

One of the oldest adobe houses in California was built here, in 1806, by Juan Jose Nieto. Through the years, additions were made to the building as ownership changed hands. Today, the adobe and its frame additions remain as they looked when the last building was added in 1906. Several outbuildings remain including a blacksmith shop and six barns. The restored home is furnished with pieces from the 1800s and 1900s. Four acres of landscaped gardens, with original and native plantings, are also maintained.

8 - *Queen Mary*
Pier "J", Long Beach (310) 435-3511

The retired British luxury liner, *Queen Mary*, was acquired by the City of Long Beach in 1967 and converted into a floating hotel and museum. Four hundred rooms have been restored which are used for the hotel. Today, it is the largest passenger liner still afloat, although it is permanently moored in Long Beach Harbor. The history of the *Queen Mary's* thirty years at sea is exhibited in the "Museum of the Sea," on board this finely preserved ship.

8 - Long Beach Historic Downtown Walking Tour
Long Beach Area Convention and Visitors Council, 1 World Trade Center, Long Beach (310) 436-3645

Among the historic 1920s buildings, preserved along Long Beach's Ocean Boulevard, are: a seven-story Mediterranean Revival structure with battlements and octagonal tower; the fully restored Spanish Revival Breakers Hotel; and a California bungalow designed by famed California architects Greene and Greene. A guide to these and other historic buildings, in the Long Beach area, are available from the Convention and Visitors Council.

9 - Long Beach Lighthouse
End of breakwater, south of Long Beach, Long Beach outer harbor

After the Coast Guard took over Long Beach's lighthouse, in 1939, it was among the first to become totally automated, with light, fog horn and radio beacon. It was also one of the first stations to be designed in other than the traditional cylinder type design.

10 - "Alamitos No. 1" Discovery Well   SHL 580
Corner of Hill Street and Temple Avenue, Signal Hill

The discovery well of the Royal Dutch Shell Company struck oil here on June 23, 1921. Hundreds of wooden oil derricks eventually covered this site which was the most productive oil field in the area.

11 - Los Alamitos Museum
11052 Los Alamitos Boulevard, Los Alamitos (310) 431-8836

Exhibited in this old fire station are displays from the early history, and families, of the Los Alamitos area, and the sugar beet industry.

12 - Anaheim Museum
241 South Anaheim Boulevard, Anaheim (714) 778-3301

Restoration of Anaheim's only remaining Carnegie Library building was completed in 1987 as part of a citizen effort to establish a museum of history in the city. This stately, 1908 landmark building houses temporary and permanent exhibits that chronicle the history of Anaheim and surrounding area. One gallery features exhibits of special interest to children.

12 - North Gate of Anaheim   SHL 112
Southwest corner of Anaheim Boulevard and North Street, Anaheim

When a colony of Germans, from San Francisco, came here in 1857 to establish the City of Anaheim, they built a fence of willow poles around the colony. Many of the willow poles took root and formed a natural barrier against the wild cattle that roamed the area. The north gate, which was erected on the main road to Los Angeles, was one of four gates that provided entrance to this 1,100-acre settlement.

12 - Pioneer House of The Mother Colony   SHL 201
414 North West Street, Anaheim (714) 774-3840

The first house constructed in Orange County was built in 1857, as headquarters for the town's manager, George Hansen. It was moved to its present location and acquired by the City of Anaheim as a museum. Artifacts on display include the colony's wine-making equipment, furnishings and clothing of the period. Outside, in the gardens, is a grape arbor that bears the same variety of grapes planted by George Hansen when the colony of German settlers came here in 1857.

12 - Hobby City Doll and Toy Museum
1238 South Beach Boulevard, Anaheim (714) 527-2323

Rare and antique dolls and toys, from around the world, are exhibited in a half-scale replica of the "White House," the centerpiece of the six-acre, Hobby City complex. Exhibits include: Campbell's Soup dolls from the early 1900s; the finely-detailed Royal Hawaiian family; stone and wood dolls from the Egyptian pyramid period that date back over 3,000 years; an exquisite English wax portrait doll, circa 1830; centuries-old ivory Chinese Doctor Dolls; Kewpies; and ten-foot-long Japanese Imperial Palace with figures that bare a likeness to the Royal Family.

Hobby City Doll and Toy Museum. Courtesy of Hobby City Doll and Toy Museum.

13 - Stanley House Museum
Garden Grove Historical Society, 12174 Euclid Avenue, Heritage Park, Garden Grove (714) 530-8871

Original furnishings of the Edward Ware family are housed in this Victorian style house, built in 1890-1891. Other historic structures in the park include: Garden Grove's original post office, built in 1877; a restored barbershop; a general store; a windmill and tank house; a replica of the city's first fire station; and an old red country barn.

14 - Westminster Museum
14102 Hoover Street, Westminster

Westminster's history, and beginnings as a temperance colony, are preserved in this museum's collection of memorabilia and artifacts from the 1870s.

15 - Pacific Electric "Red Car" Museum
707 Electric Avenue, Seal Beach (310) 596-2579

In the early 1900s, "Big Red Cars" operated on the Pacific Electric Railway, between Los Angeles and the beach communities in Orange County. Many buildings along the old line are still in use as museums, restaurants and other commercial establishments. Exhibits of local and Orange County history are on display inside this converted work car.

15 - Anaheim Landing SHL 219
Seal Beach Boulevard and Electric Avenue, Seal Beach

Orange County's pioneer seaport was developed by the Anaheim Lighter Company in the mid-1860s. From here cargo would be unloaded from coastal steamers, warehoused and shipped to Orange County communities. Service was terminated in 1875, when the Southern Pacific Railroad to Anaheim was completed.

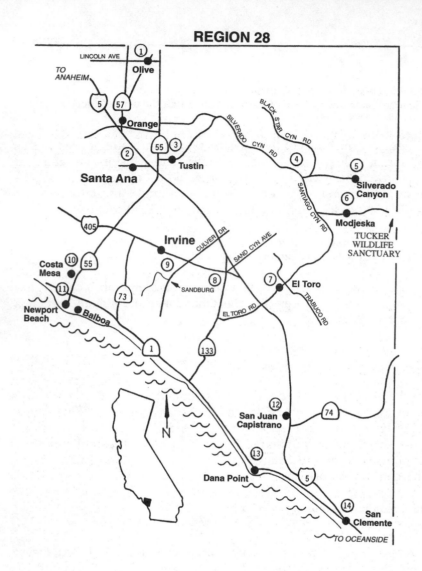

1 - Old Santa Ana   SHL 204
Orange-Olive Road, north of Lincoln Avenue, Orange

Jose Antonio Yorba, who traveled through this area as a soldier in the Portola expedition of 1769, petitioned and received a land grant encompassing this site in 1810. Several adobe homes were constructed, and a town was formed. The town was first named Santa Ana.

2 - Charles W. Bowers Museum (Bowers Museum)
2002 North Main Street, Santa Ana   (714) 567-3600

The building that houses the Bowers Museum was constructed in the Spanish Colonial style, during the early 1930s. It contains an extensive collection of Indian and early California relics, 19th century textiles, the history of Orange County's citrus industry, and other interesting and unusual exhibits.

Bowers Museum, Santa Ana. Courtesy of Bowers Museum.

2 - Discovery Museum of Orange County
3101 West Harvard Street, Santa Ana (714) 540-0404

Life at the turn-of-the-century is recreated for visitors to this fully restored, and furnished, 1898 Victorian home of Hiram Kellogg. A variety of high quality, hands-on discovery programs are offered for different age and interest groups. Student tours, children's workshops, Scout programs, and special events for adults and senior citizens, are available throughout the year by reservation.

2 - Orange County's Old Courthouse SHL 837
211 West Santa Ana Boulevard, Santa Ana

This Arizona red sandstone structure is the oldest existing courthouse building in Southern California. Erected in 1900, it was used as the Orange County courthouse until 1979.

3 - Red Hill SHL 203
Church of the Covenant Elementary School, 11911 Red Hill Road, Santa Ana

Spaniards called this hill Cerrito de las Ranas (Hill of the Frogs). An important landmark for early travelers and map makers, American settlers changed the name to Red Hill because of the color of its soil.

4 - Black Star Canyon Indian Village Site SHL 217
Black Star Canyon Road off Silverado Canyon Road, 9 miles north of Silverado (not open to the public)

Evidence of an Indian village can still be seen in the remains of mounds and grinding rocks. This canyon got its name from the Black Star Coal Mining Company that operated here in the 1870s.

5 - Carbondale SHL 228
Silverado Community Church, 8002 Silverado Canyon Road, Silverado Canyon (714) 649-2636

The mining town of Carbondale was founded here in 1878, after the discovery of coal was made in this canyon. In 1881, Southern Pacific Railroad took over the mine and operated it for several years. After the mine closed, the entire town moved away, taking with them all the town's buildings.

5 - Silverado Mining Camp SHL 202
End of paved Silverado Canyon Road, Silverado Canyon

Silver was discovered here in the late 1870s by two prospectors, Hank Smith and William Curry. In 1878, the mining town of Silverado was established. For the next three years, the town was a thriving community of miners that saw regular stage service from Los Angeles and Santa Ana.

6 - Home of Helena Modjeska SHL 205
Modjeska Canyon Road, Modjeska

Poland's Madam Modjeska, a great actress of her time, had this home built. She lived here from 1888, after her retirement from the stage. Her home, which still stands, was designed by Stanford White, the famous architect of New York's first Madison Square Garden.

6 - Flores Peak SHL 225
Northwest of Tucker Wildlife Sanctuary, Modjeska Canyon Road, Modjeska Canyon

A gang of bandits led by Juan Flores, a San Quentin Prison escapee, was captured here in January 1857, by a posse led by General Andres Pico. General Pico formed this posse after Flores and his men ambushed, and killed, Los Angeles Sheriff, James Barton, and three of his men earlier in the month.

7 - Heritage Hill Historical Park
25151 Serrano Road, Lake Forest (714) 855-2028

Four buildings of historical importance to Orange County stand on the grounds of the county's first historical park. The Serrano Adobe is the only one of the four that was originally built at this site.

Serrano Adobe SHL 199 - The last remaining adobe, built by the Serrano family, is this restored structure built around 1858-1863. Serrano raised cattle on this 10,000-acre ranchero granted to him in the early 1840s. He sold his adobe and most of his ranchero, in 1884, to Dwight Whiting, a major developer of El Toro.

7 - Heritage Hill Historical Park cont.

El Toro Grammar School - The first school in El Toro was this 1890, one-room schoolhouse. Grades 1 through 8 were instructed in this building until a new, two-room building was erected in 1914.

St. George's Episcopal Mission - Original furnishings are preserved in this 1891 Episcopal Church. It was built in a style familiar to the many English who settled in El Toro.

Bennett Ranch House - The last remaining turn-of-the-century, ranch house in El Toro was the home of the Charles Bennett family. Bennett was a pioneer Orange County citrus farmer. His son, Harvey, experimented with developing improved strains of oranges and lemons.

8 - Old Town Irvine   SHL 1004
Sand Canyon Avenue and Burt Road, Irvine

Old Town Irvine, historically known as Irvine, was founded here in 1887, as the center of the 125,000-acre Irvine Ranch. This company town served as a community center for the tenant farmers and workers, and was the shipping center for the Ranch's diversified agricultural products. In 1895, a warehouse was built and the cultivation of lima beans began. By 1909, the Irvine Ranch was farming a 54 square-mile bean field and was the world's leading producer of lima beans. The historic appearance of the 1895 warehouse, and the 1911-1916 general store, hotel and blacksmith shop, have been preserved. These structures have now been renovated into office, hotel, restaurant and retail spaces.

8 - Barton Mound   SHL 218
At the end of Sand Canyon Avenue, near the junction of I-405 and Hwy 133, East Irvine

In 1857, Sheriff James Barton and three of his men, were ambushed here and killed, by Juan Flores and his gang of outlaws. General Andres Pico formed a posse and captured the Flores gang.

9 - Irvine Historical Museum
5 San Joaquin at Sandburg (next to Rancho San Joaquin Golf Course), Irvine
(714) 786-4112

Indian artifacts, agricultural tools and history of Irvine Ranch are displayed in this century-old structure.

10 - Estancia of the Mission San Juan Capistrano SHL 227
Diego Sepulveda Adobe, 1900 Adams Avenue, Costa Mesa (714) 631-5918

In the early 1800s, an adobe building was constructed here as a shelter for Indians who tended the mission's cattle that grazed in the region. Two walls of the original adobe were used in the construction of this circa 1820-1823 house. After secularization, the Estancia became the property of Diego Sepulveda who made this adobe his home. Today, the adobe is preserved and maintained by the Costa Mesa Historical Society in Estancia Park.

10 - Costa Mesa Historical Society Museum
Anaheim and Plumer Streets, Costa Mesa (714) 631-5918

History of the Costa Mesa region is exhibited in this society's museum. One of the special collections is the history of the Santa Ana Army Air Base.

11 - Movieland of the Air Museum
John Wayne - Orange County Airport, Newport Beach (714) 545-5021

More than 50 original, and replica, airplanes are featured in this air museum. Among the exhibits featured at this interesting museum are: the history of aviation through World War II; original historical aircraft that still fly; and planes used in television programs and movies.

11 - Old Landing SHL 198
Dover Drive, north of Pacific Coast Hwy, Newport Beach

Captain S. S. Dunnells sailed into this "new port" in 1865. Seven years later he established a dock and warehouse and called it Newport Landing. In 1873, the three McFadden brothers purchased Newport Landing as headquarters for their lumber business. It became known as "Old Landing," when the McFaddens built another wharf on the ocean side of Newport Beach in 1888.

11 - McFadden Wharf   SHL 794
Newport Pier, McFadden Place between 20th and 22nd Places, Newport Beach

Four years after the McFadden brothers completed this wharf in 1888, it became the terminus of the Santa Ana and Newport Railroad. This port became the major commercial pier in Orange County, and was a major shipping point to adjoining Riverside and San Bernardino Counties.

11- First Water-to-Water Flight   SHL 775
Balboa Pier, opposite Balboa Pavilion, Newport Beach

On May 10, 1912, pioneer aviator and aircraft manufacturer Glenn L. Martin, made the first water-to-water flight from here to Santa Catalina Island. He used his own aircraft, which he built in an abandoned church building in Santa Ana, for the historic flight.

11 - Balboa Pavilion   SHL 959
400 Main Street, by the Balboa Pier and Peninsula Park, Balboa
(714) 673-5245

The Newport Bay Investment Company erected this large open-air pavilion, in 1905, to attract investors to their property on Balboa Peninsula. Upon completion of Pacific Electric's "Big Red Car" service to this point the following year, Balboa Pavilion became the center of the company's land development activity. This impressive structure is a well-known landmark in Southern California.

11 - Newport Harbor Nautical Museum
1714 West Balboa Boulevard, Newport Beach   (714) 673-3377

The history of Newport Beach, and its well-known small boat harbor is preserved here in photographs, nautical artifacts, historical films, and memorabilia. Boats and boat models, navigational instruments, fishing equipment, rigging and knot exhibits, and a 50-bottle collection of "ship-in-a-bottle" handiwork are also displayed.

12 - Mission San Juan Capistrano SHL 200
Camino Capistrano and Ortega Hwy, San Juan Capistrano (714) 493-1424

The seventh, in the chain of twenty-one, missions was established here by Father Junipero Serra, on November 1, 1776. The great sandstone church, with its seven domes, arched roof and bell tower, was completed in 1806—only to be destroyed six years later by an earthquake. The original adobe chapel has been restored and stands alongside ruins of the 1806 church. Mission San Juan Capistrano is famous for its swallows that return every year, on St Joseph's Day, March 19th.

12 - San Juan Capistrano Walking Tour
Map is available from O'Neill Museum, 31831 Los Rios, San Juan Capistrano (714) 493-8444

A visitor's guide, to a dozen historic San Juan Capistrano buildings, can be obtained from the Historical Society which has its museum and office in this circa 1870s building. Among the buildings listed are: the 1784 Rios Adobe, the oldest residence in California continuously occupied by the same family; Blas Aguilar adobe, the home of the last alcalde of the Mexican period; Garcia Adobe, the only two-story, Monterey-style adobe in Orange County; and the restored Capistrano Depot, built by the Atchison, Topeka and Santa Fe Railroad in 1894.

12 - O'Neill Museum
Albert Pryor Residence, 31831 Los Rios Street, San Juan Capistrano (714) 493-8444

The San Juan Capistrano Historical Society has restored this 1870s building, constructed by saloon-keeper, Dolores Garcia, and opened it to the public as the O'Neill Museum. Furniture from the 1880s, and Native American artifacts, are displayed. The historical society publishes a visitor's guide and conducts Sunday afternoon tours of the dozen historic buildings surrounding Los Rios Street—one of the oldest streets in the State.

13 - Dana Point   SHL 189
Gazebo at the end of the street of the Blue Lantern, Dana Point

Pirateer Hippolyte de Bouchard, known along the coast for his plundering of the missions, landed at this cove in 1818 to raid the Mission San Juan Capistrano.

Richard Henry Dana, in his book, *Two Years Before the Mast*, tells of his experiences at this cove, then known as El Embarcadero, and of his adventures along the California coast in the 1830s. San Juan Point was renamed Dana Point in honor of this legendary author.

14 - Site of First Baptism   SHL 562
100 Avenida Presidio, San Clemente

Father Francisco Gomez, a Franciscan Padre on the Portola Expedition of 1769, performed the first baptism in Alta California at an Indian Village near San Onofre. The site of the actual baptism is in Los Cristianitos Canyon, on the Camp Pendleton Marine Base. The event is also commemorated by this plaque in the civic center.

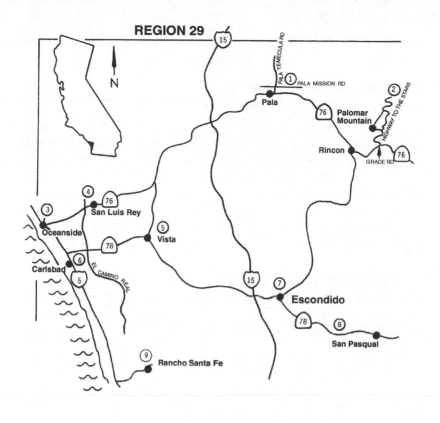

REGION 29

N

Pala

① PALA MISSION RD

Palomar Mountain ⑦⑥

Rincon

GRADE RD ⑦⑥

② HIGHWAY TO THE STARS

④ ⑦⑥ San Luis Rey

③ Oceanside

⑤ Vista

⑦⑧

⑥ Carlsbad ⑤

EL CAMINO REAL

⑮ ⑦

Escondido

⑦⑧ ⑧

San Pasqual

⑨ Rancho Santa Fe

---

1 - Asistencia de San Antonio de Pala   SHL 243
Pala Mission Road, plaque on Hwy 76, Pala   (619) 742-3317

This branch of Mission San Luis Rey was founded in 1816. It was built to serve Indians living on rancherias located twenty miles inland from the mission. Descendants of the first Indians converted by the mission padres still attend services at the chapel they helped restore. The refurbished bell tower (the only freestanding bell tower erected in the mission chain) and a small museum can also be seen at this historic site.

2 - Palomar Observatory
Highway to the Stars, northeast of Palomar Mountain, Grade Road (County Road S6) off Hwy 76, (619) 742-2119

The largest telescope in America is the 200-inch Hale telescope erected here in 1949-1950. Astronomy photographs are on display in the observatory's museum.

3 - Amphibian Vehicle Museum
Main Gate - Camp Pendleton, Oceanside Harbor Drive exit off I-5, Oceanside (619) 725-5566

Amphibious vehicles used by the Marine Corps since World War II are displayed inside this on-base museum. Driver's license, vehicle registration and proof of insurance are required for entry to the base and the self-guided tour.

3 - Las Flores Asistencia SHL 616
Main Gate - Camp Pendleton, Oceanside Harbor Drive exit off I-5, Oceanside

During the early 1820s, a mission outpost was established here in order to provide lodging for travelers between the missions San Diego and San Luis Rey. Adobe ruins are all that remain to be seen of this National Historic Landmark.

4 - Mission San Luis Rey de Francis SHL 239
4050 Mission Avenue, San Luis Rey (619) 757-3651

The eighteenth mission in California was founded here by Father Fermin Francisco de Lasuen on June 13, 1798. It was one of the largest, and most prosperous, of the California missions. The present church structure was completed in 1815 and restored in the late 1800s. In May 1893, it was rededicated as a Franciscan seminary. Today, it is one of four missions still owned by the Franciscan Order. Books from the early days of the mission, vestments and Indian artifacts are displayed in the mission's museum.

5 - Antique Gas and Steam Engine Museum
2040 North Santa Fe, Vista (619) 941-1791

Located on 35 acres of the Guajome Regional Park, this museum features over 300 pieces of equipment, making it the largest collection of operating steam and gas engines in this part of the state. It is the only "farm machinery museum" in Southern California. Articles from pioneer country kitchens and parlors are also displayed in this unusual museum.

Threshing operation, Antique Gas and Steam Engine Museum. Courtesy of Antique Gas and Steam Engine Museum.

Mission San Luis Rey. Courtesy of Mission San Luis Rey.

5 - Rancho Guajome   SHL 940
2210 North Santa Fe Avenue, Vista

Guajome Rancho was one of the few Mexican land grants awarded to Indian neophytes. Andres and Caterina Solma received part of the land originally owned by the Mission San Luis Rey and later sold it to a Los Angeles businessman, Abel Sterns. In 1852, Colonel Cave Counts and his wife, Ysidora, built this large adobe house on the rancho, which Ysidora received as a wedding gift from Sterns. San Diego County acquired the Counts' Adobe and surrounding property, and in 1973, established Guajome Regional Park.

6 - San Luis Rey Historical Society Museum
Carlsbad By The Sea, 2855 Carlsbad Boulevard, Carlsbad

Early California history is displayed here with Indian artifacts from the ancient Indian culture of this region.

7 - Escondido Historical Museum
Grape Day Park, 321 North Broadway, Escondido (619) 743-8207

Historic buildings along Escondido's Heritage Walk include: the town's first library; a barn and windmill from the early 1900s; a Victorian-style ranch house, with its tankhouse; a blacksmith shop; and an 1888 Santa Fe Railroad depot. The library building itself houses the various collections of the Historical Society.

7 - Mule Hill   SHL 452
On Pomerado Road, 1/10 mile east of I-15, 5 miles southeast of Escondido

While waiting for reinforcements to arrive from San Diego, General Stephen Kearny and his men, who had suffered many casualties in the battle of San Pasqual, were forced to eat their mules to avoid starvation. This hill, on which they camped in December 1846, was renamed "Mule Hill."

8 - San Pasqual Battlefield State Historic Park   SHL 533
3/4 mile southeast of Escondido on Hwy 78, San Pasqual Valley Road, west of San Pasqual (619) 238-3380

General Stephen Kearny and the Army of the West, en route to San Diego, encountered a superior force of Mexican horsemen at this site on December 6, 1846. The bloodiest battle of the Mexican War, fought in California, took place here, with American forces suffering major losses. The famous scout, Kit Carson, went to San Diego to get reinforcements while the remainder of Kearny's troops regrouped to the top of the hill, now called "Mule Hill," about five miles to the west.

9 - Historic Planned Community of Rancho Santa Fe   SHL 982
Via de Santa Fe and La Flecha Streets, Rancho Santa Fe

The Santa Fe Land Improvement Company, a subsidiary of the Santa Fe Railroad, acquired 8,800 acres of the old Rancho San Dieguito in 1906. On it they planted over a million eucalyptus seedlings, which they planned to grow for use as railroad ties. The eucalyptus tree program failed, but under the leadership of Santa Fe's Vice President, W. E. Hodges, Rancho Santa Fe was developed as one of California's first Spanish colonial planned communities. Land use, building design and landscape restrictions were adopted to protect the near-perfect environment. Architects, Richard Requa and Herbert L. Jackson, designed the residential areas and Lilian Jeanette Rice developed the business area. The Reitz Building (La Flecha House), which stands at this site, was designed by Lilian Rice. It was home to the manager of the Santa Fe Land Improvement company, and housed the city's first public library.

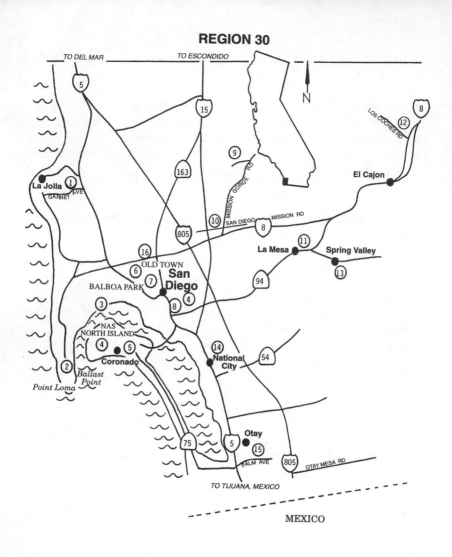

1 - Site of Kate Sessions Nursery   SHL 764
Pico Street and Garnet Avenue, west of I-5, north of Mission Bay, San Diego

The city of San Diego rented Kate Sessions thirty-six acres of land in Balboa Park, in 1892, for her use as a nursery. In exchange, she landscaped the west portion of the park and has been credited with much of the beauty of San Diego. It was here that one of her nurseries once stood.

2 - Quarantine Station SHL 61
Pier 160, Naval Oceans Systems Center, Point Loma

Foreign ships were required to stop here for inspection to prevent any disease from being brought ashore. Several barn-like hide houses, which are now gone, operated here between 1824-1846.

2 - Site of San Diego Whaling Station SHL 50
U.S. Navy Submarine Support Facility, plaque located at east side of Kephart and Page Roads, Point Loma

Two New England whaling companies operated on this site in the mid-1800s. Whales would be towed to this spot, cut-up and processed. From the "whale overlook," by the old Point Loma Lighthouse, gray whales can still be seen in these waters from December through February.

2 - Site of Fort Guijarros SHL 69
Plaque located at end of Rosecrans, south of Kerricks Road, Point Loma

A Spanish adobe fort was constructed here in 1795-1800, and manned by Catalonian soldiers, from the San Diego Presidio. The American ship *Lelia Byrd* was fired upon from this fort when attempting to trade with the Spaniards onshore—a violation of Spanish Law which prohibited foreign trade. Nothing remains of the original fort which was abandoned in 1838.

2 - Ballast Point SHL 56
At the end of Guijarros Road on San Diego Bay, Point Loma

It was here that Juan Rodriguez Cabrillo landed, in 1542, and took possession of Alta California in the name of Spain. He named the port of San Diego "San Miguel."

2 - Fort Rosecrans National Cemetery SHL 55
Cabrillo Memorial Drive, south of Woodward Road, Point Loma

Sailors and Marines who lost their lives in an explosion aboard the USS *Bennington*, on July 21, 1905, are memorialized in this national cemetery. Casualties from the December 1846, battle of San Pasqual are also buried in this place of honor.

2 - Fort Rosecrans SHL 62
White Road off Sylvester, Point Loma

The U.S. military post established here in 1898 was named in honor of General William Rosecrans, who came to San Diego in 1867. Ruins of the old fort can still be seen today.

2 - Cabrillo National Monument
Cabrillo Memorial Drive at the end of Catalina Boulevard, Point Loma
(619) 557-5450

The historic landing place of explorer, Juan Rodriquez Cabrillo, who came ashore here in 1542, and claimed the West Coast for Spain, is preserved in this national monument. Other events took place here and are identified as State Historical Landmarks.

2 - Old Point Loma Lighthouse SHL 51
Southern end of Cabrillo Memorial Drive, Point Loma

The first lighthouse on the West Coast was erected at this point, in 1854-1855. It was constructed of adobe bricks and sandstone. Some of the floor tiles came from the abandoned Fort Guijarros. Often obscured by fog, this lighthouse was replaced in 1891 by a second structure erected at a lower elevation. The original lighthouse has been restored and contains artifacts from the period 1850-1890.

3 - Site of El Desembarcadero SHL 64
U.S. Naval Training Center, southeast of Rosecrans Street, between Russell and Zola Streets, San Diego

This filled-in area, once at the mouth of the San Diego River, was the landing site for small craft that brought passengers and cargo to Old Town. Diversion of the river, to form the San Diego River Flood Control Channel, obliterated the original landing site.

3 - Beginning of Spanish Expeditions Into California SHL 891
Spanish Landing Park, Harbor Drive between Neville and Mitscher Roads, by Lindbergh Field, San Diego

Four companies of Spaniards arrived here, in 1769, to begin the founding of the missions and the settlements of California. Among those who met here to begin this historic exploration of Alta

California were Gaspar de Portola, Father Junipero Serra, Pedro Fages and Father Crespi. A monument has been erected here to mark the site of their historic landing

4 - First Military Flying School in America SHL 818
Naval Air Station, North Island, Coronado

Aviation pioneer Glenn Curtis, who made the first public aircraft flights, came here in 1911 and founded America's first military flying school. Aviation history has continued at this historic site. The Army Air Force operated Rockwell Field until 1939. The Navy's North Island Air Station, which was commissioned in 1917, is still active in military aviation.

5 - Hotel del Coronado SHL 844
1500 Orange Avenue, Coronado (619) 522-8196 or (800) 468-3533

Eleven U.S. presidents and many dignitaries from around the world have visited this famous late Victorian-style seaside hotel. Erected in 1887-1888, it stands as one of America's largest wooden buildings and one of the few remaining resort hotels of this style in the country. Thomas Edison supervised the installation of his incandescent lamps here, in what was the largest single installation at the time, outside the city of New York. Most of the hotel remains the same as when it was built over a hundred years ago.

Hotel del Coronado. Courtesy of Hotel del Coronado.

6 - Old Town State Historic Park SHL 830
Juan, Congress, Twiggs and Taylor Streets, San Diego (619) 237-6770

This six-block area was the settlement of San Diego that grew up around the presidio between 1822 and 1872. Preserved within this State Historic Park are many old adobe houses and exhibits of Mexican and early American life in California.

Mormon Battalion Visitors Center - 2510 Juan Street (619) 298-3317
An historical sculpture of a Mormon soldier from the 1847 Mormon Battalion infantry march, and an 1850 cannon, can be seen at this visitors' center. Tours and movies are also offered.

Discover San Diego - 2463 Juan Street, Galleria (619) 298-2800
The history of San Diego, from its founding to the present, is presented in a 30-minute, multi-media program by Discover San Diego.

Heritage Park - Juan and Harney Streets (619) 298-2482
The San Diego County Parks Department conducts tours of the Victorian buildings in this section of Old Town known as Heritage Park.

Derby-Pendleton House - 4017 Harney Street (619) 298-2482
This 1851 Clapboard house was built in Portland, Maine, in 1851. It was disassembled, shipped around the Horn and reassembled here. Antique furniture, from the period 1850 to 1860, are among the furnishings inside this Greek Revival style house.

Casa de Lopez SHL 60 - 3890 Twiggs Street
Built around 1835, this adobe was the home of Juan Matias Moreno, secretary to Pio Pico, the last Mexican Governor of California.

Casa de Cota Site SHL 75 - Twiggs and Congress Streets
Casa de Cota, one of San Diego's early adobe structures, was built on this site around the 1830s. It was destroyed by the Army during World War II.

6 - Old Town State Historic Park   SHL 830 cont.

Casa de Stewart   SHL 73 - Congress and Mason Streets
John C. Stewart married Rosa Machado. They lived in this adobe constructed by her father in the 1830s. Richard Henry Dana, a shipmate of John Stewart, described his 1859 visit to this home in his novel *Two Years Before the Mast.*

First Public School Building   SHL 538 - 3960 Mason Street
The first public school in San Diego was erected here in 1865. This restored frame building is a fine example of the Greek Revival style of architecture that was popular during that period.

Old Town Plaza   SHL 63 - San Diego Avenue and Mason Street
This plaza was the center of all activity in Old San Diego. It was here that the Americans established their headquarters, during their military rule of California, in 1846. The American flag was first raised over this plaza on July 29, 1846.

First San Diego Courthouse - Corner of Plaza facing San Diego Ave.
San Diego's first civic building is being reconstructed on its original site at Old Town Plaza. It will feature a period 1850s courtroom, and the offices of the mayor and city clerk. Historic events that took place here will be reenacted, docents will conduct tours and period artifacts will be displayed.

Casa de Estudillo   SHL 53 - Southeast side of Plaza
Built in the late 1820s, this 12-room, U-shaped structure was the home of Jose de Estudillo, commander of the San Diego Presidio. This restored adobe was once the center of social life in Southern California and served as a refuge for women and children during the American occupation in 1846.

Casa de Pedrorena   SHL 70 - 2616 San Diego Avenue
This old adobe house was the home of Miguel de Pedrorena, a native of Madrid, Spain, who came here in the late 1830s. He served as a delegate to California's Constitutional Convention, held in Monterey, in 1849.

6 - Old Town State Historic Park   SHL 830 cont.

The Whaley House   SHL 65 - 2482 San Diego Avenue
(619) 298-2482
Thomas Whaley built San Diego's first brick house here in 1856. Bricks used in the construction of this two-story house were fired in his own kiln. Inside this restored house are walls plastered with ground seashells, and furnishings from the 1850s and 1860s. Tales of "ghosts of the Whaley Family," thought to still be present in this home, have made the Whaley house a popular tourist attraction.

Site of the Exchange Hotel   SHL 491 - 2731 San Diego Avenue
San Diego's first three-story building was erected here in the early 1850s. In the summer of 1851, the oldest lodge of the Masons was organized in this building. The following year the structure was completely destroyed by fire.

Wells Fargo History Museum - 2733 San Diego Avenue
(619) 294-5549
The exciting history of Wells Fargo, from the Gold Rush days to the modern electronic age, is displayed. Exhibits include: a circa 1865 Concord Stagecoach; a replica Wells Fargo office, with agent's desk; historic photographs and documents; gold specimens and gold mining artifacts. Interpretive displays give visitors hands-on experience with early telegraph and gold mining equipment.

Casa de Machado   SHL 71 - 2741 San Diego Avenue
Jose Manuel Machado built several adobes similar to this for himself, and his married daughters, in the 1830s. Commandant of the California Battalion, Colonel John Fremont, had his headquarters here in July 1846.

Old Spanish Cemetery   SHL 68 - San Diego Avenue and Arista Street
This pioneer cemetery was used by the Catholic Church in San Diego from 1850 until 1880. It was the burial place of some of San Diego's most distinguished residents.

6 - Old Town State Historic Park   SHL 830 cont.

Chapel of The Immaculate Conception   SHL 49 - Conde Street, southwest of San Diego Avenue
In the 1850s Jose Antonio Aguirre purchased the adobe home of John Brown and converted it into a Catholic church. Father Antonio Ubach brought the first organ to San Diego, for this church, in 1866. In 1937, the church was reconstructed at this site, just a few feet from its original location.

Congress Hall Site   SHL 66 - 4016 Wallace Street
The last Pony Express route was operated from a two-story adobe building that once stood here. The 1867 structure was demolished in 1939.

Seeley Stables - 2648 Calhoun Street (619) 294-5183
Covered wagons, and stagecoaches, are among the horse-drawn vehicles exhibited in this reconstructed barn from the 1860s. Alfred Seeley operated the San Diego-Los Angeles Stage Line from this location in the late 1800s.

Casa de Bandini   SHL 72 - 2660 Calhoun Street,
Commodore Robert Stockton used the 1827 adobe, built by Jose and Juan Bandini, as his headquarters while he was in charge of the American forces occupying San Diego in 1846. The famous scout, Kit Carson, delivered a message here from General Kearny asking for reinforcements after the battle of San Pasqual.

6 - Site of San Diego Presidio   SHL 59
Presidio Park, off Taylor Street, northeast of Old Town San Diego

The first European settlement, on the West Coast, was made on this site in 1769. It was begun with the establishment of California's first mission and the San Diego Royal Presidio. Today, the ruins of the presidio can be seen here in Presidio Park, along with other important landmarks and monuments to Father Serra. The Junipero Serra Museum, honoring the founder of the first nine California missions, is also located within this park.

6 - The Junipero Serra Museum (Serra Museum)
2727 Presidio Drive, San Diego (619) 297-3258

This historical society museum contains artifacts and materials from California's early history, and is at the site of the first mission founded by Padre Junipero Serra, in 1769.

6 - Site of Serra Palm SHL 67
Presidio Park, off Taylor Street, northeast of Old Town San Diego

Father Junipero Serra, Gaspar de Portola and Pedro Fages established their "Spanish Camp" in this area in 1769. It was from here that they began their exploration of Alta California. Father Serra, who established the first nine of the twenty-one missions, planted the first two date palms in California near this site.

6 - Fort Stockton SHL 54
Presidio Park, off Taylor Street, northeast of Old Town San Diego

At the top of this hill, Mexico's governor of Alta California established his headquarters as the de facto capitol of California from 1825-1831. An earthen fort was constructed here in 1838. In 1846, the Americans built Fort Stockton, using the old fort as a foundation.

6 - Derby Dike SHL 244
Marker in Presidio Park, west of Old Town, San Diego

Derby Dike was built between 1853-1855 to divert the debris laden waters of the San Diego River away from the harbor at San Diego Bay. Lt. George Derby, a member of the U.S. Corp of Topographical Engineers, engineered the dike that turned the river to flow into what is now Mission Bay. During Derby's stay in Old Town he wrote many humourous articles for the _San Diego Herald_ under the pen name "John Phoenix."

6 - Casa de Carrillo SHL 74
4136 Wallace Street, San Diego

This small restored adobe is believed to be part of the original Ruiz adobe built in 1810. The Joaquin Carrillo family was said to have lived here in the 1820s when it was a much larger structure.

7 - Balboa Park
Park Boulevard, north of I-5, San Diego (619) 239-0512

San Diego's Balboa Park is among the largest municipal parks in the nation. Buildings constructed for the 1915, and 1935-1936, Expositions have been preserved and are used to house the park's museums and exhibits. Located here are eight museums, art galleries, the famous San Diego Zoo, theaters, restaurants, gardens and other interesting sites. Places of historic interest include:

Museum of Man - American Indian artifacts are exhibited with displays of the story of mankind. (619) 239-2001

San Diego Model Railroad Museum - This authentic model railroad museum features various scale model trains and layouts. Historic Tehachapi Pass is being constructed in every detail including the famous Tehachapi Loop. More than 5,000 square feet are now devoted to the Tehachapi Pass layout. (619) 696-0199

San Diego Hall of Champions - San Diego County athletes, who have achieved recognition in sports, are honored here. Special exhibits include: military sports, Olympics, disabled athlete's achievements and Special Olympics. Pictures, awards, equipment and sports memorabilia are displayed. (619) 234-2544

The Reuben H. Fleet Space Theater and Science Center - This theater's, dome shaped, Omnimax screen was the prototype for similar theaters built around the country. The science center is a hands-on museum with more than 50 exhibits. (619) 238-1168

San Diego Aerospace Museum and Aerospace Hall of Fame - More than 50 original and replica aircraft are displayed here in historic settings. A replica of Lindbergh's *Spirit of St. Louis* (the original was built in San Diego), the Navy's first plane (a 1912 Curtiss A-1) and a space capsule are part of the exhibits. The International Hall of Fame honors heroes of aviation and space history. (619) 234-8291

7 - Balboa Park cont.

House of Pacific Relations (HPR) - Cultures of 27 different nations come alive in authentic settings within this nineteen-house complex. Hosts from each member country invite visitors into these cottages every Sunday afternoon to sample their foods, music, and customs. Antique collections, costumes, furnishings and art are among the native treasures found in these home-like settings.

8 - San Diego Union Museum
2626 San Diego Avenue, San Diego (619) 297-2119

In 1868, the *San Diego Union* newspaper was founded in this building. Restored to its original condition, with 1860's furnishings, it is now a museum of early San Diego history. A scale model of Old Town, as it was in 1870, is among the interesting exhibits displayed.

8 - Firehouse Museum
1572 Columbia Street, San Diego (619) 232-3473

The oldest firehouse in San Diego is now a museum of antique fire-fighting equipment, artifacts and memorabilia. Included in the collection are old helmets and relics from around the world.

8 - San Diego Barracks Site   SHL 523
In the area bounded by Kettner Boulevard, Market, "G" and California Streets, San Diego

Established in 1851 as a military supply depot, the buildings that once stood here were first called Fort New San Diego. The name was changed to San Diego Barracks, and it served as an outpost of Fort Rosecrans until it was abandoned in 1921. A plaque commemorates where this fort once stood.

8 - La Punta de Los Muertos   SHL 57
Pacific Highway and Market Street, San Diego

Sailors and Marines, who died of scurvy, aboard the two ships sent from Spain, to survey the harbor at San Diego in 1782, were buried here at "Dead Man's Point."

8 - San Diego Maritime Museum
1306 North Harbor Drive, San Diego (619) 234-9153

Three historic ships: the 1863 windjammer, *Star of India*; the 1898 San Francisco ferryboat, *Berkeley*; and the 1904 steam yacht, *Medea*, make up this interesting floating museum. Ship models, U.S. Navy artifacts, and nautical exhibits are among the collections displayed on board these ships.

Star of India. *Courtesy of Maritime Museum Association of San Diego.*

8 - Gaslamp Quarter (William Heath Davis House)
410 Island Avenue, San Diego (619) 233-5227

Walking tours of the historical district of downtown San Diego are conducted by the Gaslamp Quarter Council. Victorian style buildings in various stages of restoration are included in the tour. Nearby, on Broadway, are the U.S. Grant Hotel and the Spreckels Theater building. Both were designed by the same San Diego architect, Harrison Albright in the early 1900s.

8 - Villa Montezuma (Jesse Shepard House)
1925 "K" Street, San Diego (619) 239-2211

San Diego's Historical Society maintains the 1887 Victorian style home of musician and author, Jesse Shepard, as a museum. Unusual architecture, interesting interior designs and art-glass windows have made this the most unusual historical residential building in the city.

8 - San Diego State College SHL 798
5402 College Avenue, San Diego (619) 594-5200

In 1897, San Diego State College was established as a two-year, normal school. After the turn-of-the-century it changed to a four-year teachers' college, and in 1935, it became a liberal arts college. On June 7, 1963, San Diego State College conferred upon President John F. Kennedy, the first doctorate to be granted by the California State College system.

9 - Mission Dam and Flume SHL 52
Mission Trails Regional Park, Old Mission Dam Historical Site, Mission Gorge Road, San Diego

Irrigation water was supplied to the mission's fields and vineyards via an aqueduct system, part of which was this granite and cement dam constructed in the early 1800s. Remains of this early irrigation project can still be seen and have been registered as a National Historic Landmark.

10 - Mission San Diego de Alcala SHL 242
10818 San Diego Mission Road, Mission Valley (619) 281-8449

Father Junipero Serra established the first of California's twenty-one missions in San Diego, on July 16, 1769. The close proximity of the presidio made it necessary for the mission to move in 1774 to its present location. Earthquakes in the early 1800s twice required rebuilding of the mission church. By 1931, when a complete restoration was undertaken, only the facade and part of a wall remained from the original mission church. The first mission site can be seen in Presidio Park.

10 - El Camino Real - Southern Terminus   SHL 784
Mission San Diego de Alcala, 10818 San Diego Mission Road, Mission Valley

On the 250th anniversary of the birth of Father Junipero Serra, this plaque was placed to mark the southern terminus of the trail he helped blaze between the missions. This trail was called "El Camino Real,"—the King's Highway, and was the major north-south route through California along the coast.

11 - La Mesa Depot (San Diego Railroad Museum)
4695 Nebo Drive, La Mesa (619) 697-7762 or (619) 595-3030

The 1894 restored depot of the San Diego, Cuyamaca and Eastern Railroad is now home of the La Mesa Depot Museum. Several locomotives and cars are exhibited, including, the Pullman car that Franklin D. Roosevelt used during his 1935 Presidential campaign.

12 - Rancho La Canada de Los Coches (Site)   SHL 425
Los Coches Monument, 13468 Old Hwy, Lakeside

The smallest Mexican land grant in California was made to Apolinaria Lorenzana, in 1843, and comprised just over 28 acres. The adobe house and gristmill he built no longer stand, but the site is commemorated by this plaque.

13 - Bancroft Ranch House   SHL 626
Memory Lane off Bancroft Drive, Spring Valley

Judge A. S. Ensworth built this adobe house, in 1856, using timbers salvaged from a ship that once operated in San Diego Bay. In 1885, Hubert Howe Bancroft purchased the home. It was here that Bancroft wrote part of his *History of California*. His home is now maintained by the Spring Valley Historical Society as a local history museum.

14 - National City Historic Tour
Chamber of Commerce, 711 "A" Avenue, National City (619) 477-9339

National City's Chamber of Commerce publishes a historical site map and guide to 32 buildings of historical importance to the community.

15 - Montgomery Memorial SHL 711
Monument at Montgomery-Walker Memorial Park, Coronado Avenue and Beyer Boulevard, Otay Mesa

The first heavier-than-air flight was made here, by John Joseph Montgomery, in 1883. Twenty years after Montgomery's successful glider flight, the Wright brothers made their famous flight at Kitty Hawk. Montgomery's pioneer aircraft experiments continued until 1911, when he died in a glider accident near Evergreen, in Santa Clara County.

16 - Site of Ryan Aircraft Facility
On grounds of Solar Turbines, Harbor Drive between Laurel and Hawthorne, San Diego (619) 544-5671

The first aircraft to be flown solo, nonstop from New York to Paris, was designed and built on this site by Ryan Aircraft, in 1927, for Charles A. Lindbergh. Lindbergh's original _Spirit of St. Louis_ is on exhibit at the National Air and Space Museum, in Washington, D.C. Although this historic site is not open to the public, an exact replica of the famous aircraft can be seen inside San Diego's Aerospace Museum, in Balboa Park.

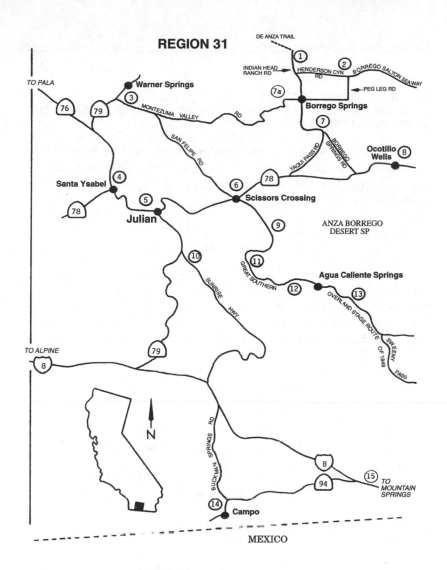

REGION 31

DE ANZA TRAIL

TO PALA

Warner Springs

INDIAN HEAD RANCH RD

HENDERSON CYN RD

BORREGO SALTON SEAWAY

PEG LEG RD

Borrego Springs

MONTEZUMA VALLEY RD

SAN FELIPE RD

YAQUI PASS RD

BORREGO SPRINGS RD

Ocotillo Wells

Santa Ysabel

Julian

Scissors Crossing

ANZA BORREGO DESERT SP

Agua Caliente Springs

GREAT SOUTHERN

OVERLAND STAGE ROUTE

SWEENY PASS

OF 1849

SUNRISE HWY

TO ALPINE

N

BUCKMAN SPRINGS RD

TO MOUNTAIN SPRINGS

Campo

MEXICO

---

1 - El Vado   SHL 634
Borrego Springs Road, 8 miles north of Borrego Springs, at the mouth of Coyote Canyon near Indian Head Ranch Road

For three days in December 1775, Juan Bautista de Anza camped here with his party of 240 colonists. They were en route to form the city of San Francisco.

1 - Santa Catarina SHL 785
Santa Catarina Springs, 10 miles northwest of Borrego Springs, Anza Borrego Desert State Park

Juan Bautista de Anza's Expedition party camped here in 1774 as they opened the trail across Southern California, from the Colorado River. A year later he returned to this camp with 240 colonists en route to settle San Francisco.

2 - "Peg Leg" Smith Monument SHL 750
Henderson Canyon Road, near Pegleg Road, Anza Borrego Desert State Park (619) 767-4684

"Peg Leg" Smith, who told of a lost gold mine in this region, was memorialized by this monument after his death in 1866. Many who heard his tales searched the desert for clues to the location of the mine. The mine, if there ever was one, was never found.

3 - Warner's Ranch SHL 311
County Road S2, east of Hwy 79, southeast of Warner Springs

Among the first Americans to have extensive land holdings in California was Jonathan Trumball Warner, who came to California in 1831, from Connecticut. Warner was a generous host and Warner Ranch became a popular place along the old emigrant trail. In 1858, Warner Ranch became a stop on the Butterfield Stage route. The remains of the old adobe are a National Historic Landmark.

4 - Chapel of Santa Ysabel SHL 369
1 and 1/2 miles north of Santa Ysabel on Hwy 79 (619) 765-0810

An outpost of the San Diego Mission was established here, in 1818. In 1924, the present chapel was built and continues as a place of worship for Indians from five area reservations. A museum of history and an Indian burial ground are maintained at the outpost.

5 - Julian SHL 412
Marker placed in Julian Memorial Park, 5th and Julian Road, Julian, Julian Chamber of Commerce (619) 765-1857

This town was the site of one of Southern California's major gold discoveries. Between 1870 and 1880, more than $5 million in placer and quartz gold was taken from the Julian area. Fruit orchards kept Julian from becoming a ghost town after the gold played out and its miners left in 1880. Many local historic sites remain, including more than a dozen nineteenth century buildings, museums and old mines.

5 - Julian Pioneer Museum
2811 Washington, Julian (619) 765-0227

Peter Myerhofer erected this building in the mid-1880s. It was later converted into a blacksmith shop. In 1950, the Julian Woman's Club took the stone wall building shell and completely restored it to serve as the town's museum. One of the state's finest lace collections is featured here, along with Indian artifacts, mining equipment, tools and period clothing.

5 - Julian Hotel
Julian Gold Rush Hotel, 2032 Main Street, Julian (619) 765-0201

This building was originally constructed as a bakery, in the 1890s, by the Robinsons, a freed Black couple. They enlarged the building and turned it into a hotel. Today, it remains as an operating hotel, filled with antiques and turn-of-the-century ambiance.

5 - Eagle and High Peak Mines
Eagle Mining Company, Hwy 78 and Hwy 79, Julian (619) 765-0036

Visitors to the 1870 Eagle Mine travel a thousand feet into an underground hard rock tunnel to tour the inner workings of an authentic gold mine. Antique engines, tools and machinery of the period, and gold bearing quartz veins are part of the interesting and educational displays that can be viewed.

6 - San Felipe Stage Station   SHL 793
County Road S2, northwest of Hwy 78, near Anza Borrego Desert State Park

Warren Hall built and operated a stage station at this site for the Butterfield Overland Stage Company, which operated between San Francisco, Los Angeles and St. Louis, from 1858 to 1861. Service was stopped along the Butterfield Route at the outbreak of the Civil War, in 1861, and this station became a military outpost. At the end of the war, it was used as a station on the Yuma-San Diego stage route.

7A - Anza Borrego Desert State Park
Visitor Center, 200 Palm Canyon Drive, Borrego Springs (619) 767-4205

Native American artifacts, Cahuilla and Kumeyaay pottery, San Dieguito tools, and the area's natural history are exhibited. The museum is housed inside a subterranean structure, built against a natural rock face, without exterior windows.

7 - San Gregorio SHL 673
Borrego Sink, southeast of Palm Canyon Road, Anza Borrego State Park
(619) 767-4684

Juan Bautista de Anza blazed the first inland trail across Southern California in 1774. He found water and food for his animals at a campsite on the floor of this valley.

8 - Los Puertecitos SHL 635
1 and 3/4 miles east of Ocotillo Wells on Hwy 78 (619) 767-5391

In 1775, Juan Bautista de Anza brought his party of 240 colonists through this pass, en route to Northern California, where they would form the city of San Francisco.

9 - Butterfield Stage Pass SHL 647
Blair Valley, 1/2 mile east of County Road S2, south of Hwy 78, Anza Borrego Desert State Park

The route of the old Butterfield Overland Stage can still be seen at this pass between Blair and Earthquake valleys. From 1858 to 1861, the famous Butterfield Stages ran over this pass, between St. Louis and San Francisco.

10 - Pedro Fages Trail SHL 858
Plaque on Sunrise Hwy, about 2 miles southeast of intersection with Hwy 79

In October 1772, Pedro Fages left San Diego and headed east searching for army deserters. He was the first European to enter Oriflamme Canyon. He traveled north from there over Cajon Pass, across the Mojave Desert and into the San Joaquin Valley. His historic journey opened many new areas of California and is commemorated here and at other points along his trail.

11 - Box Canyon SHL 472
8 miles south of Hwy 78 on the Great Southern Overland Stage Route of 1849, Anza Borrego Desert State Park

Passage for settlers, following the southern emigrant trail thorough this canyon was made possible by men of the Mormon Battalion who used axes to cut this pass through solid rock in January 1847. Butterfield Overland Mail Stagecoaches followed this canyon route between 1858-1861.

12 - Vallecito Stage Depot SHL 304
Vallecito Stage Station County Park, 5 miles north of Agua Caliente Springs, on the Great Southern Overland Stage Route of 1849

This sod building was erected in 1852. It served as a station on the Butterfield Stage Route between 1858 and 1861. Soldiers stationed here after the Civil War brought law and order to the region. In 1934 the original building was reconstructed and is now part of the Anza Borrego Desert State Park.

13 - Palm Spring Stage Stop SHL 639
Vallecito Creek Road, 1 and 1/2 miles east of the Great Southern Overland Stage Route of 1849, 4 and 1/2 miles south of Agua Caliente Springs, Anza Borrego Desert State Park

This site, also known as Pamitas Spring, was a stop for the Butterfield Stage Route. It ran between St. Louis, Los Angeles and San Francisco from 1858 to 1861. Before Warren Hall built his state stations here in 1858, Palm Spring was a natural resting place along this old trail.

14 - Gaskill's Stone Store SHL 411
Campo Stone Store County Park, 31130 Hwy 94, Campo (619) 478-5707

Across the street from this building was the site of a famous gunfight, between the Gaskill brothers, and a gang of Mexican bandits, on December 5, 1875. The Gaskill brothers, who survived injuries sustained in the gunfight, built this stone building several years after this battle.

14 - San Diego & Arizona Eastern Railway
San Diego Depot, 743 Imperial Avenue, Campo

Antique steam and U.S. Army diesel locomotives operate over the old San Diego & Arizona Eastern Railway line from this station at Campo. The new Pacific Southwest Railway Museum is located one-half mile from this station.

14 - Pacific Southwest Railway Museum
Hwy 94, Campo (619) 69-PSRMA (taped information)

Displayed at this branch of the San Diego Railroad Museum are nine locomotives and an extensive collection of passenger cars, freight cars and cabooses.

15 - Desert View Tower   SHL 939
Near a section of the old emigrant trail, west side of Hwy 8, near Boulder Park, Old Hwy 80, San Diego, Imperial County Lines

Desert View tower, a three-story circular stone structure and the surrounding sculpture, is one of the earliest examples of twentieth century environmental folk art in California. Robert Vaughn started building the tower from native stone in 1923, to commemorate the Mormon Trail. His work was continued in the 1930s, by M. T. Ratcliffe, who, in his off-time, carved animal figures in the rocks found around the tower.

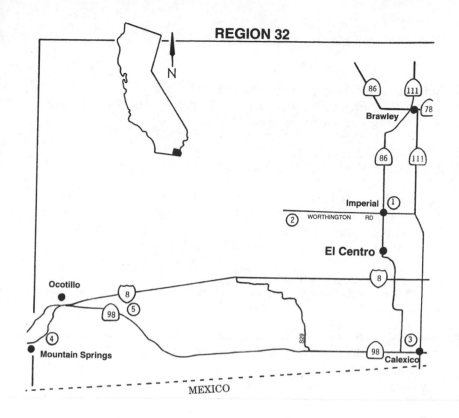

1 - Imperial Valley Pioneers Museum
Midwinter Fairgrounds, Aten Road, 204 East 2nd Street, Imperial
(619) 355-1222

Native American artifacts, pioneer farm implements and house-wares, and a pictorial history of Imperial County are exhibited in this museum.

2 - Site of Fort Romualdo Pacheco   SHL 944
West bank of New River, south of Worthington Road, 6 and 1/2 miles west of Imperial

The land route from Mexico to California, that was opened by the expeditions of Juan Bautista de Anza, in 1774 and 1775, was closed in 1781 following the massacre of Spanish soldiers, male settlers and padres, by Yuma Indians. Romualdo Pacheco established a Mexican fort here in 1825, to provide protection along the route. After an attack by Yuma Indians, in 1826, which took the lives of three Mexican soldiers, the fort was abandoned.

3 - Camp Salvation SHL 808
Plaque at Rockwood Plaza Park, at 5th and Heber, Calexico

Lt. Cave J. Couts, escort commander of the International Boundary Commission established Camp Salvation, on this site, in September 1849. This outpost served as a refugee center, for emigrants traveling the southern emigrant trail, through December of that year.

4 - Mountain Springs Station SHL 194
East of San Diego County Line on I-8, marker in Boulder Park at Desert Tower

Many historic trails were made across the Imperial Valley by explorers, settlers and Argonauts. At many places, tracks left by the emigrant wagons, old plank roads and ruins of early structures, such as this old stage station, can still be seen.

South of the In-Ko-Pah exit off I-8, via a rough dirt road, are spectacular granite rock formations and historic Smugglers Cave. Bandits, opium smugglers and outlaws of the old west used these natural hide-outs during the late 1800s and early 1900s. A map of this area's natural sites is available from the Bureau of Land Management. (714) 351-6394.

5 - Yuha Well SHL 1008
In the desert, midway between I-8 and Highway 98, southeast of Coyote Wells

This site was an important, and essential, encampment for Juan Bautista de Anza's Expeditions of 1774, and 1775-1776. Father Francisco Garces, and a Christian Indian, Sebastian Tarabal, guided the first Anza Party across the desert to these wells in March 1774. In December 1775, Anza stopped here with the 240 colonists that he was leading from Sonora to Alta California across the land route he established on his previous expedition.

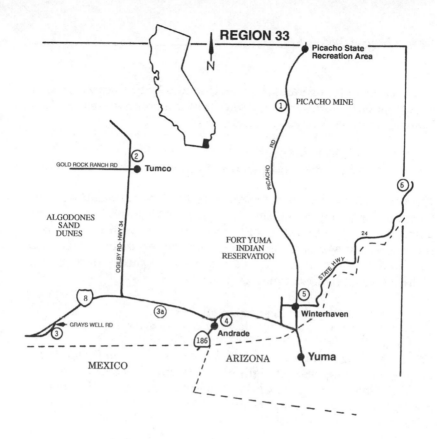

REGION 33

N

Picacho State
Recreation Area

PICACHO MINE ①

PICACHO RD

② GOLD ROCK RANCH RD ● Tumco

OGILBY RD - HWY 34

ALGODONES
SAND
DUNES

FORT YUMA
INDIAN
RESERVATION

⑥

24

STATE HWY

⑧

GRAYS WELL RD

③a

⑤

Winterhaven

③

④ Andrade

186

MEXICO

ARIZONA ● Yuma

---

1 - Picacho Mines SHL 193
4 miles south of Picacho State Recreation Area headquarters on Picacho Road (619) 339-1360

The richest placer gold area in Southern California was discovered at this site, in 1860, by an Indian. Mexican prospectors arrived in 1862, and the town of Picacho developed into a typical Mexican community, complete with arenas for bullfights. Picacho Mines are located on private property about five miles south of the town which is now Picacho State Recreation Area.

2 - Tumco Mines SHL 182
8 miles north of I-8 via Ogilby Road, east of Gold Rock Ranch Road

Ruins and old mine shafts are all that remain of the town of Tumco. It once had a population of over 2,000 people. From 1884, until 1914, gold mines were operated by the United Mines Company. The town's name, "Tumco" is an acronym of the company name, "The United Mines Company."

3 - Old Plank Road SHL 845
Plaque at Algodones Rest Area, south of I-8, 18 miles west of Winterhaven

The first automobile roads through the Imperial sand dunes were made of wooden planks. They were laid seven miles across these dunes, in 1916-1917. Teams of horses would move the 8 X 12 foot sections whenever shifting sand would cover them. This road provided the only access for cars across the dunes until a new highway was constructed in 1927.

3A - Charley's World of Lost Art SHL 939
On a dirt road northwest of Andrade, south of Hwy 8, Imperial County

Charles Kasling's sculpture garden of stone and cement figures is the largest, and youngest, of California's twentieth century folk art environments. "Driftwood Charley" began his work in 1967, creating a world of miniature villages, biblical scenes and skillfully crafted fantasy animals.

4 - Hernando de Alarcon Expedition SHL 568
5 and 1/2 miles west of Winterhaven, 1 and 1/2 miles south on Hwy 186 at All-American Canal

The first known white man to set foot on California soil was Hernando de Alarcon, in May 1540. Alarcon reached this region by sailing north from Acapulco, Mexico, to the mouth of the Colorado River. He discovered the Colorado River, and proved that Baja California was a peninsula, not an island.

5 - Site of Mission Purisima Concepcion SHL 350
St. Thomas Indian Mission, Indian Hill, on Picacho Road, Fort Yuma, 1 mile south of Winterhaven

Two missions were established by Franciscan Padres in 1780. They were situated about twelve miles apart to serve as way stations on the overland emigrant trail, between Mexico and the West Coast of California. Local Yuma Indians resented this intrusion by the white man on their lands. On July 17, 1781, after being harassed by mission soldiers, Indians attacked both missions and killed every white man . . . including the padres. Today, the Quechan Indian Church stands on the ruins of the old mission. Father Francisco Garces, the famous priest explorer, who was among the padres that lost their lives in this tragic massacre, is honored by a statue erected on this site.

5 - Fort Yuma   SHL 806
350 Picacho Road, bank of the Colorado River, Winterhaven

Fort Yuma was established on the site of the old Mission Purisima, in 1850, to provide protection along the emigrant trail. The fort was abandoned, after an attack by the Yuma Indians, in the summer of 1851. Today, a Catholic chapel stands on this site, along with a statue of Father Garces, who was massacred by Indians at the mission in July 1781.

6 - Site of Mission San Pedro y San Pablo   SHL 921
12 and 1/2 miles northeast of Winterhaven on County Road 24, intersection of LeVee and Mehring Roads

The only missions established inland from El Camino Real were along the overland emigrant trail, between Mexico and the West Coast of California. Located twelve miles apart, they were established as way-stations along this overland supply route. Local Yuma Indians resented the settlers, and mission padres, that took their land. They attacked both missions in July 1781. Following this massacre, in which every white man was killed, the Spaniards abandoned the overland trail to California.

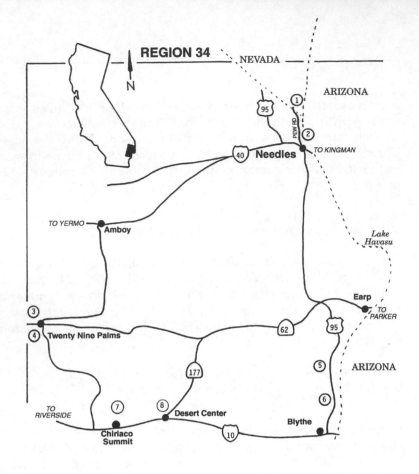

1 - Von Schmidt State Boundary Monument SHL 859
East side of Pew Road, 15 miles north of Needles

A. W. Von Schmidt made the first official survey of the California-Nevada State boundary in 1872-1873. This cast iron, boundary marker was placed in 1873, by Von Schmidt, but the actual boundary line was corrected to a location about three-fourths mile north in a later survey.

2 - Old Indian Trail Monument   SHL 781
Eastern entrance to the city of Needles, North "K" Street

The first white man to cross the San Bernardino Mountains was Spanish Padre Francisco Garces, in 1776. During 1826-1827, Jedediah Strong Smith was the first American to make this crossing. Markings on the rock at this site are Indian petroglyphs.

2 - Needles Museum
923 Front, Needles (909) 326-5678

Local historical items are displayed here, and at Pacific Federal Bank. Outdoor displays can be seen on Broadway and at Santa Fe Park.

3 - Twentynine Palms Historical Museum
6136 Adobe Road, Twentynine Palms (619) 367-3445

Operated by the Twentynine Palms Historical Society, this museum contains items of local historical importance, artifacts on loan from pioneer families and special hands-on programs for children.

4 - Joshua Tree National Monument
74485 National Monument Drive, at Utah Drive, Twentynine Palms
(619) 367-7511

The visitor center contains a museum of natural history and information about the historic Twentynine Palms Oasis.

5 - Giant Desert Figures   SHL 101
1/2 mile west of U.S. 95, 16 miles north of Blythe

An ancient Indian culture made giant figures, the largest of which is 167 feet long, by clearing this mesa of pebbles and using them to make the figure outlines. They were first sighted from an aircraft.

6 - Site of Blythe Intake   SHL 948
On U.S. 95, 4 and 1/2 miles north of Blythe at entrance to Palo Verde Diversion Dam

Thomas Blythe financed the construction of these waterworks in 1877, diverting the waters of the Colorado River for this pioneer land reclamation project.

7 - Desert Training Center, California-Arizona Maneuver Area SHL 985
General Patton Memorial Museum, #2 Chiriaco Road, Chiriaco Summit
(619) 774-7388

In February 1942, the War Department assigned Major General George S. Patton, Jr., the responsibility to establish DTC (Desert Training Center). Here, troops and equipment could be trained, and tested under conditions that they would be likely to encounter while fighting Germans in North Africa. The world's largest military training ground, a network of eleven camps, was established across an 18,000 square mile area that stretched from: Indio, California; to Prescott, Arizona; and from Searchlight, Nevada; to Yuma, Arizona. More than a million men were trained in these camps during the 23 months that DTC was in operation. Today, the General Patton Memorial Museum stands at the original site of Camp Young, where Patton had his headquarters.

8 - Site of Contractors General Hospital SHL 992
Along the Metropolitan Water District's Colorado River Aqueduct, about 6 miles west of Desert Center

Kaiser Permanente, the "granddaddy of HMOs" began in a small, wood-frame, twelve-bed hospital. It was built here in 1933, by Dr. Sidney Garfield, to bring medical care to workmen building the California Aqueduct. Dr. Garfield's practice was thriving, but wasn't profitable. Many of his depression-era patients were unable to pay in full for their personal medical care and the hospital was facing closure. Harold Hatch, of the Industrial Indemnity Company, suggested that five cents per worker, per day, from contractors' premiums for work-related injuries be pre-paid to the hospital. In return, Dr. Garfield would provide care as needed. Garfield then offered the same pre-paid plan to workers for their non-industrial medical care. Within a few years, he had two more hospitals operating along the aqueduct. He established another at Washington State's, Grand Coulee Dam, for Henry J. Kaiser. During World War II, 200,000 West Coast ship workers were covered by the plan. In 1945, the Kaiser Permanente Medical Care Program was offered to the public.

1 - Cabot's Old Indian Pueblo Museum
67-616 East Desert View Avenue, Desert Hot Springs (619) 329-7610

This Hopi Indian style, pueblo museum was built, in 1913, of earth and wood collected from the desert. Cabot Yerxa's four-story structure contains 35 rooms of Indian costumes, pottery, beads and artifacts. Among the unusual exhibits are Eskimo artifacts, an Indian monument carved from a Giant Sequoia redwood, and a tomahawk and shield from Custer's battlefield.

2 - Palm Springs Desert Museum
101 Museum Drive, Palm Springs (619) 325-0189

Primary displays include: Indian artifacts, rugs and basketry, as well as sculpture and art of the American West. A natural science center, theater, and changing exhibits are also part of this 75,000 square foot cultural center.

2 - Village Green Heritage Center
221 South Palm Canyon Drive, Palm Springs (619) 323-8197

Two historic homes, from the late 1800s, are preserved here with exhibits of period artifacts, photographs and antiques. The oldest structure is this adobe home of the area's first white settler. The second building was constructed from old railroad ties. Both were moved to this location and are preserved by the Palm Springs Historical Society.

3 - Coachella Valley Museum and Cultural Center
82-616 Miles Avenue, Indio (619) 342-6651

Housed in a 1920 adobe, this museum features Cahuilla Indian baskets, artifacts, and the history of the region's large date industry.

4 - The Living Desert
47-900 South Portola Road, Palm Desert (619) 346-5694

Pre-historic plants, exotic desert life in natural settings, a walk-through bird aviary and endangered species are featured exhibits of this wild animal park and botanical garden. Within the Cahuilla Indian Gardens, visitors learn about the plants that they used for food, fiber, medicine and housing material.

5 - Desert Christ Park
Antone Martin Memorial Park, Mohawk Trail off Hwy 62, Yucca Valley (619) 369-7212

Sculptor, Antone Martin, created this "World Peace Shrine," between 1953 and 1961. It was his concept of "peace on Earth, and goodwill toward men." Historical biblical scenes, from the life of Jesus Christ, were the inspiration for the 35 pieces he sculpted in this desert setting. Martin's impression of the "Last Supper" is displayed on a massive 125-ton, three-story facade overlooking the valley.

REGION 36

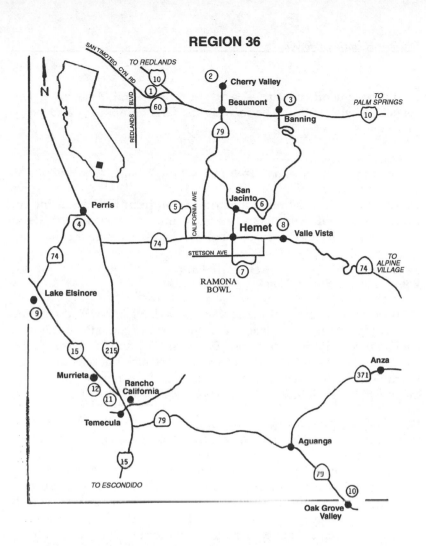

1 - Indian Village of Saahatpa   SHL 749
Marker at the Brookside Rest Area, west bound on I-10, 3 miles west of junction I-10 and Hwy 60

The leader of the Cahuilla Indians, Juan Antonio, founded the village of Saahatpa, in the San Timoteo Canyon, during the 1850s.

2 - Edward-Dean Museum of Decorative Arts
9401 Oak Glenn Road, Cherry Valley (909) 845-2626

This unusual museum features antique furniture, from the sixteenth to the nineteenth centuries, and European and Asia art. The collections also include: paperweights, fans, miniatures and ivory carvings.

3 - Malki Museum
Morongo Indian Reservation, 11-795 Fields Road, Banning (909) 849-7289

Heirlooms of the Cahuilla, and other Southern California Indian tribes, are exhibited in this Indian museum. Indians staff the Malki Museum and explain the history behind the pieces in their collection.

3 - Gilman Ranch County Historic Park
Wilson and 16th Streets, Banning (909) 922-9200

Archaeologists digging at this historic park, have uncovered remains of the oldest permanent structure in the San Gorgonio Pass, the 1854 adobe house built by Jose Pope. Between 1862 and 1879, the adobe was used as a stage stop, post office, general store, and as the home for the ranch's last owner, James Gilman and his family. Several of the ranch's original buildings have been restored.

4 - Orange Empire Railway Museum
2201 South "A" Street, Perris (909) 657-2605

This 50-acre museum features three locomotives from the 1920s; and more than 140 other pieces of interesting and unusual railroad equipment. Streetcars, trolleys and work cars are on display, as well as an old railway post office, a model train display, and a 1882 dugout-type general store. Trains and streetcars operate on a track around the museum property and along an original right-of-way. An 1887 railroad station can be seen in the town of Perris.

5 - Indian Maze Stone   SHL 557
California Avenue, 5 miles west of Hemet in Maze Stone Park (909) 787-2553

Protected in this county park is a large granite boulder on which an Indian petroglyph has been carved. Ancient Indian carvings, and paintings, are found throughout California, and in the Northwest. Their source and meaning are not known. The only other carved rock, similar in markings to this one, is in the Northwest United States.

Los Angeles Railway No. 665. Courtesy of Orange Empire Railway Museum.

Ventura County Railway No. 2. Courtesy of Orange Empire Railway Museum.

6 - San Jacinto Valley Museum
181 East Main, San Jacinto (909) 654-4952

Founded in 1939, this museum has an extensive collection of historical items from the San Jacinto Valley area, including Indian archaeological findings.

6 - Soviet Transploar Landing Site SHL 989
Near the intersection of Cottonwood and Sanderson Streets, west of San Jacinto

Three Soviet aviators landed their single-engine ANT-25 near this site on July 14, 1937. This site marks the first successful circumnavigation of the North Pole, while simultaneously establishing an international flight record for duration and distance. The nearly 6,700-mile flight from Moscow, earned the crew local and international recognition, and a personal meeting with President Franklin Roosevelt at the White House.

7 - Ramona Bowl, Site of the Ramona Pageant SHL 1009
27400 Ramona Bowl Road, Hemet (909) 658-3111

Outdoor pageants were a popular form of entertainment, throughout California, during the 1900-1929 period. The Ramona Pageant, which was first presented in this natural, open-air amphitheater, in the spring of 1923, is the state's oldest continuing outdoor drama. Garnet Holme, who was named "Pageant Master" of our national parks, wrote and directed the original Ramona Pageant, which was based on Helen Hunt Jackson's best-selling, 1884 novel, *Ramona*. Improvements have been made in, and around, the bowl, and a small history museum was added in 1952, but the pageant continues to be presented in the style that made it successful year after year.

7 - Site of Indian Village of Pochea SHL 104
3/4 mile east of the Ramona Bowl, Hemet, Marker at the Ramona Bowl

Evidence of the ancient Indian Village of Pochea can be seen in the large number of metate grinding holes in these rocks. The Indians left this village site after losing many of their tribe members to measles which they contracted from the Spaniards who came here in the 1770s.

7 - Guy B. Woodward Museum of History
645 Main Street, Ramona (619) 789-7644

This structure was built in 1886, as a "country place," by San Diego restaurateur, Theophile Verlaque. It is the only remaining adobe home of French Provincial architecture, west of New Orleans. The Ramona Pioneer Historical Society acquired Verlaque House in 1984. They have restored each room to depict the interior setting of early Santa Maria Valley settlers' homes. A baby grand piano, made in Austria in 1870, for the King of Austria, sits in the parlor. Antiques and period furniture; a horse hide trunk, lined with newspapers published from 1802 to 1815; and a circa 1880 cabinetmaker's chest, with one of the most complete sets of woodworking tools in existence, are among the artifacts on display. The Cowboy's Hall of Fame selected this museum as the exhibit center for the memorial to Casey Tibbs, World Champion rodeo rider and local resident. The outdoor ranch setting includes an 1874 cowboy bunk house, blacksmith shop, tack room, wagons, farm implements and tools.

8 - Site of Anza's Camp SHL 103
Cary Ranch, 60901 Coyote Canyon Road, southeast of Anza

Juan Bautista de Anza, the first white explorer to travel overland into California, discovered San Carlos Pass and camped here in March 1774. From here he traveled inland to Monterey. The following year he brought a party of 240 Spanish colonists through the same pass on their journey to settle the city that became San Francisco.

9 - "Chimes" House
201 West Graham, Lake Elsinore (714) 674-3456

An artesian well at this site produced hot mineral waters in the 1880s, which brought about the construction of a major health resort, known as the Crescent Bathhouse. This two-story colonial building, constructed of redwood, still stands and is now called The Chimes.

10 - Camp Wright SHL 482
Hwy 79, Oak Grove (714) 674-3456

Camp Wright was built during the Civil War to maintain communications between California and Arizona. The only encounter of the

Civil War in California, took place here, when a group of Southern sympathizers from El Monte, were captured on their way to join the Confederate Army. Across the road from this site was the Oak Grove Stage Station which was used as a hospital for Camp Wright during the Civil War (1861-1866).

10 - Oak Grove Stage Station   SHL 502
Hwy 79, Oak Grove

During the Butterfield Overland Stage era (1858-1861), part of this adobe building was used as a stage station. This building is one of the few remaining stations to be seen along the famous route. It has been registered as a National Historic Landmark.

11 - Jose Maria Gonzales Adobe
Old Adobe Plaza, Jefferson Avenue and Overland Drive, Rancho California

The 1879 adobe home of Temecula Valley pioneer, Jose Maria Gonzales, has been meticulously restored as the centerpiece of a new nine-acre Rancho California shopping center. The Basque origin of Gonzales is reflected in the Mediterranean-style design of the other 21 stores in the center.

12 - Santa Rosa Rancho   SHL 1005
22115 Tenaja Road, near Murrieta

Evidence of man's 6,000-year presence in this region is preserved in the California Nature Conservancy's, 3,000-acre, Santa Rosa Plateau Preserve. The 13-acre Santa Rosa Rancho historical site, located on this preserve contains adobe homes of the Rancho's owners from around 1840 to 1963. The Parker Dear family, who owned most of the ranch between 1876 and 1900, were well known for their hospitality. They entertained lavishly, with their annual May Day Picnic drawing over 2,000 guests. Walter Vail bought the ranch in 1904. For 60 years his family successfully operated an immense, 96,000-acre, cattle ranch that dominated the economy of several western states.

1 - Glendora Bougainvillea SHL 912
Intersection of East Bennett and North Minnesota Avenues, Glendora

The largest growth of this exotic vine plant, in the United States, was planted here in 1901, by Ruben Hamlin, one of the area's early citrus growers. This plant was discovered in South America, by Louis Antoine de Bougainville, and brought to California in the 1870s. These flowering plants now cover the bottom part of two dozen palm trees along Bennett and Minnesota Avenues.

1 - Glendora Historical Society Museum
314 North Glendora Avenue, Glendora (818) 963-0419

The history of the Glendora area, which traces its roots to Native Americans who lived here 8,000 years ago, is preserved and exhibited in its first city hall building, which was constructed in 1913. In addition to the City Hall, this restored building also housed the police and fire departments, the jail and post office. Bars of the old jail cells are still visible in some of the building's windows.

Glendora Historical Society Museum. Courtesy of Glendora Historical Society Museum.

2 - San Dimas Mansion
121 North San Dimas Avenue, San Dimas

In the late 1880s, the San Jose Ranch Co. engaged the noted California architect, Joseph Newsome, to build the San Dimas Hotel on this part of the old San Jose Rancho. Before it could be put into use, the land boom collapsed. San Dimas' largest house was purchased by Mr. and Mrs. J. W. Walker, in 1889, and subsequently lived in by six generations of their family. The first church services in San Dimas were conducted in the parlor and the basement housed the first school. Not open to the public.

2 - Carrion Adobe   SHL 386
919 Puddingstone Drive, La Verne

La Casa de Carrion was built in 1864, as the home of Saturnino Carrion, and his wife Dolores. Building materials were brought from the Pueblo de Los Angeles to this site by ox-drawn carretas. The family moved away in the early 1900s, when construction of Puddingstone Dam inundated a portion of their land. Some additions have been made to this one-and-a-half-story structure, which is now preserved as a private residence.

2 - La Verne Heritage Park
Via de Mansion, east off Wheeler, La Verne

Two circa 1908, redwood buildings have been restored in a setting reminiscent of the citrus ranches that dotted this area during the first part of the twentieth century. A small grove of lemon and orange trees, a Victorian-style gazebo, turn-of-the-century lampposts, and antique farm implements, add to the realism and help preserve the heritage of La Verne's early days.

_Weber House,
La Verne
Heritage Park._

3 - Site of Pioneer Hydroelectric Power Plant SHL 514
Mt. Baldy Road, San Antonio Canyon

The first long distance transmission of high voltage alternating current in California, was accomplished with the construction of a hydroelectric power plant here in 1892. George Westinghouse's high voltage transformers brought 10,000 volts of electricity to the town of Pomona from this pioneer power plant. Only ruins of the building's foundation remain to be seen today.

4 - Chaffey Communities Cultural Center
525 West 18th Street, Upland (909) 982-8010

Old St. Marks Church, designed in 1911, by Mission Inn architect, Arthur Benton, was moved to this site in 1965. It houses the 9,000-item collection of Upland, Ontario, Rancho Cucamonga, Montclair, and Mt. Baldy history. A 1940s citrus grove, caretaker's cottage, and a two-acre orange and lemon grove, are also maintained at this site.

4 - Madonna of the Trail
Monument at Euclid Avenue and Foothill Boulevard, Upland

Pioneer mothers, who emigrated to California by covered wagon, are honored by this monument along the National Old Trails Highway. In Spanish days, before the first American settlers arrived, Padres traveled this road between the missions. Under Mexican rule, this road was the main link between San Bernardino and Los Angeles. In November 1826, Jedediah Smith and a band of 16 trappers, the first Americans to enter California over land, followed this trail seeking a river flowing westward. Thousands of travelers passed over this roadway when it became part of the old U.S. Route 66 in the 1930s.

Madonna of the Trail Monument.

5 - Rancho Cucamonga Winery   SHL 490
8916 Foothill Boulevard, Rancho Cucamonga

California's oldest commercial winery was begun here in 1839 by Tiburcio Tapia who planted, "Black Mission Grape" cuttings, from the Mission San Gabriel. In 1858, John Rains purchased the vineyard from Tapia's daughter and built an adobe winery. Two, 1400-gallon oak aging casks, were installed in the winery. H. H. Thomas restored the winery and operated it as the Thomas Vineyards well into the twentieth century. An original structure from this pioneer winery has been preserved within this commercial development.

_Rancho Cucamonga
Winery._

5 - Route 66 Museum and Visitor Center
Thomas Winery Plaza, 8916 Foothill Boulevard, Rancho Cucamonga
(909) 948-9166

Memorabilia from the 1930s, to the 1960s, collected from along former U.S. Highway 66, are exhibited in this new museum. Road signs, period lampposts, gas pumps, historic photographs and old maps are among the items in the museum's growing collection.

5 - Site of Tapia Adobe   SHL 360
1/4 mile north of Rancho Cucamonga, marker at Rancho Cucamonga Winery, 8916 Foothill Boulevard, Rancho Cucamonga

Cucamonga Indian lands were granted to Tiburcio Tapia, in 1839, by Governor Juan Bautista Alvarado of Mexico, as a Mexican land grant. Tapia built an adobe mansion and covered its roof with tar from the La Brea Tar Pits in Los Angeles. Most of his original grant has been developed into residential home sites and nothing remains of the historic Tapia mansion.

5 - John Rains House (Casa de Rancho Cucamonga)
8810 Hemlock Street, Rancho Cucamonga (909) 989-4970

The oldest fired-brick building in San Bernardino County was constructed in 1860, by John and Merced Rains. This home, of the heiress of Rancho Chino, has been restored as part of the San Bernardino County Museum. Historical items and furnishings, from the 1860s and 1870s, are exhibited throughout the building.

6 - First Home of Pomona College   SHL 289
Marker on southwest corner of Mission Boulevard and South White Street, Pomona

Pomona College, the founding member of the Claremont Colleges, had its beginning in the small house at this site, in 1888. Five months later the college moved to an unfinished hotel (now Sumner Hall, in Claremont) donated to the college by the Santa Fe Railroad.

6 - Adobe de Palomares   SHL 372
Ygnacio Palomares Adobe
491 Arrow Hwy, Pomona (909) 623-2198

On this section of Rancho San Jose, Ygnacio Palomares built his 13-room,adobe house, in 1854. It became a popular stop for 20-mule team freighters, emigrants, and stages on this road to San Bernardino. An extensive restoration was undertaken in the 1930s, preserving this adobe and its gardens. The Historical Society of Pomona Valley maintains this adobe and its antique furnishings.

6 - The Railway and Locomotive Historical Society
Los Angeles County Fairgrounds, Gate 12, White Avenue, Pomona
(909) 623-0190

Arcadia's Santa Fe Railroad Station was built in 1895. It was moved here, in 1954, to serve as a museum for historical railroad artifacts and as the headquarters for the Railway and Locomotive Historical Society. A collection of old steam locomotives and rolling stock, including the largest steam locomotive and diesel locomotive in the world, are maintained by the society at this museum. The museum is open during the Los Angeles County Fair and at other times throughout the year.

6 - Temporary Detention Camps For Japanese-Americans SHL 934
Los Angeles County Fairgrounds, White Avenue, south of Arrow Hwy,
Pomona (909) 623-3111

After Japan declared war on the United States in 1941, all Japanese
and Japanese-Americans, on the West Coast, were ordered to report
to temporary detention camps, for relocation to permanent camps
across the United States. They were held in these camps until the
end of World War II. Population here reached a maximum of 5,434
people in the three months that the Pomona Fairgrounds operated as
an assembly center.

6 - Phillips Mansion
2640 Pomona Boulevard, Pomona (909) 623-2198

One of this area's first brick structures was the 1875 home of German
immigrant, Louis Phillips. In 1966, the Historical Society of Pomona
Valley purchased Phillips' home and restored it to its original
condition. It has been refurnished with Victorian antiques and
original pieces from the Phillips' family collection.

7 - Site of the Rancho Chino Adobe SHL 942
4440 Eucalyptus Avenue, Fire Station No. 2, Chino

Isaac Williams built an adobe mansion in the early 1840s, at this site,
on the Rancho Santa Ana del Chino. He built one of the first
gristmills in Southern California, and engaged in extensive cattle and
sheep ranching. During the Mexican War of 1846, this was the site of
a battle that cost the life of one Mexican. From 1858-1861, this was a
station on the famous Butterfield Stage route between St. Louis and
San Francisco. Nothing remains today of those pioneer structures.

7 - Planes of Fame Air Museum
7000 Merrill Avenue (World War II Cal-Aero Field, Chino Airport), Chino
(909) 597-3722

The first aviation museum in the West was established at this airport.
Historical aircraft are maintained here and flown in air shows.
Among the historic planes exhibited are: rare planes that once fought
in Europe and the Pacific; the only remaining flying Japanese Zero;
and a F4U "Corsair." On the weekends, a B-17 bomber is open for an
inside tour and many, one-of-a-kind aircraft are displayed.

7 - Yorba-Slaughter Adobe   SHL 191
17127 Pomona-Rincon Road, 5 and 1/2 miles south of Chino off Hwy 71
(909) 597-8832

Raimundo Yorba built this single story adobe house in 1850-1853, on this 47,000-acre ranchero. A relay station, for the Butterfield Stages, was maintained from 1858-1861. In 1868, Yorba sold his adobe, and 3,000 acres of land, to Fenton Slaughter, who put two additions on the building. This restored adobe and its furnishings, many of which were purchased by the Slaughter's in Boston, and shipped around the Horn, became the property of the San Bernardino County Museum in 1971. On the grounds of this fine museum is a restored winery, post office and a country store.

8 - Site of Rubidoux's First Gristmill   SHL 303
5504 Molina Way, Rubidoux, plaque at Jurupa Hills Country Club Golf Course (909) 685-7214

The first gristmill in this area was constructed in 1846-1847, by Louis Rubidoux, pioneer businessman and civic leader. One of the mill-stones has been moved to the historic Mission Inn, in Riverside. The second millstone remains here, at the mill's original site.

8 - Jensen-Alvarado Ranch Historic Park
4307 Briggs Street, Rubidoux (909) 369-6055

Captain Cornelius Jensen, a native of the Frisian Isle of Sylt, traded his life at sea, to become a merchant in Sacramento during the Gold Rush era. He came to Southern California in the early 1850s, and married Mercedes Alvarado, the daughter of one of California's prominent families. In 1856, he was elected to his first, of nine, terms as a San Bernardino County Supervisor. In 1865, Cornelius and his wife, Mercedes, purchased part of the Rubidoux Rancho. Using local labor, and materials, they built the region's first brick home. The home, a mansion for its day, was constructed in a style reminiscent of the sea captains' homes in Jensen's homeland. The original home, and brick outbuildings, are preserved in an 1880s ranch setting at this historic park.

Jensen-Alvarado House c. 1870. Photo from the Jensen-Alvarado Ranch collection, Riverside Regional Park and Openspace District.

9 - Jurupa Mountains Cultural Center
7621 Granite Hill Drive, Riverside (909) 685-5818

Located on an early Indian campsite, this museum features a collection of Indian artifacts. Natural history of the area is also exhibited.

9 - Site of Louis Rubidoux Adobe   SHL 102
5500 block of Mission Boulevard, Riverside

Louis Rubidoux settled here with his family in the 1840s and later purchased the Wilson Adobe. He became an important businessman, judge and supervisor in what was then known as West Riverside.

9 - Mission Inn   SHL 761
Mission Inn Museum, 3649 - 7th Street, Riverside (909) 781-8241

In 1875, Captain C. C. Miller built an adobe structure on this site as a guest house. The present Mission Inn was built around the old adobe cottage, which stood until 1952. The architectural influence of the 21 California Missions can be seen in the Mission Inn—the largest Mission Revival building in the state. Antique furnishings, paintings from around the world, a millstone from the historic Rubidoux gristmill, Tiffany windows, 650 bells, and historic Spanish and Mexican items are some of the interesting features of this famous inn.

9 - Riverside Municipal Museum
3720 Orange Street, Riverside (909) 782-5273

The history of the orange industry, from its birthplace in Riverside, to its influence on Southern California, is featured. Local Native American culture, and the history of early settlers who followed the De Anza Expeditions of 1774-1776 are displayed.

9 - Universalist-Unitarian Church
3657 Lemon Street, Riverside (909) 686-6515

The oldest Unitarian Church in the West was built here, in 1891, out of red sandstone from Arizona. A medievel English influence can be seen inside this Gothic-style structure.

9 - Riverside Historic Tour
Chamber of Commerce, 4261 Main Street, Riverside (909) 683-7100

Almost forty buildings and historic sites are included in Riverside's historic tour. Many of the buildings are within a short walking distance of the Mission Inn. A guide is available from the Chamber of Commerce, Mission Inn, and Riverside Municipal Museum.

9 - Parent Navel Orange Tree in California   SHL 20
Magnolia and Arlington Streets, Riverside (909) 787-7950

It was from this navel orange tree that the famous California orange industry had its beginning. In the 1870s, Mrs. Eliza Tibbets received two Brazilian seedling orange trees from Washington D.C., which she raised at her home in Riverside. By 1895, 20,000 acres of navel orange trees covered the Riverside area. All had been started from the bud stock of this tree. In 1902, one of the original trees was replanted here at this memorial where it still bears fruit.

9 - Heritage House (Riverside)
8193 Magnolia Avenue, Riverside (909) 689-1333

The founder of the California Fruit Growers Exchange, James Bettner, built this two-story mansion in 1891. Its original gas lighting fixtures were converted to electricity in 1906. Original family items, and period furnishings, can be seen in this restored home. It is now administered by the Riverside Municipal Museum.

9 - Sherman Indian Museum
9010 Magnolia Avenue, Riverside (909) 276-6719

Local Indian history is featured in this museum. It is located in what was once the center of education for young, Indian males. Originally known as the Sherman Institute, it is now the Sherman Indian High School's, administration building.

10 - Site of Anza's Crossing of the Santa Ana River   SHL 787
Marked near the Union Pacific Bridge, Santa Ana River Regional Park, south of Rubidoux

In December 1775, Captain Juan Bautista de Anza brought the first party of white settlers across the San Carlos Pass, which he had discovered the prior year. On January 1, 1776, his party crossed the Santa Ana River, at this site, on their journey to become the first white settlers of San Francisco. A child, born during this party's journey, was the first white child born in California.

11 - Corona Founders Monument   SHL 738
Marker at City Park, 1000 block of 6th Street, Corona

The city of Corona was founded from lands that were part of Rancho La Sierra of Bernardo Yorba, in 1886. This monument was placed here to honor the founders of Corona.

11 - The Heritage Room
Corona Public Library, 650 South Main Street, Corona (909) 736-2386

Corona's new library building features a local history room where memorabilia and artifacts of the "Circle City" are exhibited. Photographs displayed by the Historic Heritage Committee include: the 1913-1916 road races on Grand Boulevard—the road that encircles the city; the grand buildings which once graced the city; and the pioneer citrus industry that made Corona the "Lemon Capitol of the World."

11 - Butterfield Stage Station Site   SHL 188
20730 Temescal Canyon Road, south of Cajalco Road junction, near the fire station, Corona

The adobe building, which once stood here, was a station on the famous Butterfield Stage route between St. Louis and San Francisco. The Civil War brought an end to the Butterfield Stage in 1861, but other lines traveled this old stage route through the end of the century.

12 - Painted Indian Rock   SHL 190
East of Temescal Canyon Road and north of Dawson Canyon Road, north of Glen Ivy Hot Springs

An interesting Indian pictograph was discovered on this rock when it was originally uncovered, along the Santa Fe Railroad right-of-way in the 1920s. Vandals have since obliterated this fine example of Temecula Indian writings.

12 - Serrano Tanning Vats   SHL 186
Temescal Canyon Road, southeast off I-15, between Corona and Glen Ivy Hot Springs

In the early 1880s, Indians used these stone tanning vats, on Leandro Serrano's ranchero, to tan hides. The third adobe that Serrano constructed on his ranchero was built near here in the 1840s.

12 - Site of Third Serrano Adobe   SHL 224
Temescal Canyon Road, southeast off I-15, between Corona and Glen Ivy Hot Springs

Leandro Serrano came to these Mission San Luis Rey lands in 1818. He built the first house in Riverside County, established a sheep and cattle ranch, and in the 1840s built his third adobe, at this site near the tanning vats. Serrano died in 1852. His family continued to live here for more than forty years after his death.

12 - Carved Indian Rock   SHL 187
187 Dawson Canyon Road, northeast of Glen Ivy Hot Springs

Although severely damaged, some of the carvings made by ancient Temecula Indians can still be seen on this rock. Indian petroglyphs, such as these, exist throughout California and the Western United States.

12 - Old Temescal Road   SHL 638
Temescal Canyon at Wrangler Way, Corona

This section of Highway 71 follows the old Temescal Road used by ancient Indians; emigrants to California, along the southern emigrant trail; Argonauts; and the Overland Stages. This historic pioneer road has been commemorated by this monument.

12 - Site of First House in Riverside County   SHL 185
West of I-15, near junction of Lawson Drive and Temescal Canyon Road, north of Glen Ivy Hot Springs, site is on private property

Leandro Serrano, the son of a soldier who came to California with Father Junipero Serra, built the first house in Riverside County at this site. Serrano engaged in sheep and cattle ranching after local Indians helped him rid the area of bears and mountain cats.

13 - March Field Museum
Van Buren Boulevard, off I-215, March Air Force Base, Building 420, Riverside (909) 655-3725

Air Force uniforms, photographs, and the history of this branch of the military service are exhibited, along with a collection of 50 vintage planes. Bombers, fighters, helicopters and a U-2 spy plane, are among the Air Force's historic collection maintained at this base museum.

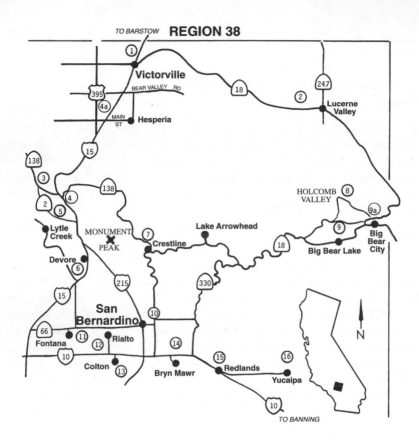

1 - Roy Rogers - Dale Evans Museum
15650 Seneca Road, Victorville (619) 243-4547

Personal and professional memorabilia of Roy Rogers and Dale Evans is exhibited here.

2 - Chimney Rock   SHL 737
Hwy 18 and Grapevine Canyon, Rabbit Springs Road, Lucerne Valley

The final conflict, between Indians and settlers in Southern California, took place at this campsite in January 1867. The Indians, who returned here to their campsite, after raiding and looting a lumber camp in the San Bernardino Mountains, were surprised by an armed posse. Many Indians were killed or wounded in the ensuing battle—a battle that brought an end to these hostilities.

3 - Mormon Trail Monument   SHL 577
Hwy 138, West Cajon Canyon

Five hundred Mormon pioneers brought their heavy wagons through this pass, in 1851, en route to eventual settlement in the San Bernardino Valley. The trail followed by these pioneer settlers is commemorated by this monument.

4A - Hula Ville   SHL 939
West side of I-15 on Amargosa Road, at the city borders of Hesperia and Victorville

A garden of poetry, inscribed on pieces of plywood, Japanese bottle "trees," and larger-than-life symbols from an earlier time, decorate Miles Mahan's road-side stretch of desert property along this section of old Route 66. Nicknames of "old-timers" he knew and respected are inscribed on homemade plaques: Freeway Annie, Old Orville, Roadrunner Dick, Dirty Neck George; as well as the more famous, Death Valley Scotty, Whiskey Pete, and Chuckawalla Slim. Mahan proudly shows visitors his desert "driving range" and "nine-hole" golf course, which are all part of this fine example of twentieth century folk art.

Thunderbird at Hulaville.

4 - Santa Fe and Salt Lake Trail Monument   SHL 576 and SHL 578
SHL 576 - Cajon Pass at Hwy 138, exit from northbound I-15, east to Wagon
Train Road (frontage road), south to end of road
SHL 578 - Cajon Pass at Cleghorn Canyon Road and I-15, in the Elsie Arey
May Nature Center

The bravery of the first explorers, traders and settlers who traveled
this early trail, through Cajon Pass, is commemorated by these
monuments. They were erected in 1917 by eight California pioneers.
This route became known as the famous "Spanish Trail." It was used
for almost 20 years, by pack trains traveling between Santa Fe, New
Mexico and Los Angeles.

5 - Angeles National Forest   SHL 717
Hwy 2 through Angeles National Forest to La Canada Flintridge
(818) 574-5200

President Benjamin Harrison designated the "San Gabriel
Timberland Reserve" as the first national forest in California, in
December 1892. The name was changed to Angeles National Forest
in 1908.

6 - Sycamore Grove   SHL 573
1 and 1/2 miles southwest of Devore, Glen Helen Regional Park

Mormon pioneers, emigrating to Southern California in 1851,
camped in this grove while their leaders negotiated the purchase of
land in the San Bernardino Valley for their settlement.

7 - Daley Toll Road   SHL 579
Hwy 18, Daley Canyon Road, Crestline

The most important pioneer wagon road built in the San Bernardino
Mountains was the 1870 Daley Toll Road, between Del Rosa and
Strawberry Peak. After 20 years of operation it was acquired by the
county. Near this marker, a section of the old toll road can be seen.

7 - Mormon Lumber Road   SHL 96
Waterman Canyon and Highway 18, west of Crestline

The first lumber road constructed out of the San Bernardino
Mountains, to the San Bernardino Valley, was built by the colony of

Mormons that arrived in this region in 1851. They used this pioneer road to bring lumber down the mountain for building their settlement and for trade with Los Angeles' residents.

7 - Garces-Smith Monument SHL 618
Monument Peak on the old Government Road (Mojave Road), 8 and 1/2 miles northwest of Crestline via a dirt road to Cajon Mountain Lookout

Padre Francisco Garces and Jedediah Strong Smith are commemorated at the summit of this pass, which they both crossed on their pioneer exploration of California. Padre Garces followed this old Mojave Indian trail in 1776. Jedediah Smith crossed this summit in 1826, and again in 1827. Smith's extensive exploration of California opened the central valleys of the state to eventual settlement.

8 - Holcomb Valley SHL 619
Holcomb Valley Road, 3 miles north of Big Bear Lake (909) 866-3437
Plaque in Big Bear City Park, Greenway Drive, Big Bear City

Southern California's largest gold discovery was made in this valley by William Holcomb, in May 1860. The resulting gold rush brought an influx of prospectors. "Boom" towns, reminiscent of the 49er towns of the Mother Lode region, of California, sprang up in Holcomb Valley. Some of the original log buildings, gold tailings and old mine sites can still be seen in this valley. A guide to the sites in Holcomb Valley is available from the Big Bear Ranger Station.

9 - Old Bear Valley Dam SHL 725
West end of Big Bear Lake

The first Bear Valley Dam was built here in 1883-1884, to provide water for the city of Redlands. It was constructed of locally quarried rocks, but its cement had to be shipped around the Horn from England. When the dam was completed, it created, what-was-then the world's largest man-made lake—Big Bear Lake. A higher dam was erected at this site in 1911-1912. Remains of the old dam are visible when the lake's water level is low.

9A - Big Bear Museum
Eleanor Abbott Big Bear Valley Historical Museum
East of airport, Greenway Drive, northeast corner of Big Bear City Park, Big Bear City (909) 585-8100

An authentic 1875 log cabin completely furnished with period items, antique toys, an extensive collection of local artifacts, and displays featuring early cattle ranching, lumbering and gold mining are among the museum's exhibits. The museum is housed in an original Big Bear City store, on property once owned by the historic Peter Dan Woodward Club (the early builders of Big Bear City).

10 - Old Mormon Fort Site   SHL 44
Arrowhead Avenue and Court Street, San Bernardino

A major colony of Mormon settlers was established here, in 1851, on land purchased from Jose del Carmen Lugo. They founded the town of San Bernardino, built sawmills, constructed roads, and erected a stockade that covered eight acres of the town. It was at this site, where the original Lugo adobe stood, that the stockade's fort was constructed. In 1857, at the request of Brigham Young, most of San Bernardino's Mormon settlers returned to Salt Lake City.

10 - The Arrowhead   SHL 977
South foot of Arrowhead Peak in the San Bernardino Mountains, north of the softball field in Wildwood Park, Waterman and 40th Streets, San Bernardino

The natural geological formation of a giant arrowhead shape, on the side of this mountain peak, was part of many local Indian legends long before the first Europeans passed this way in the late 18th century. The Gabrielino Indians associated it with the creation of the world. Other tribes said that the arrowhead represented battles between good and evil; or showed the way to good hunting grounds, and to therapeutic hot springs. The Mormons believed it was a "mark set by God to show where His people should settle." Between 1893 and 1915, the Santa Fe Railroad advertised the enormous, 1,376 foot X 479 foot, arrowhead as a site to see while on excursion trips through the region. In 1948, the Board of Supervisors adopted the arrowhead as part of the seal of San Bernardino County.

10 - California Theater of Performing Arts
562 West 4th Street, San Bernardino (909) 386-7361 or (909) 386-7353

The old California Theater is among the five remaining Art Deco theaters in California. This 1,760-seat building began as a vaudeville theater and is now a performing arts house.

11 - United States Rabbit Experimental Station (Site) SHL 950
8384 Cypress Avenue, Fontana (909) 350-6780

Between March 1928, and June 1965, this was the site of the first and only rabbit research and experimental station in the United States.

12 - Rialto Historical Society
205 North Riverside Avenue, Rialto (909) 875-1750

Unique exhibits at this historical museum include: a collection of old orange crate labels, orange industry equipment, Victorian rooms, and history of the Rialto area.

13 - Fort Benson SHL 617
10600 Hunts Lane, Colton

This is the site of an adobe fortification, constructed in 1856, by a group of independent Mormons who were in a land title dispute with their fellow colonists from Salt Lake City. This fort was manned for a year, until 1857, when Brigham Young recalled the colony to Utah. This was also the site of an ancient Indian village and a camping place used by Jedediah Strong Smith in 1827.

13 - Agua Mansa SHL 121
2001 West Agua Mansa Road, Agua Mansa Memorial Park and Cemetery, 3 miles southwest of Colton (909) 370-2091

The community of Agua Mansa was formed in 1845, by New Mexico colonists. The colonists accepted an offer of land, from Don Juan Bandini, in exchange for their protecting his stock from Indian raids. In 1862, the Santa Ana River flooded and washed away all the homes in Agua Mansa, leaving only the chapel and cemetery. Some of the original structures were rebuilt, but the town never returned to its original size and was eventually abandoned. Only the cemetery remains to be seen today.

13 - Virgil Earp House
528 West "H" Street, Colton

Virgil Earp built this home for his wife, Allie, in 1888. He was the first elected Marshal of Colton, in 1887. He also operated a gambling hall in San Bernardino in the early 1900s.

14 - Guachama Mission Station   SHL 95
Marker in field next to 25894 Mission Road, Loma Linda

The adobe building that once stood here was constructed by padres from Mission San Gabriel as headquarters for their Rancho San Bernardino. This area was originally called "Guachama Rancheria," for the Guachama Indian village that was located just south of this site in the early 1800s.

14 - San Bernardino Asistencia   SHL 42
26930 Barton Road, Redlands (909) 793-5402

In the early 1830s, construction began on this extensive adobe structure. It was designed to serve as a mission chapel at this outpost of the San Gabriel Mission. The decree of secularization ended all mission activity in California, in 1833-1834, and thus further construction of this building ceased. Over the years, the building fell into a state of ruin until little remained of the original structure. Reconstruction of this Asistencia began in 1928, using original mission records. Clay from this site was used in making the adobe bricks used in this massive restoration project. This beautiful replica of the Asistencia was completed nine years later. It is used today for special religious services and as a museum.

14 - The Old Zanja   SHL 43
North of the Asistencia, Sylvan Park, Redlands

Mission Indians, under direction of the Franciscan Fathers from Mission San Gabriel, built this irrigation ditch in 1819-1820, to bring water from mountain streams to this mission outpost. This water system also supplied the needs of the asistencia and the orchards of Rancho San Bernardino. Later, it became Redland's domestic water supply.

A. K. Smiley Public Library, Redlands.

Lincoln Shrine, Redlands.

15 - San Bernardino County Museum Association
2024 Orange Tree Lane, Redlands (909) 798-8570

Among the many collections exhibited are those that show the history, agriculture and industry of San Bernardino County. The "Hall of History" contains history dioramas, stone tools, Indian artifacts, antique horse-drawn vehicles and other historical displays. In addition, this museum administers several historic buildings in the county.

15 - Historical Glass Museum
1157 North Orange Street, Redlands (909) 797-1528

Displays of American-made, antique glassware are exhibited in this 1903, Victorian style house.

15 - A. K. Smiley Public Library   SHL 994
125 West Vine, Redlands (909) 798-0337

A. K. Smiley was one of the turn-of-the-century's, best-known philanthropists. He built this Mission Revival style library building in 1898 and gave it, and the surrounding park, to the City of Redlands. The library brought many well-known Americans to Redlands, including Andrew Carnegie, who endowed the library's Carnegie Southern California Indian Collection. Rare volumes, letters, diaries, photographs and other memorabilia, from Redland's early history, are preserved in the library's archives.

15 - The Lincoln Memorial Shrine
125 West Vine Street, Redlands (909) 798-7632, mornings or (909) 798-7636, afternoons

Robert Watchorn, government, business and union leader, built and endowed this tribute to Abraham Lincoln, in 1931. It was presented to the city as a Memorial to Lincoln, the only one in existence west of the Mississippi. The Shrine features an extensive Lincoln and Civil War Library; the famous Carrara marble bust of Lincoln; an original Norman Rockwell oil painting, *The Long Shadow of Lincoln*; rare Lincoln letters, documents, and personal memorabilia; Lincoln postage stamps from around the world; General Grant's, and

General Jackson's, personal pocket Bibles; and a large collection of Union and Confederate artifacts.

15 - Kimberly Crest Mansion
1325 Prospect Drive, Redlands (909) 792-2111

Built in 1897, on an eight-acre estate, this sixteenth century French chateau style mansion features a damask-paneled parlor installed by the Tiffany Studios of New York in 1907. European antiques, and original family furnishings, are preserved in this former home of one of the founders of the Kimberly-Clark Corporation.

16 - Yucaipa Rancheria Site   SHL 620
Plaque located at 32183 Kentucky Street, Yucaipa

Excavation of this area, by the San Bernardino Historical Society, uncovered relics of habitation by Serrano Indians who were present about the time that the Spaniards were here in the late 1700s. Yucaipa was the name of the Indian village which stood at this site.

16 - Sepulveda Adobe   SHL 528
32183 Kentucky Street, Yucaipa

The oldest house still standing in San Bernardino County was built by Diego Sepulveda in 1842. This two-story adobe was restored by the County of San Bernardino. Original Sepulveda family possessions, brought around the Horn in 1802, are included in the furnishings on display.

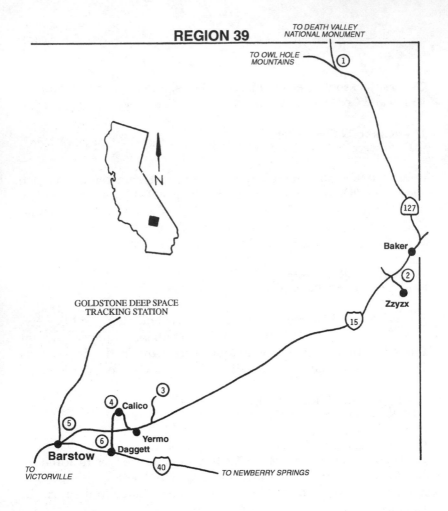

1 - Wades' Escape From Death Valley   SHL 622
Hwy 127, 30 miles north of Baker at Owl's Head Mountain cutoff

The Henry Wade family, who became trapped in Death Valley without water when crossing the desert in 1849, found this route as an exit out of Death Valley. Following a dry river bottom they reached safety at this point on the old Spanish Trail.

2 - Zzyzx
Zzyzx exit off I-15

Dr. Curtis Springer settled here in 1944 and changed the name of the town from "Soda Springs" to "Zzyzx." He developed a health spa around the mineral springs that once served as a desert oasis for ancient Indians and as an important way station on the Mojave Road during the 1860s. Roadside markers along the old Mojave Road can still be seen. Today, this is the Desert Study Center of California State University.

2 - The Mojave Road SHL 963
Between Fort Mojave on the Colorado River, across the Mojave Desert through Cajon Pass to Wilmington

Mojave Road was constructed in 1857-1858 as a government wagon road between Prescott, Arizona and Camp Drum (renamed Drum Barracks) near the Port of Los Angeles, in Wilmington. "Friends of the Mojave Road" restored 130 miles of the original road which can be traveled by 4-wheel vehicles from Camp Cady (12 miles east of Yermo) to the Colorado River. Zzyzx (originally called Soda Springs) was one of several small army outposts established to protect supplies from Indian attacks along this road.

3 - Calico Early Man Archaeological Site
I-15, Minneola Road Exit, 2 and 3/4 miles to site, Calico (909) 798-8570

Excavation of this site uncovered more than 12,000 stone tools used by prehistoric man 200,000 years ago. This is the oldest known site of man-made artifacts in the Western Hemisphere. Visitors can see the site of the actual dig, with remains still visible in its walls, and view the discoveries.

4 - Possum Trot (Site) SHL 939
North of I-15, Ghost Town Road, Calico

Desert wind powered the eighty, nearly life-sized dolls that Calvin and Ruby Black erected, and costumed, here in the 1950s to attract visitors to their rock shop and theater. Each figure represented an important person in the artists' lives. Their work was a unique example of California's twentieth century, environmental, folk art.

4 - Calico Ghost Town   SHL 782
Ghost Town Road, Calico (619) 254-2122

In the 1880s the richest silver strike in California's history was made in these hills. More than $13 million in silver was mined in ten years, swelling the town's population to over 3,000 residents. When the price of silver dropped in 1896, most miners left and Calico became a ghost town. Walter Knott, founder of Knott's Berry Farm in Buena Park, restored the town in 1954. It is now operated by the County of San Bernardino and is a major tourist attraction.

5 - Harvey House   SHL 892
Santa Fe Depot, North First Street off Hwy 58, Barstow, plaque at Mojave River Valley Museum

This immense 1910 building, "Casa del Desierto," was one of 75 Harvey Houses operated along the Santa Fe Railroad as a hotel for passengers of the line. One wing of this Spanish Moorish structure is now used as an Amtrak depot for Barstow.

1915 photo of Harvey House (Casa del Desierto), and Old Town Barstow. Courtesy of the Mojave River Valley Museum Association.

5 - Mojave River Valley Museum

270 East Virginia Way, (in Chamber of Commerce building), Barstow
(619) 256-5452

Fifty thousand years of man's existence in this region is exhibited along with more recent historical displays from the time of early pioneer settlers. Artifacts, antique furniture and Indian relics are housed here. On the grounds of the museum is an original frontier jail and a red dormitory car that once housed rail workers. A guide to local historic sites is available from the museum staff.

6 - Daggett Historical Tour

Points of historical interest in Daggett are identified by "covered wagon historical markers" throughout the town. The site of the American Borax Works, and structures erected before the turn-of-the-century, are among the sites. More recent history was made when Solar One, the first solar electric power plant in the nation, was put into operation. Information about Solar One can be obtained from their visitor center, in Daggett.

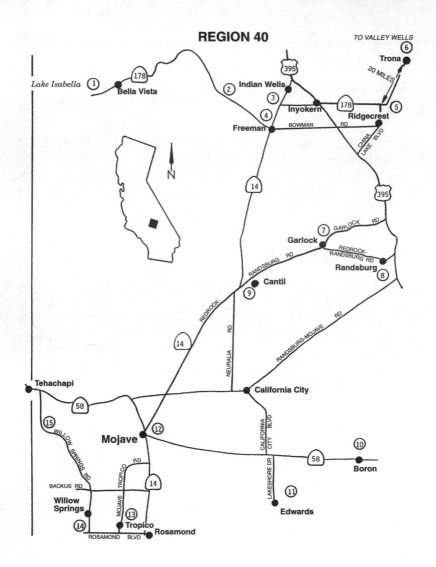

REGION 40

TO VALLEY WELLS

Trona ⑥

Lake Isabella ① ⑰⑧ Bella Vista

⑤⑨⑤

Indian Wells ② ③

⑦⑧ Inyokern

④ Ridgecrest ⑤

Freeman BOWMAN RD

CHINA LAKE BLVD

⑭

⑤⑨⑤

Garlock ⑦ GARLOCK RD

REDROCK-RANDSBURG RD

Randsburg ⑧

RANDSBURG RD

Cantil ⑨

REDROCK-

⑭ NEURALIA RD

RANDSBURG-MOJAVE RD

Tehachapi

California City

⑤⑧

⑮ WILLOW SPRINGS RD

Mojave ⑫

CALIFORNIA CITY BLVD

⑩

MOJAVE TROPICO RD

⑤⑧ Boron

BACKUS RD

⑭

LAKESHORE DR

⑪

Willow Springs

⑬ Tropico

Edwards

⑭ ROSAMOND BLVD Rosamond

330

1 - Site of Edward Kern Campsite   SHL 742
Marker located at entrance to Old Isabella Road Recreation Area, Hwy 178, Lake Isabella

It was near this spot, where the north and south forks of the Kern River met, that the Talbot party of Captain Fremont's third expedition camped, in the winter of 1845-1846. The river and county were named in honor of Edward Kern who was topographer for the expedition.

2 - Walker's Pass   SHL 99
8 miles west of Freeman Junction and Hwy 14 at summit of Hwy 178

Joseph Walker discovered the Kern River Valley, in 1834, when looking for a southern pass out of the San Joaquin Valley, where he had spent the summer on a trapping expedition. He returned to this pass as a wagon train guide in 1843, and again in 1845, with a party that included topographer Edward Kern. Kern mapped the upper waters of the Kern River. His name was also given to Kern County and the city of Kernville.

3 - Indian Wells   SHL 457
On Hwy 14, 4 miles north of Freeman Junction

The spring at Indian Wells was used by many of the 49ers heading west during the gold rush days. The Jayhawker party found water here after they had battled Indians, the Mojave Desert and Death Valley, in 1849-1850. Indian Wells also served as a freight and stage station during the 1860s.

4 - Freeman Junction   SHL 766
Marker located on Hwy 178, 1/4 mile west of Hwy 14

This junction of old Indian trails was an important cross-road in early California history. Joseph Walker passed this junction after making his discovery of Walker Pass in 1834. Death Valley 49ers traveled to the California gold fields by taking the trails that went west and south of this junction. A stage stop and store were located here from 1873, until railroads brought an end to stages and freight wagons, in 1909.

5 - Maturango Museum
100 East Las Flores, Ridgecrest (619) 375-6900

Indian relics, from the area now occupied by the China Lake Naval Weapons Center, are featured exhibits. Museum staff members also arrange tours, to the Weapons Center, to see some of the 13,000 rock carvings (petroglyphs) made by ancient Indian inhabitants of this valley.

6 - Searles Lake Borax Discovery SHL 774
Roadside Rest Area, Trona Road (Hwy 178), Trona

While prospecting this area in 1862, John Searles discovered crystals of borax on the surface of a lake which then covered this region. Searles Lake is now a dry lake bed covering an area of about 36 square miles. In addition to borax, other chemicals are now taken from this dry lake bottom.

6 - Valley Wells SHL 443
Trona Wildrose Road at Valley Wells, northeast of Trona

Some of the 49er emigrants that crossed Death Valley, came here for water, only to find it too salty to drink. It was with great difficulty that they were able to continue in their quest for civilization.

7 - Garlock SHL 671
Garlock Road, 1 mile north of Redrock-Randsburg Road

Garlock was once the site of four stamp mills that crushed gold ore from Randsburg's Yellow Aster Mine in the 1890s. When water was piped from here to Randsburg, and a stamp mill was constructed at the Yellow Aster Mine, Garlock's population dwindled. Today, only ruins of a few of the town's old buildings remain to be seen.

8 - Randsburg Desert Museum
161 Butte Street, Randsburg (619) 374-2111

History of the Rand Mining District and the founding of Randsburg are displayed in the collections of this desert museum. Mining tools and Indian artifacts are featured exhibits.

8 - Rand Mining District SHL 938
Randsburg Road exit east of U.S. 395

This area produced a variety of minerals including tungsten, gold and silver. The Yellow Aster Mine yielded gold ore worth more than $16 million in the late 1890s. Many of the old buildings and mine headframes stand today in the city of Randsburg.

9 - Desert Spring SHL 476
Pappas Road, 1/2 mile south of Valley Road, 3.7 miles east of Cantil Post Office, off Hwy 14, Cantil

The Jayhawker party, and other emigrants that headed west through Death Valley, stopped here for water after leaving Indian Wells to the north. Desert Spring also served as a freight station on the line between Los Angeles and the Cerro Gordo Mines.

10 - Open Pit Borax Mine
30 miles east of Mojave on Hwy 58, Boron

Discovery of the world's largest deposit of borax at this site eliminated the need for 20-mule teams to haul borax 165 miles from Death Valley to Mojave. This large borax pit measures one-half mile across and is deeper than a 40-story building.

11 - Edwards Air Force Base
East of Rosamond via Rosamond Boulevard, Edwards

Most of the major advances in modern aviation have occurred at this Air Force Test Center. The first jet aircraft to fly in the U.S. was tested and flown here in 1942. This same site was used by Captain Charles Yeager when he broke the sound barrier in 1947. Flight testing of the space shuttle took place here; and the first of many landings in the manned space shuttle program was on this dry lake bed.

12 - Mojave 20-Mule-Team Borax Terminus SHL 652
Marker located opposite 16246 Sierra Hwy (west side of Hwy 14), Mojave

The 20-mule-team, borax wagons, that brought borax ore 165 miles across the desert from Death Valley, unloaded their payload at the Southern Pacific Railroad loading dock here in Mojave. These teams operated from 1884, until 1889, when new borax discoveries at Boron ended the need to transport ore out of the Mojave Desert.

13 - Burton's Tropico Gold Camp and Mine
Mojave Tropico Road, north of Rosamond Boulevard, Rosamond
(805) 256-2179

One of California's leading mine museums is located here, with 16 antique buildings from the surrounding area. Relics, mining drills and tools add to the atmosphere of this gold mining location.

14 - Willow Springs SHL 130
Marker at junction of Tehachapi-Willow Springs Road and Rosamond Boulevard, 8 miles west of Rosamond

Willow Springs was a famous stopover place for many of the area's first exploration parties. Padre Garces first camped here in 1776; Fremont's Party in 1844; and the Jayhawker party, that crossed Death Valley enroute to Los Angeles, in 1858. Willow Springs was also a stage depot on the route from Havilah to Los Angeles. Stone buildings from the early 1900s can still be seen.

15 - Oak Creek Pass SHL 97
Southeast of Tehachapi between Hwy 58 and Oak Creek Road on Tehachapi-Willow Springs Road, plaque is on northeast side of the road among the windmills

Padre Francisco Garces, the first white man to view the Kern River, traveled over Oak Creek Pass in 1776, on his return from exploring the San Joaquin Valley and Colorado River regions. Fremont used this pass in 1834 and again when leaving California in 1844. This was the only route through the Tehachapi Mountains before the railroad was built.

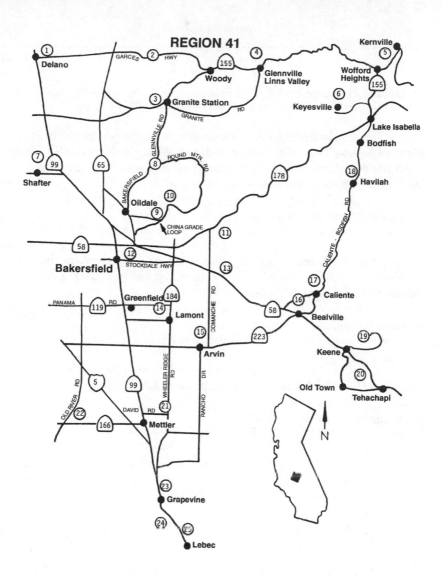

REGION 41

Kernville

Delano

GARCES HWY

155

Woody

Glennville
Linns Valley

Wofford
Heights

155

Granite Station

GRANITE RD

Keyesville

Lake Isabella

Bodfish

99

ROUND MTN RD

Shafter

65

GLENNVILLE RD

BAKERSFIELD

178

CALIENTE - BODFISH RD

Havilah

Oildale

CHINA GRADE LOOP

58

Bakersfield

STOCKDALE HWY

COMANCHE RD

Caliente

17

16

58

Bealville

PANAMA RD

119

Greenfield

184

14

Lamont

223

Keene

19

Arvin

WHEELER RIDGE RD

RANCHO DR

Old Town

20

Tehachapi

OLD RIVER RD

5

99

DAVID RD

21

22

166

Mettler

N

23

Grapevine

24

25

Lebec

335

1 - Delano Heritage Park
Garces Hwy and Lexington Street, Delano (805) 725-6730

Several historic buildings from the Delano area are preserved in this park; including the 1876 Delano jail and the 1916 Jasmine School. Local historical artifacts are exhibited in this park's museum. Tours are arranged by appointment only.

2 - Garces Baptismal Site SHL 631
Marker in shape of a cross on Garces Hwy, 7 miles east of Hwy 65

Padre Francisco Garces recorded the first Christian baptism, in the San Joaquin Valley, on May 3, 1776, when he baptized a dying Yokuts Indian boy at this site.

3 - Granite Station
Granite and Bakersfield-Glennville Roads, 6 miles south of Woody

This railroad stop was established in 1870 as a way station for freighters from Bakersfield, Linns Valley and Glennville.

3 - Mountain House SHL 589
8 miles southwest of Woody on Bakersfield-Glennville Road

The Butterfield Overland Stage operated along the Stockton-Los Angeles Road during the period 1858-1861. None of the stations established to serve this historic line remain today.

4 - Glennville Adobe SHL 495
Hwy 155 at Glennville, Linns Valley

Kern County's oldest known residence, now restored by the Kern County Museum, was built in 1850 as an Indian trading post. The town of Glennville was named after an earlier settler, James Madison "Matt" Glenn, in 1857. The county's oldest religious structure, Mt. Carmel Presbyterian Church, was erected in Glennville in 1866.

4 - Lavers Crossing SHL 672
Marker located 1 mile north of Glennville on White River Road

Lavers Crossing was the principal community in Linns Valley during the 1860s. Kern County's first school class was held here in 1854.

5 - Kern Valley Museum
49 Big Blue Road at Whitney Road, Kernville (619) 376-6683

This museum's displays include: many objects used by the first known Indian inhabitants of the area; significant items of early-day ranching; tools from the lumber industry; gold mining tools, with samples of gold from the local area; and other items of historical interest from the Kern River Valley.

5 - Kernville SHL 132
Monument in front of cemetery, 4 miles north of Wofford Heights, Kernville

First founded as a "makeshift" saloon (a plank across two whiskey barrels), the town of Kernville was originally named Whiskey Flat. Within two years it had a hotel, stores, saloons and three stamp mills. It had also become a trading center for traffic that crossed Walker Pass to the desert mining areas. The town was renamed Kernville in 1864. It was moved to its present location in 1952, when the newly created Lake Isabella flooded the area.

6 - Keyesville SHL 98
Keyesville Road east of Hwy 155

The discovery of gold in 1853, by Richard Keyes, brought the settlers that formed Southern California's first gold rush mining town. The town was first called Hogeye, then renamed Keyesville. Now, it is often called Keysville because of a misspelling of the name, when the post office opened, in 1857. To protect Keyesville from an anticipated Indian attack in 1855, miners built a fort out of brush covered with dirt, the outline of which can still be seen.

7 - Site of the Flight of the *Gossamer Condor* SHL 923
Marker located at Shafter Airport, 1 mile west of Hwy 99 (805) 746-6711

Aviation history was made at this site in August 1977, when the Kremer Circuit (a one-mile figure-eight course) was successfully completed by a man-powered aircraft. A plaque at this site commemorates this aviation first by the *Gossamer Condor*.

8 - Posey Station SHL 539
Intersection of Round Mountain Road and Bakersfield-Glennville Road

The Butterfield Overland Stage operated along the Stockton-Los Angeles Road during the period 1858-1861. None of the stations established to serve this historic line remain today, but their sites have been commemorated.

9 - Gordon's Ferry on Kern River SHL 137
Marker at south end of bridge, west of county gun club at foot of China Grade Loop

Major Aneas Gordon operated an overhead cable ferry across the Kern River, at this point, in the 1850s. In 1858, it became a stop on the Butterfield Overland Mail Stage Route.

10 - Discovery Well of Kern River Oil Field SHL 290
South of Round Mountain Road, across the Kern River from county gun club

Discovery of this oil field was made by two brothers, Johnathon and James Elwood, who dug this first well by hand in 1899. That same year the first commercial well was drilled in this region just 400 feet north of this site.

11 - Garces Kern River Crossing SHL 278
Marker 8 miles east of Bakersfield on Hwy 178 between Comanche and Rancheria Roads

Padre Francisco Garces was carried across the Kern River by Yokuts Indians, in 1776, as he explored the area searching for a shorter route from Sonora, Mexico, to Monterey, California. He named the river, Rio de San Felipe.

12 - Garces' Circle Statue SHL 277
Intersection of Chester Avenue and 30th Street, Bakersfield

This monument was erected to the memory of Franciscan Padre Francisco Garces, the first white man to reach this Indian ranchera, which is now known as Bakersfield. When he first visited here in 1776, Padre Garces named it San Miguel de los Noches por el Santa Principe.

Blacksmith shop from Calloway Ranch. Courtesy of Kern County Museum.

12 - Kern County Museum
3801 Chester Avenue, Bakersfield (805) 324-4052

Sixty interesting and unusual buildings, representative of Kern County in the 1860s to 1900s, are maintained in a 14-acre setting. Some of the original buildings have been restored. Other structures are re-creations. Indian artifacts, antique vehicles, firearms and oil well relics are also exhibited.

12 - Site of Alexis Godey's Home   SHL 690
Marker located 414 - 19th Street, just east of Central Park, Bakersfield

Alexis Godey, a guide for General John Fremont when he explored the Kern River Valley in 1843-1844, built his last home on this site in 1873.

12 - Colonel Thomas Baker Statue   SHL 382
In front of Bakersfield City Hall at 1501 Truxtun Avenue, Bakersfield

This statue is a memorial to Colonel Baker, who was the county's first permanent settler, and for whom the town of Bakersfield was named.

12 - Site of Elisha Steven's Home   SHL 732
Marker located at entrance to condominiums on West Columbus by Union Avenue, Bakersfield

One of Bakersfield's first permanent settlers was the noted American western pioneer and emigrant party leader, Elisha Stevens. Stevens lived on this homesite after serving under Commodore Stockton during the Mexican War.

13 - Jedediah Strong Smith Trail   SHL 660
Remains of marker 11 miles east of Bakersfield at Intersection of Hwy 58, Old Bena and Tower Line Roads

Jedediah Smith's fur trapping party of 1827 was the first group of Americans to reach this region of California, which was then a part of Mexico. His wide travels throughout the territory west of the Mississippi opened rich fur trapping country and trails that were soon frequented by pioneers going to California.

14 - Kern River Slough   SHL 588
2 miles east of Greenfield on Panama Road

The Butterfield Overland Stage operated along the Stockton-Los Angeles Road during the period 1858-1861. None of the stations established to serve this historic line remain today, but their sites have been commemorated.

15 - Garces Statue   SHL 371
At east limit of Arvin, in front of St. Thomas Church on Bear Mountain Boulevard

This monument was erected in memory of Padre Francisco Garces who passed this site in 1776. This was the outermost point in the south San Joaquin Valley visited by Padre Garces as he opened new trails between Mexico and Monterey, California.

16 - Bealville   SHL 741
Marker located south of Caliente, on Bealville Road, 1 mile north of Hwy 58

When the Southern Pacific Railroad established their depot here in 1876, they named it for Edward F. Beale. Beale's name is associated with many areas of California's early history. He aided Stephen

Kearny during the Mexican War, at the battle of San Pasqual, by crawling through the lines with Kit Carson to get help. Beale made several cross-country trips and was the first to bring news of California's gold strike to the East. He established an Indian reservation on his ranch and was appointed Superintendent of Indian Affairs for California and Nevada. Beale also brought camels to Fort Tejon to use for desert transportation by the U.S. Army.

17 - Caliente SHL 757
2.3 miles north of Hwy 58 on Bealville Road, Caliente

A major land boom struck Caliente when it seemed that the railroad would not be able to be built across the 4,000-foot Tehachapi Mountains and that Caliente would become the terminus of the line. William Hood, who would later become chief engineer of the Southern Pacific Railroad, used a unique engineering technique and was able to construct a route to the summit. His design of the Tehachapi Loop and the efforts of three thousand Chinese laborers resulted in the completion of the Los Angeles-San Francisco line.

18 - Havilah SHL 100
8 miles south of Bodfish on Caliente-Bodfish Road

The discovery of gold in the summer of 1864 led to the organization of the Clear Mining District which was later to become the town of Havilah. Asbury Harpending laid out the town, gave it its name and began Kern County's first real estate development. By 1866, the town had become the county seat, with 10 mills, 30 businesses and twice weekly stage service from Los Angeles and San Francisco. Havilah was sustained for more than 50 years by its many small mines, but as the larger mines closed, more and more of its residents moved. Bakersfield became the county seat in 1874, when farming and the railroads assumed the major part of the county's economy. Fires, floods and the loss of residents eventually turned Havilah into a ghost town.

19 - Tehachapi (Walong) Loop SHL 508
Keene exit north of Hwy 58, northeast of Keene

Three thousand Chinese laborers were hired to lay 28 miles of railroad track, from Caliente, over the 4,000-foot summit of the

Tehachapi Mountains. Eighteen tunnels were blasted through a total of 8,240 feet of mountain, but it was the construction of the Tehachapi Loop that became known as one of the world's outstanding engineering feats. To gain elevation, a train with 85 or more cars will pass over itself, going around the loop, and be 75 feet above the end cars trailing through the tunnel below.

20 - Old Town SHL 643
Marker located 4 miles west of Tehachapi on Tehachapi-Woodford Road

The first community in Tehachapi Valley was established here in the 1860s. When the railroad was completed in 1876, at Greenwich, residents from Tehachapi moved there and later renamed it Tehachapi.

21 - Sinks of the Tejon SHL 540
Intersection of David Road and Wheeler Ridge Road, near Mettler

The Butterfield Overland Stage operated along the Stockton-Los Angeles Road during the period 1858-1861. None of the stations established to serve this historic line remain today, but their sites have been commemorated.

22 - Fages-Zalvidea Crossing SHL 291
Marker on Hwy 166, 7 miles west of Mettler Station

Commander Fages, who left the first written record of exploration of the south San Joaquin Valley, crossed this trail in 1772. Father Jose de Zalvidea crossed this same spot, in 1806, while on an expedition in search of mission sites.

23 - Sebastian Indian Reservation SHL 133
8 miles south of Mettler on I-5

General Edward Beale, who would later became Superintendent of Indian Affairs for California, established this Indian reservation in 1853. It was one of several reservations established in California to protect the Indians. More than 1,000 Indians lived here until they were transferred to other reservations in 1864.

23 - Rose Station   SHL 300
Marker 8 miles south of Mettler on I-5

An adobe stage station was built here, in 1875, by William Rose as part of the Butterfield Overland Mail Route. It was a popular stopover place for travelers between Los Angeles and Bakersfield during the 1860s and 1870s.

24 - Fort Tejon   SHL 129
Fort Tejon State Historic Park, 35251 Fort Tejon Road, 3 miles north of Lebec on I-5 (805) 248-6692 or (805) 765-5004

Fort Tejon was established in 1854, by the U.S. Army, to safeguard early settlers against Indian attacks and to protect the San Sebastian Indian Reservation fifteen miles to the south. Military presence also suppressed stock rustling and crimes associated with the gold rush. Fort Tejon was a main link in the Butterfield Stage route between Los Angeles and points north. The first stage of this famous line arrived in 1858, the same year that saw the arrival of a camel train from the Near East. It was believed that camels could provide desert transportation for the Army, but the camel's tender feet couldn't adapt to the area's rocky soil. Restored buildings, parade grounds and a museum, with exhibits of military life at this fort, are maintained in this state historic park.

25 - Top of Grapevine Pass (Tejon Pass)   SHL 283
Marker located 1/2 mile south of Lebec, near the Grapevine summit

Commander Pedro Fages, the first white man to cross the Tehachapi Mountains, first saw the San Joaquin Valley from this historic pass in 1772. A memorial to Fages was placed at this pass to mark his historic journey from San Diego to San Luis Obispo.

REGION 42

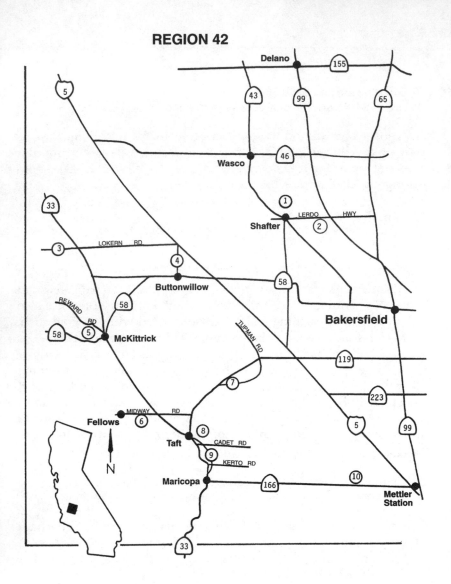

1 - Shafter Depot Museum
150 Central Valley Hwy, Shafter (805) 746-1557 or (805) 746-4423

When the railroad was completed in this area, in 1898, a siding was named here to honor General William Rufus "Pecos Bill" Shafter, commanding general of the American forces in Cuba during the Spanish-American war. Property lots for the town were sold, and in 1917, this Santa Fe depot was erected. The completely restored depot depicts a period agent's office with original equipment and documents. Some of General Shafter's personal effects are also displayed. An outdoor display of farm machinery, used in the region between 1915 and 1945, shows the transition from hand and animal-powered implements to motorized equipment.

1 - Green Hotel
530 James Street, Shafter (805) 746-1913

The Kern County Land Company built this hotel in 1913, to provide lodging for prospective buyers of lots, in the new city of Shafter. The completely restored and furnished hotel is the city's oldest commercial building and is used for community activities.

2 - Site of the Flight of the *Gossamer Condor* SHL 923
Marker located at Shafter Airport, 1 mile west of Hwy 99 (805) 746-6711

Aviation history was made at this site in August 1977, when the Kremer Circuit (a one-mile figure-eight course) was successfully completed by the *Gossamer Condor*, a man-powered aircraft.

3 - Site of Buena Vista Refinery SHL 504
10 miles north of McKittrick on Hwy 33 at intersection of Lokern Road

Buena Vista Refinery was California's first commercial oil refinery. Illuminating oil was produced from 1864 to 1867, and shipped to San Francisco, but the high cost of transportation brought it to an end.

4 - Buttonwillow Tree SHL 492
1 mile north of Buttonwillow off Hwy 58, on Buttonwillow Avenue

The ancient Yokuts Indians used this area as their dance ground. It was later used as cattle rodeo grounds, and as the Miller and Lux

Ranch headquarters. The town of Buttonwillow was named for this lone Buttonwillow tree in 1895.

5 - California Standard Oil Well No. 1   SHL 376
West of Hwy 58 on Reward Road, McKittrick

The second oil field discovered in 1899, McKittrick Field, was started with the drilling of this well which produced oil for the next 30 years.

5 - Site of McKittrick Brea Pit   SHL 498
1/2 mile south of McKittrick on Hwy 58

An ancient natural animal trap was discovered at this site in the 1920s. Excavation of the site yielded bird and mammal bones of prehistoric creatures once native to this area. The site of this ancient tar pit has since been filled in, but bones recovered during twenty years of excavation are on display in the Kern County Museum, in Bakersfield.

6 - Midway Gusher   SHL 581
1/4 mile off Fellows on Broadway Road

When "Well 2-6" blew on November 27, 1909, the great west side oil boom began. It was called one of the greatest oil booms California ever experienced.

7 - Tulamniu Indian Village   SHL 374
West shore of Buena Vista Lake, Tupman Road, south of Hwy 119

Both Spanish Commander Fages and Father Zalvidea recorded this Yokuts Indian Village when they explored the San Joaquin Valley in the late 1700s. The village was occupied for several centuries and was excavated by the Smithsonian Institution in 1933-1934.

8 - Replica of Fort Sutter
Southwest corner of Ash and Lincoln Streets, Taft

This fort is a slightly larger replica of the famous Fort Sutter in Sacramento. It houses county, state and federal offices in Taft.

9 - Lakeview Gusher No. 1   SHL 485
Petroleum Club Road, between Kerto and Cadet roads, 1 and 1/2 miles north of Maricopa

On March 10, 1910, the world's greatest known oil gusher blew in at this site. The flow of oil reached an uncontrolled 100,000 barrels per day, and brought in 9 million barrels of oil in 18 months.

10 - Fages - Zalvidea Crossing   SHL 291
Marker on Hwy 166, 7 miles west of Mettler Station

Commander Fages, who left the first written record of exploration of the south San Joaquin Valley, crossed this trail in 1772. Father Jose de Zalvidea crossed this same spot in 1806 while on an expedition in search of mission sites.

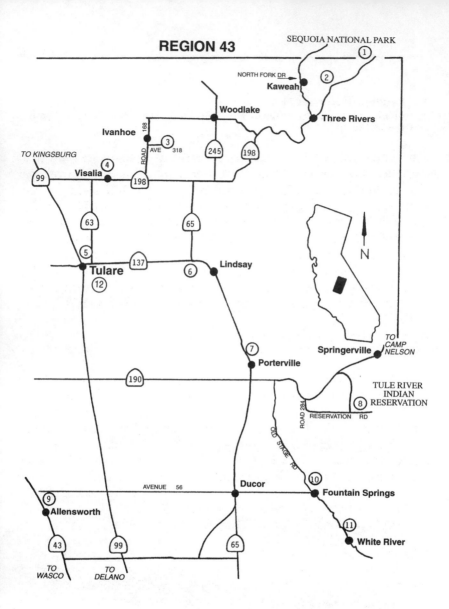

REGION 43

SEQUOIA NATIONAL PARK

①

NORTH FORK DR ②
Kaweah

Woodlake

Ivanhoe

③

Three Rivers

Visalia ④

TO KINGSBURG

99

198

63

65

5

137

⑥ **Lindsay**

Tulare
⑫

⑦

Porterville

190

Springerville

TO CAMP NELSON

TULE RIVER INDIAN RESERVATION

⑧

RESERVATION RD

ROAD 284

OLD STAGE RD

AVENUE 56

Ducor

⑩

Fountain Springs

⑨ **Allensworth**

⑪

White River

43

99

65

TO WASCO

TO DELANO

N

1 - Sequoia National Park
Accessible only from the west via Hwy 198 Visalia, or Hwy 180 from Fresno
(209) 565-3134

The "Giant Forest" contains the largest living things in the world—
the Giant Sequoia trees. The first "white man" to see these giant trees
was Hale Tharp in 1856. He made his first cabin inside a fire-
hollowed sequoia log that had fallen. It was known as Tharp's Log
and can still be seen inside the park at Log Meadow. In 1890,
Sequoia became the country's second National Park, preserving these
giants for many future generations to see. A guide to the Park's
trails, Moro Rock, some of the trees of historical significance and
Crystal Cave is available at the park entrance and visitor's center.
The Park's museum is located on the main road in Lodgepole.

2 - Kaweah Colony   SHL 389
2 and 3/4 miles north of Three Rivers on North Fork Drive, Kaweah

A socialist colony was established here, from 1886 until 1892, to
demonstrate the "advantages of cooperation in social and industrial
life." It planned to support itself by logging in what is now Sequoia
National Park. The famous General Sherman Tree was originally
named the Karl Marx Tree by these colonists. They also constructed
a sawmill and an 18-mile logging road. Today, the only reminder of
the colony's existence is what remains of the Kaweah post office.

3 - Election Tree   SHL 410
North of Hwy 198 via Road 168 to Avenue 318, near Ivanhoe

When Tulare County was established in 1852, Major James Savage
held an election under this tree that resulted in the organization of
this new county. The first county seat remained under this tree for
two years, but the "legal" location was at Wood's cabin about half a
mile to the south.

4 - Visalia Heritage Tours
Visalia Chamber of Commerce, 701 West Mineral King, Visalia
(209) 734-5876

The Historic Preservation Advisory Board and Chamber of
Commerce have published two tour guides to more than 50 of

Visalia's historic homes and buildings. Each guide is designed as a walking tour.

4 - Tulare County Museum
27000 Mooney Boulevard, Visalia (209) 733-6616

Historical buildings from the 1890s, an 1854 log cabin, and an 1872 jail are on display with wagons, buggies and other reminders of pioneer days in the region.

5 - Tulare Historical Tour
Tulare Chamber of Commerce, 260 North "L" Street, Tulare (209) 686-1547

A guide to the dozen homes built in the late 1800s, that remain in Tulare, has been published by the Historical Society and can be obtained from the Chamber of Commerce.

5 - Tulare City Historical Museum
444 West Tulare Avenue, Tulare (209) 686-2074

San Joaquin Valley's newest museum preserves the history of the Yokuts Indians, who lived here when most of Tulare County was covered by Tulare Lake—one of the largest bodies of water west of the Mississippi. The museum also traces the history of the city of Tulare, since its founding by the Southern Pacific Railroad in the early 1870s, and the county's conversion to farmland with the draining of Tulare Lake. A large collection of historic agricultural implements and turn-of-the-century home furnishings are among the featured exhibits.

5 - Temporary Detention Camps for Japanese-Americans   SHL 934
Tulare County Fairgrounds, off Hwy 99, west on Bardsley Road, Tulare (209) 686-4707

After the United States was attacked by Japan and entered the Second World War, Japanese and Japanese-Americans were ordered to report to temporary detention camps, for relocation to permanent camps across the United States until the end of the war. The Japanese population reached a maximum of 4,978 people in the five months that this facility served as an assembly center.

5 - Butterfield Stage Route - Lindsey SHL 471
Junction of Hwy 65 and Hwy 137, west of Lindsey

The Butterfield Overland Stage route followed the Stockton-Los Angeles Road, an old emigrant trail, through here from 1858 to 1861. Passengers and mail traveled on a regular schedule, between St. Louis and San Francisco, until the outbreak of the Civil War when service was discontinued.

7 - Site of Tule River Stage Station SHL 473
Main Street and Henderson, north of Hwy 190, Porterville

Porter Putman purchased the Tule River Stage Station in 1859, from its original builder, Peter Goodhue, and developed it into a popular stopping place and hotel on the Butterfield Overland Stage route. The town of Porterville grew up around what was then known as Porter's Station. A memorial to the town's founder was erected at this historic site.

7 - Porterville Historical Museum
257 North "D" Street, Porterville (209) 784-2053

Constructed in 1913, as a passenger station for the Southern Pacific Railroad, this building now houses the Porterville Historical Museum. Displays include Yokuts Indian artifacts and relics from early pioneer days.

7 - Zalud House
393 North Hockett Street at Morton Avenue, Porterville (209) 782-7548

Built in 1891, this is one of the few houses of its era that has not been remodeled. It remains today, as it was originally constructed. Most of the original furnishings and memorabilia of the Zalud family are maintained at the home. To add to the historic atmosphere, staff members wear costumes of the period when showing this house.

8 - First Tule Indian Reservation SHL 388
Southeast of Porterville on Reservation Road

At the end of the Tule River Indian War, in 1857, several different Indian tribes were brought here for resettlement. In 1873, the reservation was moved to its present location, as the original site did not prove satisfactory. A plaque marks the site of the first Tule Indian Reservation.

9 - Colonel Allensworth State Historic Park
4099 Douglas Avenue, 17 miles north of Wasco, Hwy 43 (800) 444-7275

The only California town founded and governed by Black Americans, was here at Allensworth, in 1908. Colonel Allensworth's restored home, the school, and some of the town's other buildings are preserved in this historic park. An interpretive museum exhibits the history of this former black community.

10 - Fountain Springs SHL 648
Old Stage Road, north of Avenue 56, Fountain Springs

About 1 and 1/2 miles to the north stood the Fountain Springs Stop on the Butterfield Overland Stage route. Fountain Springs was located at the crossroads of the Stockton-Los Angeles Road and the road to the Kern River gold mines. A monument now marks the site of this pioneer stage stop.

11 - Tailholt SHL 413
South of Fountain Springs on Old Stage Road

This 1856 gold mining camp was known by several different names, until 1870, when the name White River was established. During the Kern River gold rush period this town had a substantial population. It was also known for its two cemeteries: one was for the respectable . . . the other for renegades and outlaws. Nothing remains today of this former gold camp.

REGION 44

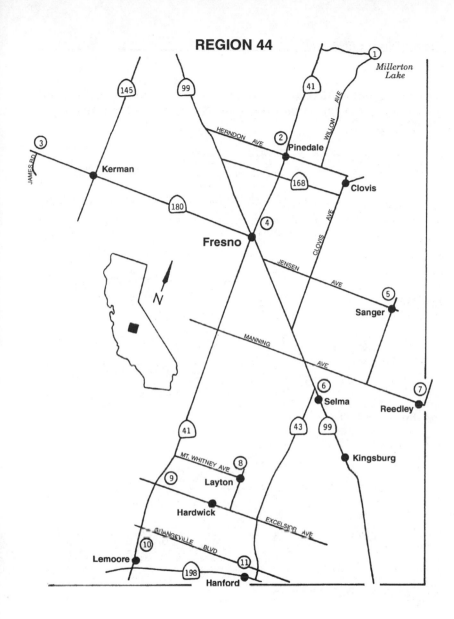

1 - Fort Miller   SHL 584
Millerton Lake State Recreation Area, east of Hwy 41, 15 miles northeast of Fresno (209) 822-2661

Camp Barbour was established at this site, in 1850, to provide miners with protection from the region's Indians. The "Mariposa Indian War Treaty" was signed at this camp on April 29, 1851. Later that year the camp was renamed Fort Miller and remained an active U.S. Army Post until 1856. The Fort's blockhouse was relocated to Roeding Park, in Fresno, before the site of the original fort was covered by Millerton Lake in the 1940s.

2 - Temporary Detention Camps for Japanese-Americans   SHL 934
Pinedale Industrial Area, northwest of Herndon Avenue and Hwy 41, Pinedale

After the outbreak of World War II, Japanese and Japanese-Americans were ordered to surrender themselves to temporary detention camps throughout California. Fresno County Fairgrounds, and industrial buildings then located in Pinedale, were two of those temporary detention centers. The Japanese population reached a maximum of 4,792 people in the two months that these facilities were used as assembly centers.

3 - Fresno City (Site)   SHL 488
Junction of Hwy 180 (Whites Bridge) and James Road, west of Fresno

Fresno City existed at the head of navigation of the Fresno Slough for about 20 years, from 1855-1875. With the completion of the Central Pacific Railroad, the City of Fresno was established in 1872, about thirty miles east of here. No trace of Fresno City remains today.

4 - Kearney Mansion Museum
7160 West Kearney Boulevard, Fresno (209) 441-0862

The museum is established in the beautifully restored home of landowner and industrialist, M. Theodore Kearney. It features: furniture from the late 1800s, in settings of the period; original Kearney furnishings; and a collection of glass photographic negatives of local history.

4 - Forestiere Underground Gardens SHL 916
5021 West Shaw Avenue, Fresno (209) 485-3281

Baldasare Forestiere, a Sicilian immigrant, built a 10-acre underground retreat. Over a period of forty years he designed a maze of 60 rooms, constructed curved ceilings without pillars, elegant archways, atriums, a winery, reading room, a chapel and bell tower . . . all 10 to 20 feet underground. Forestiere planted fruit trees, flowering shrubs, grape pergolas and cascading vines in these subterranean gardens. He was an expert horticulturist and through grafting techniques, was able to grow grapefruits, lemons, oranges, tangerines, and other citrus fruits on the same trees. Skylights brought in sunlight, rain water and provided ventilation. His gardens were opened to the public after his death in 1946 and, for the next 40 years, were a popular tourist attraction. Efforts are being made to preserve this landmark, and to reopen it the public.

4 - Fresno Metropolitan Museum
Old *Fresno Bee* Building, 1555 Van Ness Avenue, Fresno (209) 441-1444

Housed in this 1922, Italian Renaissance style building are the collections of the Fresno Metropolitan Museum. The exhibits include antique woodworking tools and a collection of historic photographs by the famous landscape photographer, Ansel Adams.

4 - Site of the Fresno Free Speech Fight of the Industrial
Workers of the World SHL 873
Plaque in concrete tree planter south of clock tower on the Fulton Mall, Van Ness Avenue and Fresno Street, Fresno

The Industrial Workers of the World, known to their opponents as "Wobblies," demonstrated at the corner of Mariposa and "I" Streets, from October 1910, to March 1911, in their effort to organize Fresno's unskilled labor force. Their campaign, which they called a "fight for the right of free speech," was the first of its type in California.

4 - Site of First Junior College in California SHL 803
Marker at Stanislaus and "O" Streets, Fresno

California's first junior college was established at this site in 1910. Originally, the school was a postgraduate school for high school students. Within a few years the state had the nation's first system of junior colleges.

4 - Meux Home Museum
1007 "R" Street, Fresno (209) 233-8007

This Victorian home was built in 1889, by Dr. Thomas Meux, and was a family residence until 1970. Most of the house remains the same as when it was constructed in 1889-1890. Its rich wood interior and wall coverings have been well-preserved along with original family furnishings. It is now operated as a museum of local history.

4 - Temporary Detention Camps for Japanese-Americans SHL 934
Fresno County Fairgrounds, Kings Canyon Road and Maple Avenue, Fresno

After the outbreak of World War II, Japanese and Japanese-Americans were ordered to surrender themselves to temporary detention camps throughout California. Fresno County Fairgrounds, and industrial buildings then located in Pinedale, were two of those temporary detention centers. The Japanese population reached a maximum of 4,792 people in the two months that these facilities were used as assembly centers.

4 - The Discovery Center
1944 North Winery Avenue, Fresno (209) 251-5531

Indian baskets and artifacts are among the exhibits featured at this six-acre, participatory, science museum. Many interesting hands-on displays make this museum appealing to young people.

5 - Sanger Depot Museum
Sanger Civic Center, in blocks bounded by Jensen, West and Hoage Avenues, and Seventh Street (209) 875-4720

This building of the Southern Pacific Railroad depot, in Sanger, was the arrival point for the settlers that established this new town in 1887. This depot served as the town's center of commerce until the 1930s. It was relocated to its present site, in Sanger's Civic Center, in 1977, and was restored to its original condition. The depot displays items from the community that are of historical significance.

6 - Selma's Points of Local Historical Interest
Selma District Chamber of Commerce, 1802 Tucker Street, Selma
(209) 896-3315

The Selma Chamber of Commerce publishes a guide to the city's local historical sites. Included in the guide's listings are: early houses of unusual construction, one built completely of cobblestone, and the home of Sierra explorer and inventor, Frank Dusy.

6 - Selma Pioneer Village and Museum
1880 Art Gonzales Parkway, Selma (209) 891-2320

Preserved on this 15-acre site are: St. Ansgar's Lutheran Church, a Queen Anne style house, a turn-of-the-century schoolhouse, a railroad depot and other local historic buildings. Among the related displays are a collection of agricultural implements and tools, household furnishings, toys, and medical and office equipment.

7 - Reedley Museum
10th Street, Reedley (209) 638-1913

Reedley's first city hall was built in 1913. It is now the site of the Reedley Museum, which features an extensive collection of Indian artifacts from this area. Farm machinery, which played an important part in the beginning of the town, is exhibited along with photos of the town and its people through the years.

7 - Reedley's Points of Local Historical Interest
Reedley Chamber of Commerce, 1613 - 12th Street, Reedley (209) 638-3548

Many of Reedley's historic buildings are centrally located in town, between Reed and East Avenues, and Dinuba and North Avenues. Within this area are homes, churches, hotels, schools, and public buildings constructed as early as 1889. The 1903 opera house, at 101 "G" Street, has been restored and is open to the public.

8 - Kingston Ghost Town   SHL 270
Kingston Park, Douglas Avenue, 1 and 1/2 miles southwest of Laton

L. A. Whitmore established a ferry crossing here in 1854. Within two years, the city of Kingston was formed. The town was a stopping place for the Butterfield Stage that used the ferry to cross the Kings River. In 1873, a toll bridge was built to replace the ferry. It was over this bridge that the notorious bandit, Tiburcio Vasquez, and his gang, fled after a daring raid on the town's inhabitants. Nothing remains of this town today.

9 - Mussel Slough Tragedy   SHL 245
1/2 mile east of Grangeville-Hardwick Hwy, between Elder and Everett Avenues, southeast of Hardwick

A dispute between settlers and railroad agents, over title to this land, cost the lives of five ranchers and two railroad agents in a battle fought here on May 11, 1880.

10 - El Adobe de Los Robles Rancho   SHL 206
Hwy 41, at Hanford-Armona Road, 3 miles north of Lemoore

This 1856 adobe is among the oldest restored houses in Kings County. It was built by Daniel Rhoads, who with his brother, John, organized the first relief expedition to attempt the rescue of the Donner Party, at Donner Lake, in the winter of 1847. Both Daniel and John are buried here. John's grave is marked for his heroism in carrying one of the children of the Donner Party, on his back, through miles of snow.

10 - Sarah A. Mooney Memorial Museum
528 West "D" Street at Martin, Lemoore (209) 924-3947

This 1893 two-story brick house contains many artifacts and items of local historical interest. It was built at a time when Lemoore was the largest wool shipping center in the United States.

11 - Chinese Taoist Temple
#12 China Alley, Hanford

Hanford had a large Chinese population—more than 800 families by 1890. This temple was built in 1893, as a meeting hall, sleeping quarters, school and place of worship. It has been restored and is among the oldest temples of its kind in California. It contains many artifacts of the period.

11 - Fort Roosevelt Natural Science and History Museum
870 West Davis, Hanford (209) 582-8970

Within the grounds of Fort Roosevelt is the 1893 Hanford Railroad Freight Depot, and a hands-on history museum for children of all ages. Other features include: an Indian dwelling, a log cabin, an operating hand water pump, a windmill, a cactus garden, a pond and animal exhibits.

11 - Hanford Historic Tour
Chamber of Commerce, 200 Santa Fe Avenue #D, Hanford (209) 582-0483

Hanford's historic China Alley, Courthouse Square and La Bastille (two-story Roman style sheriff's office and jail) are among the turn-of-the-century structures preserved in this community which once had the largest Chinese population in the state. The Chamber of Commerce prints a guide to the town's historic buildings, which is available from their office, or from the Visitor Development Committee at 5 China Alley.

11 - Hanford Carnegie Museum
109 East 8th Street, Hanford (209) 584-1367

Built in 1905, as one of the famous Carnegie Libraries, it now houses the history collection of Hanford and Kings County. Furniture, artifacts, and old photographs are featured exhibits.

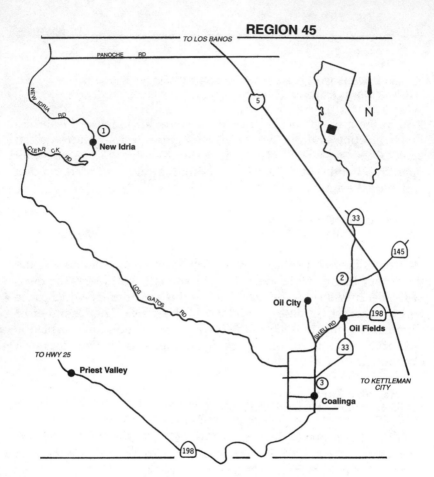

1 - New Idria Quicksilver Mine SHL 324
West of I-5 via Panoche Road, turn south on New Idria Road and follow signs to mine

More than 200 men worked here, in the 1860s, at this country's most productive quicksilver mine. Miles of tunnels were cut into these mountains which continued to produce mercury for more than a century.

2 - Arroyo de Cantua SHL 344
West of Hwy 198/33, between I-5 and Shell Road, north of Coalinga

In the mid 1800s, some of California's most notorious bandits had their principal hideouts in the nearby hills. Joaquin Murietta's gang, who raided mining camps and held-up stages, frequented the Joaquin Rocks. It was here, at Arroyo de Cantua, that he was killed in 1853 by a posse of State Rangers.

3 - R. C. Baker Memorial Museum
297 West Elm Avenue, Coalinga (209) 935-1914

The geological and historical lore of the Coalinga area is preserved through displays of fossils, oil field equipment and turn-of-the-century artifacts from some of the early settlers of this "wild frontier boom town." Early Yokuts Indian history is also displayed. This museum survived the disastrous 1983 earthquake that struck Coalinga, but other buildings and historical/cultural homes were destroyed or heavily damaged.

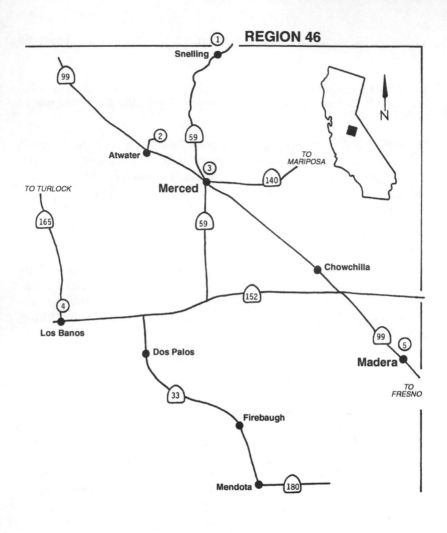

1 - Snelling Courthouse SHL 409
Hwy 59, monument in front of the courthouse, center of Snelling

This 1857 courthouse was the first courthouse erected in Merced County, when Snelling was the county seat. The county seat was moved to Merced in 1872, but the courthouse was still used as a justice court until 1977. A monument was erected in 1930, commemorating the 75th anniversary of the organization of Merced County and is dedicated to the pioneers who settled here.

362

2 - Castle Air Museum
Castle Air Force Base, Santa Fe Drive, north of Hwy 99, Atwater
(209) 723-2178

Restored, vintage, military aircraft from World War II, the Korean War and Vietnam Conflict periods are exhibited here. Among them is "The British Vulcan," which is still in use today, and the only nuclear bomber of its type on public display in the United States. An inside museum has displays of: Army Air Corps and Air Force uniforms; the once top secret, Nordon bombsight; and personal military items including a Congressional Medal of Honor.

3 - Temporary Detention Camps for Japanese-Americans   SHL 934
Merced County Fairgrounds, 8th and "J" Streets, Merced   (209) 722-1506

Following the start of World War II, Japanese and Japanese-Americans were ordered to report to temporary detention camps for relocation until the War's end. From here, they would be moved to permanent centers across the United States. The Japanese population here reached a maximum of 4,508 in the four months that this facility served as an assembly center.

3 - Merced County Historical Society and Courthouse Museum
21st and "N" Streets, in Courthouse Park, Merced   (209) 723-2401

Construction of Merced County's courthouse was completed in 1875, three years after Merced was named the county seat. Several county offices are housed in this restored three-story Italiante Renaissance Revival style structure which operates primarily as a historical museum. The treasurer's office has been completely renovated and features such details as antique typewriters, oil lamps and wire teller cages at the counter.

4 - Canal Farm   SHL 548
1/2 mile east of the Los Banos business district and railroad tracks, Los Banos

Henry Miller and his partner, Charles Lux were the state's best-known cattle and sheep ranchers. During the last half of the nineteenth century they acquired more than a million acres of land throughout California and turned desert property into productive fields through irrigation. Miller and Lux established their head-quarters at the Canal Farm site in 1873. The name "Canal Farm" came from the gravity irrigation system developed on this site in 1871. The present Canal Farm Inn was built on the foundation of Miller's ranch house.

4 - Los Banos   SHL 550
At junction of Hwy 165 and Hwy 33/152, Los Banos Chamber of Commerce (800) 336-6354

Padre Arroyo de la Cuesta named this place Los Banos (which means "the Baths" in Spanish) for the pools of water that padres would frequent here, on their travels to the San Joaquin Valley, in the early 1800s.

4 - Ralph Milliken Museum
905 Pacheco Boulevard, Los Banos (209) 826-5505

Military uniforms, Indian relics and displays of local historical interest are featured exhibits of this museum.

5 - Madera County Historical Society Museum
210 West Yosemite Avenue, Madera (209) 673-0291

Madera County's first courthouse, built here in 1900, is now the home of the historical society's museum. Local Indian artifacts, home furnishings and the history of Madera's lumber industry are displayed. A large collection of old photographs show the growth of Madera County since it was organized in 1893.

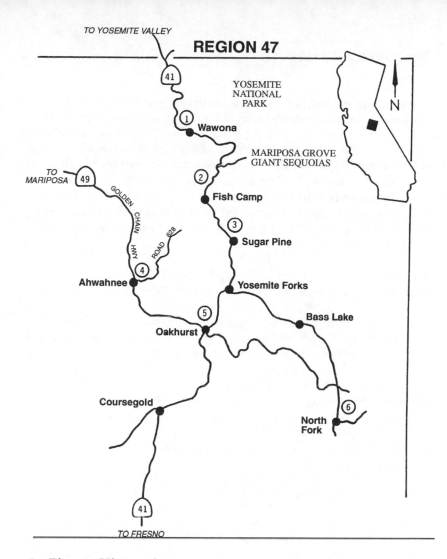

TO YOSEMITE VALLEY

41

YOSEMITE
NATIONAL
PARK

N

1 Wawona

MARIPOSA GROVE
GIANT SEQUOIAS

TO
MARIPOSA 49

2

Fish Camp

GOLDEN CHAIN HWY

ROAD 628

3

Sugar Pine

4

Ahwahnee

Yosemite Forks

5

Bass Lake

Oakhurst

Coursegold

6

North
Fork

41

TO FRESNO

1 - Pioneer History Center
Hwy 41, 6 miles south of Yosemite Park, Wawona

Galen Clark discovered the Mariposa Grove Big Trees, eight miles
from here, in 1857. He built a covered bridge the following year. It
was restored in 1956. Now, this covered bridge is the center of an
outdoor display featuring several historic buildings relocated from
Yosemite National Park for permanent preservation. A collection of
horse-drawn wagons and original mine equipment, from the Great
Sierra Mine Company, is also exhibited.

2 - Yosemite National Park-Southern Entrance
Hwy 41, 2 miles north of Fish Camp (209) 372-0265

Yosemite Valley was discovered in 1851, by Major John D. Savage, while in pursuit of Indians. From this southern entrance to the park, it's a short drive to Mariposa Grove Big Trees to see some of the world's largest living things—the Sequoia Gigantea trees. This route also provides access to Glacier Point and Yosemite tunnel. At the end of the tunnel is a spectacular view of Yosemite Valley with its rugged peaks and waterfalls.

3 - Yosemite Mountain Sugar Pine Railroad
56001 Hwy 41, 2 miles south of Fish Camp (209) 683-7273

Sugar Pine lumber was brought out of Sierra National Forest by narrow gauge logger trains which still operate over this four-mile railbed. Rough-cut lumber would then be sent from Sugar Pine, to Madera, via a 63-mile flume—one of the longest flumes in the world. The history of this region is told during a 45-minute ride on the restored, 1928 Shay steam locomotive and Model "A" powered railcars. Yosemite Mountain also features the Thornberry Museum.

4 - California Native American Ceremonial
Roundhouses (Thematic) SHL 1001
Wassama Roundhouse State Historic Park, Hwy 628 and Hwy 49 near Ahwanee (209) 822-2332

The ceremonial roundhouse is the Miwok Indian Village's most spiritual and respected structure. It is where the village leader lived, the site of dances, religious ceremonies, and social events. When the leader died, the roundhouse was burned and another was built when a new leader was chosen. This authentically reconstructed round-house continues to serve the cultural needs of the local Miwok people. Other Indian structures include a sweat house and several bark lean-tos. Nearby, on the grounds of the old Ahwanee Sanatorium, is the burial place of a U.S. Army officer and several Indians. They died in a battle when captured Indians were being moved from Yosemite Valley, in 1851. Ahwanee is also the site of the famous 63-mile flume that carried cut lumber from Sugar Pine to Madera.

5 - Fresno Flats Historical Park
49777 Road 427 off Road 426, Oakhurst (209) 683-6570

This historic park was established to capture the flavor of family life in Fresno Flats (now called Oakhurst) from the 1860s to the 1880s. An old log cabin, two houses (one with original furnishings), two jail houses, a reconstructed blacksmith shop and the second schoolhouse in Madera County are part of this large outdoor exhibit. Also displayed is a section of the flume that carried lumber 63 miles, between Sugar Pine and Madera, and a collection of horse-drawn wagons.

6 - Sierra Mono Museum
Junction of Roads 228 and 225, North Fork (209) 877-2115

Operated entirely by Indians, this museum is dedicated to the preservation of the Mono Indian culture. Members of the Mono Tribe donated the many Indian baskets and artifacts on exhibit.

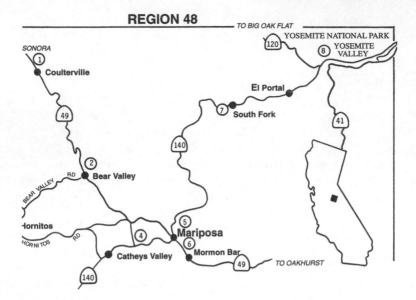

1- Coulterville SHL 332
Hwy 49, 28 miles north of Mariposa

George Coulter came and established a store, in this mining town in 1849-1850. He built the town's first hotel, which stood across the street from the Jeffrey Hotel. An old mine steam locomotive, and the hangman's tree, stand in front of the Wells Fargo building along Coulterville's main street.

2 - Bear Valley SHL 331
Bear Valley Road, 16 miles north of Mariposa, Bear Valley

Colonel John Fremont, who moved the location of his Mexican land grant on two prior occasions, "floated" his grant in 1848 to include the gold rich hills of the Mariposa region. Bear Valley became the headquarters for his vast holdings where he built the town and his elegant home. A few of the original stone and adobe buildings can still be seen from the days when this town of 3,000 was a rich gold mining community.

3 - Hornitos SHL 333
West of Mariposa at junction of Hornitos and Bear Valley Road

The town of Hornitos means "little ovens," in Spanish, and may have gotten its name from the little oven-shaped graves built above the ground. Some of the graves can still be seen in the cemetery by the Catholic Church. Hornitos was first settled by Mexicans who were driven out of neighboring Quartzburg. It was a wild, lawless town and was said to have been frequented by the infamous Joaquin Murieta. As the placers at Quartzburg gave out, law-abiding citizens moved here, incorporated the city (the first and only incorporated city in Mariposa County) and passed laws that brought order to the town. Several of the town's old buildings still show bullet holes from the gun battles that took place here.

4 - Aqua Fria SHL 518
Hwy 140, between Catheys Valley and Mariposa on Aqua Fria Road

In 1850-1851, the first county seat of Mariposa County was located here. At the time, the town was an important mining community and the existing county comprised about 20 percent of the state's area. In 1852, additional counties were formed, the size of the county was reduced, and the county seat was moved to the town of Mariposa. Nothing remains to be seen of the original town.

5 - Mariposa Museum and History Center
5119 Jessie Street, Mariposa (209) 966-2924

This historical museum has interesting exhibits of several typical 49er Gold Rush buildings, a five stamp quartz mill, wagons and mining equipment. The collections also include Indian artifacts and items of local historical interest.

5 - Mariposa Historic Sites
Library and History Center, Jessie and 12th Streets, Mariposa (209) 966-2140

A guide to Mariposa's historical buildings is available at the History Center. Many of Mariposa's buildings date back into the 1849-1870 Gold Rush era.

Interior Mariposa Museum and History Center. Courtesy of Mariposa Museum and History Center.

5 - Mariposa County Courthouse   SHL 670
Bullion Street, between 9th and 10th, one block east of Hwy 140, Mariposa
(209) 966-3222

Mariposa's residents erected this courthouse in 1854, after the town became the county seat. It is the oldest active courthouse in California. Many of the building's original furnishings are still being used. Since there are no active incorporated cities in Mariposa County, the entire county is governed from this building.

5 - California State Mining and Mineral Museum
Mariposa County Fairgrounds, on Hwy 49 about 2 miles south of Hwy 140, Mariposa (209) 742-7625

Leaf gold, wire gold, nuggets and some of the finest specimens of crystallized gold from the Mother Lode, are displayed in this unique museum where visitors can explore an underground mine tunnel, or operate a working scale model of a five stamp quartz mill. Also exhibited are: diamonds, minerals and meteorites, discovered in California; and Benitoite, the state gemstone. With 20,000 gems and minerals, it is one of the largest collections in the world. Historic mining artifacts are used to depict the state's gold mining history in one wing of the museum.

6 - Mormon Bar   SHL 323
2 miles southeast of Mariposa at Hwy 49 and Ben Hur Road

Mormons settled here in 1849, and worked this area for a short time, in search of gold. Others worked this area as well, including thousands of Chinese. The original town site was obliterated when the present highway was widened through this area.

7 - Site of Savage's Trading Post   SHL 527
8 miles west of El Portal on Hwy 140, South Fork

John Savage established a trading post near here in 1849, but concern about possible Indian attacks forced him to move in less than a year. In 1851, Savage and a volunteer battalion pursued the Indians into Yosemite Valley. His discovery of Yosemite Valley opened the area to tourists in just four years.

8 - Yosemite Valley   SHL 790
Arch Rock entrance, east of El Portal, Hwy 140   (209) 372-0265

Yosemite Valley was discovered in 1851, by Major James Savage, of the Mariposa Battalion, when he entered the valley in search of Indians. Within just a few years, regular tourist traffic began and the first hotel was built. In 1864, President Lincoln granted Yosemite Valley, and the Mariposa Big Tree Grove, to the State of California. This first state park in the country was returned to the federal government, in 1906, so that it could become part of Yosemite National Park.

Several historic buildings are maintained in the valley, including the Old Village Chapel (built from children's donations) and the Ahwanee Hotel with its original antique furnishings. Yosemite's museums feature outstanding collections of Indian artifacts, military uniforms, historic photographs, and displays that depict the culture of the Native Americans that lived in this valley.

The grandeur of Yosemite's natural beauty makes a lasting impression on those who see this National Park. Its waterfalls are among the highest in the world; and its landscape of open meadows, and domes of ice-shaped granite, remain today much as they were when Major Savage first saw the valley.

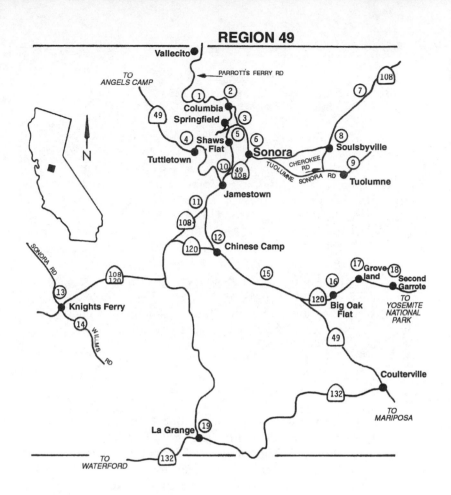

1 - Parrott's Ferry   SHL 438
Parrott's Ferry Road, between Columbia and Vallecito at the Stanislaus River

In 1860 a ferry was put into operation to cross the Stanislaus River at this site. Ferry service continued until the first bridge was built in 1903.

2 - Columbia State Historic Park   SHL 123
4 miles north of Sonora off Hwy 49, Columbia   (209) 532-4301

More than $80 million in gold was shipped from this town of several thousand residents, in the early 1850s. The entire 12-square block town of Columbia has been preserved as a California State Historic Park, with many of its original buildings being operated as hotels, restaurants, shops and businesses. Overnight guests can stay at the ornately furnished, 1856 City Hotel, or the 1857 Fallon Hotel, which was restored and reopened in 1986. Hidden Treasures Gold Mining offers tours of their active mine. The 1857 Fallon House Theater features year-round stage productions. The state's oldest continually operating barber shop and a newspaper operating since 1855, the *Columbia Gazette*, link visitors to the past. Every building in this historic town has been identified and listed in the park guide. Original furnishings of the period, stages and horse-drawn buggies add to the atmosphere of this living museum.

3 - Springfield   SHL 432
1 mile southwest of Columbia

Water, for placer mining, was in such abundance from this town's springs that miners would bring their gold-bearing earth by the cartload to be washed. The town was laid out over a square mile, with a central plaza, shops, a schoolhouse and a church. Springfield's old brick church still remains in the central plaza.

3 - Sawmill Flat   SHL 424
3 miles southeast of Columbia and 1 and 1/2 miles south of Yankee Hill, on Sawmill Flat Road

The need for timbers in the gold mines brought about the construction of two pioneer sawmills, on Wood's Creek, in the 1850s.

4 - Mark Twain's Cabin   SHL 138
1 mile west of Tuttletown off Hwy 49

Mark Twain (Samuel Clemens), the American writer and humorist, was a guest of the Gillis brothers and stayed at their cabin, in 1864-1865. The original cabin was destroyed by fire. This replica cabin was built around the same fireplace and chimney, which still stands.

Street scene and blacksmith shop. Courtesy of Columbia State Historic Park.

Wells Fargo Express. Courtesy of Columbia State Historic Park.

4 - Tuttletown SHL 124
6 miles northwest of Sonora on Hwy 49

The first permanent house to be built in Tuolumne County was a log cabin, constructed in 1848, by Anson Tuttle, the county's first judge. Mark Twain (Samuel Clemens) lived nearby and would trade at Swerer's store in town. Another of the town's famous writers was Bret Harte, who was said to have been a clerk at Swerer's store where he waited on Mark Twain.

5 - Shaw's Flat SHL 395
Shaw's Flat Road, 2 miles north of Sonora

The large, 1850s, gold camp of Shaw's Flat was named for Mandeville Shaw, who planted an orchard here in 1849. Mississippi House was built here in 1850, as a bar, store and post office. It contains many original furnishings. The miner's bell, that was used to call men to work or announce meetings, is now displayed at the schoolhouse.

6 - St. James Episcopal Church and Museum SHL 139
North Washington Street, at Snell Street, Sonora
(209) 532-7644 or (209) 532-0104

Built in 1859-1860, St. James Episcopal Church is California's second oldest Episcopal Church of frame construction. The "Red Church," with its fine stained glass windows, is considered one of the finest frame buildings in California from that era. Its Norwegian designer, the Reverend John G. Gassman, was also the church's first pastor. History of the famous church is displayed in the church's upstairs social hall.

6 - Big Bonanza Mine Site
House at 61 West Snell Street overlooks site, Sonora

Sonora was a gold-rich region of California. More than $40 million in quartz gold was mined within a couple mile radius of the city. The Big Bonanza Mine was one of the most famous, and productive, pocket mines in the state. During one week, in the 1870s, the Bonanza was said to have yielded half a million dollars in gold. No part of the mine can be seen today, but many homes built during the period have been preserved around the mine site.

6 - Tuolumne County Museum and History Center
158 West Bradford Street, Sonora (209) 532-1317

Tuolumne County's restored, 1857, jail building now houses artifacts and archives of the county's historical and genealogical societies. An extensive collection of more than 17,000 photographs; the Tuolumne County gold collection; pioneer firearms; and the history of the westward migration to California and Oregon, between 1841-1860, is displayed.

6 - Sonora Historical Tour
Tuolumne County Museum and History Center, 158 West Bradford Street, Sonora (209) 532-1317

Sonora . . . A Guide to Yesterday, is published by the county museum as a guide to more than fifty of the city's Gold Rush era and turn-of-the-century homes and businesses. Some of the structures described in the guide include: an 1856 cast iron front building; the Brandford building, with its copper doors and ornate dome; imposing Victorians; the old Sonora Grammar School, with its silvery dome; an original 1857 adobe-type brick home; and the three-story Roman pressed brick building that houses the county courthouse.

6 - Sonora Fire Department Museum
City Hall, 94 West Washington Street, second floor, Sonora (209) 532-7432

Vintage fire equipment, uniforms and memorabilia from the 100 year history of the Sonora Fire Department are exhibited. A fine collection of historic fire fighting photographs is also displayed.

7 - Sonora-Mono Road   SHL 422
Monument is 14 miles northeast of Sonora on Hwy 108 at Sonora Pass

Emigrants, supply wagons and passenger stages followed this approximate route, to cross the Sierra Nevada, through Sonora Pass. Travel over this difficult terrain was improved with the completion of the Sonora-Mono Road in 1864.

8 - Soulsbyville SHL 420
1 mile south of Hwy 108 via Soulsbyville Road

Benjamin Soulsby brought in hundreds of Cornish miners from England, in the 1850s, to work in his quartz gold mine. More than $6 million in gold was mined by the first of the century. Soulsbyville's predominate landmark is the old lumber mill refuse burner near the site of the Soulsby Mine.

8 - Cherokee SHL 445
Cherokee Road just southeast of Soulsbyville

The first placer gold in this region was discovered in 1853 by the Scott brothers, who were descendants of Cherokee Indians.

9 - Tuolumne SHL 407
East of Sonora on the Tuolumne-Sonora Road

The first settlers to this gold mining camp were the Summers, who named the town Summersville. The town, which was located near the center of the East Belt placer gold rush of 1856-1857, was later renamed Tuolumne.

10 - Jamestown SHL 431
3 and 1/2 miles southwest of Sonora on Hwy 49/108

Colonel George James founded Jamestown during the gold rush of 1848, just north of where Tuolumne County's first gold discovery was made. Some of the original buildings, from the late 1800s, are preserved in "Jimtown" and are still being used as businesses.

10 - Railtown 1897 State Historic Park
5th Avenue and Reservoir Road, Jamestown (209) 984-3953

Sierra Railroad operates from its depot at this historic park, on a 12-mile round trip, over this famous line. Sixty pieces of railroad equipment, an operating roundhouse and Sierra Railroad shops are part of this unique working railroad park. One of the park's vintage locomotives was built in 1891 and is still in operation.

11 - Montezuma   SHL 122
3 miles south of Jamestown at the junction of Hwy 49 and Hwy 108

Montezuma was a town of vast underground gold mines and an important community on the road between Sonora, and the stage headquarters, at Chinese Camp.

12 - Chinese Camp   SHL 423
South of Jamestown at junction of Hwy 49 and Hwy 120

Five thousand Chinese mined this area during the 1850s. Their city became the headquarters for stage lines that ran throughout the county. The post office, built in 1854, is still being used. The 1855, St. Francis Xavier Catholic Church, was restored in 1949. In 1856, a disagreement between two Chinese Tongs (Sam Yap and Yan Woo) was resolved in a battle between the two groups. Twenty-one hundred Chinese were engaged in the war, but casualties were light because only homemade weapons were used.

12 - Wells Fargo Building   SHL 140
Chinese Camp off Hwy 49

Only partial ruins remain of this 1849 building that served the town of Chinese Camp, as a general merchandise store, and Wells Fargo office.

13 - Knights Ferry   SHL 347
Hwy 120 and Sonora Road

William Knight emigrated to California with the Workman-Rowland party, in 1841, and established a ferry operation north of Sacramento two years later. In 1848, he started the first ferry crossing of the Stanislaus River, providing prospectors access to the rich claims to be found along the river. Killed in a gunfight a year later, his operations were taken over by the Dent brothers, who built a covered bridge, sawmill and gristmill. The flood of 1862 destroyed the bridge and gristmill. Both were rebuilt and can be seen today. The Dent house, iron jail house, Masonic Hall and general store (the oldest continuously operated store in the state) are among the gold rush period structures that can be seen in town.

14 - Willms Ranch   SHL 415
2 miles southeast of Knights Ferry on Willms Road

Pioneer merchants, John Willms and John Kappelmann, began acquiring land from miners and settlers in 1850. By 1852 they had a total of 3,600 acres under the "KW" brand. After Kappelmann's death in 1881, Willms continued to operate the ranch, increasing it to almost 10,000 acres by 1910. This pioneer ranch is still run by the Willms family and is not open to the public.

15 - Jacksonville   SHL 419
Hwy 120, northwest approach to Don Pedro Bridge at the Tuolumne River

In 1849, Colonel A. M. Jackson opened a trading post and established the town of Jacksonville along the banks of the Tuolumne River. The county's first orchard was planted here, by Julian Smart, that same year. Jacksonville, which grew to become the county's second largest city, is now covered by the waters of the Don Pedro Dam and Reservoir.

16 - Big Oak Flat   SHL 406
Priest's Grade (Hwy 120), 2 miles west of Groveland

Before the town of Big Oak Flat was given its present name, it was called Savage Diggins . . . for John Savage who found gold here in 1849. Two years later, Savage became the first white man to see Yosemite Valley as he pursued Yosemite Indians into this unexplored region. In the town of Big Oak Flats, miners, seeking their share of the $25 million in gold that this area produced, undermined the huge oak that stood in the center of town by digging for gold at its roots. Pieces from the tree have been preserved in the monument at this site.

17 - Groveland   SHL 446
Plaque on Main Street, Groveland   (209) 962-6416

The first adobe homes were built here, in 1849, around the region's rich placer mines. The town was originally called "First Garrote," because of the hanging of a horse thief here. Its name was later changed to "Groveland." A few restored adobe buildings from the 1850s can still be seen in this historic town.

18 - Second Garrote   SHL 460
2 miles east of Groveland on Hwy 120

Mines in this area produced gold for those who lived in the town of "Second Garrote." The town is said to have gotten its name from its famous "hangman's tree," where up to 60 men were hung.

19 - La Grange   SHL 414
Hwy 132, west of Coulterville

The town was originally known as "French Bar," when it was settled by French miners, in 1852. La Grange ("barn" in French) had a population of 5,000, in 1855, when it became the county seat. Evidence of gold mining can be seen in the area's immense tailing piles, and the old gold dredge, now on display at the town's park. Several buildings remain from the 1850s, including: the Wells Fargo building; the La Grange jail; St. Louis Catholic Church; and the adobe museum. The entire historic town of La Grange is listed on the National Register of Historic Places.

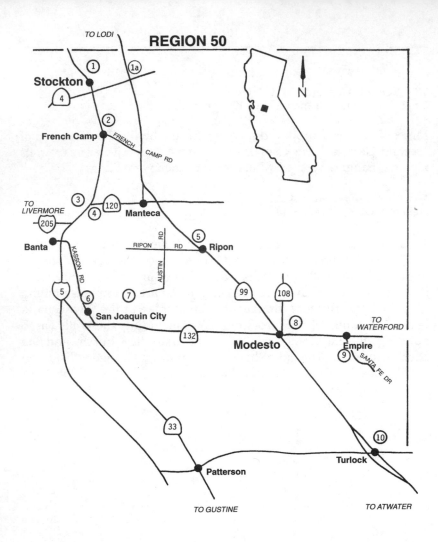

REGION 50

TO LODI

Stockton

French Camp

FRENCH CAMP RD

Manteca

TO LIVERMORE

Banta

KASSON RD

RIPON RD

AUSTIN RD

Ripon

San Joaquin City

Modesto

Empire

SANTA FE DR

TO WATERFORD

Patterson

Turlock

TO GUSTINE

TO ATWATER

N

1 - Haggin Memorial Gallery and Pioneer Historical Museum
1201 North Pershing Avenue, Stockton (209) 462-1566

Most of the art shown in this museum was collected by Louis Haggin, a pioneer Stockton cattle rancher. Historic artifacts, Indian relics, and replicas of local historic interiors are among the featured exhibits.

1 - Burial Place of John Brown SHL 513
1100 East Weber Avenue, Stockton

John Brown, who was known as California's Paul Revere, used a relay of horses and road 500 miles to San Francisco, to warn Commodore Stockton of the Mexican siege of Los Angeles, in 1846. He spent the last years of his life in Stockton and was buried at Citizen's Cemetery that once stood near this site.

1 - Weber Point SHL 165
Plaque at the intersection of Center Street and Miner Avenue, Stockton

Charles Weber, who established San Joaquin Valley's first white settlement at French Camp, also laid out this town, which became Stockton in 1847. Weber incorporated this city in 1850, before California was admitted to the Union, and named it in honor of Robert Stockton, U.S. Naval Commander in the Mexican War. It was the first city in California to receive an American name. Weber built his two-story adobe and frame house, at this site, in 1850. He occupied it until his death in 1881.

1 - Site of First Building in Stockton SHL 178
Lindsay Point, at the west end of Lindsay Street, behind City Hall, Stockton

Thomas Lindsay, a pioneer settler of this region in 1844, built Stockton's first structure on this site. Indians killed Lindsay in the spring of 1845, and burned the tule hut he had built here. A plaque to the memory of this pioneer was placed at Stockton's City Hall, which stands near Lindsay's original homesite.

1 - Temple Israel Cemetery SHL 765
Located on blocks bounded by Acacia, Pilgrim, Poplar and Union Streets, Stockton

Founder of the city of Stockton, Charles Weber, donated the land and established this Jewish cemetery in 1851. It is the oldest Jewish cemetery, in continuous operation, west of the Rocky Mountains.

1 - Reuel Colt Gridley Monument SHL 801
Stockton Rural Cemetery, Cemetery Lane north of Harding Way, Stockton

Reuel Gridley raised $275,000, to aid Union soldiers during the Civil War, by selling and reselling a "sack of flour." His humanitarian relief effort was commemorated, with the erection of this monument at his grave, in 1887.

1 - Pollardville Ghost Town
10464 Hwy 99, Stockton

Old buildings from surrounding communities, and structures used for movie sets, were relocated to form this "ghost town." Main Street is reminiscent of the Old West of the 1800s.

1 - Temporary Detention Camps for Japanese-Americans SHL 934
San Joaquin County Fairgrounds, Stockton (209) 466-5041

After Japan declared war on the United States, and the U.S. became involved in World War II, all Japanese and Japanese-Americans on the West Coast were ordered to report to detention camps for relocation. From these temporary detention camps, they were sent to permanent camps across the United States, until the end of the War. Japanese population reached a maximum of 4,271 in the five months that this facility served as an assembly center.

1A - Trail of the John C. Fremont 1844 Expedition SHL 995
Northwest corner of Junction Hwy 88 and Calaveras River, San Joaquin County

Lt. John C. Fremont's report to Congress, of his 1844 Expedition into California, had world-wide impact and was a turning point in the state's history. Fremont's highly publicized and well-documented report, a descriptive account of the Eden-like lands he explored, followed on the heels of the admission of Texas into the Union, and whetted the appetite of expansionists who wanted a United States stretching from the Atlantic to the Pacific. One of the sites of that famous expedition is commemorated here.

2 - French Camp   SHL 668
Between 2nd and 4th Streets on Elm, French Camp

French-Canadian fur trappers and their families camped here every spring and summer, between 1832 and 1845. These employees of the Hudson Bay Company trapped beaver, mink, and bear along the San Joaquin River. Charles Weber established San Joaquin Valley's first permanent white settlement at this site in 1843. Weber would later be the founder of Stockton.

2 - California Chicory Works (Site)   SHL 935
1672 West Bowman Road, French Camp

During the period 1890-1910, one of America's major producers of chicory had a processing plant at this site. Chicory, a coffee substitute, was roasted, ground and shipped to markets all around the United States from this facility.

3 - First Transcontinental Railroad-Completion Site   SHL 780.7
1 mile east of I-5 and Hwy 120 junction, where the Southern Pacific Bridge crosses the San Joaquin River near Stewart and Manthey Roads

Completion of the San Joaquin River Bridge, in September 1869, was the final link that connected San Francisco to Sacramento, and it was the last part of the first transcontinental railroad to be completed. Travel by rail, between San Francisco and St. Louis, Missouri was now possible for the first time. This historic bridge still remains to commemorate this important milestone in coast-to-coast transportation.

4 - Landing Place of Sailing Launch *Comet*   SHL 437
Monument on Hwy 120, west of Manteca near the San Joaquin River

It was here that the sailing launch, *Comet*, landed in 1846 with twenty Mormon pioneers, who were on their way to establish the colony of

New Hope. Two years later a ferry operation was established at this point.

5 - New Hope SHL 438
Monument at Fourth and Locust Streets, Ripon

The first settlers in the town of New Hope were twenty pioneer Mormons, who established a colony nearby, in 1846. They erected three log cabins, brought in farm equipment and planted acres of wheat. The rains that came that first winter flooded them out. By the fall of 1847 the entire colony left.

6 - San Joaquin City SHL 777
West side of San Joaquin River, below the mouth of the Stanislaus River via Kasson Road, 10 miles southeast of Banta

An agricultural settlement was begun here in 1849 and served as a terminal for boats that plied the San Joaquin River during the gold rush days. Several businesses and homes were built, but nothing remains of this town today.

7 - Battle of the Stanislaus SHL 214
Bank of Stanislaus River, 6 miles west of Ripon, 2 miles from junction of San Joaquin River in Caswell Memorial State Park

It was on this site, in the late spring of 1829, that Mexican troops under the command of General Vallejo, fought the Cosumnes Indians in an attempt to halt their raids against local ranches. It was one of the few battles in California where a cannon was used.

8 - McHenry Museum
1402 "I" Street, Modesto (209) 577-5366

This museum's unique displays of Modesto County's, and Stanislaus County's, pioneer lifestyles include: turn-of-the-century rooms, clothing, a doctor's office and historic artifacts. The nearby Victorian style, McHenry Mansion, was constructed in 1883, by one of the town's first families and has been restored to its original condition.

8 - Miller California Ranch and Buggy Display
9425 Yosemite Boulevard (Hwy 132), Modesto (209) 522-1781

The late Pierce Miller's collection of antique "rolling stock" is displayed on his former ranch. Horseless and horse-drawn vehicles, steam engines and antique household items are among the interesting exhibits. Also on the grounds of the ranch is an authentic general store, blacksmith, and a turn-of-the-century barber shop. Open for group tours by appointment only.

9 - Empire City   SHL 418
Monument 1/2 mile west of cemetery, Lakewood Memorial Park, 1 mile south of Empire on Sante Fe

Floods in 1852 nearly destroyed Empire City, which, at that time, was located on the Tuolumne River, at the head of navigation. The town rebuilt and served as the county seat for about a year. All that remains today of the original town site is the pioneer cemetery, which is part of Lakewood Memorial Park.

10 - Temporary Detention Camps for
Japanese-Americans   SHL 934
Intersection of Main Street and Hwy 165, Turlock

In 1942, after Japan bombed Pearl Harbor and declared war on the United States, Japanese and Japanese-Americans on the West Coast were ordered to report to temporary detention camps, until they were relocated to permanent camps across the United States. One of those temporary camps was located here. The Japanese population reached a maximum of 3,661 in the four months that this facility served as an assembly center.

11 - Oakdale Museum
212 West "F" Street, Oakdale (209) 847-9229

The 1869 home of Oakdale's first postmaster, the oldest home in the city, now houses the collections of the Oakdale Museum. History of the area is displayed in old photographs, artifacts and memorabilia.

REGION 51

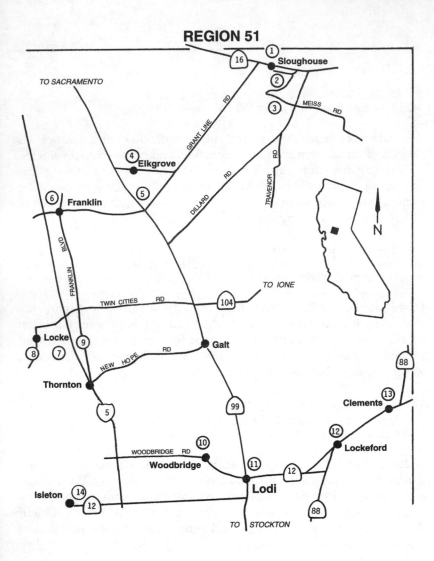

1 - Slough House SHL 575
Hwy 16 (Jackson Road), Sloughhouse

Jared Sheldon, owner of a Mexican land grant in this region, built a hotel on this site in 1850 and called it the "Slough House." The original hotel burned in 1890. It was reconstructed that same year, on this site, where it still stands today.

2 - Site of Sheldon Gristmill SHL 439
1 mile southeast of Sloughhouse on Meiss Road

Jared Sheldon erected a gristmill at this site, in 1846-1847, on land that was part of his Mexican land grant. He became involved in a serious confrontation with miners when the dam he built to provide water for his mill flooded their claims. He built a fort, and equipped it with a cannon to warn the miners, but they captured his fort. When Sheldon brought in reinforcements, he and two men were killed in the ensuing battle. A year after this battle, Sheldon's dam was washed away in the floods of 1851-1852.

3 - Michigan Bar SHL 468
North of the junction of Dillard and Tavernor Roads, south of Hwy 16

Two men from Michigan founded this gold camp, in 1849, along the shore of the Cosumnes River. By the early 1850s, the town's population had increased to 1,500. Introduction of hydraulic mining destroyed most of the original town site and the town's landmarks.

4 - Site of First County Free Library Branch SHL 817
9125 Elk Grove Boulevard, Elk Grove

At this site, the first free county library branch in California was established in 1908. This important first in this state's history is commemorated here.

4 - Grave of Elitha Donner Wilder SHL 719
Elk Grove Masonic Cemetery, Elk Grove

Elitha Donner, a daughter of George Donner, was rescued by the first relief party to reach their snowbound party in the winter of

1846-1847. She married Benjamin Wilder in 1853 and was buried here in July 1923.

5 - Murphy's Ranch SHL 680
West of Hwy 99 at Grant Line Road, Elk Grove

Concerned that the Mexican government had plans to force all American settlers out of California, a group of pioneers formed the Bear Flag Party with plans to form an independent republic. The first action of the "Bear Flag Revolt" took place when the Americans overpowered the Mexican Army and took their horses from this ranch. Four days later, on June 14, 1846, General Vallejo was captured and the Bear Flag raised over Sonora.

6 - Grave of Alexander Hamilton Willard SHL 657
Franklin Cemetery, Hood Franklin Road, Franklin

In 1804, President Jefferson sent out the Lewis and Clark Expedition to discover the course of the Missouri River. One of the last surviving members of that historic expedition was Alexander Willard, who came to California, in 1852. He was buried here in 1865.

7 - Benson's Ferry SHL 149
3 miles north of Thornton off I-5

A ferry crossing, of the Mokelumne River, was established here in 1849. It became "Benson's Ferry" when John Benson purchased it the following year. Benson's son-in-law operated the ferry for several years after Benson was killed by an employee in 1859. A bridge now stands near the site of this pioneer ferry crossing.

8 - Locke Historic District
Bounded by the Sacramento River, Locke Road, Alley and Levee Streets, Locke

Commercial structures in this part of town remain much the same as when they were built in the early 1900s. Locke was settled by the Chinese in 1915. The community continues to be almost exclusively Chinese today.

9 - Mokelumne City (Site) SHL 162
Junction of the Cosumnes and Mokelumne Rivers, 3 miles north of Thornton, via Franklin Boulevard

Within a few years after Mokelumne City was founded at the junction of the Mokelumne and Cosumnes Rivers, it became the second most populous city in the county. This prosperous city was devastated by the floods of 1862. It never fully recovered. Nothing remains of the city today.

10 - Woodbridge SHL 358
2 miles northwest of Lodi between I-5 and Hwy 99

The town of Woodbridge was established on the south side of Woods' toll bridge. It was an active community during the late 1850s and early 1860s. A few of the town's pre-1900 buildings remain standing along this once popular stage route.

10 - San Joaquin Valley College SHL 520
Lilac Street, Woodbridge

This campus was erected in 1878-1879, as Woodbridge Academy. It became San Joaquin Valley College two years later and continued to operate until the early 1900s. The school building that stands today was built after the original structure was demolished in 1922.

10 - Woods Ferry and Bridge SHL 163
Mokelumne River, approximately 250 feet north of Woodbridge Irrigation District Diversion Dam, Woodbridge

The first crossing of the Mokelumne River, in this region, was by a ferry established in 1852, by Jeremiah Woods. Woods erected a toll bridge, in 1858, to replace the ferry after this became a popular stage route between Sacramento and Stockton.

11 - Lodi Arch SHL 931
Pine and Sacramento Streets, Lodi

Built for the Tokay Carnival of 1907, this is one of two ceremonial arches remaining in California. The Tokay Carnival is now celebrated annually, in September, as the Lodi Grape Festival. Ninety-seven per cent of the world's Flame Tokay Grape is grown in this area.

11 - San Joaquin County Historical Society and Museum
11793 North Micke Grove Road, Lodi (209) 368-9154

Some of the most extensive collections of local historic materials and unique personal collections, to be found in California museum exhibits, are featured here, including: 3000 hand-powered and foot-operated tools, agricultural implements, tractors and mine collections. The museum's latest addition is the re-created 1890s home of Stockton's founder, Charles Webber.

12 - Lockeford SHL 365
Northeast of Lodi on Hwy 12

Dr. Locke came to California as a physician, in 1849, and with his brother, bought land around the Mokelumne River. Within the next few years, the city of Lockeford was established and became a shipping point on the Mokelumne River. The growth of the city ebbed as the mines played out and the railroad became the prime mover of goods . . . but the city didn't die. Many of the town's original buildings can still be seen today.

13 - Lone Star Mill (Site) SHL 155
1 mile north of Clements via the old Ione Road, Hwy 12/88

In 1854, the first business established in this area was the Lone Star Mill, a sawmill on the Mokelumne River. The following year, a flour mill was added, which continued to operate for 30 years. Nothing remains of these mills which were abandoned in 1885.

14 - Bing Kong Tong Building
Mid point on two city blocks of historic Main Street, Isleton Chamber of Commerce (916) 777-5880

This historic building was the Chinese cultural meeting center for the Tong Society, grammar school and church. It is being restored as a museum to house the collections of the Isleton Historical Society. A Shintu Shrine, art, furniture and historical artifacts will be displayed.

REGION 52

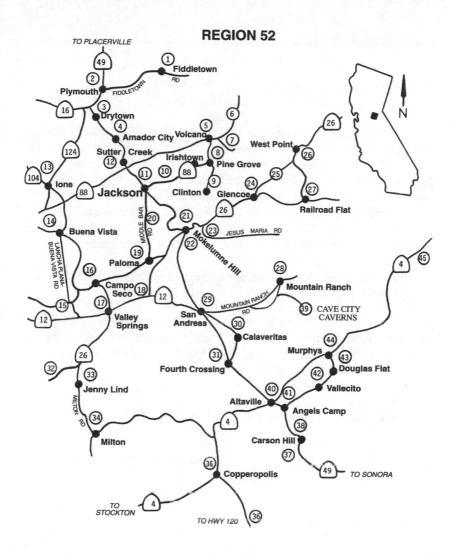

1 - Fiddletown   SHL 35
6 miles east of Plymouth via Fiddletown Road   (209) 296-4519

Locally made brick was used in the construction of several buildings that still stand along Fiddletown's main street.   Fiddletown was a center of trade during the gold rush days and is best known from Bret Harte's story, "An Episode of Fiddletown."   The Chew Kee Store, and Chinese Museum, is housed in a rammed earth adobe, one of the few remaining in California from the 1850s.   Chinese and pioneer artifacts are featured in the museum's collections.   Historic buildings from the 1850s and 1860s are on the grounds of the museum.

2 - Plymouth Consolidated Mining Company Office   SHL 470
Main Street, Plymouth

Built in 1857, this brick building was used into the 1940s as the office and commissary of the Plymouth Mining Company.   Other buildings constructed from the 1860s through the end of the century, can still be seen along Plymouth's Main Street.

2 - D'Agostini Winery   SHL 762
Sobon Estates, 14430 Shenandoah Road, Plymouth   (209) 245-6554

Established in 1856, this winery still uses some of its original Zinfandel vines for production.   Handmade oak casks are used in the original stone cellar, which is made from locally quarried stone.

3 - Drytown   SHL 31
3 miles north of Amador City on Hwy 49   (209) 223-0350

Named for the nearby dry creek, Drytown was one of the first gold mining towns in Amador County.   In 1857, about the time local gold deposits played out, fire swept through the town and destroyed most of its dwellings.   Several brick and adobe buildings from the 1850s, and historic points of interest, remain in this old mining town.

4 - Amador City
2 miles north of Sutter Creek on Hwy 49

Known as the smallest incorporated city in California, Amador City was once the site of placer and quartz gold mining activity.

Buildings in the city date back to the late 1850s, many of which have been restored, and are in use today. Among them are the Imperial Hotel, and the Mine House Inn, which was once used as the headquarters for the Keystone Mine. The headframe of the Keystone Mine can be seen south of town.

5 - Volcano SHL 29
Northeast of Pine Grove off Hwy 88

The hills around the city of Volcano yielded more than $90 million in gold during the 1850s and 1860s. The city was a rich cultural center, boasting the state's first circulating library, a private law school, a debating society, an astronomical observation site and a theater group. Many historic buildings and sites remain and have been marked throughout the town. Guests can still stay at the historic St. George Hotel built in the early 1860s. The Civil War cannon "Old Abe," on display by the Masonic Hall, was used as a deterrent to prevent Confederate sympathizers from getting to the gold mined in this area.

6 - Site of First Amateur Astronomical Observatory SHL 715
Snake Ridge Road, 3/4 mile north of Volcano

It was at this site, in 1860, that George Madeira built the first known amateur astronomical observatory in California. With his three-inch, refractor telescope, he discovered the Great Comet of 1861.

7 - California Native American Ceremonial
Roundhouses (Thematic) SHL 1001
Chaw'se Indian Grinding Rock State Historic Park, 14881 Pine Grove -Volcano Road, Pine Grove (209) 296-7488

The ceremonial roundhouse is the Miwok Indian Village's most spiritual and most respected structure. It is where the village leader lived, and is the site of dances, religious ceremonies and social events. When the leader died, the roundhouse was burned and another built when a new leader was chosen. This authentically reconstructed roundhouse continues to serve the cultural needs of the local Miwok people. Miwok Indian women used the nearby 14,000 square foot limestone rock, as a community gristmill, to grind nuts and berries into meal. More than a thousand mortar holes remain in this ancient grinding rock. Hundreds of petroglyph designs can also be seen in this historic park.

8 - Irishtown SHL 38
Junction of Hwy 88 and Clinton Road, 8 miles northeast of Jackson

Evidence of the popularity of this site, as an Indian camping ground, can be seen in the hundreds of mortar holes cut into the rocks. No trace of the "white" settlement of Irishtown, where prospectors stopped on their way to the mines, remains today.

8 - Roaring Camp Mining Co.
Hwy 88, Pine Grove (209) 296-4100

Roaring Camp was once a camp for 49ers on the Mokelumne River. Ruins and foundations of Spanish, Chinese and Indian settlements can be seen in this private gold camp. Relics and artifacts are displayed in the museum as well. Access is by tour guide only.

8 - Pine Grove Walking Tour
Northeast of Jackson on Hwy 88, Pine Grove

The town of Pine Grove got its start in 1855, with the construction of an inn along the Volcano-Jackson emigrant road. Standing today is the century-old, Pine Grove Hotel, which was built as a stage stop to replace the original inn. Also preserved is the school and town hall, constructed in 1869-1879, and the 1860 pioneer cemetery.

9 - Clinton SHL 37
Clinton Road south of Hwy 88

Placer and quartz gold was mined here from the 1850s until the 1880s. The historic 1877 Catholic Church still stands in this community.

10 - Jackson Gate SHL 118
1 and 1/3 miles northeast of Jackson via Main Street and Jackson Gate Road

The first mining ditch in the county was dug here in 1850, where 500 miners worked the gravel for gold. An old building from the 1850s still stands.

11 - Argonaut and Kennedy Mines   SHL 786
Kennedy Tailing Wheels Park, North Main Street and Jackson Gate Road,
Jackson, contact Amador County Museum for tours of operating models at
(209) 223-6386

Two of the deepest mines in the world are located across the
highway from each other, at the site of several deep quartz gold
mines. The Argonaut Mine was discovered in the early 1850s and
produced millions into the twentieth century. In 1922, forty-seven
miners lost their lives when fire trapped them below ground in this
mine. The Kennedy Mine's vertical shaft, of 5,912-feet, is the deepest
in the United States. The Kennedy Mine was among the most
productive gold mines in the country, yielding more than $50
million. About 1/2 mile east of the Kennedy are several 58-foot
tailing wheels. They were used to bring mill waste to the top of this
hill for disposal and are now part of the county park.

11 - Pioneer Hall   SHL 34
113-115 Main Street, Jackson

The Native Daughters of the Golden West were organized here, in
1886. This order has been active throughout the West in identifying
and marking historic places.

11 - Amador County Museum
225 Church Street, Jackson (209) 223-6386

The 1859 brick home of A. C. Brown, houses the county's collections
of western history items and photographs, along with Indian,
Chinese and gold mining artifacts. It is located in the historic district
of the city, where it and other buildings are maintained in excellent
condition. Tours of operating mine models are provided by the
museum.

11 - Site of First Jewish Synagogue In Amador County   SHL 865
Church and North Streets, on Jackson Elementary School Grounds, Jackson

It was at this site, in 1857, that the first Jewish Synagogue in the
county was established. The congregation outgrew the building in
1869. It then became a schoolhouse. Nothing remains today of this
pioneer structure.

11 - Jackson Walking Tour
Amador County Chamber of Commerce, 30 South Hwy 49/88, Jackson
(209) 223-0350

Jackson, a gold mining camp in the center of the Mother Lode Country, became the county seat when Amador County was established in 1854. Just a few of the town's original buildings survived the 1862 fire that ravaged Jackson. Plaques mark some of the historical sites that were destroyed in that fire, such as the 1850's "hanging tree." A guide, to Jackson's twenty-five points of historic interest, is published by the Amador County Chamber of Commerce.

11 - Butte Store   SHL 39
1/2 mile past Middle Bar Road, on Hwy 49, just south of Jackson

Ginocchio Store is the only surviving structure of the once thriving mining camp of Butte City. Originally built in 1854, as a bakery, it was converted into a merchandising store, in what was once a settlement of a thousand miner's cabins.

12 - Sutter Creek   SHL 322
4 miles north of Jackson on Hwy 49 (209) 223-0350

The creek is named for John A. Sutter, who operated a sawmill here in 1846, and mined the creek in 1848. The discovery of quartz gold at this site led to extensive mining in the hills. The Lincoln Mine was financed by Sacramento businessman, Leland Stanford, who would later become Governor of California. The return of Stanford's investment was so great that he was able to begin the financing of the Central Pacific Railroad as part of the first transcontinental railroad. Many historic buildings, churches and homes, built in the period from 1857-1873, have been restored or reconstructed in this well-kept community. A guide to the region's historic sites is available from the Amador County Chamber of Commerce.

12 - Knight Foundry   SHL 1007
81 Eureka Street, Sutter Creek (209) 267-5543, for tours call (209) 267-1449

The oldest continually-operating, water-powered foundry and machine shop in California, was established here in 1873, by Samuel Knight and George Horne, to supply machinery for the area's hard rock mining industry. In addition to Knight's famous water wheels, which were used throughout the West to drive mining and manufacturing equipment, Knight also developed and manufactured all types of mining equipment and water control accessories. This water-powered foundry remains today as an excellent example of how these shops operated before the introduction of electricity.

13 - D. Stewart Store   SHL 788
Junction of Hwy 104 and Hwy 124, Ione

The first brick store to be built downtown was constructed here in 1856 as a general merchandise store for the Stewart family. The family continued to operate the store until it was sold in 1973.

13 - Methodist Episcopal Church   SHL 506
Junction of Hwy 104 and Hwy 124, Ione

The first church to serve this region was the Methodist Episcopal Church organized in 1853. Its second home was this Gothic style structure, erected in 1862-1866, of locally fired brick.

13 - Preston School of Industry   SHL 867
Waterman Road off Hwy 104, Ione

This massive castle-like structure was built in 1890-1894, as the Preston School of Industry, for the rehabilitation of juvenile offenders. The state closed this facility in 1960.

14 - Cook's Store - Buena Vista
5 miles south of Ione on Ione-Buena Vista Road, Buena Vista

This century-old stone building was once located six miles from here, in the town of Lancha Plana. William Cook, the store's owner, made a deal with the Chinese who wanted to mine the land under his store. If they would move his store to this site and rebuild it, they could mine the land under the old store site. Within a few weeks the move was made and Cook's store has been standing here ever since. The original store site in Lancha Plana is now inundated by the Camanche Reservoir.

15 - Camanche SHL 254
South Shore Recreation Area, Camanche Parkway, north of Hwy 12

Nothing remains of the town of Camanche, which had a population of 1,500 during the Gold Rush period. The town, and its neighboring mining camps, are now inundated by the Camanche Reservoir.

16 - Lancha Plana SHL 30
South of Buena Vista via Lancha Plana-Buena Vista Road

A busy ferryboat landing was once located here, where miners and their supplies would be taken across the Mokelumne River, in the 1850s. Hydraulic mining, in the late 1850s, uncovered a major gold field in the surrounding hills. Today the area is inundated by the Camanche Reservoir.

16 - Campo Seco SHL 257
Paloma/Campo Seco Roads, 3 miles north of Valley Springs

Campo Seco went from a placer mining camp in the 1850s, to a copper center in the 1860s, when the Penn Copper Mine was located here. Ruins of the Adams Express Building, Chinatown district and pioneer cemetery can be seen in this old mining town.

17 - Valley Springs SHL 251
10 miles west of San Andreas on Hwy 12

A railroad and supply center was located here in 1885, at the Valley Springs terminus, of the San Joaquin and Sierra Nevada Railway.

18 - Double Springs SHL 264
3 and 3/4 miles east of Valley Springs at junction of Hwy 26 and Hwy 12

The first county seat of Calaveras County was established at Double Springs in 1850. Camphor wood, shipped from China, was used in the construction of the first courthouse. One section of the original building still stands and is located behind the 1860 sandstone house built by Alexander Wheat.

19 - Paloma   SHL 295
Monument located 1 mile southeast of Gwin Mine in Paloma

Quartz gold was discovered in 1851, at the Gwin Mine, located just north of the placer gold fields that were worked here in 1849. William Gwin, a member of the state constitutional convention and one of the first U.S. Senators from California, owned the Gwin Mine. It produced millions in gold before it closed in 1908.

20 - Middle Bar   SHL 36
On Middle Bar Road, south of junction with Hwy 49, 4 and 1/2 miles south of Jackson

Waters from the Pardee Dam, six miles downstream, now cover this region of the Mokelumne River. Gold was mined here during the '49 Gold Rush period and again in the 1920s.

21 - Big Bar   SHL 41
On Hwy 49, north of Hwy 26 near Mokelumne Hill, 4 miles south of Jackson

Gold was mined from the Mokelumne River here at Big Bar, in 1848. Equally important was the 1850 Whale Boat Ferry, and toll bridge erected in 1852-1853, that provided access across the river to the northern mining areas.

22 - Mokelumne Hill   SHL 269
Southwest corner of Main and Center Streets, Mokelumne Hill

Mokelumne Hill became the center of the richest placer gold mining region of the county. In the early days of "Mok Hill," violence was commonplace. The 1849 "Chilean War" was followed by the "French War," in 1851, with many killings in-between. Mokelumne Hill was the county seat, and leading city in the Mother Lode area, between 1862 and 1866. Many of its original stone buildings are standing today.

22 - Congregational Church   SHL 261
Northeast corner of Main and Church Streets, Mokelumne Hill

The oldest standing Congregational Church building in California was erected here at Mokelumne Hill, in 1856.

22 - International Order of Odd Fellows Hall   SHL 256
Hwy 49, Mokelumne Hill

In 1854, this stone building was erected as the Wells Fargo office. Seven years later, a third floor was added as the I.O.O.F. Lodge, making it the first three-story building in the Mother Lode region. Today it is known as the I.O.O.F. Building.

22 - Calaveras County Courthouse and Hotel   SHL 663
Hotel Leger, 8304 Main Street, Mokelumne Hill   (209) 286-1401

When the county seat was moved from Mokelumne Hill to San Andreas in 1866, George Leger acquired the old courthouse building and made it a part of his hotel, which was located on the adjoining property. The Hotel de France originally stood here until it burned in 1854. George Leger rebuilt it in 1854, and again in 1874, after another fire. It is open today as the Leger Hotel and includes the old courthouse building.

22 - Chili Gulch   SHL 265
1 mile south of Mokelumne Hill on Hwy 49

In 1849, Chili Gulch was among the richest placer mining areas in Calaveras County. The Chileans use of peon labor to work their claims upset the anti-slavery miners and resulted in laws being passed banning the use of slave, or peon, labor. Chileans fought the Americans over this issue and lost the "Chilean War."

23 - Jesus Maria   SHL 284
Plaque located on Jesus Maria Road, 5 miles from intersection with Hwy 26, 2 miles east of Mokelumne Hill

Ruins are all that remain today of the small town of Jesus Maria that once stood here. During the early 1850s, it was the site of placer mining, and was named for the Mexican farmer who ranched here.

24 - Glencoe   SHL 280
12 miles northeast of Mokelumne Hill on Hwy 26, Glencoe

Mexicans first worked placer gold here, in the early 1850s, when the town was known as Mosquito Gulch. The discovery and mining of quartz gold could not sustain the town once the gold played out. Some ruins of the town's original buildings can still be seen.

25 - Sandy Gulch   SHL 253
3 miles west of West Point on Hwy 26, near Associated Mine Road junction

Once the home of the Miwok Indians, Sandy Gulch became an 1850s quartz mining area, with its own custom stamp mill. Only the old pioneer cemetery remains to mark the site of this community.

26 - West Point   SHL 268
Hwy 26 and Main Street, West Point

Scout, Kit Carson, named this place while looking for a pass over the Sierra Nevadas. It was a busy trading post and, during the Gold Rush, a quartz mining area. Some of the buildings erected during the mid-1800s can be seen in the town's business district.

27 - Railroad Flat   SHL 286
Monument on Ridge Road commemorates the Petticoat Mine at Railroad Flat

A mule-powered ore car was used in mining gold-bearing quartz from the mines in this town. The remains of a store, post office and some of the old homes can still be seen.

28 - El Dorado (Mountain Ranch)   SHL 282
Mountain Ranch Road east of San Andreas

The town of El Dorado took the name Mountain Ranch when Mountain Ranch's post office relocated to El Dorado in 1868. The remains of the Mountain Ranch sawmill, and some other early Gold Rush buildings, can still be seen.

29 - San Andreas   SHL 252
Calaveras County Museum, 30 North Main Street, San Andreas
(209) 754-6513

Mexican miners first settled here in 1848, and worked the rich gravel for gold. Several old buildings can still be viewed in the old downtown district, including: the I.O.O.F. Hall, built in 1856; and the

1866 courthouse, where the notorious stage robber, Black Bart, was tried and sent to San Quentin's prison. The old courthouse is now the Calaveras County Museum. Artifacts from pioneer settlers and Indians are on display.

29 - Pioneer Cemetery SHL 271
West of the center of town on Hwy 12, San Andreas

Calaveras County's oldest cemetery is located here, with graves that date back to the early 1850s. Pioneer graves, from the Poverty Bar Cemetery, were moved here before their original site was inundated by the waters of the Camanche Reservoir.

30 - Calaveritas SHL 255
6 miles southeast of San Andreas on Calaveras Road

Almost all Calaveritas' buildings were destroyed by fire in 1858, bringing an end to the town that Mexican miners founded in 1849. Today, only ruins of some of the original buildings remain.

31 - Fourth Crossing SHL 258
West side of Hwy 49, midway between San Andreas and Angels Camp, at crossing of San Antonio Creek

This rich placer gold mining town became a stage and freight depot in the late 1800s. Its 1857 stone bridge, over the Calaveras River, is the oldest bridge in California still standing at its original location. Also at this site, is the historic 1860 Reddick Hotel and placer gold tailings.

32 - Stone Corral SHL 263
1/3 mile east of San Joaquin-Calaveras County line on Hwy 26, 12 miles southwest of Valley Springs

On the road eastward from Stockton, to the gold mines of the Mother Lode, stood the famous Red House where many travelers spent the night. The inn and its barns are gone, as are others like it that once stood along this roadway. Only the stone corral of the Red House remains to be seen.

33 - Jenny Lind SHL 266
2 and 3/4 miles south of Hwy 26 on Milton Road

In the 1850s, the center of mining activities along the lower Calaveras River was here in Jenny Lind. Today, only a few old homes and the ruins of an adobe store remain.

34 - Milton SHL 262
7 and 1/2 miles south of Hwy 26 on Milton Road

Milton was the first town in Calaveras County to have a railroad when the Southern Pacific completed its line here, in 1871. Passengers and freight would be moved from here by wagon or stage to other cities in the county.

35 - Copperopolis SHL 296
State Department of Forestry Station, 375 Main Street, Cooperopolis

Copper was discovered here in 1860. By 1868, more than 2,000 people lived here in what had become California's primary copper producing area. Remains of the headframe and buildings, of the Copper Consolidated Mining Company, can still be seen. The 1862 brick Congregational Church was used as an I.O.O.F. Hall and community center.

36 - O'Byrne Ferry SHL 281
Plaque located on north side of bridge, over New Melones Lake on O'Byrne's Ferry Road

The Stanislaus River was crossed by ferry, until the first toll bridge was erected, in 1853. It was replaced by a covered bridge in 1862. The bridge stood for 90 years, until construction of the Tullock Dam eliminated the need for it.

37 - Robinson's Ferry SHL 276
Plaque located at New Melones overlook on Hwy 49, 6 miles south of Angels Camp

Now inundated by the waters of New Melones Lake, Robinson's Ferry was once the site of a ferry crossing over the Stanislaus River during the Gold Rush period. Established in 1848, Robinson's Ferry hit its peak in the summer of 1849, when it took 20,000 passengers across the river in just six weeks.

38 - Carson Hill SHL 274
South of Angels Camp on Hwy 49

A 195-pound gold nugget, the largest ever mined in California, was found here in 1854. Considered one of the richest camps in the Mother Lode, mining continued here until 1942.

38 - Archie Stevenot Memorial SHL 769
Plaque at Carson Hill Rest Stop, east side of Hwy 49, 5 miles south of Angels Camp, birthplace - west side of Hwy 49, 1/2 mile south of Carson Hill

Archie Stevenot, who earned the name "Mr. Mother Lode" by promoting California's gold country in the 1900s, was honored with this memorial. Stevenot was born near here, in 1882, to one of Carson Hill's pioneer families.

39 - California Caverns (Moaning Caves) SHL 956
Cave City Road, approximately 4 miles from Mountain Ranch Road, 11 miles east of Hwy 49 (209) 736-2708

These historic California Caverns were explored by John Muir, who wrote about his adventure, and the crystal chambers, in his book, _Mountains of California_. Professionally guided tours are available.

40 - Altaville SHL 288
1 mile north of Angels Camp at junction of Hwy 4 and Hwy 49

The oldest iron foundry in California was established here, in 1854, where most of the mining machinery and stamp mills were produced for the surrounding counties. The foundry is still operating at its original site.

40 - Prince-Garibardi Building SHL 735
Junction of Hwy 4 and Hwy 49, Altaville

Constructed in 1852, this two-story stone block building, with its iron doors and shutters, is an impressive Altaville landmark. This well-preserved building is still in use today.

40 - Pioneer Red Brick Schoolhouse   SHL 499
Junction of Hwy 4 and Hwy 49, State Division of Forestry grounds, Altaville

Constructed of red brick, in 1858, this building was used as a grammar school until 1950. It now stands on the grounds of the State Highway Maintenance Station.

41 - Angels Camp   SHL 287
Hwy 49

Located along the streets of this gold mining town is the historic Angels Hotel (where Mark Twain stayed) and the Stickle Store. There are also several stone buildings, from the 1850s, with iron shutters. Utica Mine, now the site of Utica Park, produced millions in gold in what was a major quartz mining region in the Mother Lode.

41 - Angels Camp Museum
753 South Main Street, Angels Camp (209) 736-2963

The rich history of gold mining in the Mother Lode country is displayed in this museum's collection of artifacts, old mining equipment, and other mementos of the 49er Gold Rush period. On the grounds of this museum, antique rolling stock is exhibited.

41 - Angels Hotel   SHL 734
Main Street at Birds Way, Angels Camp

It was in this two-story stone hotel, in 1865, that a bartender told Mark Twain a tale that he would later use to write his famous story, "The Celebrated Jumping Frog of Calaveras County." The city of Angels Camp holds a Jumping Frog Jubilee, every May, in commemoration of Mark Twain's visit.

42 - Vallecito   SHL 273
5 miles east of Angels Camp on Hwy 4

Along this town's main street are two remaining structures from the 1850s—the Wells Fargo building and Dinkelspiel Store. Nearby are the famous Moaning Caves which were once an Indian burial site.

42 - Vallecito Miner's Bell   SHL 370
In front of Union Church on Main Street, Vallecito

This bell was cast in Troy, New York, and brought around the Horn, in 1854. It was mounted in an oak tree and used to summon miners to Sunday services. When the tree fell in 1939, the bell was remounted on top of this monument.

43 - Douglas Flat   SHL 272
2 miles north of Vallecito on Hwy 4

The Central Hill Channel, on which Douglas Flat was located, was an ancient river deposit that yielded thousands in gold. The Gilleado Building, that once served as this town's store and bank, is the only remaining structure from that period.

44 - Murphys   SHL 275
Hwy 4 east to Murphys, 9 miles from Hwy 49

Two brothers, John and Daniel Murphy, discovered gold and mined this region in 1848-1849. The town that grew-up around "Murphy's Diggings" mushroomed to a population of 5,000, with many businesses and 500 frame homes. Many of the town's well-preserved buildings are those constructed of stone, that replaced frame structures that were damaged, or destroyed, in the town's three major fires. A large number of buildings, from the 1850s, through the end of the century remain, including churches, businesses, and commercial establishments now operating in this historic town.

44 - Sperry (Mitchler) Hotel   SHL 267
Murphys Historic Hotel, 457 Main Street, Murphys (209) 728-3444

Built in 1856, to provide lodging for visitors to the Calaveras Big Trees (now a State Park), the Sperry Hotel was the largest building in town. Ownership, and the hotel's name, has changed over the years but it remains one of the oldest operating hotels in California.

44 - Peter L. Traver Building   SHL 466
Old Timer's Museum, across the street from the Murphys Hotel, Murphys

The oldest stone building in town was constructed in 1856, across the street from the historic Sperry Hotel. Clad with iron-shutters, this building is now the home of the "Old Timer's Museum." Its collections feature Gold Rush memorabilia and Indian artifacts. A pioneer blacksmith shop stands behind the building.

44 - Brownsville   SHL 465
1 mile east of Murphys on Pennsylvania Gulch Road

During the 1850s and 1860s, Brownsville was a thriving mining camp with rich placer claims. Nothing remains of the town or its structures.

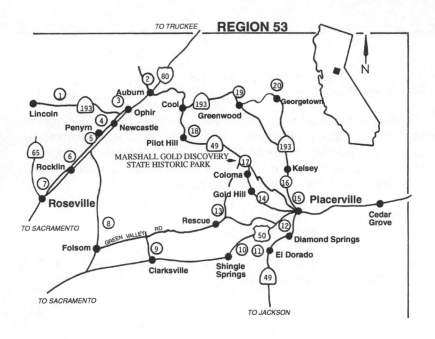

1 - Virginiatown SHL 400
Virginiatown Road, 4 and 1/4 miles east of Lincoln, north of Hwy 193

Virginiatown was an early 1850s gold mining town where Philip Armour, who is said to be the same Armour that founded the Armour meatpacking company, ran the town's butcher shop. Only a monument remains in this gold rush town that once was home to 2,000 miners.

2 - Auburn SHL 404
Junction of I-80 and Hwy 49

Claude Chana founded the city of Auburn after his discovery of a rich surface gold deposit here in 1848. Auburn became the county seat for Sutter County in 1850. When Placer County was formed in 1851, Auburn was again designated as the county seat. Many local historic sites are preserved in this area of Auburn, known as "Historic Old Auburn," including: the first city hall; the old fire house; Chinese homes; and California's oldest post office still housed in its original building.

410

2 - Gold Country Museum
1273 High Street, Gold Country Fairgrounds, Auburn (916) 885-9570

The history of gold mining in the region is displayed. Exhibits include: an operational, stamp mill model; a walk through a mine shaft; hands-on gold panning demonstrations; and exhibits depicting the lifestyle of the men who worked the region's mines.

2 - First Transcontinental Railroad - Auburn Depot   SHL 780.4
Off Lincoln Way at foot of slope leading to Southern Pacific Depot, Auburn

Auburn's importance as a freight distribution point and stage stop greatly increased with the arrival of the Central Pacific Railway in May 1865. The additional stage and freight traffic helped Auburn grow into a community that was not dependent on gold mining for its economic survival.

2 - Auburn Historic Tour
Auburn Area Chamber of Commerce, 601 Lincoln Way, Auburn
(916) 885-5616

The flavor of the Gold Rush period is preserved in the style and architecture of Auburn's buildings. In addition to the historic sites preserved in the "Old Auburn" section of town, there are some locally important sites that can be seen along Lincoln Way and High Street, such as: St. Luke's Church, Kaiser Brewery, Masonic Hall and the Methodist Church—all constructed in the 1850s.

2 - Bernhard Museum Complex
291 Auburn-Folsom Road, Auburn (916) 889-4156

This restored 14-room house was built in 1851 and is furnished with late Victorian pieces. An 1854 winery is also located here.

2 - Placer County Courthouse
On hilltop overlooking Old Town, Auburn

Erected in 1894, this courthouse replaced two prior buildings, and was the site of the first cemetery and public hanging grounds. The building was constructed of marble that was mined in the Colfax area, granite from Rocklin, slate from Slatington and lime and bricks from the Auburn area.

3 - Ophir SHL 463
I-80, southwest of Auburn

Residents of the mining camp of Spanish Corral changed the town's name to Ophir, when a rich quartz gold discovery was made there, in 1850. By 1852, it had become the largest town in Placer County. Most of the town was destroyed by fire in 1853. A restored feed store and several of the town's old homes are all that remain of its original buildings.

4 - First Transcontinental Railroad - Newcastle   SHL 780.3
Southern Pacific Depot, off I-80, Newcastle

The Central Pacific Railway completed its line to Newcastle in June 1864. Further construction of the line stopped until the following April because of political opposition and a lack of money. Restored buildings, from the 1860s, now house various businesses.

5 - Griffith Quarry SHL 885
Griffith Quarry Park and Museum, corner of Taylor and Rock Springs Road, Penryn (916) 663-1837

High quality granite was produced from these quarries, which were established by G. Griffith, in 1864. Granite was shipped from here and used in buildings in San Francisco and Sacramento, including the state capitol in Sacramento. In 1874, California's first successful granite polishing mill was established at this site. The Griffith Quarry Museum features displays on the history of this region's granite industry, including a re-creation of part of the Penryn Granite Works office. Three miles of nature trails offer views of the old quarry sites.

6 - First Transcontinental Railroad - Rocklin SHL 780.2
Taylor Road, Rocklin

Completion of the Central Pacific Railway, to Rocklin, in May 1864 gave Rocklin's granite quarries a greatly improved transportation system. By 1890, thirty quarries were shipping granite to San

Francisco, Stockton and other cities around the area. The relocation of the railroad's roundhouse, from Rocklin to Roseville, in 1908, was the beginning of the end to Rocklin's importance on the line. Several old railroad cars have been converted into a museum of railroad artifacts at this site.

7 - First Transcontinental Railroad - Roseville   SHL 780.1
Southern Pacific Depot, Atlantic Street, Roseville

After the Central Pacific Railway completed its line to Roseville, in April 1864, regularly scheduled runs were made between Sacramento and Roseville. In 1908 the roundhouse was moved from Rocklin, to Roseville, and the city became a major railroad distribution center. The largest railroad marshalling yard, west of the Mississippi, is located here and operated by the Southern Pacific Railroad.

7 - Roseville Art Center/Hamon House
424 Oak Street, Roseville (916) 783-4117

Roseville's historic 1909 Victorian Hamon House has been restored as a luncheon restaurant and art center. Old photographs, antiques and temporary exhibits of art and historic items can be seen on tours of this old home.

8 - Folsom Lake State Recreation Area
Plaque located on Green Valley Road about 4 miles northeast of Folsom
(916) 988-0205

Historic mining towns and camps were inundated by Folsom Lake in 1955, when the dam was constructed at this site. Mormon Island, Negro Hill, Salmon Falls and Condemned Bar are commemorated here for their role in the history of California's Gold Rush period.

8 - Mormon Island   SHL 569
Mormon Island Drive off Green Valley Road, southeast edge of Folsom Lake

Less than two months after Marshall's famous 1848 discovery of gold in Coloma, a second major gold discovery was made here by two members of the Momon Battalion. The announcement of their find brought 150 Mormons, and other miners to the site, which they named " Mormon Bar." Within five years, the population swelled to 2,500. Fire destroyed the town in 1856, and in 1955 the site was inundated by Folsom lake.

8 - Mormon Island Memorial Cemetery
Mormon Island, north of Green Valley Road, Folsom Lake State Recreation Area

Before Lake Folsom inundated the mining towns and campsites of Mormon Island, Negro Hill, Salmon Falls and Condemned Bar, the pioneers who were buried there were re-buried in this memorial cemetery.

8 - Condemned Bar SHL 572
East side of Folsom Lake near Peninsula Campground

This was the site of the Condemned Bar Bridge, one of the many toll bridges constructed to cross the American River and its forks. Fortunes were made by the operators of the many ferries and toll bridges that provided access to the nearby gold fields.

8 - Salmon Falls SHL 571
East side of Folsom Lake at mouth of Sweetwater Creek

During the 1850s, the town of Salmon Falls grew to a population of over 3,000 as men came to work the nearby mines.

8 - Pioneer Express Trail SHL 585
Folsom Road, south of Hidden Valley, Folsom Lake State Recreation Area (916) 988-0205

Between 1849 and 1854, mail was delivered between the mining camps along the American River by Pioneer Express riders. Most of those camps are now inundated by Folsom Lake.

Mormon Tavern SHL 699
Bass Lake Road, off U.S. 50, Clarksville

In 1849, Mormon Tavern was built to serve stage passengers who stopped at this point on the route of the old Clarksville-White Rock

Emigrant Road. It became a Pony Express stop and remount station for the Central Overland Pony Express in April 1860, when the first rider stopped here on the eastbound leg of the historic route.

10 - Shingle Springs SHL 456
Mother Lode Drive near post office, Shingle Springs

The shingle mill constructed in 1849 gave the town its name. Some of the original buildings can still be seen. A monument has been erected to commemorate the Boston-Newton Company that camped here in 1849, on their cross-country journey to Sutter's Fort.

11 - Mud Springs SHL 486
Hwy 49, El Dorado

This camp, on the old Carson Emigrant Trail, got its name from the muddy ground around the springs where emigrants would stop. It was an important mining, freight and stage center, and was renamed El Dorado during the 1850s. Most of the town's original buildings were destroyed by fire in 1923. One remaining building, which housed the Wells Fargo office, is now restored as a restaurant.

11 - El Dorado-Nevada House (Mud Springs) SHL 700
Pleasant Valley Road near Church Street, El Dorado

Many of the remount stations for the Central Overland Pony Express have been commemorated throughout the state. This station was originally a trading post for emigrants to California who stopped at these "mud springs" to water their stock. With the discovery of gold in this area, a mining camp was established, bringing regular freight and stage traffic to this site.

12 - Diamond Springs SHL 487
Monument at intersection of Pleasant Valley and China Garden Roads, Diamond Springs

Diamond Springs was one of the richest gold areas around Placerville. A 25-pound gold nugget, among the largest found in the county, was discovered here in 1850. Several restored buildings remain in this small town including the 1852 I.O.O.F Hall.

13 - The Coloma Road - Rescue   SHL 747
Marker at junction of Green Valley and Deer Valley Roads, Rescue

John Sutter and James Marshall first marked this road from Sutter's Fort, in Sacramento, to his sawmill in Coloma. After Marshall's discovery of gold in Coloma, this trail became a well-traveled road as prospectors came to the gold fields. Around this area were several roadhouses, including the "Gordon House," north of Rescue.

13 - Pleasant Grove House   SHL 703
On Green Valley Road, 9 and 1/2 miles east of Folsom, near Rescue

Miners and early pioneers marked the first trails through this region. These trails would become the roads followed by emigrants to California and by pioneer stage lines. It also served as a remount station for the Central Overland Pony Express during 1860-1861.

14 - Wakamatsu Tea and Silk Farm Colony   SHL 815
Gold Hill and Cold Springs Road, Gold Hill

The first Japanese-influenced, agricultural attempt in California was made here in 1869, by a colony of Japanese immigrants. Their tea and silk farm was not successful in this area and the colony disbanded two years later.

15 - Placerville   SHL 475
Marker at Bedford and Main Streets, Placerville

A gold mining town, by the name of "Old Dry Diggins", sprang up here in 1848 with the first discovery of gold. As the town grew, so did the influx of criminals. Justice was swift and soon the town became known as "Hangtown"—a name it kept for five years. The town was incorporated as Placerville, in 1854, and became the county seat three years later. Many century-old buildings of historic interest have been restored.

15 - Placerville Pony Express Office   SHL 701
Main and Sacramento Streets, Placerville

Placerville played an important role in the brief history of the Central Overland Pony Express. From April 4, 1860 to June 30, 1861, this building served as a relay station. The transcontinental telegraph brought an end to the Pony Express on October 26, 1861.

15 - Gold Bug Mine
Gold Bug Park, Bedford Avenue, Placerville (916) 622-0832

Miners dug this mine in the 1850s as they followed a rich gold-bearing vein into the hill. Two shafts, 147 feet and 362 feet respectively, are lighted and are open to the public for self-guided tours. Gold ore, from this mine, was processed at the stamp mill located in the park across the street.

15 - Hangman's Tree   SHL 141
305 Main Street, Placerville

The citizens of "Hangman's," as Placerville was originally called, were quick to bring action against the town's growing criminal element. The tree that once stood here was the Hangman's Tree where justice was meted out in the 1850s.

15 - Studebaker Blacksmith Shop   SHL 142
543 Main Street, Placerville

In the early 1850s, John Studebaker made wheelbarrows and repaired wagons in the rear of this shop. Studebaker later moved to Indiana where he went into wagon manufacturing. With the coming of the automobile, the Studebaker family became car distributors and eventually manufactured a car under their name.

15 - Methodist Episcopal Church   SHL 767
1031 Thompson Way near Cedar Ravine Street, Placerville (916) 622-0273

The Methodist Episcopal Church, built in 1851, is the oldest church building in the county. It was relocated here as a pioneer memorial.

15 - El Dorado County Historical Museum
El Dorado County Fairgrounds, 100 Placerville Drive, west of Placerville (916) 621-5865

Historical artifacts from the county, Indian artifacts, an original studebaker wheelbarrow, mining equipment and other displays are featured in the museum's collections. A full-sized Wells Fargo stage coach, a replica of a general store and furnishings from the 1850s are also on exhibit.

16 - Marshall's Blacksmith Shop   SHL 319
Hwy 193 at Kelsey

James Marshall, who made the famous discovery of gold at Sutter's Mill in Coloma, spent the last years of his life here as a blacksmith and carpenter. His shop has been preserved, but its contents moved to the museum at Sutter's Fort Historical Monument, in Sacramento.

17 - Marshall Gold Discovery State Historic Park
8 miles north of Placerville on Hwy 49, Coloma (916) 622-3470

The discovery of gold by James Marshall, at Sutter's Mill in 1848, would change California forever. Marshall, who was constructing a sawmill for John Sutter, discovered "some shining flecks in the water" by the mill. Within a few months, Coloma's population soared to several thousand and the Gold Rush was on. Most of the town of Coloma is now included inside this State Historic Park. Its historic landmarks, buildings and museums are well marked, and comprise one of the best "living museums" in the country. Some of the most notable include: the gold discovery site (SHL 530), a reconstructed Sutter's Mill, and a monument to James Marshall (SHL 143). A complete guide to these mid-1800s buildings and historic sites is available at the park headquarters.

17 - The Coloma Road - Coloma   SHL 748
Marshall Gold Discovery Park, Hwy 49, north of Coloma

The road from Sutter's Fort, that John Sutter and James Marshall laid out to get lumber from the mill in Coloma to Sacramento, had its northern terminus here, in Coloma. Thousands of gold seekers traveled this road seeking their fortunes at Coloma.

18 - Old Grange Hall   SHL 551
1/2 mile north of Pilot Hill on Hwy 49

This brick building was built as a hotel by Alcondor Bayley, in 1862, in anticipation of the passenger traffic the railroad would bring. The Central Pacific Railway chose a different route for its line and Bayley's hotel was a financial failure. The first grange, in California, was organized on this property in 1870.

19 - Greenwood SHL 521
East of Cool on Hwy 193

An old trapper, John Greenwood, established a trading post in this area in 1848-1849. By 1850, this town was formed. Among the town's businesses was one of the first theaters in the county. California song writer, John A. Stone, lived here. His gravestone is in the town's pioneer cemetery.

20 - Georgetown SHL 484
Marker on Main Street in front of VFW Hall, Georgetown

The residents of Georgetown rebuilt their town after it was razed in a disastrous fire in 1852. Determined to keep fires from spreading, they made the new main street 100 feet wide, and the side streets 60 feet wide. The new town flourished. Many of the town's reconstructed buildings stand today, including the Georgetown Hotel, the picturesque American Hotel, and the Shannon Knox House which was built from lumber shipped around the Horn.

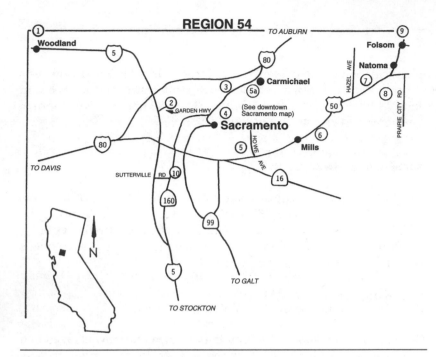

1 - Woodland Opera House SHL 851
320 - 2nd Street, Woodland Opera House State Historic Park, Woodland (916) 666-9617

This brick building was constructed in 1891, on the site of the first opera house, in the Sacramento Valley. It stands today in a section of Woodland that contains other buildings from the 1890s.

1 - Gable Mansion SHL 864
659 First Street, Woodland

Pioneer settlers of Yolo County, Amos and Harvey Gable, erected this Victorian style home in 1885. It was among the last of its size and style to be constructed in California.

1 - Hays Antique Truck Museum
2000 East Main Street, Woodland (916) 666-1044

Autocar, Fageol, Jumbo, Patriot, Traffic . . . forgotten makes of trucks from the past . . . but they are not forgotten here at the country's

420

largest collection of vintage trucks. Most of the museum's 187 trucks, representing 132 different makes produced between 1901 and 1956, have been restored. The indoor, two-acre exhibit illustrates the twentieth century evolution of engines, transmissions, tires and other truck components. Innovative ideas that led to the development of today's safe, fuel-efficient, computer-controlled trucks, as well as some that failed, are displayed here.

1 - Yolo County Historical Museum
512 Gibson Road, Woodland (916) 666-1045

Prominent Yolo County pioneer, William Byas Gibson, built this two-story brick Greek Revival style home between 1857 and 1877, to serve as his residence and ranch headquarters. It remained a family residence until 1963. An extensive renovation of the house, out-buildings and grounds was undertaken after the property was acquired in 1975 for use as a county museum. Period furnishings, representing Renaissance Revival, Eastlake, Mission/Art Nouveau, Eclectic and Cottage styles, are displayed in individual room settings to depict life in Yolo County, from the 1850s to the 1930s. Outbuild-ings contain antique farm equipment and related artifacts.

2 - Nisipowinan Indian Village Site SHL 900
Garden Hwy exit off I-5, east 1 block to Discovery Park Drive, Sacramento

Excavation of mounds at this Indian Village yielded artifacts that establish the existence of this tribe's ancestors as early as 1000 B.C. Evidence of this tribe's contact with John Sutter, in 1840-1850, was also uncovered at this site.

3 - First Transcontinental Railroad
Presidential Decree SHL 780.8
Plaque at Haggin Oaks Golf Course, 3645 Fulton Avenue, Sacramento

President Abraham Lincoln decreed that the western base of the Sierra Nevada began where the Central Pacific Railroad crossed Arcade Creek. This action by the President, in January 1864, increased government subsidies and provided additional funds to complete the line over the Sierra Nevada.

3 - Temporary Detention Camps for Japanese-Americans   SHL 934
McClellan Air Force Base, north of Haggin Oaks Golf Course, Sacramento

Japanese and Japanese-Americans were ordered to report to temporary detention camps, for relocation, after Japan declared war on the United States and involved this country in World War II. From this center they were relocated to permanent camps across the United States. Japanese population here reached a maximum of 4,739 in the one month that this facility served as an assembly center.

3 - Sacramento Science Center and Junior Museum
3615 Auburn Boulevard, Sacramento (916) 277-6180

Exploratory physical science exhibits, computers and a live animal hall are among this museum's featured collections. Rotating displays include historical artifacts and early commercial products.

4 - Downtown Sacramento - See Region 55

5 - Pony Express Remount Station   SHL 697
Guy West Bridge, California State University, 6000 "J" Street, Sacramento

Five Mile House was the first Pony Express remount station on the eastward leg of the express route leaving Sacramento.

5A - Effie Yeaw Nature Center
Ancil Hoffman County Park, 6700 Tarshes Drive, Carmichael (916) 489-4918

The Center includes nature trails through 75 acres of undeveloped woodlands and a replica Maidu Indian Village that introduces visitors to the cultural heritage of this region. Although most of the Indian artifacts are re-creations, the village scene with its tule huts, shade shelters, granary, grinding rock, fire pit and leaching pit is a good example of a typical summer setting along the American River.

6 - Pony Express Remount Station   SHL 698
White Rock Road, south of Folsom Boulevard, 4 miles east of Mills

Operated as a stage station, this location became known as Fifteen Mile House, on the Pony Express Route. It was the second remount station on the route eastward, from Sacramento, to Missouri.

6 - Silver Wings Aviation Museum
Mather Air Force Base, Rancho Cordova (916) 364-2906

World War I military and civilian aircraft are displayed at this military museum. The history of the Air Force and Mather Air Force Base, from World War I to the present, is also exhibited.

7 - Nimbus Dam SHL 746
Hazel Avenue exit off I-80

This marker commemorates the trail that James Marshall followed to report his discovery of gold at Sutter's Mill in 1848.

8 - Prairie City (Site) SHL 464
2 miles south of U.S. 50 on Prairie City Road at Alder Creek

More than 100 buildings stood here in the 1850s and 1860s, when Prairie City was a booming gold town. Today, nothing remains of this once bustling town of 3,000.

9 - California's First Passenger Railroad
Folsom Terminal SHL 558
In Leidesdorff Plaza, on Sutter Street near Reading Street and Folsom Boulevard, Folsom

California's first passenger railroad line, the Sacramento Valley Railroad, was built by Theodore Judah in 1855-1856, between the towns of Sacramento and Folsom. It is believed that the first depot was built at this site. The second depot was destroyed by fire. A third depot building was erected in 1913, by the Southern Pacific Railroad (where it now stands) at 200 Wool Street. The Folsom Chamber of Commerce now occupies this restored depot which is listed in the National Register of Historic Places. The 1868 Ashland Freight Depot was moved here and is the oldest standing station west of the Mississippi River.

9 - Folsom Historic Sites
Chamber of Commerce, 200 Wool Street, Folsom (916) 985-2698

The Folsom Chamber of Commerce has a guide to its historic buildings, churches and other sites of historic interest. Structures dating from the 1850s have been restored and are located throughout the city.

9 - Folsom Pony Express Terminal   SHL 702
Sutter Street near junction with Decatur Street, Folsom

The western terminus of the Pony Express was changed from Sacramento, to Folsom, in July 1860, with the completion of the Sacramento Valley Railroad between those two cities. Mail was taken the final leg from Folsom, to Sacramento, by the newly completed railroad.

9 - Old Folsom Powerhouse   SHL 633
Folsom Lake State Park off Greenback Lane, near Leidesdorff Street, Folsom (916) 985-2895

In exchange for land, for a new state prison, inmate labor from Folsom Prison was used to build this powerhouse in 1895. Electricity from this powerhouse was transmitted 22 miles to Sacramento, the longest distance that electric power had ever been transmitted. It continued to operate until 1952 and has since been donated to the state for preservation.

9 - Folsom Valley Railway
Folsom City Park, Natoma and Stafford Streets, Folsom (916) 355-7285

Scale models of the type of locomotives that operated in Folsom during the 1860s are in use on this park's 12-inch gauge railroad. Freight wagons and farm implements, from the 1860s, are exhibited near the entrance to this scale model railroad station.

9 - Folsom Prison
North off East Natoma Street on Prison Road, Folsom (916) 372-6060

Construction began here in 1880, with most of the prison built by inmates using rock from the local quarry. Called the "end of the world" by the inmates who first came here, this state prison's solid granite walls are as formidable now as when they were first built. A small museum, near the prison entrance, presents a video history of the prison and exhibits, which include: a collection of weapons confiscated from prisoners; photographs; original handcuffs and manacles; a handmade raft used in an escape attempt; vehicle license plates manufactured at the prison; and a handwritten log of Folsom's early inmates by name, inmate number, type of crime committed and sentence. An inmate-operated gift shop sells paintings and various crafts made by prisoners.

10 - Site of Sutterville   SHL 593
Sutterville Road exit off I-5, across from William Land Park Zoo, Sacramento

John Sutter laid out the town of Sutterville in 1844, five years after he established Fort Sutter. This site was identified for years by the brick buildings erected here in the 1840s and 1850s.

10 - Camp Union   SHL 666
Sutterville Road exit off I-5 at Del Rio, Sacramento

During the Civil War, this was the site of Camp Union where California Volunteers were trained for duty against Confederate Troops.

REGION 55

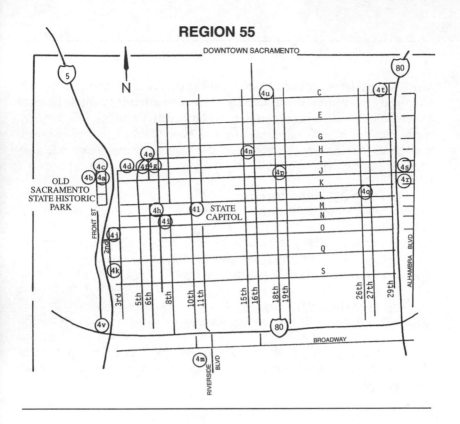

4A - Old Sacramento   SHL 812
Old Sacramento State Historic Park, Front Street, west of I-5, Sacramento
(916) 443-7815

John Sutter founded the city of Sacramento here, in 1848. This section of town is now called "Old Sacramento" and is preserved as a state historic park. The forty historic buildings located here have been restored, or rebuilt, and represent the highest concentration of 1852-1875 buildings in the state. It was here that the Pony Express and Overland stages terminated their runs from Missouri, the first transcontinental telegraph was received, and the transcontinental railroad route over the Sierra Nevada was begun.

4A - Big Four Headquarters (Site)   SHL 600
Old Sacramento, 220-26 "K" Street

California officially retired this state landmark number when the

426

three buildings that served as headquarters of the "Big Four" were included in Old Sacramento State Historic Park. Leland Stanford, Collis Huntington, Mark Hopkins and Charles Crocker, the "Big Four" who financed construction of the Central Pacific Railway as part of the first transcontinental railroad in 1863, had offices here.

4A - Pony Express Monument
Old Sacramento, 2nd and "J" Streets

The inscription at the base of this monument tells the brief history of the Central Overland Pony Express: "This statue commemorates the glory of the Pony Express, which started here at 2:45 a.m. on April 4, 1860, when Sam Hamilton galloped into a blinding rain storm for the first lap of the 1,966-mile trip to St. Joseph, Missouri. During its eighteen month existence its 121 riders and 500 ponies carried 35,000 pieces of mail with the loss of but one pouch. This venture founded by Russell, Majors and Waddell, ended California's isolation from the rest of the Union."

Pony Express Rider monument in Old Sacramento. Photo by Jennifer Roberts.

4A - *Sacramento Union* SHL 605
Old Sacramento, 121 "J" Street

The *Sacramento Union* newspaper occupied this building in 1852. The newspaper which once called itself "The Oldest Daily in the West," was published from March 1851 until October 1993. The newspaper published its final edition on January 14, 1994.

4A - Eagle Theater SHL 595
Old Sacramento, 923-25 Front Street (916) 446-6761

When built in 1849, the Eagle Theater was the first building constructed as a theater in California. In 1974, a replica of the original building was reconstructed on this site. Performances are once again offered.

4A - B. F. Hastings Bank Building SHL 606
Old Sacramento, southwest corner of Second and "J" Streets (916) 445-4209

The first eastward journey of the Pony Express started here in 1860. Restored chambers of the California Supreme Court, which first met in this building, can be seen along with an operating Wells Fargo Office and exhibits from the 1850s.

4A - Wells Fargo History Museum
Old Sacramento, 1000 Second Street, Sacramento (916) 440-4263

Old photos, documents and artifacts trace the history of Wells Fargo, from the days when craftsmen built stagecoaches by hand and agents were both banker and telegraph operator, to today's sophisticated computer age. Museum displays include: original gold scales, a Concord Stagecoach model, a Pony Express exhibit, and a re-created Wells Fargo office with agent's desk.

4A - Orleans Hotel SHL 608
Old Sacramento, 1018 Second Street

The original building erected at this site operated as the Orleans Hotel and stage depot from 1852 until 1870. A replica of the Orleans Hotel now stands on this site.

4A - Lady Adams Building SHL 603
Old Sacramento, 113-15 "K" Street

Material brought around the Horn, by the ship *Lady Adams*, was used in the construction of this building. It remains among the oldest buildings in Sacramento.

4A - Site of Newton Booth Home SHL 596
Old Sacramento, 1015-21 Front Street

California Governor, and later U.S. Senator, Newton Booth, had his home and business at this site. The original buildings no longer remain, but other buildings owned by him on this same street still stand.

4A - Site of Sam Brannan House SHL 604
Old Sacramento, 112 "J" Street

Sam Brannan constructed seven buildings between 1853 and 1865. One of his first buildings was constructed on this site.

4A - Old Telegraph Station SHL 366
Old Sacramento, 1015 Second Street

State Telegraph Company operated here until 1868. From then until 1915 it was a Western Union Office.

4A - Adams and Company Building SHL 607
Old Sacramento, 1014 Second Street

Wells Fargo and Company occupied this building when it was the western agent for the Pony Express.

4A - What Cheer House SHL 597
Old Sacramento, southeast corner of Front and "J" Streets

During the 49er gold rush days, What Cheer House was a popular stopping place. In 1931, the original hotel burned to the ground and this replica was built in its place.

4A - Ebner's Hotel   SHL 602
Old Sacramento, 116 "K" Street

Constructed in 1856, this original three-story building has been restored and remains as it appeared during the gold rush days.

4A - Pioneer Mutual Volunteer Firehouse   SHL 612
Old Sacramento, 1112 Second Street

Engine Company Number One, the oldest fire company in California, was located in this 1854 building.

4A - First Transcontinental Railroad   SHL 780
Old Sacramento, Front and "K" Streets

The western link of the first transcontinental railroad, the Central Pacific Railroad, was planned by Theodore Judah, who built California's first passenger railroad. Judah met with four Sacramento merchants (the "Big Four") and convinced them of the merits of a transcontinental railroad. Leland Stanford, a member of the "Big Four," and California's eighth Governor, broke ground at this site in 1863, for the beginning of the railroad that would join with the Union Pacific May 10, 1869, at Promontory, Utah.

4A - Early Stagecoach Terminal   SHL 598
Old Sacramento, Front and "K" Streets

During the 1850s, this was a stage terminal for stage lines. It was here that construction of the Central Pacific Railroad began in 1863.

4A - D. O. Mills Bank Building   SHL 609
Old Sacramento, 226 "J" Street

This was the first banking house on the Pacific Coast. Mills became first President of the Bank of California in 1864.

4A - Overton Building Site   SHL 610
Old Sacramento, 3rd and "J" Streets

In 1852, Sacramento's post office was housed in the Overton Building at this site. It was later used as a state office building.

4A - Western Hotel Site SHL 601
Old Sacramento, 209-21 "K" Street

In 1875, the Western Hotel was built as one of the largest hotels in California. Material from this building was used in the restoration of other structures in this old section of Sacramento.

4A - *Sacramento Bee* Site SHL 611
Old Sacramento, 1016-20 - 3rd Street

One of the first buildings occupied by the *Sacramento Bee* newspaper stood at this site. The *Sacramento Bee*, which began publication in 1857, is now headquartered at 21st and "Q" Streets.

4B - Central Pacific Passenger Station
Front and "J" Streets, Sacramento (916) 445-4209

Historic steam locomotives operate from this reconstructed 1876 Central Pacific Railroad passenger station, on round trips along the Sacramento River, to Miller Park. Old steam locomotives and railroad cars, from the 1870s, are on display at this station.

4C - California State Railroad Museum
111 "I" Street, Sacramento (916) 445-7387 or (916) 448-4466

Included in this museum's historic collection are 60 engines and cars restored to their original condition. Rolling stock is exhibited in natural settings with special effects that add realism to these fully equipped cars. Private cars; a working refrigerator car; a post office car; and a sleeping car, that gives the "feel" of a moving car at night, are part of the interpretive displays featured here.

4D - China Slough SHL 594
4th and "I" Streets, Sacramento

This site was the location of China Slough during the Gold Rush period. Now, the Southern Pacific Depot stands here.

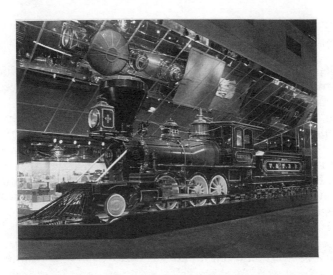

California State Railroad Museum. A California State Railroad Museum photo.

4E - Old Folsom Powerhouse - Sacramento Station   SHL 633.2
6th and "H" Streets, Sacramento

Station A was constructed by the Sacramento Electric Power and Light Company to receive electric power being transmitted from the Folsom Powerhouse. When the first transmission of electricity was made, in 1895, from Folsom to this station 22 miles away, it was the longest distance that electric power had ever been transmitted.

4F - Site of Pioneer Memorial Congregational Church   SHL 613
915 - 6th Street, Sacramento

Sacramento's first church was built across the street from this site in 1849. It was replaced in 1854, when the original building was destroyed by fire. Services were held here until the 1920s.

4G - First State Capitol Site   SHL 869
7th and "I" Streets, Sacramento

California's state capitol was located here twice before moving into the present capitol location. In 1852, and again in 1854, the state legislature met here at the site of the county's first courthouse. The original structure burned in 1854. It was replaced by a second building, where state business was transacted until 1869.

4H - First Congregationally Owned Synagogue SHL 654
7th Street, between Capital and "L" Streets, Sacramento

In 1849, this prefabricated building was shipped around the Horn from Baltimore. It was originally used by the Methodist Episcopal Church, until 1852, when it was sold to three officers of a Jewish association. This building then became the first congregationally owned Jewish Synagogue on the Pacific Coast.

4I - Stanford-Lathrop Home SHL 614
800 "N" Street, Sacramento (916) 324-0575

Governor Leland Stanford and his wife, Jane Lathrop Stanford, lived here from 1861 to 1874, while he was Governor of California and a U.S. Senator. Stanford University was named for the Stanford's only child, who was born in this house, and died at the age of sixteen.

4J - Crocker Art Gallery SHL 599
216 "0" Street, Sacramento (916) 449-5423

This building was erected in the 1870s, next to the residence of Judge E. B. Crocker and his wife, to house their private collection of paintings. Following the death of Judge Crocker, his wife donated the gallery to the City of Sacramento.

4K - California's First Passenger Railroad
Sacramento Terminal SHL 526
Monument at Second and "L" Streets, Sacramento

Sacramento Valley Railroad, California's first passenger railroad, was begun here by Theodore Judah in 1855. The original terminal was replaced by this structure in the early 1920s.

4L - Cathedral of the Blessed Sacrament
1017 - 11th Street, Sacramento (916) 444-3070

With its design inspired by the Eglise de la Trinite Church of Holy Trinity in Paris, the Cathedral of the Blessed Sacrament was built in

1886-1889, at a cost of $250,000, to be the largest church west of the Mississippi. Its 175-foot high dome and 216-foot center spire are visible from many parts of the Sacramento Valley. Stained glass windows from Austria, painted ceilings and oil paintings hanging on the cathedral walls add to the beauty of this magnificent structure.

4L - California's State Capitol Building SHL 872
"L" and "N" Streets and 10th and 15th Streets, Sacramento (916) 324-0333

Construction of California's capitol took place between 1861 and 1874. The most expensive restoration of a historical landmark was undertaken a century later, when this capitol was completely renovated. The buildings, 35-acre Capitol Park, and the California State History Museum provide an impressive look back into California's early history. Within the capitol rotunda are murals depicting the history of California, a marble statue of Queen Isabella, and flags that have flown over the state. Historic offices, original furnishings, and displays from every county in the state are located throughout the building.

4L - Wells Fargo History Museum
400 Capitol Mall, Sacramento (916) 440-4161

Authentic history of Wells Fargo from the Gold Rush days, to the modern electronic age, is displayed. Realistic exhibits include: a circa 1865 Concord Stagecoach, and the coach builder's tools; a replica Wells Fargo office, complete with agent's desk; working telegraph and original documents; and gold specimens and gold mining artifacts.

4M - Sacramento City Cemetery SHL 566
1000 Broadway at 10th Street, Sacramento (916) 448-5665

Three of California's early governors, John Bigler, Newton Booth, and William Irwin, are buried in this 1850s Sacramento cemetery. Some of the other California pioneers memorialized here are: Mark Hopkins, Judge E. B. Crocker, General George Wright, and President Alexander Hamilton's youngest son.

4M - Tower Cafe
Land Park and Broadway, Sacramento (916) 441-0222

This 100-foot tower marks the location of the city's oldest, continuously operated, movie theatre and the birthplace of one of the world's largest record distribution companies. The Tower was built in 1939, as Sacramento's premiere motion picture house, and home to several retail businesses. It was in one of these businesses, Tower Cut-Rate Drugs, that Clayton Solomon had the idea of selling used jukebox records. Thus, Tower Records was born. The original drugstore site is now home to Tower International Cafe.

4N - Governor's Mansion State Historical Monument SHL 823
16th and "H" Streets, Sacramento (916) 323-3047

Between 1903 and 1967, thirteen of California's governors lived in this 1878 Victorian Gothic mansion. Today it is operated as a museum that gives visitors an opportunity to view well-preserved furnishings from a great period in this state's history.

4P - Sacramento Heritage Walking Tour
Convention and Visitor's Bureau, 1421 "K" Street at 15th Street, Sacramento (916) 264-7777

Sacramento's evolution, from John Sutter's 1839 Fort, to the center of California's state government is chronicled in the wide array of architectural styles preserved within the city. Among the sixteen homes listed in the Alkali Flat Tour (the city's oldest remaining residential district) is the 1854 brick Greek Revival style, J. Neely Johnson House, the oldest house in the city. It was home to Peter Burnett, the first Governor of California; and the residence of J. Neely Johnson when he was elected governor. The Capitol Tour and Downtown Tour guides describe the rich architectural heritage that can be seen today in the city's government and commercial buildings.

4P - Sacramento History Museum
101 "I" Street, Sacramento (916) 264-7057

Historic items from early Sacramento, newspapers, horse-drawn equipment, railroad materials and nineteenth century clothing tell the story of this region's growth and development. The Center's million-dollar, Gold Rush Exhibit shows many examples of the precious metals and tools used by 49ers. Unique computerized video stations give visitors an opportunity to view many old photographs and documents from the region.

4P - Sacramento Central Library
828 "I" Street, Sacramento (916) 440-5926

The second floor of the city's original 1918 Carnegie Library building has been restored and refurbished as the "Sacramento Room." It now houses rare books and maps, Sacramento area historical reference materials and special collections. Among the interesting treasures preserved here are: a book printed by Benjamin Franklin; a fifteenth century, hand-lettered manuscript; and an original map depicting California as an island. A glass arch-topped atrium now joins the original structure to the new six-story central library building.

Sacramento Central Library. Courtesy of the Library, photo by Don Burns.

4Q - Coloma-Sutter's Fort Road-Western Terminus SHL 745
Sutter's Fort State Historic Park, 2701 "L" Street, Sacramento (916) 445-4422

John Sutter constructed a sawmill in Coloma to supply his fort with lumber. The road between his fort in Sacramento and the Coloma mill became a well-used trail during the Gold Rush days. This old road, which also served as a stage route, is commemorated at four locations. The western end of the trail is marked at this fort.

4Q - Sutter's Fort State Historic Park SHL 525
2701 "L" Street, Sacramento (916) 445-4422

John Sutter established this fort in 1839, as a trading post, a place of refuge for travelers, and for protection of his Mexican land grant. In 1841, Sutter purchased livestock and equipment from the Russians who were abandoning Fort Ross, and transported them to his fort. Fort Sutter became the center of all political and economic activity in this region of California. Rescue parties were dispatched from here to aid emigrants stranded in the winter snows of the Sierra Nevada. The most famous rescue effort was for the Donner Party. The original adobe fort was restored and its outer walls reconstructed in 1890-1893, to preserve this important landmark in California's history. Sutter's Fort Museum contains some of the best known relics from the pre-Gold Rush period.

4Q - State Indian Museum SHL 991
2618 "K" Street, Sacramento (916) 324-0971

The first state-operated Indian museum was built here in 1940 to house the state Indian collection. B. W. Hathaway's popular 1926 California Indian Exhibit, and the first Ishi (California's last Yashi Indian) Exhibit and film were designed and exhibited here. In the 1950s, local Indians erected models for the museum. Today they participate in the development of museum programs that reflect both historic and modern Indian culture. This landmark museum is one of the largest and best-known Indian museums, and the only designated state Indian museum in California.

4R - Chevra Kaddisha SHL 654.1
33rd and "K" Streets, Sacramento

California's first Jewish cemetery was established here in 1850 as the "Chevra Kaddisha," or Home of Peace Cemetery.

4S - New Helvetia Cemetery   SHL 592
Alhambra Boulevard between "I" and "J" Streets, Sacramento

On this site once stood Sacramento's first cemetery, which John Sutter established in 1849. Sutter Junior High School is now located on these grounds.

4T - Sutter's Landing Site   SHL 591
29th and "B" Streets, Sacramento

John A. Sutter, a Swiss immigrant, landed here in 1839, at what was then a bank of the American River. It was near this site that Sutter established the first white settlement in the Sacramento Valley and built his famous fort.

4U - California's Almond Growers Exchange   SHL 967
1802 "C" Street, Sacramento (916) 442-0771

California Almond Growers Exchange Processing Plant operates from this 90-acre facility, where seventy percent of California's almond crop is processed. Constructed in 1915, as the Sacramento Shelling Plant, this 33-city block plant is now the largest almond processing plant in the world. Processing of California's number one food export can be seen on tours offered at the plant's visitor center.

4V - Towe Ford Museum
2200 Front Street, Sacramento (916) 442-6802

One hundred and fifty Ford cars and trucks, representing every year and every model of Ford, for the first fifty years (1903 - 1953), have been relocated here from the Towe Ford Museum in Montana. Included in the collection is Henry Ford's personal Model T, a rare Model B (only four are known to exist), and a 1957 Fairlane with retractable hardtop.

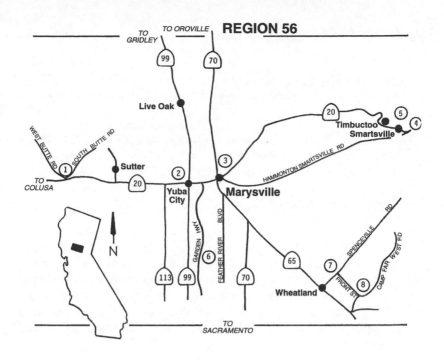

1 - Thompson Seedless Grape Site   SHL 929
West Butte Road at Hwy 20, 8 miles west of Yuba City

The Thompson Seedless Grape was introduced to California in 1875, by William Thompson. Nine years after settling here with his family in 1863, Thompson planted cuttings that were to produce this "new" type of grape in California. Thousands of acres of this variety of grape are now grown in the state.

2 - Community Memorial Museum of Sutter County
1333 Butte House Road, Yuba City   (916) 741-7141

This museum features settings, from various phases of pioneer life, in the Yuba City area. John Sutter's desk is exhibited in the "Pioneer Corner." "The Barn" has displays of antique tools. Period furnishings and clothing are shown in: "Great Grandma's Parlor," the "Children's Center," and "The Wedding of 1866."

439

3 - Mary Murphy Covillaud Memorial
Marysville Cemetery, Catholic Cemetery north of Marysville, over the levee on Hwy 70

This cemetery marks the final resting place of Mary Murphy Covillaud, a survivor of the Donner Party, who married a founding father of this city and for whom the town of Marysville was named.

3 - Mary Aaron Memorial Museum
704 "D" Street, Marysville (916) 743-1004

This Gothic style residence was built in 1856. It was given to the city as a museum, in the memory of Mary Aaron. The second floor has been restored and contains architectural documents from the original builder. Mining equipment, furnishings and various items from the 1850-1900 period are on display in the museum. On the grounds is the County Store Museum, antique farm equipment and an old sheriff's office.

3 - Bok Kai Temple (Chinese Joss House)   SHL 889
Yuba River Levee at "D" and 1st Streets, Marysville (916) 743-6501

Built in 1880, this is the only Chinese Temple erected in the United States as a place of worship to Bok Kai, the Chinese River God. Hydraulic mining had raised the river bed 70 feet and the Chinese community, fearing floods, built this temple to their River God of Good Fortune. Miles of levees were eventually constructed along the Yuba River to protect the city. The interior of the temple was renovated in 1971 and it is now used as a place of worship.

3 - Temporary Detention Camp for Japanese-Americans   SHL 934
Near junction of Broadway, Feather River and Arboga Road, south of Marysville

After the Japanese attack on Pearl Harbor in 1941, and the entry of the United States into World War II, thousands of Japanese and Japanese-Americans living on the West Coast were ordered to report to temporary detention camps. Then they were resettled in permanent camps across the United States. The Japanese population reached a maximum of 2,451 in the month that this facility served as an assembly center.

4 - Smartsville SHL 321
Main and O'Brien Streets, Smartsville

Smartsville was a rich mining area in the 1850s, and a site of extensive hydraulic mining in the 1860s and 1870s. When hydraulic mining was made illegal, in 1883, most of the town's population left. The most imposing structure in town today, the Church of the Immaculate Conception, was constructed in 1861.

5 - Timbuctoo SHL 320
Northwest of Smartsville and north of Hwy 20

Mining for gold began in the nearby hills and valleys in the early 1850s. By 1855, successful hydraulic mining made the town of Timbuctoo the largest in Eastern Yuba County. Ruins of the Wells Fargo office and the Stewart Brothers store are all that remain.

6 - Hock Farm SHL 346
5320 Garden Hwy at Messich Road, 8 miles south of Yuba City

John Sutter, the first white settler in Sutter County, built an adobe here in 1841. It served as part of the headquarters for his cattle ranch, which he called "Hock Farm." When General Sutter retired, he built a mansion near the first adobe house where he lived until 1868. All that remains is the iron wall from the fort at Hock Farm. Nothing remains of the adobe or mansion.

7 - Overland Emigrant Trail SHL 799.3
Spenceville Road, Wheatland

The last leg of the overland emigrant trail was made from this point, to Johnson's Ranchero, where the first settlement west of the Sierra was made. Thousands of emigrants followed this trail from the Nevada border, in the late 1840s and early 1850s, to settle in California or to seek their fortune in the gold fields.

8 - Johnson's Ranchero SHL 493
3 miles east of Wheatland on Front Street

The first settlement reached by emigrants, after crossing the Sierra through Donner Pass, was at this site near the present town of

Wheatland. Five women and two men, from the Donner Party, reached this settlement in the winter of 1846-1847 to get aid for their friends and relatives, who were snowbound at Donner Lake.

8 - Site of the Wheatland Hop Riot of 1913   SHL 1003
Intersection of "A" and Sixth Streets, Wheatland

Working and living conditions during the early 1900s were very poor for many of California's migrant farm workers. Members of the International Workers of the World, known as "Wobblies" to their opponents, met here on August 3, 1913, to demand better living conditions for the 2,800 men, women and children, working on Ralph Durst's hop ranch. When an attempt was made to arrest Richard Ford, the main IWW organizer in the camp, the situation got out-of-control, a riot ensued and four people died. The events in Wheatland that day aroused public opinion, and resulted in the formation of a new State Commission on Immigration and Housing, to help improve working conditions.

REGION 57

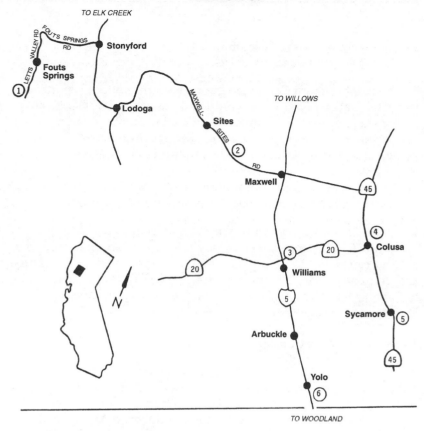

TO ELK CREEK

LETTS VALLEY RD

FOUTS SPRINGS RD

Stonyford

Fouts Springs

(1)

Lodoga

MAXWELL-SITES

Sites

(2)

RD

TO WILLOWS

Maxwell

45

(4)

Colusa

(3)

20

20

Williams

5

Sycamore

(5)

Arbuckle

45

N

Yolo

(6)

TO WOODLAND

1 - Lett's Valley   SHL 736
Southwest of Stoneyford via Fouts Spring, Mendocino National Forest
(916) 983-6118

This campground and lake was once part of the settlement of Jack and David Lett who came here in 1855. Both brothers lost their lives, in 1877, when trying to prevent squatters from settling on their land.

2 - Granville Swift Stone Corral   SHL 238
6 miles west of Maxwell on Maxwell-Sites Road

Granville Swift used this natural corral as part of his vast cattle operations in the Sacramento Valley. He is credited with building this stone fence in the 1850s. It has been restored.

3 - Sacramento Valley Museum
1491"E" Street, Williams (916) 473-2978

The history of Colusa County, in the nineteenth century, is portrayed in a combination of indoor and outdoor exhibits. A blacksmith shop, barber shop, apothecary shop and a collection of farm equipment are displayed, as well as reproductions of rooms from an early settler's home. Indian artifacts and period clothing are also featured.

3 - Dr. Robert B. Semple Monument
Williams Cemetery, Crawford Road, south of Williams (916) 473-5444

Dr. Robert Semple, founder of the town of Benicia and President of California's first Constitutional Convention, is memorialized in this pioneer cemetery. Dr. Semple was a member of the Bear Flag Party and marched with General Fremont to Monterey in 1846. His brother, Colonel Charles Semple, founded the city of Colusa, at a site Dr. Semple selected when he first visited this area in 1847.

4 - Colusa County Courthouse   SHL 890
546 Jay Street, Colusa (916) 458-5146

This white, Southern style courthouse was built in 1861, by Colusa's early settlers, who were predominantly Southerners. It is now the oldest remaining courthouse in the Sacramento Valley and the second oldest seat of county government in California.

5 - Sycamore Brick Shrine
1 and 1/2 miles south of Sycamore on Hwy 45

The first Roman Catholic Mass said in Colusa County was at this site on May 2, 1856. A 27-foot wooden cross was erected to commemorate the event. In 1883, this brick shrine was erected as a place of worship and the original cross replaced with one of concrete.

6 - Alta Schmidt House Museum
936 Fourth Street, Yolo (916) 865-5444

Artifacts, photographs, documents and records that trace the history of the Orland area are maintained, by the Orland Historical and Cultural Society, in this pioneer home of Alta Schmidt.

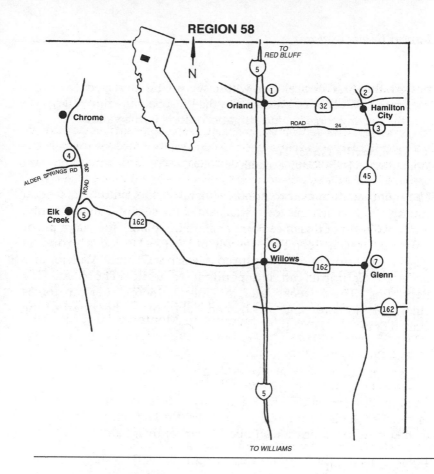

Orland

Chrome

Hamilton
City

Elk
Creek

Willows

Glenn

TO
RED BLUFF

ALDER SPRINGS RD

ROAD

ROAD

TO WILLIAMS

1 - Swift Adobe   SHL 345
On Hambright Creek north of Orland

Granville Swift was among the first settlers in this valley. The adobe
he built on Hambright Creek was the headquarters for his extensive
cattle operations. He was also the first to plant barley in this region.
Fortune hunters undermined the adobe by digging for gold that was
rumored to have been buried there by Swift.

2 - William S. Green Irrigation Notice   SHL 831
Site is 3 and 1/2 miles north of Hamilton City, on the west bank of the
Sacramento River, near the Glenn-Colusa Irrigation District Plant

On December 18, 1883, on an oak tree near this spot, Will Green posted the first notice that water would be diverted from the Sacramento River to irrigate land in the West Sacramento Valley. He was the driving force behind irrigation efforts in the valley.

3 - Monroeville Ghost Town
Monument on Hwy 45 at the mouth of Stony Creek

The monument erected to honor William B. Ide, who held several county offices when this town was named the seat of Colusa County, is all that is left of this once popular stopping place. Ide was a major influence in the Bear Flag Revolt of 1846. He led a group of Americans into Sonoma, captured Mexico's General Vallejo, and declared California an independent republic (The Bear Flag Republic). Three weeks later, on July 9, 1846, American forces landed at Monterey and proclaimed California to be a part of the United States.

4 - Grindstone Creek
Site is on private property, north of Alder Springs Road off Road 306

The first known manufacturing activity in this part of the state was established at Grindstone Creek, in 1845. Rocks from the creek were made into grindstones and shipped as far south as San Francisco.

5 - Bidwell Point
South of Elk Creek and Hwy 162

General John Bidwell and his Indian guide camped at this point on Conical Hill, July 3, 1844. They were exploring the region to find an acceptable land grant, for the children of the American Consul, Thomas O. Larkin.

6 - Willows
16 miles south of Orland at I-5 and Hwy 162

The second adobe built by Granville Swift, in Glenn County, was here at "The Willows," a noted landmark on these plains in the late 1800s. From here, Swift operated a corral where he controlled access to the only watering hole for miles around. Willows became the county seat when Glenn County was formed, in 1891.

7 - Glenn
15 miles south of Hamilton City at Hwy 45 and Hwy 162

Both the city and county were named in honor of Dr. Hugh Glenn, a Missouri physician, who came to California in 1849. He began purchasing land in 1867, until he had acquired 55,000 acres along the Sacramento River, on which he planted 45,000 acres of wheat. More than 100 eight-mule teams were needed to harvest the nearly one million bags of grain that his land produced in 1880. This harvest earned Dr. Glenn the title, "World's Wheat King." Dr. Glenn's land was subdivided, after he was shot to death by his secretary, in 1883. Today, only the town that bears his name remains.

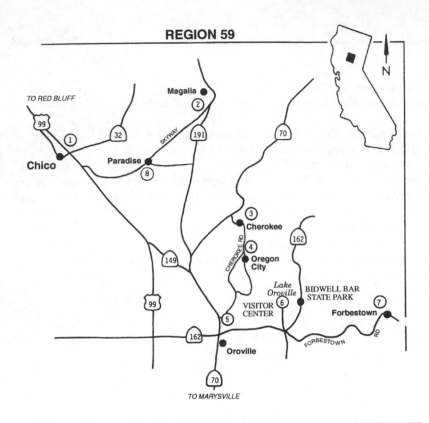

1 - Sir Joseph Hooker Oak Tree   SHL 313
Bidwell Park on Manzanita Avenue, between Vallombrosa and Hooker Oak Avenue, Chico

Named in honor of the English botanist, Sir Joseph Hooker, who visited General John Bidwell in 1877, this American Oak was among the largest in the region. It was over 1,000 years old, and measured 28-feet in circumference, before it fell in a 1977 storm.

1 - Experimental Forestry Station and Nursery   SHL 840.2
In the Cedar Grove section of Bidwell Park, 4th Street and Cypress Avenue, Chico (916) 895-4972

General John Bidwell's interest in horticulture prompted his donation of land, to the state in 1886, for use as an experimental forestry station. It was one of the first stations of its type in the Nation.

Preserved in the Cedar Grove section of this park are trees from all over the world.

1 - Stansbury Home Victorian House Museum
307 West Fifth Street, Chico (916) 895-3848

The 1883 home of Chico pioneers, Dr. and Mrs. Oscar Stansbury, has been preserved by the city and the Stansbury Home Preservation Association in its original, unaltered condition. The two-story home, a classic example of Victorian Italianate architecture, contains about eighty-five percent of its original furniture and family mementos. All but one room has its original wallpaper and wall coverings, making this one of the best-preserved examples of Victorian wallpapering in California.

1 - Chico Museum
141 Salem Street, Chico (916) 891-4336

Chico's 1904 Carnegie library building was remodeled and enlarged in 1939, to serve as the city's museum. Items reflecting the history of Chico and the surrounding area are displayed. A featured exhibit of the museum is the late-1800s Chinese Temple which was shipped here in pieces and reassembled.

Stansbury Home. Courtesy of Stansbury Home Victorian House Museum.

1 - Bidwell Mansion State Historic Park   SHL 329
525 The Esplanade, Chico   (916) 895-6144

In 1852, Indians built an adobe home for General John Bidwell on his 26,000-acre Rancho Chico. Bidwell developed the town of Chico on his ranch in 1860, and donated land for schools and churches. He used his land to grow hundreds of varieties of fruit trees and vineyards that helped develop California's agriculture as we know it today. This restored and refurnished 26-room brick mansion was built in 1865 as the center for his social, humanitarian and political activities. Important visitors, such as President Hayes, Generals Grant and Sherman, and Susan B. Anthony, were entertained here.

2 - Dogtown Gold Nugget   SHL 771
Northeast of Chico on Skyway in Magalia

The largest known gold nugget found in Butte County weighed 54 pounds and was discovered in the Willard Mine on August 14, 1859. This monument marks the site of that famous discovery.

3 - Cherokee Museum
4226 Cherokee Road, Oroville   (916) 533-1849

This mining town was founded and operated successfully by a band of Cherokee Indians, who came here from the Oklahoma Territory, in 1853. The largest diamond find in North America was made here in 1863, with the discovery of 300 diamonds. Scars left in these hills from hydraulic mining, and stone ruins of the town's assay/mine office can still be seen. The old Stage Stop now houses the Cherokee Museum which contains various items from the city's past.

4 - Oregon City   SHL 807
Between Oroville and Cherokee on Oregon Gulch Road

Among the 49er emigrants that came to California from Oregon was Peter Burnett. He was a founder of Oregon City. A year after his arrival, Burnett became the first civilian Governor of California.

5 - Oroville
Hwy 70 and Hwy 162

Many of Oroville's early homes and businesses have been restored. Their history is told in a guide available from the Chamber of Commerce. The "green line" painted down the center of Oroville's streets can be followed to all the city's historical landmarks.

5 - Chinese Temple and Garden   SHL 770
1500 Broderick Street, Oroville (916) 538-2496

Built by Oroville's Chinese population in 1863, this temple served the 10,000 laborers who lived and worked here. It has since been restored and features objects of folk art, priceless costumes, tapestries, and one of the few Chinese gardens open to the public.

5 - Butte County Pioneer Memorial Museum
2332 Montgomery Street, Oroville (916) 532-0107

The museum, fashioned after a gold miner's cabin, features relics from Butte County, in displays that depict the history of the area.

5 - Judge C. F. Lott Memorial Home
Sank Park, 1067 Montgomery Street, Oroville (916) 538-2497

Lott came to California in 1849 and began a law practice at Bidwell Bar. He was elected State Senator and built his home here in 1856. His home was willed to the city. It is now a cultural repository for decorative art objects typical of those found in the homes of Oroville's pioneer families. The collection includes furniture, paintings, rugs, textiles, clothes, silver and glassware from 1849-1910.

5 - Yana Indian Memorial
Bicentennial Park, downtown Oroville

Ishi, the last of the Yana Indian Tribe, and the last known, wild Native American Indian found in the United States, was immortalized by local high school students who created this hand-carved statue. The statue was installed in 1976, outside the jail that was Ishi's first home after he was found in 1911.

5 - Discovery Site of Last Wild American Indian   SHL 809
Oroville-Quincy Hwy at Oak Avenue, Oroville

Ishi, the last known survivor of the Yana Indians was found here in 1911. He was the last, wild Native American found in the United States. The last five years of his life were spent at the University Museum of Anthropology, in San Francisco, where he contributed much to the understanding of primitive Indian history and culture.

6 - Oroville Dam
Lake Oroville State Recreation Area, Kelly Ridge Road north of Hwy 162 (916) 538-2200, Visitor's Center (916) 538-2219

Built in the 1960s, Oroville Dam, is the tallest dam of its type in the United States, measuring 770 feet.

6 - Bidwell Bar   SHL 330
Lake Oroville State Recreation Area Visitor Center, Kelly Ridge Road off Hwy 162 (916) 538-2200

General John Bidwell discovered gold here in 1848. Within five years Bidwell Bar grew to become the county seat for Butte County. Oroville became the county seat after Bidwell Bar's mines played-out and its residents left for other towns. Today, Bidwell Bar is covered by the waters of the Oroville Reservoir.

6 - Bidwell Bar Suspension Bridge   SHL 314
Bidwell Canyon Drive, Bidwell Canyon Recreation Area, Lake Oroville

California's first suspension bridge was brought around the Horn from New York, and built at Bidwell's Bar, in the 1850s. When Oroville Dam was built in 1964, the bridge and its toll house were moved to its present site, where it is preserved as an important historical landmark.

6 - Mother Orange Tree
Bidwell Canyon Drive, Bidwell Canyon Recreation Area, Lake Oroville

Judge Joseph Lewis planted a two-year-old orange tree, in 1856, on the approach to the Bidwell Bar Suspension Bridge. As the tree grew, miners would use seeds from its fruit to raise their own orange trees. From this "mother" tree came many of Northern California's orange groves. When the Bidwell Bar Suspension Bridge was moved in 1964, the tree, one of the oldest orange trees in the state, was relocated here.

7 - Forbestown
18 miles east of Oroville on Forbestown Road

The restored Masonic Hall, built in 1857, is all that remains of the town that was the center of this area's mining activities for forty years.

7 - Yuba-Feather Historical Museum
Forbestown Park, New York Flat Road, Forbestown (916) 675-1025

Vintage printing presses still operate in this museum's turn-of-the-century era printing room. A 19th century general store, a blacksmith shop, and items from the area's mining and logging pursuits are also exhibited.

8 - Gold Nugget Museum
502 Pearson Road, Paradise (916) 872-8722

Gold Rush era artifacts, and history of the region's Native Americans and early settlers, are featured at this living museum. A country store, miner's cabin, simulated gold mine, and an extensive turn-of-the-century doll collection are exhibited. The all-volunteer staff reconstructed a small Western town on the museum grounds.

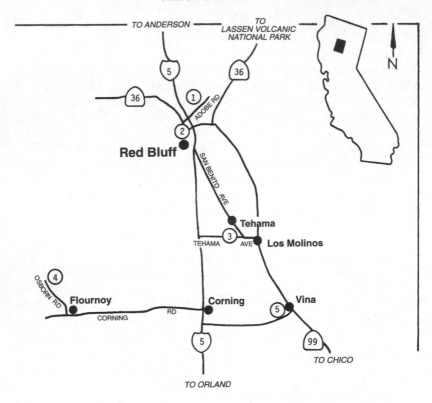

1 - William B. Ide Adobe State Historical Park   SHL 12
21659 Adobe Road, Red Bluff (916) 527-5927

This monument, restored adobe house, and other buildings are a memorial to William B. Ide, commandant of the Bear Flag Revolt of 1846. Ide, with a group of other pioneers, having learned that Mexican officials were planning to drive all Americans out of California, marched to Sonoma, captured Mexican General Vallejo and declared California an independent republic. Three weeks later, American forces landed at Monterey and raised the American Flag, making California a territory of the United States.

2 - Mrs. John Brown's Home SHL 117
135 Main Street, Red Bluff

The pro-Union community of Red Bluff raised funds to build this home for Mary Brown, widow of Civil War abolitionist and Harper's Ferry martyr, John Brown. Mrs. Brown and her children came to California at the close of the Civil War, in 1864. They lived in this home for the next six years.

2 - Kelly-Griggs House Museum
311 Washington Street, Red Bluff (916) 527-1129

This 1880 house and museum features: antique furniture; early Chinese memorabilia; old photographs; artifacts from local pioneer families; and original possessions of Ishi, the last surviving wild Indian in North America. The Isensee Indian exhibit in the Ishi room contains Ishi, Yani and Maidu artwork, baskets and tools.

3 - Site of First Tehama County Courthouse SHL 183
Second and "D" Streets, Tehama

The town of Tehama was an important ferry crossing and stage center, along the Oregon Road, in the mid-1800s. The first seat of Tehama County was established at Judge Hall's ranch. It is commemorated by a plaque, on private property, at the site of his original two-story Union Hotel.

3 - Robert Thomes Monument
Tehama Cemetery, 1 and 1/2 miles west of Tehama on Tehama Avenue

A granite monument to Tehama's pioneer settler, Robert Thomes, was erected here after his death in 1878. Thomes was the only American to be awarded a Mexican land grant without marrying a Spanish or Mexican citizen to qualify.

4 - Nomi Lackee Indian Reservation SHL 357
Monument on Osborn Road, 4 miles north of Flournoy

As many as 2,500 Native Americans, displaced by white settlers, were quartered on this reservation, from 1854 until 1866. Then they were relocated to Round Valley, in Mendocino County. A monument marks the site of this early Indian reservation.

5 - Vina
Monument on Hwy 99E at Deer Creek, Vina

Peter Lassen, Tehama County's first white settler, received a Mexican land grant of 25,000 acres in 1843, on which he laid out the town of Benton City. He returned to Missouri and brought back settlers, across the Lassen Trail in 1848 to live here, but the gold fields lured them away. Masons erected a monument in this town to honor Peter Lassen. He brought the first Masonic Lodge Charter to California in 1848.

1 - Bass Hill   SHL 148
Off ramp to Bay Bridge, I-5, north of Mountain Gate

A monument to the memory of Williamson Smith, the division stage agent of the California and Oregon Stage Company, and the company's pioneer stage drivers, was placed along this remnant of the old stage road at a point where their stages were frequently held-up.

2 - French Gulch   SHL 166
Trinity Mountain Road, 3 miles north of Hwy 299

One of this region's richest gold mining centers in the 1850s was French Gulch. The Feeney Hotel (now known as the French Gulch Hotel) has been restored and is operating as a hotel today. Other buildings from the 1860s can be seen in the town's historic district.

3 - Whiskeytown   SHL 131
11 miles west of Redding on Hwy 299

Whiskeytown, which is said to have gotten its name when a pack mule dumped a barrel of whiskey in Whiskey Creek, was a gold mining town during the 1849 Gold Rush period. Today, the town is inundated by the Whiskeytown Reservoir and is part of the Whiskeytown-Shasta-Trinity National Recreation Area. The National Park Service has restored the 1892 home of pioneer settler, Charles Camden, which is at the west end of Whiskeytown Lake.

4 - Old Town Shasta   SHL 77
Shasta State Historic Park, Hwy 299, 6 miles west of Redding
(916) 243-8194

Founded in 1849, as "Reading's Springs," the town was renamed "Shasta" in 1850. Shasta was the center of gold mining for this area and was the county seat between 1851 and 1888. The 1855 Shasta County Courthouse building has been restored and houses a state history museum. Original Western paintings, Indian artifacts, displays of pioneer life and frontier justice are exhibited. The personal collection of Mae Helen Bacon Boggs, who spearheaded the 1915 San Francisco Exposition, is a featured exhibit. The restored 1855-1856 Litsch Store and brick ruins of the town's once flourishing business district can be explored.

The Litsch Store as it was in the 1800s, has been completely restored. Courtesy of Shasta State Historic Park, California Dept. of Parks and Recreation.

4 - Father Rinaldi's Church Foundation   SHL 483
1/2 mile from Hwy 299W on Red Bluff Road, (on private property) Shasta

Father Raphael Rinaldi, who came to Shasta in 1855, as the new parish priest, laid this foundation for a new church to be built of cut stone. This foundation, and the cornerstone which was laid in 1857, is all that was ever built.

4 - Pioneer Baby's Grave   SHL 377
3/4 mile west of Shasta on Hwy 299

This headstone marks the grave of a pioneer Jewish child, buried here in 1864. Engineers planning a road through here, in 1923, discovered this burial site and altered the planned direction of the road.

5 - Redding Museum and Art Center
Caldwell Park, 56 Quartz Hill Road, Redding (916) 225-4155

A permanent exhibit of Indian baskets and items of historical interest are part of the museum's collections. Redding's history as a railhead, county seat, and copper trading center is a featured part of their historical exhibits.

5 - Shasta College Museum
1065 North Old Oregon Trail, Redding
Research Office (916) 225-4621

The Shasta College Museum and Research Center is housed in a building that resembles the Pierson B. Reading Adobe, the home of the first white settlers in Shasta County. Exhibits focus on the history of the northern Sacramento Valley and include: farming equipment from the 1850s to the 1930s, mining and logging tools, and a 6-ton petroglyph.

6 - Reading's Bar   SHL 32
Marked at Clear Creek Bridge, 7 miles west of Hwy 273 on Clear Creek Road

Major Reading went to Sutter's Mill after the discovery of gold was made there in 1848. He examined the soil and figured that the soil on his own ranchero was similar, and might also contain gold. He returned to his ranchero and, with the help of Indians, found the first gold in Shasta County at what was to become Reading's Bar.

7 - Clear Creek   SHL 78
Clear Creek Road at the end of Clear Creek Bridge, 6 miles west of Hwy 273

The first discovery of gold in Shasta County was at Reading's Bar, here on Clear Creek, in 1848. The town that once numbered 1,000 along this creek no longer remains, but Reading's historic gold discovery site is commemorated here.

8 - Bell's Bridge   SHL 519
Clear Creek Road and Hwy 273

During the 1850s, J. J. Bell operated a toll bridge near here that crossed Clear Creek into the Shasta, Trinity and Siskiyou gold fields. Bell also established an inn above the bridge, where he provided lodging and food, for many of the travelers along this part of the Oregon Road.

9 - Anderson Museum
Anderson Chamber of Commerce, 2086 Balls Ferry Road, Anderson
(916) 365-8095

Anderson's Chamber of Commerce maintains a collection of artifacts from the local area depicting the history of the city. Two rooms at the Chamber office are devoted to the museum.

9 - California-Oregon Road   SHL 58
1 and 3/4 miles north of Anderson on I-5

The main artery of travel used by pioneers between Oregon and California was along this trail (which Interstate 5 closely follows today). The northern most point of travel for riverboats on the Sacramento River was at this point on the California-Oregon Road.

10 - Fort Reading   SHL 379
3 and 1/2 miles east of junction of Dersch and Airport Roads

The first and largest U.S. Army post in Northern California was established here in 1852 and named in honor of Major Pierson Reading. Most military activity at the post ended in 1856 and the last soldiers left in the summer of 1857. The fort was officially closed in 1866 and the buildings sold. Nothing remains of the fort today except the land where it once stood.

11 - Dersch Homestead SHL 120
7 and 3/4 miles east of junction of Dersch and Airport Roads

In 1863, Indians raided the home of George and Marie Dersch, on land they homesteaded in 1860. Three years later, Indians again raided their home, this time killing Mrs. Dersch. Settlers, unable to get help from Fort Reading, took matters into their own hands by tracking down the Indians responsible for the attack and executing them. A replica of the Dersch home has been reconstructed at this site.

12 - Reading Adobe (Site) SHL 10
Adobe Lane, 7 miles east of Cottonwood via Balls Ferry Road

Pierson Reading received a 26,000-acre land grant in 1845 which ran 19 miles along the west bank of the Sacramento River. After serving under John Fremont, as a major in the Mexican War, Reading returned to his ranchero in 1847 and built his adobe at this site. It was in this adobe that Shasta County's first seat of government was established on February 18, 1850. Nothing remains today of Reading's adobe which stood here for more than a century.

13 - Cottonwood Historic District
Front Street, Cottonwood

Several brick buildings are preserved in this district of Cottonwood as local historic points of interest.

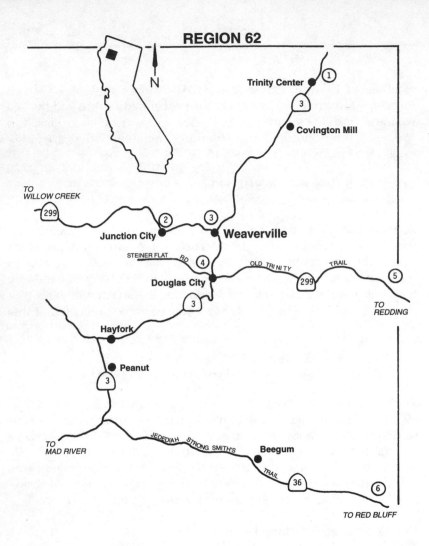

N

Trinity Center ● ①

③

● Covington Mill

TO
WILLOW CREEK

299

② Junction City ●

③

● Weaverville

STEINER FLAT RD. ④

OLD TRINITY TRAIL

299 ⑤

Douglas City ●

TO
REDDING

③

Hayfork ●

● Peanut

③

TO
MAD RIVER

JEDEDIAH STRONG SMITH'S

● Beegum

TRAIL

36 ⑥

TO RED BLUFF

462

1 - Scott Museum of Trinity Center
1/2 mile east of Hwy 3 on Airport Road, Trinity Center

This museum contains a large collection of various types of barbed wire—nearly 500 samples of the 700 known patents. Also exhibited are authentic models of the type of stage that once stopped at this center on the Oregon California Road. Among the unusual displays are horse snowshoes and pack saddles.

2 - La Grange Mine   SHL 778
4 miles west of Weaverville on Hwy 299

Opened in 1851, La Grange Mine became one of the largest hydraulic placer mines in the world. More than 100 million yards of gravel were processed before the mine closed in 1918. To provide enough water for this large operation, a series of ditches, tunnels and flumes were constructed over a distance of 30 miles to Stuart's Fork.

3 - Weaverville Joss House   SHL 709
Oregon and Main Streets, Weaverville (916) 623-5284

The Chinese population in Weaverville numbered over 2,000 during the Gold Rush period. Their first place of worship burned in 1873. It was replaced, at this site, in 1874. This well-preserved building contains many of the furnishings, originally brought from China, that were saved when the first building burned. It is still used as a place of worship by the Chinese community.

3 - Weaverville Walking Tour
Trinity County Chamber of Commerce, 317 Main Street, Weaverville (916) 623-6101

Weaverville's Chamber of Commerce and Trinity County Historical Society publish a guide to the city's historical homes and business establishments. Included in the 119 listings is the historic downtown district, which borders Main Street between Forest and Brannon, are many two-story buildings with outside spiral staircases. Most of the listed buildings were constructed before the turn-of-the-century.

3 - J. J. (Jake) Jackson Memorial Museum
Trinity County Historical Park, 508 Main Street, Weaverville (916) 623-5211

A collection of antique firearms was the centerpiece of the country's first museum, which was originally established in the basement of the old Court House, through the efforts of Jake Jackson. In 1968, this new building became the county's new museum. Its displays include: mining equipment; old bottles and kitchen utensils; history of the region's Native Americans; medical artifacts; and items from the Chinese community. The adjacent historical park exhibits a replica of an original Weaverville blacksmith shop, a re-constructed miner's cabin, and a restored steam-powered 2-stamp mill.

3 - Weaverville Drug Store
Main Street Historical District, Weaverville

The state's oldest continuously-operating drug store was begun in this building in 1862. Displays of old patent medicines, remedies, potions, and a collection of old medicine bottles are exhibited.

4 - Reading's Bar
Bureau of Land Management Campground, Steiner Flat Road, Douglas City

The first discovery of gold in Trinity County, was at Reading's Bar in July 1848, by Major Pierson Reading.

5 - The Old Trinity Trail
Hwy 299

The Old Trinity Trail was used by 49ers on their way to the Trinity gold fields and by trappers in the 1830s and 1840s. Today's State Highway 299 follows the approximate route of the Old Trinity Trail.

6 - Jedediah Strong Smith's Trail
Hwy 36

Jedediah Smith and his party were the first white men to make the journey from California, to Oregon, and were among the first to explore Trinity County. State Highway 36, the Red Bluff-Eureka Highway, is generally the route that was followed by these first explorers in 1828.

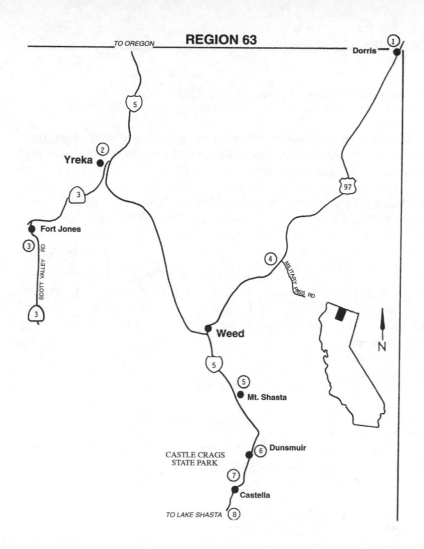

1 - Herman's House of Guns
204 South Oregon Street, Dorris

On exhibit is a historic collection of guns, cannon and military weapons. Also displayed are farm and household items, gas and steam engines, and antiques.

2 - West Miner Street - Third Street Historic District   SHL 901
Yreka Historic Preservation Corporation, 115 South Oregon Street, Yreka (916) 842-1649

The discovery of gold by Abraham Thompson, in 1851, led to the founding of the town of Yreka, which later became the county seat for Siskiyou County. Restored homes and businesses, from the mid- to late-1800s, are preserved in this historic section of town. Below the streets are tunnels and mine shafts that were carved out by miners in search of gold.

2 - Siskiyou County Museum
910 South Main Street, Yreka (916) 842-3836

This museum has both indoor and outdoor exhibits. An 1856 log cabin, 1870 miner's cabin, schoolhouse, country store and other buildings are part of the outdoor exhibit. Inside the museum are: Indian artifacts, firearms, gold and relics from the days when trappers worked this area.

2 - Siskiyou County Courthouse
311 - 4th Street, Yreka (916) 842-3531

Gold nuggets, from various mines in Siskiyou County, are exhibited in this extension of the Siskiyou County Museum. This interpretive display shows the variations in the colors of gold taken from different areas of the county. Photographs of the mining areas, various mining equipment and samples of "black sand" are also showcased.

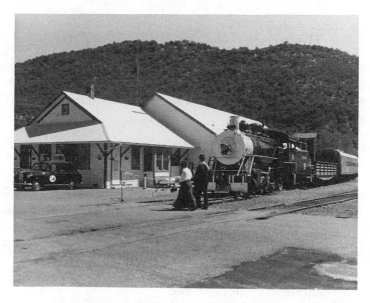

Yreka Western Railroad Company. Photo by Gordon Loomis.

2 - Blue Goose Shortline Railroad
East side of I-5, Yreka (916) 842-4146

In January 1889, Yreka Railroad was built to connect the city of Yreka with the main line at Montague, 7 and 1/3 miles to the east. This shortline railroad has been in continuous operation more than 100 years. In 1965, the City of Eureka inaugurated the "Blue Goose" steam passenger train, a summer excursion service to Montague. The historic station contains original furnishings, railroad memora bilia, old photographs and documents. "Old Number 1," a 1915 Baldwin 2-8-2 steam locomotive, is among the rolling stock still operated on this pioneer line.

3 - Fort Jones Museum
11913 Main Street, Fort Jones (916) 468-5568

This stone building displays the history of Fort Jones. The museum collections include: relics from the 1850s, guns, Indian artifacts, and Northern California Indian baskets. Outside is the Indian rain rock that Indians claimed brought torrential rains to the area.

3 - Fort Jones SHL 317
1 mile south of Fort Jones on Scott Valley Road (916) 468-5568

Fort Jones was established as a U.S. Army post, during the 1850s, to protect settlers from Indian attacks. Although the fort no longer stands, the Fort Jones Museum in town tells the history of the region.

4 - Old Emigrant Trail SHL 517
Military Pass Road, junction with U.S. 97

The first wagon road from Sacramento Valley to Yreka, crossed near this old emigrant trail, and the old Military Pass Road from Fort Crook. In the early 1850s, overland emigrants crossed this trail en route to settle Northern California. This trail later became a well-traveled stage road. Ruts from those early stages can still be seen in many areas at Sheep Rock.

5 - Mysterious Stone Circles of Weed
Both northbound and southbound rest areas, I-5, North Weed

Plaques at this rest area describe the strange stone circles that stretch over a 600-acre area. Each mound is alike, measuring about 60' in diameter and 2' high. The origin of the circles remain a mystery.

5 - Strawberry Valley Stage Station SHL 396
Old Stage Road, Mt. Shasta

The city of Mt. Shasta began as a settlement in Strawberry Valley in the 1850s. Justin Sisson, the first postmaster, built a hotel and for many years the town bore his name. Sisson's post office (established under the name Berryvale) is located across the road from this site near the old stage station.

5 - Sisson Hatchery Museum
One Old Stage Road, Mount Shasta (916) 926-5508

In 1888, Mount Shasta Hatchery was established. It has been in continuous operation ever since. The Sisson Hatchery Museum was named for Justin Sisson, who began stocking local streams with trout in 1877. Its exhibits tell the history of the hatchery, and the history of the region's logging, skiing and mountain exploration.

6 - Dunsmuir/Dunsmuir Museum

4101 Pine Street, between Dunsmuir and Sacramento Avenues, Dunsmuir
(916) 235-0733

Dunsmuir began as a railroad camp called "Pusher," for the wood burning pusher engines that had to be added to get trains over the summit. One of these old engines, No. 1727, is on display at the city park. Dunsmuir's museum (at Pine and Sacramento Avenue) depicts the history of this region and the downtown business district which is on the National Register of Historic Places.

6 - Railroad Park Resort/Caboose Motel

100 Railroad Park Road, Dunsmuir (916) 235-4440

One hundred year old, antique railroad cars have been restored and converted for use as part of the resort's restaurant and motel. A 1927 Willamette Shay engine, and other rolling stock, are displayed at this unusual motel.

7 - Battle Rock   SHL 116

Castle Crags State Park, west of I-5, Castella (916) 235-2684

Rumors of gold, and the "Lost Cabin Mine," brought many prospectors here in the 1850s. Indians, who lived in the area, fought the "white man" that came into this region and killed or drove off the Indian's fish and game. The Battle of the Crags, took place here at Battle Rock, between Indians and settlers. It cost lives on both sides and was one of the conflicts that led to the Modoc Indian War.

8 - Southern's Hotel and Stage Station   SHL 33

7 miles south of Castella on I-5, 1/2 mile south of Sims Road junction

Simeon Southern's cabin, built in 1859, was an important stage stop in the early 1870s. It also became a well-known summer resort. During the 1880s it was enlarged and remodeled to accommodate an ever increasing number of guests. The guest list was impressive and included President Hayes, General Sherman and other famous people of the period. No trace of the original hotel remains today.

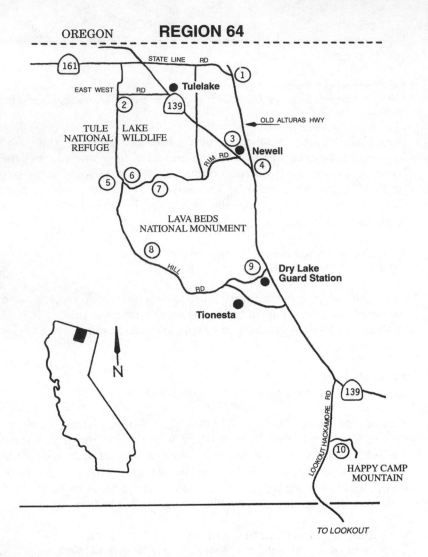

REGION 64

OREGON

161

STATE LINE RD

EAST WEST RD

● Tulelake

139

1

2

TULE NATIONAL REFUGE

LAKE WILDLIFE

OLD ALTURAS HWY

3

RIM RD

● Newell

4

5

6

7

LAVA BEDS NATIONAL MONUMENT

8

HILL RD

9

● Dry Lake Guard Station

● Tionesta

N

139

LOOKOUT HACKAMORE RD

10

HAPPY CAMP MOUNTAIN

TO LOOKOUT

1 - Bloody Point   SHL 8
Near Tulelake at the junction of State Line Road and Old Alturas Highway

Bitter conflicts, between white men and Indians, went on for almost forty years in Modoc County. In 1850, an emigrant party of about 90 men, women and children were attacked at this site. All, but one man, were massacred. Other emigrant parties were also attacked at this location, a favorite Indian ambush spot.

2 - Lower Klamath Wildlife Refuge and Tule Lake
Wildlife Refuge
Headquarters on Hill Road, south of East West Road, 4 miles west of Tulelake

One of the first wildlife reserves in the country was established at Lower Klamath Lake, in 1908, and has since been registered as a National Historic Landmark. Tule Lake and Lower Klamath Lakes are home to migrating waterfowl, including the American Bald Eagle.

3 - Tulelake Relocation Center   SHL 850.2
7 miles southeast of Tulelake off Hwy 139, Newell

Barracks were constructed here in 1942, when Tulelake Relocation Center was established as one of ten internment camps in the United States for Japanese and Japanese-Americans during World War ll.

4 - Fremont's Camp   SHL 6
11 miles southeast of Tulelake on Old Alturas Hwy, 3/4 mile north of junction with Hwy 139

John Fremont, explorer and pathfinder, camped here with his guides, in May 1846, while exploring this region between Fort Sutter and Upper Klamath Lake. Among the guides was the well-known Kit Carson.

5 - Guillem's Graveyard   SHL 13
Hill and Rim Roads, Lava Beds National Monument (916) 667-2282

During the Modoc Indian War of 1872-1873, the American losses, which numbered almost 100, were buried here in a common grave.

Twenty years later their bodies were removed and laid to rest at Arlington National Cemetery, in Washington, D.C. The original burial site has been under the protection of the National Park system since 1925.

6 - Canby's Cross SHL 110
Rim Road, 1 mile east of Hill Road, Lava Beds National Monument
(916) 667-2282

In an effort to negotiate a peaceful settlement with the Modoc Indians and their leader, Captain Jack, a meeting was held in April 1873, under a flag of truce. At this gathering were the Indians, General E. R. S. Canby, the Reverend Thomas and four others. During the conference, Captain Jack killed the General and Reverend Thomas, and wounded the others in the party. A large wooden cross was erected, by the soldiers who served under General Canby, near the place where he was killed.

7 - Captain Jack's Stronghold SHL 9
Rim Road, west of Hospital Rock, Lava Beds National Monument
(916) 667-2282

The natural, rugged terrain of this area provided the Indian forces of Captain Jack with protection, from U.S. Army troops, which were sent to capture them, in 1872-1873. The Modoc Indians lost only one man, while the Americans had many casualties each day of this four month battle. Captain Jack killed the American's General Canby, under a flag of truce, and escaped with his men in April 1873.

8 - Lava Beds National Monument
Monument Headquarters on Hill Road, west of Hwy 139 (916) 667-2282

The rugged landscape of the surrounding area was created by molten rock and lava from volcanic activity. This natural fortress, its lava tubes and ice caves, provided protection for the Modoc Indians, during their war with the U.S. Army in 1872-1873. Various historic sites of that war have been marked throughout the monument's grounds. The lava tubes and ice caves can be explored and the monument's museum has an interesting collection of Modoc Indian artifacts and history of the area.

9 - Land's Ranch   SHL 108
1/2 mile west of Dry Lake Guard Station on Hwy 139

The rear guard, of an Army supply train escort, was ambushed by Indians hiding behind the rocks along this road, in 1872. Two U.S. Cavalry soldiers were killed, and several wounded, adding to the growing number of casualties in the Modoc Indian War.

10 - Old Emigrant Trail   SHL 111
Pit River - Happy Camp Road, off Lookout Hackamore Road, south of Hwy 139, Modoc National Forest

In 1848 Peter Burnett, who would later become the first civil governor of California, brought his party of emigrants from Oregon, over this trail, which they blazed south to the Pit River. This section of the old emigrant trail was followed by many gold seekers and emigrants to California in 1849-1850.

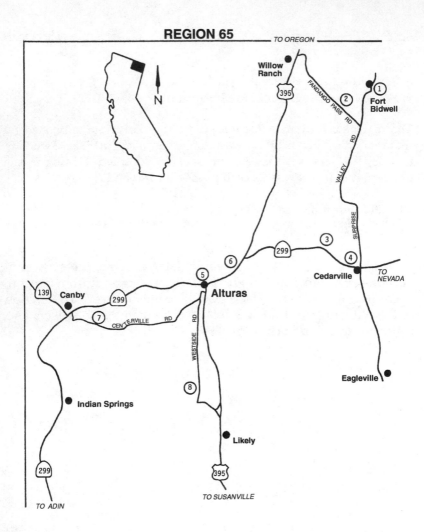

1 - Site of Fort Bidwell   SHL 430
Surprise Valley Road, 5 and 1/2 miles north of Fandango Pass junction, Fort Bidwell

U.S. Cavalrymen were stationed at Fort Bidwell, from 1865 to 1893, to provide protection for settlers and to control the menacing Indians that roamed this region of California, Oregon and Nevada. The fort was used as a government school for Paiute Indians until 1930, when the barracks were torn down.

2 - Fandango Pass   SHL 546
Fandango Pass Road, southeast of U.S. 395 and Willow Ranch

Pioneers following the Applegate and Lassen Trails crossed this pass over Warner Mountain, during the period 1846-1850. Fandango Pass was heavily traveled by emigrants who came from the Humboldt River region of Nevada to settle in California and Oregon.

3 - Bonner Grade   SHL 15
6 and 1/2 miles west of Cedarville on Hwy 299

The first road from Cedarville to Alturas was constructed in 1869, through the efforts of John Bonner, proprietor of the county's first trading post in Cedarville. The present highway, which closely follows the first road through this area, was named in his honor.

4 - Cressler and Bonner Trading Post   SHL 14
Cedarville Park, Center Street, Cedarville

The oldest building in Modoc County is this log structure erected in 1865, by James Townsend. After Townsend was killed by Indians, his widow sold this property to William Cressler and John Bonner. They, in turn, established the county's first commercial business, a general store. Other log cabin dwellings were built by early settlers around the area where this historic building now stands.

5 - Historic Walking/Driving Tour of Alturas
Alturas Chamber of Commerce, 522 South Main, Alturas (916) 233-2819

A guide to Alturas' historic buildings is available from the Chamber of Commerce and the Modoc County Historical Museum. Included in the thirty-one sites listed in this guide, are buildings constructed between 1876 and 1938, some of which are listed in the National Register of Historic Buildings. The 1910 Ford building contains a historic automobile display. Other buildings contain interiors that serve as a living museum of Alturas' historic past.

5 - Modoc County Historical Museum
600 South Main Street, Alturas (916) 233-2944

Over 4,000 Indian arrowheads, spear points and other artifacts from the Modoc Indians are displayed. Antique guns and firearms are also exhibited in this collection of historic items. Tours of local historic sites are conducted by the museum staff.

6 - Chimney Rock SHL 109
7 and 1/4 miles north of Alturas on U.S. 395

The second building constructed in Pit Valley was erected on this site, in the 1860s, by Thomas Denison. He used this rock as a chimney, by cutting a fireplace and flue out of it, and then built his home around "chimney rock."

7 - Evans and Bailey Fight SHL 125
4 and 3/4 miles southeast of Canby on the Centerville Road to Alturas, a white marker is on the hill to the right of the road

S. D. Evans and Joe Bailey were driving 900 head of cattle from Oregon to Virginia City, Nevada, when they were attacked by Indians at this site in July 1861. Their men survived the attack, but both Evans and Bailey were killed.

8 - Infernal Caverns Battleground SHL 16
16 and 1/2 miles south of Alturas on Westside Road near Bayley Reservoir

This natural fortification of rocks and caves enabled about 100 Indians to wage a costly, two-day defense, against the 65 U.S. Army soldiers that were sent to arrest them in 1867. These Indians, who had terrorized settlers in Idaho, Nevada and this region of California, were driven from this stronghold after suffering many casualties and killing eight army soldiers. The graves of six of those soldiers can still be seen at this battleground site.

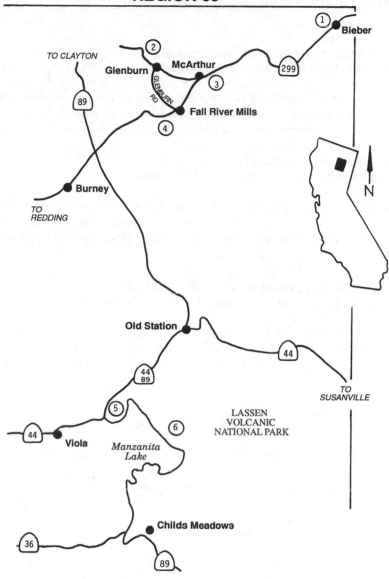

1 - Lassen Emigrant Trail - Bieber   SHL 763
Marked in Clara Bieber Memorial Park, Bieber

Peter Lassen opened this trail for emigrants in 1848, but it presented many hardships for travelers. In 1852, a better route was found, and travel across this trail came to a virtual halt within a year.

2 - Site of Fort Crook   SHL 355
5 miles northwest of Glenburn on McArthur Road

Early settlers and pioneers of this area were given protection against Indian attacks, with the establishment of Fort Crook, by Lt. George Crook in 1857. The post was abandoned in 1869. Its buildings were sold and removed from the site.

3 - Site of First School in Fall River   SHL 759
3 and 1/2 miles east of McArthur on the south side of Hwy 299

The first school to be constructed in the Fall River Valley was on this site in 1868. This simple log building had no windows. It wasn't until a sawmill was built, two years later, that the school had a floor and desks.

4 - Fort Crook Historical Museum
Fort Crook Avenue and Hwy 299, Fall River Mills (916) 336-5110

This museum features relics from settlers who inhabited the area in the 1800s. Indian artifacts, early transportation, pioneer industry exhibits, and a collection of period photographs are displayed.

4 - Lockhart Ferry   SHL 555
1/3 mile west of Fall River Mills on Hwy 299

Sam and William Lockhart came to this region in 1856, and established a ferry on the California-Oregon road, where it crossed the Pit River. William was killed in an Indian attack the following year. His brother, Sam, survived and re-established their ferry operation. In 1859, Sam built a bridge across the Pit River only to have it washed away in the great flood of 1862.

5 - Noble Pass Road   SHL 11
Lassen Park Road (Hwy 89), Lassen Volcanic National Park, northwest of
Manzanita Lake (916) 595-4444

An 1852 pioneer wagon trail over the Sierra Nevada was marked by
William Noble across Lassen National Park and Noble Pass to the
Sacramento Valley. The route of this old emigrant trail through
Lassen National Park is shown on maps available at the park en-
trances.

6 - Lassen Volcanic National Park
Lassen Park Road (Hwy 89), between Viola and Childs Meadows
(916) 595-4444

Lassen Peak, and this National Park, were named for pioneer mountain man, Peter Lassen, who explored this region in the 1840s.
Lassen Peak, a plug dome volcano, was last active between 1914 and
1921. It is now considered to be dormant, but other volcanic activity
is evident in features like the symmetrical Cinder Cone, active hot
springs, steaming fumaroles and sulfurous vents. Manzanita Lake
Visitor Center houses the park museum and its collection of historic
items.

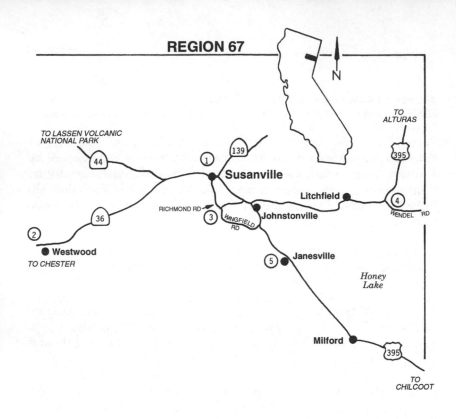

REGION 67

TO LASSEN VOLCANIC
NATIONAL PARK

TO
ALTURAS

44

139

Susanville

Litchfield

RICHMOND RD

WINGFIELD
RD

Johnstonville

WENDEL RD

36

Westwood
TO CHESTER

Janesville

Honey
Lake

Milford

395

TO
CHILCOOT

---

1 - Fort Defiance/Roop's Fort SHL 76
North Weatherlow Street, Susanville City Park, Susanville (916) 257-5721

Isaac Roop founded the city of Susanville and Lassen County. He built this log cabin as a trading post for emigrants traveling Noble's Trail, in 1854. Later it would be called Fort Roop (Fort Defiance) during the "Sagebrush War." Residents of Honey Lake held-up in Roop's Fort during a dispute, over county boundary lines, following the creation of the Nevada Territory in 1861. Both Plumas and Lake Counties claimed Honey Lake. The dispute was settled by the formation of Lassen County.

2 - Lassen Emigrant Trail - Westwood SHL 678
2 and 1/2 miles west of Westwood on Hwy 36

Forty-niners, and wagon trains bringing emigrants to California, used this trail that Peter Lassen opened in 1848.

3 - Peter Lassen Monument   SHL 565
2550 Wingfield Road via Richmond Road, 5 miles southeast of Susanville

Peter Lassen, for whom Lassen County was named, was one of Northern California's first white settlers. He was well-known as an explorer, wagonmaster and trailblazer. Many emigrants came into California using trails that he opened. When Lassen was killed by Indians in 1859, his friends buried him in this valley, near the creek that now bears his name.

4 - Noble Emigrant Trail   SHL 677
North of Honey Lake on U.S. 395 at junction with Wendel Road

While seeking a better route than the Lassen Trail, William Noble found, and later surveyed, a wagon road between Susanville and Shasta. That road, from which early travelers could see Honey Lake, went northwest from this point to Susanville, and westward to Shasta, over Noble Pass.

5 - Site of Fort Janesville   SHL 758
3/4 mile from Janesville off U.S. 395

Residents of Honey Lake Valley built themselves a fort, which they called Fort Janesville, as protection from an Indian attack—an attack that never came. Nothing remains of Fort Janesville today.

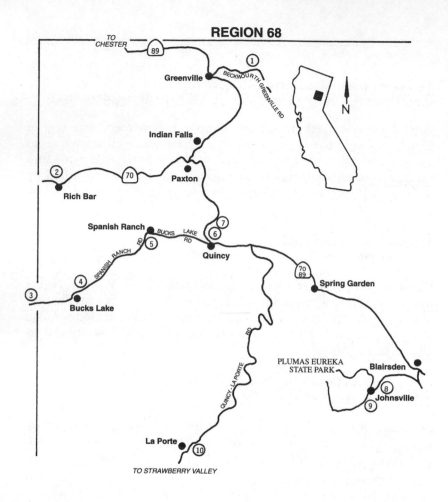

TO CHESTER

89

1

Greenville

BECKWOURTH GREENVILLE RD

N

Indian Falls

2

70

Paxton

Rich Bar

Spanish Ranch

BUCKS LAKE RD

7

6

5

SPANISH RANCH RD

Quincy

4

70
89

3

Bucks Lake

Spring Garden

QUINCY-LA PORTE RD

PLUMAS EUREKA
STATE PARK

Blairsden

8

Johnsville

9

La Porte

10

TO STRAWBERRY VALLEY

1 - Site of Peter Lassen's Cabin   SHL 184
Beckwourth-Greenville Road, 4 and 1/2 miles east of Greenville off Hwy 89

Peter Lassen, the first white settler in Indian Valley, built a log cabin, trading post on this site in 1851, to conduct trade with miners. In 1855, Lassen moved to the Susanville area, where he played an important part in that region's early history. In 1859, he was ambushed and killed by Indians while prospecting.

2 - Rich Bar   SHL 337
12 miles west of Paxton, just south of Hwy 70

Rich Bar got its name from the value of the gold claims at this site. So rich were the finds that the size of each claim was limited to a space of ten by ten feet. The once flourishing town no longer remains, but the published, *Letters from the California Mines*, written by Louise Clappe to her sister, gives a good account of life at Rich Bar during the Gold Rush days.

3 - Linthiouh Monument   SHL 212
Buck's Lake Road, west of Buck's Lake

P. Linthiouh, a 19-year-old pioneer boy, was robbed and killed by bandits as he was returning from one of the nearby mines in 1852. He was buried under a tree on which a friend carved his name and age. The tree no longer stands, but the original inscription has been reproduced on a granite monument that was erected to the memory of this young pioneer at his grave site.

4 - Buck's Ranch (Site)   SHL 197
Buck's Lake, south end of lake, via Buck's Lake Road West

In the early 1850s, Buck's Ranch was an important stage station, and overnight stop for miners. Buck's Dam and Reservoir was constructed in 1925. Now, the waters of Buck's Lake cover the former town site.

5 - Spanish Ranch - Meadow Valley SHL 481
North of junction of Spanish Ranch and Buck's Lake Roads, west of Quincy

Two Mexican settlers established a ranch in this area, where they raised cattle and sold meat, to miners that worked the surrounding area. A log hotel was constructed in 1852 and the town became a distribution point for several express companies. More than $100 million in gold was mined from the Spanish Ranch - Meadow Valley region, until 1863, when hydraulic mining was prohibited. None of the original Spanish Ranch buildings remain today.

6 - Masonic Hall Building
Harbison Avenue between Jackson and Main Streets, Quincy

The oldest building in Quincy is the Masonic Hall, which was moved here from Elizabethtown in 1855, after Quincy was named the county seat.

6 - Site of Bradley's American Ranch and Hotel SHL 479
355 Main Street, Quincy

James Bradley, owner of the American Ranch, was one of the commissioners that formed Plumas County. He built this town's first sawed-lumber building, at this site, in 1854. Using his influence, he was able to establish the new county seat at his hotel, around which he laid out the town of Quincy. A plaque marks the site of this county's first seat of justice.

6 - Site of the Plumas House SHL 480
Court and Main Streets, Quincy

In 1866, James and Jane Edwards built the Plumas House as a hotel. When fire destroyed the hotel in 1923, Hotel Quincy was erected in its place. It too was destroyed by fire in 1967. The site of Quincy's pioneer hotels is now a city park.

6 - Plumas County Museum
500 Jackson, Quincy (916) 283-6320

Located behind the courthouse, the Plumas County Museum takes a look at the history of the county and its culture. An outstanding collection of Maidu Indian baskets and artifacts, costumes and items of historical interest from the local area, are the primary exhibits.

6 - Plumas County Pioneer Schoolhouse SHL 625
Plumas County Fairgrounds, 2 miles east of Quincy, via Main Street and Plumas Fairgrounds Road (916) 283-6272

This restored schoolhouse was the first built in Plumas County. It was constructed by American Valley's pioneer residents in 1857.

7 - Elizabethtown SHL 231
North of Quincy on Purdys Road, northwest of Hwy 70

The gold mining camp of Elizabethtown was named after the daughter of an early settler, Lewis Stark, who came to this area with his family in 1852. As the local mines played out, Elizabethtown's residents began moving to the new county seat at Quincy. In 1855, the Masonic Hall building was moved to Quincy, where many of the town's homes were built using lumber from homes vacated at Elizabethtown. Tailings are all that remain from the old gold camp.

8 - Pioneer Ski Area of America SHL 723
Plumas-Eureka State Park off Hwy 70/89 on County Road A14
(916) 836-2380

In this region of the Sierra, La Porte, Jamison City, Johnsville and five other surrounding mining towns organized ski clubs, and held annual winter sport competitions, as early as 1860. A century of sport skiing in California was commemorated, in 1960, when the winter Olympics were held at Squaw Valley.

8 - Jamison City, Eureka Mills, Johnstown
     and Eureka Mine SHL 196
Plumas-Eureka State Park and Museum, 310 Johnsville Road, Blairsden
(916) 836-2380

In the Plumas-Eureka State Park area are reminders of the once booming, gold mining towns that stood here in the mid to late-1800s. The 48-stamp Plumas-Eureka Mill and other original buildings have been restored as part of this state park. Eureka Mine's former bunkhouse and office are now used to house a collection of Indian artifacts, and historical items from the famous mine. The nearby town of Johnsville (Johnstown) has well-preserved buildings, including an old church and firehouse. The towns of Jamison City and Eureka Mills no longer remain.

10 - Rabbit Creek Hotel   SHL 213
Southwest corner of Main and Church Streets, La Porte

The town of Rabbit Creek, which later became La Porte, was founded when gold was discovered in 1850. The Rabbit Creek Hotel was built on this site, in 1852, as the town's first house. Hydraulic mining made this an important mining center until 1883, when hydraulic mining was made illegal, because of the serious damage it caused to the land. Little remains of the original town buildings, but the site of the Rabbit Creek Hotel and the discovery of gold is commemorated by this monument.

REGION 69

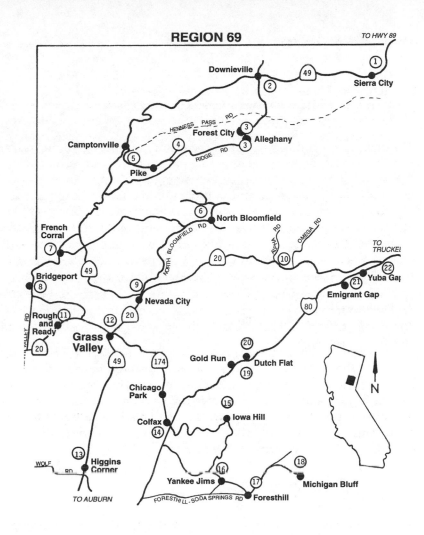

1 - Kentucky Mine Museum
1 mile east of Sierra City on Hwy 49, Sierra Country Historical Park
(916) 862-1310

The main focus of this museum is the history of mining. It includes a restored miner's cabin, a stamp mill and a mine entrance. A tour of the 10-stamp mill, one of the few remaining still in operation, shows how gold ore is processed through the mining and milling process. The tour does not go underground from the mine entrance. Other displays feature logging history and local items of interest from early settlers and Indians. A guide to Sierra City's points of historical interest is available at the museum. It points out notable buildings from 1880-1890, several of the town's older homes, and mine sites.

2 - Downieville
Main and Commercial Streets, Downieville (916) 289-3113

Many historical buildings are preserved in this 1850s gold mining town. As the county seat, justice was administered in the old courthouse which stood on the outskirts of town. The county gallows, erected in 1857 and last used in 1885, can be seen near the site of the old courthouse. Many of the town's merchants have a guide to the history and location of all the buildings in town that were constructed before the turn-of-the-century.

2 - Downieville Museum
Main Street, Downieville (916) 289-3261

Sierra County's museum is housed in this 1852 stone building, known as "Old State House." This building was first used as a Chinese store and gambling house. Its collections include a scale model of a gold stamp mill; horse snowshoes; and artifacts from Indian, Chinese and early settlers of the area.

2 - Sierra County Sheriff's Gallows   SHL 971
Sierra County Jail Yard, Downieville

In 1885, twenty-year-old, James O'Neil was hung from this gallows for the murder of local dairyman, John Woodward. That execution, conducted by Sheriff Samuel Stewart, approximately 100 feet west of this site, was the last legal execution in Sierra County. Changes in state law, in 1891, ended local executions in California. Further legal changes, in 1941, ended hanging as a means of legal execution within the state.

3 - Forest City
Ridge Road, south of Downieville off Hwy 49

Fires destroyed many of Forest City's original businesses. Those remaining were constructed in the late 1800s and can be seen along the town's main street. Two old mine tunnels remain along Oregon Creek, at the east end of town, and are now the property of the "16 to 1 Mine."

3 - Alleghany
Ridge Road, south of Downieville off Hwy 49

Alleghany was one of the few gold camps in California to remain an active gold mining area into the twentieth century. The "16 to 1 Mine" continued to operate until 1965 and today is being worked again. More than a dozen businesses and homes, constructed in the mid- to late-1800s, can be seen throughout the town. A walking tour map, compiled by the Sierra County Chamber of Commerce, can be obtained from most of the businesses in Alleghany.

4 - Site of the Plum Valley House SHL 695
Monument is 4 miles past the Pike turnoff on Ridge Road

In this area of wild plums, John Bope built his home in 1854. His home served as a toll station, on the Henness Pass Road, between Marysville and Virginia City, Nevada. The site of Bope's home is marked by this monument along the old emigrant trail.

5 - Henness Pass Road SHL 421
Southwest corner, intersection of Ridge and Henness Pass Roads, 3 miles west of Alleghany

Emigrants used this trail in 1849 to cross Henness Pass between Marysville and Virginia City, Nevada. It later became a toll road and was the only road over Henness Pass.

6 - North Bloomfield Mining and Gravel Company   SHL 852
Malakoff Diggins State Historic Park, 16 miles northeast of Nevada City on North Bloomfield Road, North Bloomfield (916) 265-2740

The North Bloomfield Mining and Gravel Company operated this major hydraulic gold mining project until hydraulic mining was outlawed in 1883. The hills were "washed away" by water pressure, from giant hydraulic nozzles, in the search for gold. A giant hydraulic nozzle is on display and the park's museum features exhibits on the history of hydraulic mining.

7 - World's First Long Distance Telephone Line   SHL 247
Pleasant Valley Road, north of Bridgeport, French Corral

The Milton Mining and Water Company office, which once stood here, was the French Corral terminus of the world's first long distance telephone line. The line connected French Corral with French Lake, 58 miles away.

8 - Bridgeport Covered Bridge (Nyes Crossing)   SHL 390
Pleasant Valley Road, north of Hwy 20

One of the many toll bridges, constructed by individuals, was erected here by David Wood in 1862. Bridgeport's restored, covered bridge is the oldest covered bridge in the West. Its length of 233-feet makes it the longest bridge of its type in the U.S. The bridge is now closed to traffic and will soon be the centerpiece of a new state park.

9 - Miners Foundry and American Victorian Museum
325 Spring Street at Bridge Street, Nevada City (916) 265-5040

The famous Pelton Water Wheel was manufactured here in 1878, for use in the North Star Mine in Grass Valley. This historic building now houses the American Victorian Museum, a collection of Victorian period artifacts, and an 1871 pipe organ.

9 - Nevada Theatre (Cedar Theatre)   SHL 863
401 Broad Street at Bridge Street, Nevada City (916) 265-6161

California's oldest theater was built here in 1865 and has since been renovated and beautifully restored. It was once the stage for artists and celebrities such as Mark Twain and Jack London. Today it is a place of entertainment in this historic section of Nevada City.

9 - National Hotel SHL 899
211 Broad Street, Nevada City (916) 265-4551

Built in the 1850s, the National Hotel is made up of four adjoining brick buildings and is the oldest continuously-operating hotel in California. The hotel's Victorian dining room and historic tavern, accompanied by 1850s antiques in the guest rooms, uphold the atmosphere of this Gold Rush era building.

9 - Nevada City Historical Preservation District
Bordered by Cottage, Prospect, Nevada and Spring Streets, Nevada City (916) 265-2692

A guide to the gas-lit, downtown historical district of Nevada City is available from the Chamber of Commerce. Within this district are ten restored buildings, from the period 1850-1870, and historic museums.

9 - South Yuba Canal Office SHL 832
134 Main Street, Nevada City

Water, for use in hydraulic mining, was furnished by the South Yuba Canal Water Company. It was the first company incorporated to supply water to the mines. The company occupied these offices from 1857 to 1880. Nevada County Historical Society now maintains this building.

9 - Carriage House
Pioneer Park, Nimrod Street and Park Avenue, Nevada City (916) 265-2521

A logging truck, stagecoach, beer wagon and fire-fighting equipment from Nevada City's early days are on display

9 - Searls Historical Library
214 Church Street, Nevada City (916) 265-5910

This 1872 building was originally the law office of Niles Searls. It now houses a museum, and library of historical information, about

Nevada City. Early photographs, records and maps tell the story of Nevada City's mines, its first residents and businesses.

9 - Firehouse Museum #1
Nevada County Historical Society, 214 Main Street, Nevada City
(916) 265-5468

This 1861 building was headquarters for Nevada City's Firehouse No. 1. It is now the county museum. On display are relics of the Donner Party, a complete altar from a Chinese Joss House, and artifacts from the Maidu Indians. Exhibits also feature the beginning of mining, railroads and communications in the county.

Firehouse #1, Nevada County Historical Society Museum. Courtesy of Nevada City Chamber of Commerce.

10 - Alpha and Omega Hydraulic Mines   SHL 628 and SHL 629
On Hwy 20, 18 miles east of Nevada City

These sister mines were the site of extensive hydraulic mining that undermined most of the original townsites of Alpha and Omega. Millions in gold were taken from these two mines—with mining continuing at the Omega site until 1949. Evidence of the far-reaching mining activity of this region can still be seen in the tailings and diggings that remain.

11 - Rough and Ready   SHL 294
5 miles west of Grass Valley on Hwy 20

One of the first mining towns in Nevada County was established here, in 1849. Its founders were a group of men who called themselves the "Rough and Ready Company," after the hero of the Mexican War, General Zachary Taylor. In a protest over a miner's tax, the town seceded from the Union in 1850. The citizens drafted their own Constitution and elected Colonel E. F. Brundage its first President. Secession lasted just a few months, but it would be another 100 years before a post office would be established here.

12 - Holbrooke Hotel   SHL 914
212 West Main Street, Grass Valley (916) 273-1353

The bar inside the Holbrooke Hotel is the old Golden Gate Saloon. The present Holbrooke Hotel was built around the Golden Gate Saloon in 1862, and is the oldest operating saloon in the region.

12 - Home of Lotta Crabtree   SHL 293
238 Mill Street, Grass Valley

Lotta Crabtree lived in this home, which was operated as a boarding house for miners, with her family in the 1850s. She became the child protégé of Lola Montez, the internationally known dancer, who was her neighbor. Lotta was a successful child star in the California mining camps. She then went on to enjoy a successful stage career across the United States.

12 - Lola Montez Home SHL 292
248 Mill Street, Grass Valley (916) 273-4667

Born Marie Dolores Eliza Rosanna Gilbert in Ireland, in 1818, she took the name Lola Montez when she began a career as a dancer. Her beauty and charm led her into many marriages and affairs across Europe and America. She moved here in 1852, and settled in this home where she taught Lotta Crabtree, her neighbor, to sing and dance. This building is a replica of Lola's original house which was condemned in 1975.

12 - North Star Mine Powerhouse SHL 843
Pelton Wheel Mining Museum, on Allison Ranch Road at south end of Mill Street, Grass Valley (916) 273-4255

A 30-foot Pelton Water Wheel, the largest in the world, was used to provide power to operate the North Star Mine. Extensive mining of gold-bearing quartz, to depths of over a mile, were made possible by this powerhouse. Machinery, tools and photographs are exhibited at the mining museum. Millions of pounds of tailings from the mines can still be seen in this area.

12 - Quartz Gold Discovery Site SHL 297
On Jenkins between Hocking and French Streets, Grass Valley

The beginning of quartz mining in California was said to have begun here on Gold Hill, with the 1850 discovery of gold-bearing quartz, by George Knight. In less than seven years, Gold Hill Mine produced more than $4 million in gold.

12 - Mount St. Mary's Academy SHL 855
Grass Valley Museum and Pacific Library, 410 South Church at Chapel Street, Grass Valley Museum (916) 272-4725, Library (916) 273-4117

Mount St. Mary's Academy operated for more than a century as a convent and academy. When first constructed in 1865, it was used as an orphanage for this community. The restored building is now home to the Grass Valley Museum and the Pacific Library. The museum's exhibits include: an original classroom, parlor, music room, doctor's office, and memorabilia from Grass Valley's early days. The library contains a collection of 10,000 scientific, reference and history books, dating from the early sixteenth century, and displays of early scientific artifacts and pictures.

12 - Empire Mine State Historic Park   SHL 298
10791 East Empire Street, Grass Valley (916) 273-8522

California's largest, deepest and richest gold mine was operated here in the 1850s, by George Roberts. The Empire and North Star mines combined, and together they brought out more than $100 million in gold, during the century that these mines were active. This park is built on the site of the Empire Mine and its 367-miles of underground passages. The historic mine yard, and its main shaft, can be seen along with a model of the underground site.

13 - Old Emigrant Trail   SHL 799
Between Auburn and Grass Valley, on Hwy 49 at Wolf Creek Bridge

Emigrants crossing the Sierra Nevada used this trail extensively in 1849 to reach the gold fields of California. It was at this point that the emigrant trail crossed the present highway.

14 - First Transcontinental Railroad - Colfax   SHL 780.5
Colfax Caboose Museum, Main Street off Hwy 174, Colfax

In September, 1865, the Central Pacific Railroad began service to Illinoistown, which had been an important supply point for the area's mining camps since 1849. The town was renamed "Colfax," in honor of Vice President Schuyler Colfax, who served under Ulysses Grant.

15 - Iowa Hill   SHL 401
East of Colfax on Iowa Hill Road

Three fires destroyed most of the town's businesses, between 1857 and 1922, and hydraulic mining on both sides of Iowa Hill, all but washed the town away. Iowa Hill survived to produce more than $20 million in gold. Some of the town's older buildings, including an early saloon, are operating today.

16 - Yankee Jim's SHL 398
3 miles west of Foresthill on Yankee Jim's Road

There were many stories about how this town got its name, all of them colorful and believable. It was, however, among the most important mining towns in Placer County during the 1850s. No buildings remain today from this old Gold Rush camp.

17 - Foresthill SHL 399
Northeast of Auburn on Foresthill-Soda Springs Road

The real growth of Foresthill came about after the opening of the "Jenny Lind Mine," in 1852. By 1880, more than a million dollars in gold came from that single mine. A few of the town's old buildings, with their wooden sidewalks, can still be seen in the town's business district.

17 - Foresthill Divide Museum
Leroy Botts Memorial Park, 24601 Harrison Street, Foresthill (916) 367-3988

This museum's permanent exhibits tell the history of the Foresthill and Iowa Hill Divides. A scale model of the Foresthill Logging Company, pioneer fire-fighting equipment, depictions of life during the Gold Rush era and early modes of transportation are featured.

18 - Michigan Bluff SHL 402
4 miles east of Foresthill, south of Foresthill-Soda Springs Road

Before Leland Stanford became Governor of California, he had a business in the town of Michigan City. It was located about a half mile from here. The mountainside, on which Michigan City was built, became unstable and began to slide. As a result, the city was abandoned by its residents, who moved here, and renamed their town Michigan Bluff in 1858-1859.

19 - Gold Run SHL 405
Northeast of Colfax on I-80

Hydraulic mining yielded $6 million in gold, from the surrounding hills, between 1862 and 1882. In 1883, a court-imposed ban on hydraulic mining in California, brought an end to large scale, gold mining operations. This, in turn, led to the departure of most of the town's population. The old Union Church is its last remaining building from the Gold Rush days.

20 - Golden Drift Museum
32820 Main Street, Dutch Flat (916) 389-2126

Nestled in the heart of the city's historic district, the Golden Drift Museum exhibits community, mining and railroad history, of the Alta, Gold Run and Dutch Flat region.

20 - Dutch Flat SHL 397
Northeast of Gold Run, 1 and 1/2 miles north of I-80 at Monte Vista turnoff

Placer gold and hydraulic mining were instrumental in the growth of Dutch Flat, the largest town in Placer County in the mid-1860s. It was here that the first money was raised to build the western link, of the first transcontinental railroad, over the Sierra Nevada. Many of the town's original buildings, constructed in the 1850s, remain in use today. Authentic structures along Main Street preserve the Old West appearance of this town.

21 - Emigrant Gap SHL 403
I-80, Emigrant Gap Vista Point on Emigrant Gap Road

Pioneer settlers followed the old emigrant trail over the Sierra Nevada, into Northern California, for almost 20 years during the mid-1800s. Covered wagons would have to be lowered by rope, from the top of these cliffs to the valley floor, before they could continue their westward journey. This was the most dangerous part of their travel.

22 - Overland Emigrant Trail SHL 799.2
Big Bend Ranger Station, adjacent to I-80 at Yuba Gap Road

Beginning in 1845, thousands of pioneers came to California, bringing their covered wagons over the emigrant trail through the Sierra Nevada. Thirty thousand people were estimated to have used this trail in 1849. Marks, from the wheels of those early pioneer's wagons, can still be seen embedded in the rocks along this old trail.

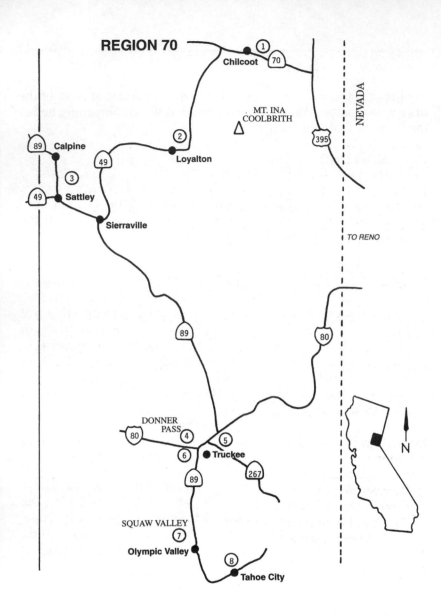

REGION 70

1 - Beckwourth Pass SHL 336
Hwy 70, east of Chilcoot

James Beckwourth discovered this pass in 1851 while on an expedition across the Sierra Nevada. At 5,200-feet, it is the lowest pass over the Sierra and was the eventual route of many emigrants to California. In 1852, Ina Coolbrith, then 11-years-old, crossed into California over this pass. Years later she became California's first poet laureate. The mountain peak six miles south of this pass would be renamed Mount Ina Coolbrith in her honor.

2 - Sierra Valley Historical Museum
Loyalton City Park, Loyalton (916) 993-6754

The agriculture and logging history of the Sierra Valley is featured in displays of equipment, artifacts and household items. A guide to Loyalton's historic, 1864-1910 buildings and other points of historical interest are available from many of the town's local businesses.

3 - Calpine, Sattley and Sierraville
Near junctions of Hwys 49 and 89 southwest of Loyalton

Interesting points of local, historical interest can be seen in these three towns. Calpine was a "company town," for the Davis-Johnson Lumber Company, in the early 1900s. Sattley was also built around the lumbering industry, with its first sawmill constructed in 1882. Sierraville was known for its mineral hot springs as early as the 1850s. A guide to the historic sites and buildings in these towns is available from local merchants.

4 - William Berry Western America Skisport Museum
I-80, at Castle Peak exit, Boreal Ridge Ski Area, Donner Pass (916) 426-3313

California's ski history is exhibited, along with a collection from the Western North America Skisport Hall of Fame. A monument stands here to honor "Snowshoes Thompson," a pioneer mail carrier who brought mail across the Sierra Nevada, by ski, in the winter months. He aided many settlers during his 20-year career in the 1800s.

5 - Truckee Historical Landmarks
Truckee-Donner Chamber of Commerce, Truckee (916) 587-2757

Twenty-five saw mills once operated around the Truckee area, producing lumber for the Central Pacific Railroad and the silver mines in Nevada. Buildings from Truckee's past have been restored in the downtown area, and can be seen on a walking tour, of Commercial Row, Church Street, Main Street and West River Street. Among the town's oldest landmarks is an 1863 log cabin, which stands behind the 1885 Truckee Hotel. A guide to these landmarks and old buildings is available from the Chamber of Commerce.

5 - First Transcontinental Railroad - Truckee   SHL 780.6
Southern Pacific Depot, Truckee

Completion of the Central Pacific Railway Line, through the Sierra Nevada, was made when the line reached Truckee, in April 1868. Thirteen months later, the first transcontinental railroad was completed, with the joining of the eastern and western rail lines at Promontory, Utah. Buildings near this site have been restored to reflect how the area would have appeared during that period.

5 - Truckee-Donner Historical Society Museum
10144 Jibboom Street, Truckee (916) 582-0893

The museum's collections, which include artifacts from Truckee's history, and memorabilia from the late 1890s, are housed in the town's 1875 jail.

6 - Emigrant Trail Museum
12593 Donner Pass Road, Truckee (916) 587-3841

Located within the Donner Memorial State Park, this museum features collections that recall the westward emigration to California. A 38-foot monument to the Donner party is displayed, along with furnishings, tools and related items of historical interest.

6 - Donner Monument SHL 134
Donner Memorial State Park, east end of Donner Lake, south of I-80, west of Truckee (916) 582-7892

Nowhere is there a more stirring account of the American pioneer spirit than the history of the Donner Party, who emigrated to California in 1846-1847. This party of eighty-nine men, women and children suffered unbelievable hardships, and death to almost half their group, in their quest to settle in California. They chose a "shortcut" on their way to California that cost them time and half their cattle and oxen. An early winter, that proved to be the worst in 30 years, trapped them without enough provisions. Half of those who set out on foot, to get help, perished along the way. Those who stayed, waited four to five months for relief parties, and only survived by eating their oxen and, at the end, some by cannibalism. Their complete story is retold in this Memorial Park.

7 - Pioneer Ski Area of America/Squaw Valley SHL 724
West of Hwy 89 at Olympic Valley Road, Squaw Valley

Ski clubs were organized by pioneer miners, and by 1860, competitive races were being run in the Sierra Nevada, 60 miles from here. A century of sport skiing in California was commemorated in 1960, when the VIII Olympic Winter Games were held here.

8 - Lake Tahoe Outlet Gates SHL 797
On Hwy 89, south of Hwy 28 junction, at the Truckee River, Tahoe City

These outlet gates were built in 1870. A 20-year dispute over their control, between Lake Tahoe property owners and water users along the Truckee River, was settled by James Church, in 1910-1911, when he developed techniques for determining the water content in snow. His discovery made possible the accurate prediction, and control, of the seasonal rise in lake and river levels.

8 - Gatekeeper's Log Cabin Museum
William B. Layton Park, 130 West Lake Boulevard, Tahoe City
(916) 583-1762

The 1981 hand-carved, log cabin, at this 3 and 1/2 acre park, features the history of Lake Tahoe, its settlers and the region's Native

Americans. This reconstructed cabin was built on the foundation of the original, circa 1910-1916 Gatekeeper's Cabin, which was destroyed by fire in 1978. Native American artifacts are exhibited; along with an interpretive display that illustrates how Gatekeepers regulated Tahoe's water level, by using a hand-turned winch system, at each of the dam's eleven gates.

8 - Watson Cabin Living Museum
560 North Lake Boulevard, Tahoe City (916) 583-8717

Logs from the surrounding area were used by Lake Tahoe pioneer, R. M. Watson, and his son, Robert, to build this cabin in 1908. A year later, Robert and his wife, Stella, were married and took up residence here. Stella Watson, one of California's first woman bus drivers, lived in this cabin until 1950. The restored cabin is a "living museum," depicting the life of an early 1900s pioneer, Lake Tahoe family. The Indian grinding stone in front of the museum was used by Washoe Indians who frequently visited the Watsons at their log cabin home.

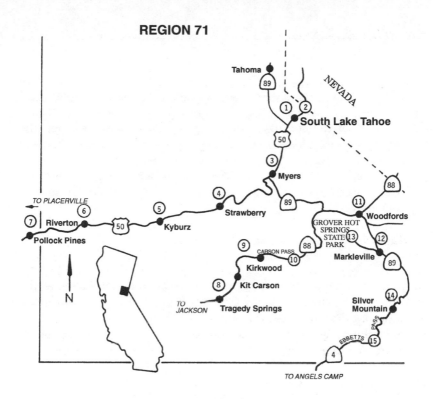

California Overland Pony Express Route

The Pony Express began in April 1860, as a mail relay service between St. Joseph, Missouri, and Sacramento, California, a distance of about 2,000-miles. Riders would change horses at "remount" stations, every 10 to 15 miles, and continue without stopping until the mail was turned over to another rider at periodic "relay" stations. The entire trip would be completed in eight days—the fastest method of communication yet devised. Completion of the transcontinental telegraph, in October 1861, ended the need for Pony Express service just eighteen months after it began. The east to west route of the Pony Express, across El Dorado County, closely follows much of the present U.S. Route 50. Remount and relay stations along this route are marked as State Historic Landmarks.

1 - Tallac Historic Site
Hwy 89 on the lake's south shore, north of South Lake Tahoe (916) 541-5227

Three, turn-of-the-century, summer estates that were once the property of wealthy Bay Area families, are now held in public trust by the U.S. Forest Service at this historic site. Information about tours of the Pope, Valhalla and McGonagle-Lucky Baldwin estates, and the Tallac Museum, is available at the adjacent Forest Service Visitor Center.

1 - Sugar Pine Point State Park
1 mile south of Tahoma on Hwy 89 (916) 525-7982

Among the historic buildings preserved in this state park is the hand-hewn log cabin, built by General Phipp, and the 1903 Queen Anne style Ehrman Mansion, constructed for San Francisco banker Isaias Hellman. Tours of the 11,700 square foot, refurbished, stone mansion are offered daily.

1 - Emerald Bay State Park
North of Camp Richardson on Hwy 89, South Lake Tahoe (916) 541-3030

In 1928-1929, this 38-room, Vikingsholm summer home was constructed by two hundred workmen. It is considered to be the most authentic reproduction of Scandinavian architecture in the United States. The roof of one wing is covered in sod and planted with wildflowers—a common practice in some European countries. The home was furnished with authentic pieces and hand-crafted reproductions.

1 - South Lake Tahoe Historical Museum
3058 U.S. 50, South Lake Tahoe (916) 541-5458, summer or (916) 544-2312, winter

This museum features artifacts of the early history of South Lake Tahoe including: Washoe Indian baskets; arrowheads, photographs; a 140-year-old pipe organ; and a model of the SS *Tahoe*, the largest ship to ever sail Lake Tahoe.

2 - Friday's Station   SHL 728
U.S. 50, 3/4 miles east of California State Line, south end of Lake Tahoe

This easternmost station of the California division of the Pony Express was located in Nevada on the old Placerville-Carson City Road. It was originally built as a stage stop in 1858, and became a remount station at the inception of the Pony Express in April 1860.

3 - Yank's Station   SHL 708
Yank's Station Shopping Center, southwest corner of U.S. 50 and Apache Avenue, Meyers

The station that stood here was erected in 1851 as a trading post, and later became a stage stop and Pony Express relay station on the Placerville-Carson City Road.

4 - Strawberry Valley House   SHL 707
Monument on U.S. 50, 9 miles east of Kyburz, Strawberry

The beauty of this valley made this stop a popular resort for teamsters and passenger stages in the 1850s. In April 1860, it also became a Pony Express remount station.

5 - Webster's Sugar Loaf House   SHL 706
1 mile west ot Kyburz, U.S. 50

Wagon teams frequently stopped at this station during the Comstock silver rush of the 1850s. It was a remount station for the Central Overland Pony Express from April 1860, to October 1861.

6 - Moore's (Riverton) Station   SHL 705
At intersection of U.S. 50 and Ice House Road, 9 miles west of Kyburz

The station that stood at this site is commemorated for the eighteen months it served as a remont station on the Pony Express route.

7 - Sportsman's Hall   SHL 704
5622 Old Pony Express Trail, Cedar Grove

This hotel that stood at this site became a relay station for the riders of the Central Overland Pony Express between April 1860 and October 1861.

8 - Old Emigrant Road   SHL 662
Hwy 88, near Tragedy Springs

It was near this site on the emigrant trail, in 1848, that three scouts of the Mormon Battalion were killed in an Indian massacre. The names of the scouts, and the tale of their tragedy, were carved on a tree that once stood here. The section of the tree that bears their legacy is housed in the museum at Sutter's Fort, in Sacramento.

8 - Maiden's Grave   SHL 28
2 miles west of Tragedy Springs on Hwy 88, west of Kirkwood

A memorial to a pioneer girl, whose life ended on the Kit Carson emigrant trail, was erected here, at her grave site.

9 - Kirkwood's Log Stage Station   SHL 40
8 miles northeast of Tragedy Springs, between Kit Carson and Kirkwood, Hwy 88

Zack Kirkwood built this log cabin, in 1864, to serve as a stage stop, inn and post office. When Alpine County was formed, the new county line went through the center of the inn's barroom.

10 - Kit Carson Emigrant Trail   SHL 661
Hwy 88, 3 miles west of Carson Pass, 17 miles west of Woodfords

Early emigrants followed this trail through Kit Carson Pass; as did the Mormon Battalion, in their march from Los Angeles to the Great Salt Lake.

10 - Kit Carson Pass   SHL 315
Marked at the summit, with bronze memorial plate, on Hwy 88, west of Woodfords

Kit Carson led Captain John Fremont and his party over the Sierra Nevada, in the first mid-winter crossing made by white men. When Carson discovered this pass, he marked his name on a tree, returned to camp and brought the Fremont party back over the pass, to Sutter's Fort in the Sacramento Valley. That section of the tree showing Carson's name, as he inscribed it in 1844, is now on display at Sutter's Fort.

10 - Pioneer Odd Fellows Memorial   SHL 378
Marker is 1/4 mile east of the summit of Carson Pass on Hwy 88, 14 miles west of Woodfords

A party of 49ers inscribed their names, and the symbol of their organization, the Independent Order of Odd Fellows (I.O.O.F.), on these rocks when they reached the summit of Kit Carson Pass.

11 - Woodfords Pony Express Station   SHL 805
Old Pony Express Road, junction of Hwy 88 and Hwy 89, Woodfords

The first white settlement in Alpine County was established here in 1847 and was known under several names. A Pony Express remount station operated at Cary's Barn for five weeks, when the service first began, in 1860.

11 - "Snow-Shoe" Thompson Monument
Monument is near the site of Thompson's home, Diamond Valley Road, Diamond Valley

John "Snow-Shoe" Thompson was a heroic mail carrier. From 1856 to 1876, he braved the Sierra Nevada winters, fought the elements, and helped those in need as he delivered the mail to early settlers. His homemade skis, which were called snowshoes by those early pioneers, enabled him to cross the snow covered mountains. They are now on exhibit at the museum in Sutter's Fort.

12 - Markleeville
Hwy 89, south of Woodfords

Many of Markleeville's original buildings were destroyed by fire in the late 1880s. The old stone courthouse still remains at its original location, on the site of Jacob Marklee's original cabin. The old Webster School has been restored, and can be seen on Montgomery Street, along with the wooden jail and county historical museum.

12 - Jacob J. Marklee Homesite   SHL 240
Alpine County Courthouse, Hwy 89, Markleeville

Jacob Marklee, the region's first permanent inhabitant, built his cabin at this site in 1861. By the time of his death, in a gunfight two years later, the town of Markleeville had begun forming around his homesite. The Comstock Lode silver strike, in Nevada, brought the town's population to over 2,000 by 1864. Markleeville was named the county seat in 1875 and a county courthouse was built of stone on the site of Marklee's original cabin.

12 - Alpine County Museum
Historical Complex, Montgomery Street near old Webster School, Markleeville (916) 694-2317

Mining, lumbering and carpentry tools, toys, dolls, Indian crafts, rocks and gems, old bottles, pictures and farm implements, are among the items displayed by the Historical Society of Alpine County in their museum.

13 - Grover Hot Springs State Park
3 miles west of Markleeville, on Hot Springs Road (916) 694-2248 or (916) 525-7232

Captain John Fremont and his scout, Kit Carson, used this area as a winter camp during their 1843 crossing of the Sierra Nevada. It is now a state park.

14 - Silver Mountain Ghost Town
On Hwy 4, 5 miles southwest of junction with Hwy 89

The silver mining town of Silver Mountain was the first county seat of Alpine County. Only the ruins of the county's first jail remain where the town once stood.

15 - Ebbetts Pass   SHL 318
Marked at the summit on Hwy 4

In the early 1850s, John Ebbett discovered a pass that soon afterward became part of the emigrant trail to Angels Camp. This pass became a heavily traveled supply route with the discovery of silver, at the Comstock Lode in Nevada, in 1864.

REGION 72

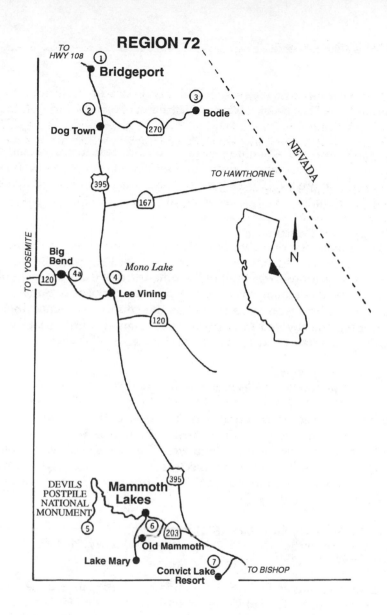

1 - Mono County Museum
Bridgeport City Park, behind Memorial Hall, north of U.S. 395
(619) 932-5281

Housed in an 1880 schoolhouse, the museum features a valuable collection of Mono, and Paiute, Indian baskets (one basket was appraised at more than $35,000), as well as Indian artifacts and items of interest from the county's historic past.

1 - Bridgeport Courthouse
On U.S. 395 in Bridgeport (619) 932-7620

This 1880 courthouse was built of handmade brick from the town of Bodie. It is now among the oldest, active courthouses in America. The town of Bridgeport has served as the county seat since 1863, when it was discovered that Aurora, the original county seat, was actually in the state of Nevada.

2 - Dogtown SHL 792
On U.S. 395, just south of Bodie Road turn-off (Hwy 270)

The first gold discovered, on the eastern slopes of the Sierra Nevada, was the 1857 find along Virginia Creek. The miners who came here that year formed the town of Dogtown. The promise of richer gold fields, elsewhere, lured the prospectors away less than two years after Dogtown was founded. Tailings from those first mines are clearly visible from the highway.

3 - Bodie State Historic Park SHL 341
13 miles east of junction with U.S. 395 on Bodie Road (Hwy 270)
(619) 647-6445

The discovery of gold by W. S. Body (Bodie), in 1859, started the gold mining town of Bodie; but it wasn't until twenty years later, when a rich gold strike was made, that the town boomed. With gold coming from the mines by the millions of dollars, and the population growing to over 10,000, violence and lawlessness became a way of life. One hundred-fifty buildings remain of what was once the "wildest" mining town in the West. The entire community of Bodie is now protected by the State Park system as an authentic ghost town.

4 - Mono Lake
Mono Lake Information Center, U.S. 395, Lee Vining (619) 647-6595

Mono Lake, a vast "dead sea," is California's largest salt lake. It was formed when the sun, and hot lava flows, evaporated most of the lake's water, leaving behind its minerals and making the water saltier than the Pacific Ocean. Volcanic craters and white rock deposits dot the lake's surface. Brine shrimp provide nourishment for San Francisco's seagulls that migrate here every summer. Ephyda fly pupae, which thrive in the brine, were an important part of the diet of the Paiute Indians who lived in this region.

4A - Trail of the John C. Fremont 1844 Expedition   SHL 995.1
Big Bend-Mountain Gate area of the Toiyabe National Forest, off U.S. 395, Mono County

Lt. John C. Fremont's report to Congress, of his 1844 Expedition into California, had world-wide impact and was a turning point in the state's history. Fremont's highly-publicized and well-documented report, a descriptive account of the Eden-like lands he explored, followed on the heels of Texas' admission into the Union. This further whetted the appetites of expansionists who wanted a United States stretching from the Atlantic to the Pacific. One of the sites of that famous expedition is commemorated here.

5 - Devil's Postpile National Monument
Mammoth Lakes Visitor's Center, Hwy 203, west of U.S. 395 (619) 934-2289

Devil's Postpile was created nearly a million years ago as hot lava cooled, solidified and cracked. It formed basalt columns, 40-60 feet high, that resemble a giant pipe organ. The National Park Service operates a museum within the park that features the history of the region and its volcanic rock formations.

5 - Mammoth City Historical Site
Old Mammoth Road, south of Hwy 203 (619) 934-2505

This town, in the Mammoth Lakes Recreation Area, was a gold mining camp in the late 1800s. Still in evidence, along the foot trails, are four tunnels dug by the Mammoth Mining Company, tailings, and a 14-ton flywheel that was once part of this town's stamp mill.

511

6 - Mammoth Historical Museum
In Mammoth Creek Meadow near Sierra Meadows Equestrian Center, Mammoth (619) 934-6918

The Southern Mono Historical Society displays antiques, photos, and memorabilia of Mammoth Lakes history in this 1830s era, log cabin, museum.

7 - Convict Lake
Convict Lake Road, west of U.S. 395, Convict Lake Resort

Convicts, escaping from the prison at Carson City, Nevada, were encountered here by Sheriff Morrison and his posse in 1871. In the gunfight that followed, Sheriff Morrison was killed. The convicts escaped, but were later captured ten miles to the south.

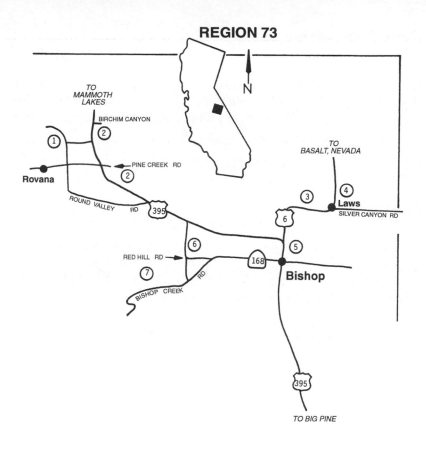

REGION 73

N

TO MAMMOTH LAKES

BIRCHIM CANYON

② ①

PINE CREEK RD

Rovana

②

TO BASALT, NEVADA

③ ④

ROUND VALLEY RD ⑮ 395

Laws

SILVER CANYON RD

6

⑥ ⑤

RED HILL RD →

⑦ 168

RD

Bishop

BISHOP CREEK

395

TO BIG PINE

1 - Mayfield Canyon Battleground   SHL 211
North of Rovana off Round Valley Road about 1/2 mile north of Ranger Station Road

On April 8, 1862, U.S. Army troops joined with settlers to battle the Paiute Indians on this battleground. One of the troopers was killed, as was a settler named Mayfield, for whom the canyon was named. Within a month the valley was in the possession of the Paiutes and most of the white settlers left.

2 - Bishop Petroglyphs
At two sites along U.S. 395, south of Pine Creek Road and at Birchim Canyon

Throughout northern Inyo County, and southern Mono County, are the largest group of petroglyphs (rock markings) in this part of the state. These markings are found on the courses of stream beds, on walls at the base of the Inyo Mountains, along natural trails and even in secluded areas. Little is known about the age or meaning of these early writings.

3 - Site of First White Man's Dwelling   SHL 230
U.S. 6, turn-off at Silver Canyon Road, near Laws

Before A. Van Fleet built a cabin here in 1861, and became Owens Valley's first permanent white settler, the only population around consisted of transient prospectors and travelers. More than fifty homestead claims, of 160 acres each, were taken up by new settlers in the next two years in this vicinity. Remains of an early stone corral can still be seen.

4 - Laws Historical Railroad Museum   SHL 953
Silver Canyon Road, off U.S. 6, Laws (619) 873-5950

The Laws Railroad Depot was built in 1883. It now houses a collection of railroad artifacts and memorabilia from the narrow gauge railroad that operated here until 1960. A large collection of narrow gauge rolling stock is displayed, including a rare, two cupola caboose and a brill self-propelled car. A hand-operated, gallows-type turntable and the station agent's residence is also on the grounds of this museum. Antique collections and artifacts, from the late 1800s, are displayed in: Laws' former post office, an old country store, a Wells Fargo building, and a frontier doctor's office. Outdoor displays include mining machinery, farm wagons and a collection of antique bells from Bishop schools.

5 - Paiute-Shoshone Indian Cultural Center
2300 West Line Street, Bishop (619) 873-4478

Displays of winter-time Indian life in the Owens Valley are of special interest in this center built by a consortium of local tribes.

6 - San Francis Ranch   SHL 208
Red Hill Road, 3 miles southwest of Bishop via Hwy 168

Samuel A. Bishop, for whom the town of Bishop and the creek by this ranch were named, was a 49er emigrant who settled here with his wife in 1861. He and the other settlers attempted to prevent conflict with the Indians by signing a treaty, but it would be five years before there was peace in this valley. The site of this pioneer's home is commemorated by this marker.

7 - Bishop Creek Battle Ground   SHL 811
5 miles southwest of Bishop, at junction of Bishop Creek Road (Hwy 168)

On April 6, 1862, before U.S. Army troops could arrive to protect Bishop Creek's settlers, fifty to sixty pioneers under the leadership of John T. Kellogg engaged more than 500 Paiute Indians on this battleground. Three of the settlers were killed in the battle.

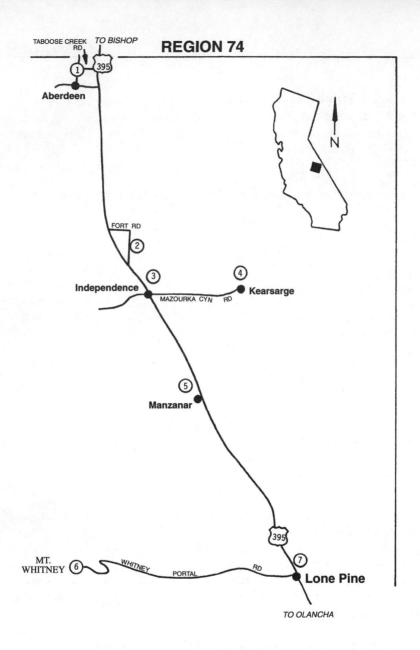

REGION 74

TABOOSE CREEK RD

TO BISHOP

395

①

Aberdeen

FORT RD

②

③ Independence

④ Kearsarge

MAZOURKA CYN RD

⑤ Manzanar

395

MT. WHITNEY ⑥

WHITNEY PORTAL RD

⑦ Lone Pine

TO OLANCHA

N

1 - Harry Wrights Stage Station
1 and 1/2 miles north of Aberdeen, on Taboose Creek

This site was a stage stop on Taboose Creek and a popular gathering place in the 1860s and 1870s.

2 - Camp Independence SHL 349
Intersection of Hwy 6 and Silver Canyon Road, northeast of Bishop

Camp Independence was established July 4, 1862, to protect settlers from the Paiute Indians and to be a barrier in the event of an invasion, by the Secessionists, from the Nevada and Arizona Territories. The former home of the camp's commander was moved to the town of Independence and has been restored. The caves occupied by the camp's soldiers and the cemetery is all that remains of this abandoned camp.

3 - Mary Austin's Home SHL 229
253 Market Street, Independence

Mary Austin designed and supervised the building of this home in Independence, where she wrote, *The Land of Little Rain* and other books about the Owens Valley region.

3 - Site of Putnam's Cabin SHL 223
139 Edwards Street off U.S. 395, Independence

Inyo County's first permanent home was built at this site, by Charles Putnam, in 1861. His stone house was used as a trading post, hospital, and fort, by the area's early settlers who first called the town "Putnam." The town changed its name to Independence a year later when nearby Camp Independence was established. Independence became the county seat when Inyo County was organized in 1866.

3 - Eastern California Museum/Inyo County Museum
155 Grant Street, Independence (619) 878-2010

This museum houses relics of the steamships, *Bessie Brady* and *Molly Stevens*. They were an important link in the mining of the Inyo Mountains. Special exhibits on Camp Independence, the Cerro

Gordo Silver Mine, and Manzanar Japanese Relocation Center are featured in this local history museum. Also on the museum grounds are: "Little Pine Village," a collection of historic homes; and antique farm and mining equipment.

4 - Bend City SHL 209
Mazourka Canyon Road, Kearsarge, west of Independence

Bend City, a mining town of about sixty adobe houses in the 1860s, was named the county seat of Coso County—a county which was never formed. The first county bridge across the Owens River was built here, but the 1872 earthquake changed the river's course, and left Bend City on the bank of an empty ravine. Nothing remains of this town site today.

5 - Manzanar Japanese Relocation Center SHL 850
6 miles south of Independence on U.S. 395

Originally this was the site of the first two-story, frame dwelling in Owens Valley, the Shepherd ranch house, which also served as a stage stop for several years. The town of Manzanar was built here in the early 1900s. During World War II, 10,000 Japanese people, most of them American citizens, were interned here in what was the first of ten such camps in the United States. Some ruins of this camp, which is now a National Registered Historic Landmark, can still be seen.

6 - Mt. Whitney
West of Lone Pine on Whitney Portal Road

The highest point in the continental United States is Mt. Whitney at 14,495 feet.

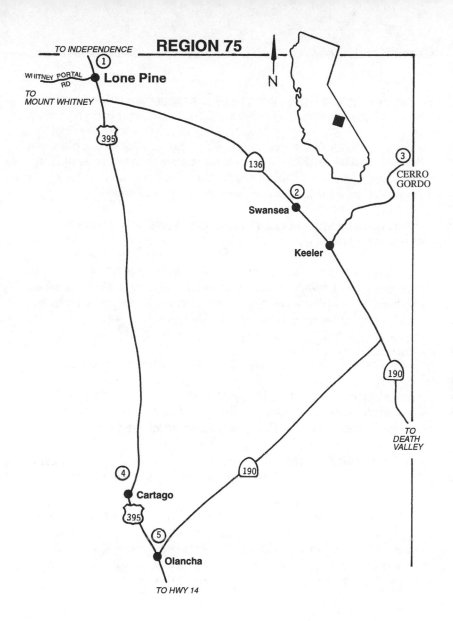

TO INDEPENDENCE

① Lone Pine

WHITNEY PORTAL RD

TO MOUNT WHITNEY

395

N

136

② Swansea

Keeler

③ CERRO GORDO

190

TO DEATH VALLEY

④ Cartago

395

⑤ Olancha

190

TO HWY 14

1 - Grave of 1872 Earthquake Victims SHL 507
1 mile north of Lone Pine off U.S. 395

The town of Lone Pine was heavily damaged, and 27 people were killed, in the March 1872 earthquake that opened a twelve-mile long fault north of the city. More than a dozen of the town's residents were buried in a common grave near the edge of the fault.

2 - Owens Lake Silver-Lead Company SHL 752
Hwy 136 at Swansea

Two mills were constructed by the Owens Lake Silver-Lead Company; one here in Swansea, the other at Cerro Gordo. These smelters were built to eliminate the high cost of transporting ore from the Cerro Gordo Mines, to San Pedro, for processing.

3 - Cerro Gordo
20 miles northeast of Olancha, Cerro Gordo Road, northeast of Keeler

The most productive mines in Inyo County were located here in the 1870s. More than $28 million in silver, lead and zinc were produced. Many buildings remain in this well-preserved ghost town.

4 - Cottonwood Charcoal Kilns SHL 537
North of Cartogo off U.S. 395, on Cottonwood Road, west shore of Owens Lake

Wood was turned into charcoal in these kilns. It was then taken by steamboat, across the Owens Lake (which is now dry), to the smelters at Cerro Gordo. Charcoal was necessary for the continued production of silver as all the available wood in the Cerro Gordo area had already been used. The hive-like kilns can still be seen.

5 - Olancha Mill Site SHL 796
Marker placed approximately 1 mile east of Olancha Creek, on U.S. 395 and Williams Road

M. H. Farley explored the Owens Lake area, in 1860, and discovered the pass out of the southern end of the lake that now bears his name. He built the first mill in the Owens Valley, on Olancha Creek, in 1862. Nothing remains of Farley's pioneer mill which operated near this site through the late 1800s.

REGION 76

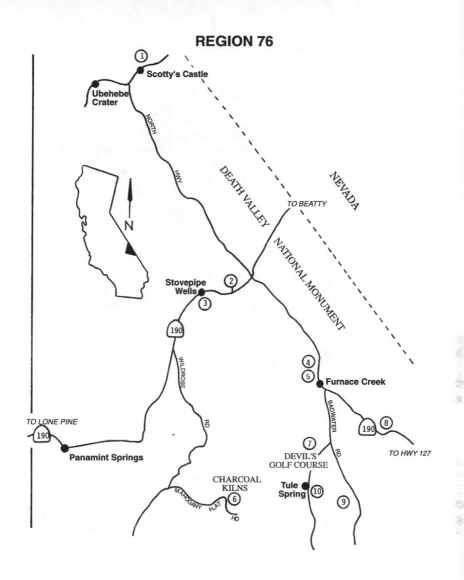

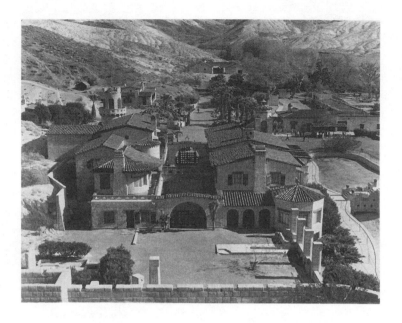

Scotty's Castle, Death Valley National Monument. Courtesy of National Park Service, photo by Richard Frear.

1 - Scotty's Castle
Extreme northern section of Death Valley on North Highway,
Death Valley National Monument (619) 786-2392 or (619) 786-2325

Built in the 1920s, at an estimated cost of between $2-3 million,
Scotty's Castle is an incredible mansion of Scottish-Moorish design.
Eight miles from Scotty's Castle is the 3,000 year-old, 800-foot deep,
Ubehebe Volcanic Crater.

2 - Old Stove Pipe Wells SHL 826
1/4 mile north of Hwy 190, on Sand Dunes Access Road, Death Valley
National Monument

The only known source of water, in the sand dune area of Death
Valley in the 1860s, was at this location. The name came from a
length of stovepipe, inserted in the water hole, so it could be found
when sand covered its location.

3 - Eichbaum Toll Road SHL 848
Hwy 190, Stovepipe Wells, Death Valley National Monument

In 1926, the first maintained road into Death Valley was opened as a
toll road, by H. W. Eichbaum. Tourism became the principal industry as a result of the opening of this road. In 1933, Death Valley
became a National Monument.

3 - Burned Wagons Point SHL 441
Hwy 190 by Stove Pipe Wells Hotel, Death Valley National Monument

Emigrants that crossed Death Valley's northwestern route, under the
Jayhawkers in 1849, burned their wagons here, dried the meat of
some of their oxen and continued westward on foot to eventual
safety.

4 - Old Harmony Borax Works SHL 773
Borax Mill Road, north of Furnace Creek Ranch, and west of Hwy 190, Death
Valley National Monument

The Harmony Borax Works were built in 1881, to process borax for
shipment to Mojave, 165 miles and a 20-day trip by mule team across
the desert. Borax is still present in Death Valley, but the discovery of
borax at points closer to the rail lines in Mojave, made it too costly to

continue to ship across the desert and the operation closed. Ruins are all that remain of the original structure.

5 - Death Valley National Monument
Hwy 190, between Olancha and the California-Nevada State Line
(619) 786-2331

Preserved within this two million-acre national monument are several state historical landmarks, museums, unusual structures, remnants of gold and borax mining, and several unusual natural sites.

5 - Death Valley Monument Headquarters
On Hwy 190 at Furnace Creek, Death Valley National Monument
(619) 786-2331

Furnace Creek Ranch was the northern terminus, for the 20-mule teams, that hauled borax across the desert to Mojave. The first frame house in Death Valley was moved to this visitor center and now houses the collection of the Borax Museum.

6 - Wildrose Charcoal Kilns
7 miles east of Wildrose Ranger Station on Mahogany Flat Road, Death Valley National Monument

These kilns were built more than a century ago, to burn nearby pinon trees into charcoal, for shipment to silver smelters.

7 - Devil's Golf Course
Can be seen for 15 miles along the west side of Badwater Road, Death Valley National Monument

Many 49ers that crossed Death Valley came across this field of jagged salt crystals. Some of the crystals are up to two feet high.

8 - Death Valley Gateway   SHL 442
Hwy 190, east entrance to Death Valley National Monument

In late December of 1849, over one hundred emigrants entered Death Valley at the mouth of Furnace Creek, seeking a shorter route to the California gold fields. Suffering from thirst and near starvation they split into two groups. The Manly Party continued southward and the Jayhawkers went northwest with other groups. Both groups were to suffer tragic losses in their attempt to cross Death Valley.

9 - Badwater
Badwater Road, 17 miles south of Furnace Creek, Death Valley National Monument

This pool of undrinkable water is near the lowest point in the continental United States—282 feet below sea level.

10 - Bennett Arcane   SHL 444
Last Camp, marker 1/4 mile off Westside Road on Bennett Wells Road, Death Valley National Monument

Forty-niner emigrants, led by William Manly, crossed the salt flats from Furnace Creek and found water here at Tule Springs. Manly and John Rogers left the party at this camp and set out on foot to get help. When they returned a month later only two families had remained in camp. Most of the others that left camp were never accounted for and were presumed to have died.

BIBLIOGRAPHY

Assembly Center Location, Construction and Equipment, from US Army, Western Defense Command. *Japanese Evacuation From The West Coast,* Final Report 1942, Washington D.C., 1943, pp. 151-185

Bay Area Historic House Museums, Hayward, CA, 1989

Benbow, Nancy and Christopher, *Cabins, Cottages and Mansions - Homes of the Presidents of the United States,* Thomas Publications, Gettysburg, PA, 1993

California Department of Parks and Recreation, *California Historical Landmarks,* State of California, Sacramento, CA, 1982

California Department of Parks and Recreation, *California Inventory of Historic Resources,* California - The Resources Agency, Sacramento, CA, 1978

California Department of Parks and Recreation, *Shasta State Historic Park: Brief History and Tour Guide,* State of California - The Resources Agency, Sacramento, CA 1985

Cohen, Marvin H., *Steam Passenger Service Directory,* Empire State Railway Museum, Inc., Middletown, NY, 1985

Covici, Jr., Pascal, Editor; *The Portable Steinbeck,* Penguin Books USA Inc., 1976

Crump, Spencer, *252 Historic Places You Can See In California,* Trans-Anglo Books, Los Angeles, CA, 1964

Curl, Alan, *Riverside Historic Landmarks,* Riverside Municipal Museum, A to Z Printing Company

Donley, Michael W., *Atlas of California,* Pacific Book Center, Culver City, CA, 1979

Foster, Lee, *Adventures in California Country,* Beautiful America Publishing Company, 1981

Gibbs, James A., *Sentinels of Solitude,* Graphic Arts Center Publishing Co., Portland, OR, 1981

Gudde, Erwin G., *California Place Names, The Origin and Etymology of Current Geographical Names,* University of California Press, Berkeley and Los Angeles, 1960

Haas, Irvin, *Historic Homes of the American Presidents,* Dover Publications Inc., New York, NY, 1991

Harris, William H. and Levey, Judith S., *The New Columbia Encyclopedia,* Columbia University Press, New York and London, 1975

Knowland, Joseph R., *California: A Landmark History,* Oakland Tribune, 1941

Lothrop, Gloria Ricci, *A Guide to Historical Outings in Southern California,* Historical Society of Southern California, Glendale, CA, 1991

Map from Edward H. Spicer, Edward Holland, *Impounded People, Japanese-Americans in the Relocation Centers*, The University of Arizona Press, Tucson, AZ, 1969

McGrath, Nancy, *Frommer's Dollarwise Guide to California and Las Vegas*, Frommer/Pasmantier Publishers, New York, NY, 1985

Official Museum Directory, 23rd Edition, R. R. Bowker, New Providence, NJ, 1992

Orange County Historical Commission, *Visiting Orange County's Past*, Santa Ana, CA, 1984

Rand McNally, *Rand McNally Auto Tour Series California*, Rand McNally & Co., 1983

Reece, Daphne, *Historic Houses of California*, Chronicle Books, San Francisco, CA, 1983

Reed, Merrill A., *Historical Statues and Monuments in California*, San Francisco, CA, 1956

Rensch, H. E., Third edition revised by William N. Abeloe, *Historic Spots in California*, Stanford University Press, Stanford, CA, 1966

Roberts, Bruce and Jones, Ray, *Western Lighthouses: Olympic Peninsula to San Diego*, The Globe Pequot Press, Old Saybrook, CT, 1993

Scott, Quinta and Kelly, Susan Croce, *Route 66 - The Highway and Its People*, University of Oklahoma Press, 1988

Shasta Interpretive Association, *Shasta State Historic Park*, Shasta, CA

Snyder, Tom, *The Route 66 Traveler's Guide and Roadside Companion*, St. Martin's Press, New York, NY, 1990

Stewart, Tabori & Chang, Inc., *Sierra Club Guide to the National Parks of the Pacific Southwest*, New York, NY, 1984

Sunset Books, *California Travel Guide*, Sunset Publishing Corp., Menlo Park, CA, 1991

Sunset Books, *Gold Rush Country*, Lane Publishing Co., Menlo Park, California, 1981

Sunset Books, *San Francisco Sunset Pictorial*, Menlo Park, CA, 1986

Thaxton, John, *Lodges and Cabins (State & National Parks)*, Burt Franklin & Company, Inc., New York, NY, 1985

Tomb, Eric, *A Coloring Book of California Authors*, Bellerophon Books, Santa Barbara, CA, 1992

US Government, *National Park System and Related Areas*, US Government Printing Office, 1982

Vorspan, Max, *History of the Jews of Los Angeles*, Huntington Library, 1970

INDEX